W9-BYW-617

China into Film:
Frames of Reference in Contemporary Chinese Cinema

ENVISIONING ASIA

Series Editors: Homi Bhabha, Norman Bryson, Wu Hung

In the same series

Fruitful Sites
Garden Culture in Ming Dynasty China
Craig Clunas

Camera Indica
The Social Life of Indian Photographs
Christopher Pinney

In the Image of Tibet
Tibetan Painting after 1959
Clare Harris

CHINA INTO FILM

Frames of Reference in
Contemporary Chinese Cinema

JEROME SILBERGELD

REAKTION BOOKS

Reaktion Books Ltd
79 Farringdon Road
London EC1M 3JU, UK

First published 1999

Series design by Ron Costley
Printed and bound in Italy

British Library Cataloguing in Publishing Data

Silbergeld, Jerome
    China into film : frames of reference in contemporary
    Chinese cinema. – (Envisioning Asia)
    1. Motion pictures – China 2. Motion picture industry – China
    I. Title
    791.4′3′0951

    ISBN 1 86189 050 8

Contents

Preface

There are a few things to be said at the outset of this book, beginning with the reasons why I would like to emphasize its being considered 'art historical'. For a historian of Chinese visual arts, the arrival of a new generation of films like *Yellow Earth* (1984) and *Black Cannon Incident* (1985) – the so-called 'Fifth Generation'[1] – was a long time in coming and yet entirely unexpected. No sooner was this pair of films available than they became the concluding event in my introductory course on Chinese art history, with an incautious claim to their representing the most successful artistic event of China's turbulent twentieth century. As with the Chinese visual arts in general, my appreciation of this genre of newly emerged, intellectually engaging Chinese films (the 'New Chinese Cinema', China's 'art' films, China's 'avant-garde cinema') has rested not on a simple aesthetic of good looks but rather on the ability of such works to communicate deeply and richly, to create and effectively interrelate image and text, to engage subject and context, to artistically and convincingly raise complex social and philosophical issues dear to China and informative to the rest of the world about China. Led by a generation of young film-makers shaped by the Cultural Revolution and China's subsequent disavowal of hardline Maoism, the sudden elevation of the long-moribund Chinese cinematic tradition to this artistic level was cause for celebration.

In the ten-plus years since this genre of Chinese films suddenly burst on the international scene, a considerable body of literature has followed in its train. It should have come as no surprise that colleagues in other academic disciplines, with other agendas, would read these films differently than I would myself. What I was not adequately pre-pared for was that some, both in China and in the West, have been disposed to treat these films quite so harshly, so negatively (and here I do not mean to conflate these academicians with Party hacks whose task is to defend against the kind of probing historical inquiries raised by such films). The range of voices, however, has proved challenging at the same time as it has reaffirmed the basic virtue of the university: stimulus through diversity. Surprisingly lacking, however, has been a specifically art-historical voice. And it is that voice which I hope to raise here, adding it to the chorus already being heard from such disci-plines as cinema studies, critical theory, women's studies, anthropology, comparative literature and urban studies.

Needless to say, there is no singular art-historical 'voice'. But there are a few distinctive characteristics to its sound which may enrich the chorus. First and foremost in this approach is a relatively greater focus on image as compared to text than is normally found in other disciplines, though all disciplines draw in different measure on a broad range of visual, textual, contextual and conceptual resources. The art historian, more than other colleagues, will bring to bear a way of looking that is steeped in the knowledge of traditional imagery and concerned with the relationship of images to relevant texts and contexts. Whether convincing or not, my emphasis on the deep structure of analogy and allegory in Chinese thought and visualization (such analogy is *inherently* visual, I believe) derives from this outlook and disposes me rather differently towards some of the more controversial issues raised by other writers, especially as related to gender and nationalism. Secondly, the art historian is always in some limited part an art critic but unlike the critic is consciously disposed to see that historical inquiry plays a considerably greater role than does critical assertion. Film-makers, like all 'art workers' in China, have long had to answer to other people's agendas, to adjust their artistry to ideology. But sometimes, their answer to the censor has come not in the form of text (which the censor may understand all too well) but in the departure from text through cinema's visuality (which censors apparently know much less well). Ironically, as we shall see, such strategy has often made for artistry, not only moulding the visual referencing of meaning but enhancing and helping to define the aesthetic of this entire cinematic venture. The Great Critic, Chairman Mao, understood the difference between artistry and politics and was clear about their problematic engagement; he proclaimed:

Insofar as a work is reactionary, the more artistic it is the more harm it can do to the people and the more it should be rejected. The common characteristic of all literature and art of exploiting classes in their period of decline is the contradiction between their reactionary political content and their artistic form. What we demand, therefore, is a unity of politics and art, a unity of content and form, a unity of revolutionary political content and the highest artistic form possible. [2]

Politicians may demand a unity of style and ideological content; censors and critics alike are free to do so also. But the art historian's task is not to dictate ideology nor to reject it – rather, it is to explain. That is no simple matter, never quite sufficient, and always a humbling engagement. The bias here is clearly towards history and historical continuities, the old informing and becoming part of the new, framed in cinematic displays of gender, allegory, dramatic form, and modes of referencing style to effect a visual rhetoric. But where I have exaggerated and erred or been naïve and seemed dilettantish, I hope that art historians will join in this cinematic discourse to bring improvement.

This art-historical voice is not intended to rise above or drown out any others but rather to add to the whole, even if it may sometimes be out of tune with certain other voices. No one can pretend to have in their work no critical bearing. But unlike some of the agendas – legitimate agendas – which shape the writing on this subject, in which a present-mindedness is quite intentionally brought to bear critically and which holds the cinematic subject to account, my own art-historical inquiry is satisfied by the effort merely to understand the complex and subtle strands of signification out of which such art works are creatively woven, by which these works are tied to both past and present, and through which they illuminate the ways in which the present is tied to the past. The virtue of an important film lies neither in 'good' looks nor in its delivering any 'right' message. Indeed, many a good-looking film is just that and nothing more, visual attractiveness having long been suspect in Chinese art; and the would-be right message has often been delivered most artlessly. The 'right' message no more likely makes for good art than the 'wrong' message makes for bad art. Indeed, if there is a 'good' or 'bad' for the China art historian it lies, subjectively, in the ability of the art work to give form and stimulus, unusually well, to an enriched visual and conceptual experience.

What seems to be well contained within the cinematic frame is actually, through outward reference, not contained at all. By 'reference' I mean to suggest an engagement of the historical, whether past history or living history. The means of such reference may be textual or purely visual or the two combined; whichever, our understanding of reference and references must acknowledge and become conversant with these means. Many things turn on the difference between a historically-based and a purely contemporary interpretation. To cite one such thing: as we shall later see, artistic production presented by Chinese male filmmakers as 'gender liberation' has sometimes been understood as nothing more than 'female appropriation', a display of 'male desire' and nationalist hegemonism. A historical perspective which respects analogy and allegory as the historical root of Chinese rhetorical strategy and which appreciates the language historically employed in this analogic may fundamentally change that perception. We shall see.

A sympathetic attention to historical reference alters our perceptions of the entire cinematic medium. For example, considered in strictly contemporary terms, the very 'Chineseness' of China in a Chinese film, and of Chinese film itself, can be alienated, derogated by its employment of a modern 'foreign mechanicity'. Reference to the historical role of mimesis in traditional Chinese image-making, which was often written of as a sacred or near-sacred process, strongly suggests otherwise, but consider the following critique:

By presenting the problem of recording at an 'originary' moment of a socialist revolution such as the Chinese one, [Chinese film director] Chen [Kaige] reveals the fascistic (because mechanized) control of mass society that Western theorists are able to capture more readily in their own cultural contexts through the palpable forms of technical apparatuses but that are equally imminent in a modernized non-Western state . . . What is 'in ruins' [in *Yellow Earth*] is not only the myth of communist progressiveness but also the notion that critique itself can stand independent of the machines that allow its articulation. Because *Yellow Earth* uses the cinematic apparatus inherited from the West, and because it circulates in the world film market, it becomes, like other films, an instrument for representing a certain China . . . [What] constitutes the 'aura' of the Loess landscape – the earth, the sky, the peasants, and their quiet way of life – disappears the moment we see it on the cinema screen, because what we see is already the result of a reassembling (of the 'original') through technology and commodification.[3]

Notwithstanding the fact that film and other mechanics of replication and display (television, videotape, FAX, email, the 'Web') serve today as a fundamental challenge to the state's hegemonic control of information and knowledge in China (demonstrating that mechanicity *per se* is neither inherently fascist nor anti-fascist),[4] the above (Western) logic, if carried to its natural conclusion, builds a great cultural wall around the Chinese film-makers – essentializes, orientalizes, primitivizes, colonizes and disenfranchises them – all of which, I have assumed, runs counter to the above critic's actual intent.

By contrast, a visual historian would not very likely regard filmic replication as lacking for purely Chinese foundations on which to build: informed by the Confucian concepts of modelling and of the central role of image replication and miniaturization in the Daoist and Buddhist traditions, traditional aesthetic discussions of mimesis tell us otherwise. An art historian would not likely regard modern filmic replication as some kind of rupture with traditional Chinese principles of representation and reproduction – as put into practice in landscape painting and garden design, in the traditional carving of calligraphic examples into stone and the taking of repeated rubbings from these, in printed texts with multiply-reproduced woodblock print illustrations, in funerary-substitute sculptural figurines (*mingqi*), in model-mould bronze casting and pottery moulding, and in urban planning and architecture – and so there is little cultural basis by which to essentialize film's mechanistic dependence on 'the West' or to ascribe some 'fascistic' privilege to its mechanicity. A significant body of thoughtful literature attests to this.[5] Moreover, a historian of China may well prefer not to cede the construction of 'modernity' to the West (the essentialized 'West'), to equate Chinese 'modernity' with 'Westernization'. As the films discussed here indicate, a Chinese modernity, yes, even a Chinese avant-garde, can be built and perhaps can *only* be built on a Chinese past: the modern extends into the past and the past survives well into the modern. In these films and in their reference to the arts which surround them, past and present, a concern for rhetoric, its devices and traditions, their translation of text to image, couched in analogue, captured in allegory and melodrama, gendered and reflexive as to self and cultural identity, negotiated through film censorship: these things are of the deepest interest to an art historian and underlie the essays which follow.

These films are by no means free of Western ('Hollywood') reference, but for the most part, and varying from film to film, they operate by their own rules: by Chinese rules, one might say. Shot-countershot is often ignored in favour of long steady shots; crossing the 180° line, often declared inviolate in Hollywood film, occurs frequently. While comparison with Western film is valuable, comparison with historical examples of Chinese visuality, as seen in traditional Chinese painting, is invaluable. To achieve this, film frames are projected here alongside images from the past. The examples of traditional painting chosen for illustration are selected not as unique examples nor as particular works which directly influenced particular film-makers. Rather they function as stylistic types, visual signifiers of cultural modes so conventionalized as to represent common solutions to common problems: generally-known solutions, and yet collectively so diverse as to speak against a conception of 'Chinese tradition' as unchanging or uniform, or even as binary, or as lacking for diverse and complex aesthetic alternatives. Most of these paintings, like most of the films featured in these essays, represent visual solutions to the presentation of pre-extant narrative texts. Like the films discussed, they make extraordinary adjustments to accommodate content and convey message. And so, they prepare us to look for this in film and to look at film in certain ways. My intention is not to prove a rightness of viewpoint but rather to show how – and how differently from many others – an art historian might view Chinese film.

The choice of films for discussion in these essays accords with that subjective 'goodness' referred to above: these are all films which communicate eloquently, if not always agreeably, and they are films which any scholar may continue to learn more and more from even on a slightly wearying fourth or fifth consecutive viewing. They all speak to basic issues confronting China in its ongoing saga of modern identity formation. They speak *from* and sometimes directly about the modes that have long served to identify Chinese visual and textual rhetoric, even as they may vary, diverge from, redefine and renew that rhetorical tradition. That is to say, they speak with their own historical (and often, art-historical) consciousness, a creative consciousness of tradition very much like that once characterized by T. S. Eliot:

The historical sense involves a perception, not only of the pastness of the past, but of its presence; the historical sense compels a man to write not merely with his own generation in his bones, but with a feeling that the whole of literature . . . has a simultaneous existence and composes a simultaneous order.[6]

And so, I have not sought unnecessarily to establish a new canon. Rather, this selection conforms to my impression that those works which have recently been made available in the West, both on film and videotape, are for the most part among the intellectually richest offerings produced by the Chinese film industry. That is not to deny that any film, every film, offers a meaningful basis for exploration. But as art works, not all films achieve the same depth through their own filmmakers' direct efforts. A film like *Love on Mt Lu* (1980) admirably encodes the early Deng-Xiaoping-era hopes for an opening up to the West and reconciliation with Taiwan on terms that are strictly Beijing's own, while the 1950s Doris-Day-like aesthetic of the film, painfully glib and chokingly saccharine, unintentionally betrays the hopeless naïveté of that position. One viewing is sufficient to plumb its shallowness. For the films chosen here for more extensive discussion, on the other hand, it has seemed to me that – even after reading all I have been able to read about them – further viewing and consideration of their imagery and textuality has continued to offer still more to think about and discuss, and that they will offer viewers still more to discover even after reading these essays; this is a mark of their artistic achievement. Moreover, since there is little point to hearing films discussed that one has no opportunity whatsoever to view, the general availability of most of these films on videotape is a happy coincidence.

These films, by the very nature of their analogical mode, construct an open-ended frame of reference. Translations of the public sphere into art, they *enter* the public sphere and require their own translators. My translations, like theirs, make no pretence towards completeness and they are bound to leave one aware of limitations, subjectivity, and the distance shy of the original subject. The writer's eternal frustration at the slippage between object and interpretation is well expressed in Vladimir Nabokov's gnawing phrase,

How ludicrous these efforts to translate
Into one's private tongue a public fate!
Instead of poetry divinely terse,
Disjointed notes, Insomnia's mean verse![7]

With Nabokov uncertain about grasping *his own* experience, how much more slippage is there bound to be in my writing about films produced in another culture, about another culture, and bound up visually and textually in the rhetoric of another culture. And yet, while these essays have embraced the open frame and all its attendant frustrations, it is a *historical* sensibility which I hope has kept them more or less 'true' and which defines their intended contribution. I hope that my efforts – my insomnia! – will help to make these film-makers' translations of contemporary Chinese culture more meaningful and more accessible to others.

In acknowledging my gratitude to others, first must come those who have already written on this subject. To cite a few will inevitably draw a line that shouldn't have to be drawn between the named and the unnamed. But these essays would never have been written if not for the stimulus of other scholars, even those voices with which I am sometimes in disagreement but which are no less valued for that fact. Foremost among these I include Chris Berry, Nick Browne, Rey Chow, Paul Clark, Ann Kaplan, Leo Lee, Bonnie McDougall, Tony Rayns, Paul Pickowicz, George Semsel, Esther Yau, Eugene Wang and Jianying (Jane) Zha, and certainly other names should be included. More personally, I am most grateful for the encouragement and scholarly assistance, in ways both large and small, of my publisher, Michael Leaman; Wu Hung and Norman Bryson, both of whom read a complete draft and provided invaluable editorial criticism; as well as Stanley Abe, Ann Anagnost, Julia (Judy) Andrews, Tani Barlow, Maggie Bickford, Judy Boltz, Shawn Brixey, Susan Bush, James Cahill, Chang Tsong-zung (Johnson Chang), Stella and John Chien, Joan Cohen, Ding Xiaoqi, Patricia Failing, Merle Goldman, Wenda Gu, Stevan Harrell, Esther Jacobson, George Latsios, Leo Lee, Andrea Lingenfelter, Ning Qiang, Bob Sitton, Hsingyuan Tsao, Eugene Wang, staff members at the University of Washington's Center for Advanced Research Technology in the Arts and Humanities, and the students in my Chinese cinema classes here at the University of Washington and at Harvard University.

This study is dedicated to my family, Michelle, David and Emily, who now get me back for a while.

1–3 *Yellow Earth*. At the rain ceremony, a plain brown jar floats in a body of water . . . Seen again, the jar 'lies motionless' . . . In the third shot, the jar 'gradually sinks'.

4, 5 *Yellow Earth*. Led by Cuiqiao's father, prayers for rain . . . to the Dragon King.

1 Drowning on Dry Land: *Yellow Earth* and the Traditionalism of the 'Avant-garde'

A plain brown jar floats in a shallow body of murky brown water. A red textile wrapping, loosely attached, floats beside it. The image is seen three times. The first and second times, the jar 'lies motionless' on the water's surface. The third time, it 'gradually sinks' into the dim water, filling with liquid and giving off bubbles as it sinks, disappearing beneath its red mantle which floats visibly just below the surface of the water.

This image occurs in the final scene of *Yellow Earth* (illus. 1–3). By this point in the film, the young heroine has already drowned trying to cross the Yellow River, drought lies heavy on the land, and the Communist call to modernize has fallen on the deaf ears of peasants massed before a spirit-tablet of the Dragon King in a ancient ritual prayer for rain (illus. 4, 5). Cut into this four-and-a-half-minute prayer sequence, these three shots together last a mere seven seconds.[1] The image is fleeting – one can watch the film intently and hardly notice it – yet the imagery endures. Much has been written about *Yellow Earth*, and this depiction of peasants kneeling beneath the scorching sun, wreaths of green leaves wrapped around their heads, prostrating themselves before their dragon idol, has been much criticized, derogated by many of the film's mainland critics as 'primitive', 'superstitious' and 'embarrassing'. Yet the image of this jar in water has gone unmentioned in the critical literature, although it seems in retrospect to embody the essence of the film, both in content and style.[2]

There is no explanation whatsoever given in the film for this jar, no visual linkage established between the peasant prayer taking place on this dusty, bone-dry yellow land and the frame-filling image of muddy waters without embankment. There is no temporal linkage either: what we see could just as well be a flashback to another time and place as it could be part of the ceremony. Only from the director's notes do we learn that this is a jar of 'holy-water'.[3] Yet the notes disclose merely this and nothing more. What the image has to do with the peasant's prayers for rain, what it has to do with *Yellow Earth*, is left uncertain. Worked into the texture of the film with evident forethought and care, this imagery suggests the gendered aspects of the film at the same time as it embodies the peasant's shamanic resistance to the socialist call for modernization.[4] And it exemplifies the allusiveness, the elusiveness, and the ambivalence which lie at the heart of *Yellow Earth*.

Why would the film-makers put so much into so little? Or better put, how can they get so much from what *seems*, at first, to be so little? Why would they intentionally leave the audience, the urban audience at least, at such a remove from the inner workings of their film? How does such a 'simple', momentary image, more a painterly tableau than a cinematic montage, not only encapsulate their subtle message but also express the very nature of their cinematic artistry? This esoteric image is not a visual preface but a summation; the 'answer' to these questions lies not at the beginning but at the end.

Following three decades of unambiguous, propagandist movie-making, the profound, haunting realism, the gripping *uncertainty*, of *Yellow Earth* seemed to have come all at once out of nowhere (illus. 6). But its origins were already evident. By 1984, voices of social dissent had long ago appeared in literature (known as 'scar literature', from the wounds left by the Cultural Revolution) and in painting (see illus. 141). In fact, by 1984, 'scar literature' and related painting had already given way to a romantic encounter with rural Chinese 'primitivism' and a critical examination of China's rustic cultural 'roots'. A critical film tradition had also begun to appear, albeit more slowly, as the complex, expensive, and mechanized film industry took longer to reconstruct after the Cultural Revolution than other media and was more the government's own agent. In the film world, with its collectivist production and gerontocratic leadership, attitudes were more resistant to change and changing attitudes slower to appear than in other media. Through the mid-1980s, government functionaries in the film world had managed to direct most criticism against the Cultural Revolution's excesses; any broader target signalled a deviation from the ever-shifting but always-correct official line. 'Fifth Generation' film, at last, shifted critical attention from the Cultural Revolution to China's cultural roots. The emergence of *Yellow Earth* finally meant that an independent-minded cultural critique of the entire socialist experiment in China could be read through the framework of China's own government-controlled film industry. Departing from the formulas of the past three decades, engaging the vague and imparticular rather than championing the determined and heroic, *Yellow Earth* turned a political corner and staked out new cinematic territory.[5]

Official disagreement over the film stood in the way of its consideration for China's Hundred Flowers awards for films of 1984.[6] But given the strength of support for *Yellow Earth* by some of the critical factions within the film industry, a political compromise was worked out at the subsequent Golden Rooster awards and a prize was given for photography – nothing more.[7] This was the only award *Yellow Earth* would ever receive in China.[8] But a month later, in April 1985, *Yellow Earth*

6 *Yellow Earth*. Cuiqiao as water-bearer.

suddenly became a sensation at the Hong Kong International Film Festival. After the film was shown, director Chen Kaige and cinematographer Zhang Yimou were mobbed by the audience and one member of the audience is said to have stood up and proclaimed emotionally, 'For all these years I had despaired for China. Now I see hope!'⁹ *Yellow Earth*, on that occasion, heralded the arrival of a new Chinese film culture. In the next six days in Hong Kong, more than a million tickets to *Yellow Earth* were sold.¹⁰ In China, despite critics' claims about its impenetrability, *Yellow Earth* then found an audience: once re-released to the public, already made a curiosity by its Hong Kong success, it became the fifth most popular film of the year in China. For Bonnie McDougall, who has made in this the most extensive study of any Chinese film, the controversy over *Yellow Earth* lay at the very heart of the film's historical importance:

... its success, and the controversy about its success, constituted altogether such an event in Chinese film history that the Chinese film world has never been the same since. Internationally, its creativity and maturity demand that Chinese films no longer be judged by patronizing double standards but against the best the rest of the world has to offer.¹¹

With *Yellow Earth*, a new film era was born in China.

In the realm of aesthetics, the aesthetic principles articulated in 1942 by Mao Zedong at the Yan'an 'forum on literature and art' and

7 *Yellow Earth*. At the wedding, wooden fish are served to peasants who cannot afford the real thing.

subsequently enshrined as Communist dogma had insisted on projecting ideological clarity, grounding everything in class struggle and rejecting anything that smacked of 'art for art's sake', abstraction, or ambiguities that might muddy the line between good politics and bad, national friend and class enemy.[12] By 1984, Mao's guiding principles had been altered in theory and were beginning to change in practice.[13] Central to Maoist aesthetic standards was the elimination of so-called 'middle characters' – meaning anyone a Western audience might think of as real people, characters with complex or unresolved motives and attitudes. Yet in *Yellow Earth*, essentially *all* the characters are middle characters. Its peasants, rather than heroic vanguards of the revolution, are portrayed as superstitious victims of their environment.

Set in 1938, *Yellow Earth* was filmed in northern Shaanxi province, on the edge of the ancient 'cradle of Chinese civilization', a dusty, desert highland through which the Yellow River bears water from distant western mountains to a distant eastern sea. At the wedding with which the movie opens, the peasants are so poor and so bound to tradition that when the obligatory offering of fish to the guests cannot be afforded, it is substituted for by platters of carved *wooden* fish passed around to the guests, served up with sauce (illus. 7). The ritual prayer for rain which draws the film to a close is understood as a reversion to China's most primitive tribal origins. In the end, as in the beginning, the yellow land towers magnificent, terrible and ageless over all those whose lives it enfolds, seeming intractable to modern socialist mechanization. Most controversial of all, the potency of the People's Liberation Army, with the future it once promised on behalf of the Communist Party, is rendered ambiguous (illus. 8). Previously, Jiang Qing, Mao Zedong's wife who reigned as cultural czar of the Cultural

Revolution, reduced Maoist aesthetics to her 'Three Principles of Stress', which for nearly ten years dominated stage and screen:

Of all the characters, stress the positive ones. Of the positive characters, stress the heroic ones. Of the main [heroic] characters, stress the central one.[14]

In practice, 'All creation and production in the ten years of the Cultural Revolution started from those theories,' according to former Film Bureau vice-director Ding Jiao.

If we wanted to describe a main hero, he could have no shortcomings, no shaky ideas. He had to be very tall, very complete and a perfect man, with no love affairs. He always looked ahead, not sideways. After he came on stage, all others had to step aside . . . If an actor wanted to praise, it was done with an arm outstretched to the sky. If he despised something, he pointed to the earth strongly. If he got excited, he put his hand to his heart.[15]

But no heroes appear in *Yellow Earth*, and no villains; no theatrics, no stress; only ambiguity. The greatest tension in *Yellow Earth* appears not on the screen, but *between* the screen and the government-controlled film-making industry.

Many official critics felt *Yellow Earth*'s portrayal of Chinese peasants to be sullen and uninspiring, found their long silences boring and incomprehensible, and argued that they should have been shown as resolutely

8 *Yellow Earth*. Gu Qing arrives and immediately begins to inscribe the peasants' songs.

demanding a better life. The masses, they claimed, 'couldn't under-stand it'. Typical of such criticism was that by film director Yu Yanfu, who said:

They've paid a great deal of attention to the composition of a lot of the shots and visually the result is stunning. But what happens in these scenes has absolutely nothing to do with the inner working or actions of their characters. All in all, it's a bit like a foreign art film. There are a lot of shots in which the camera simply doesn't move, and the characters remain immobile and silent for long periods. You can't really tell what they're supposed to be thinking . . . [The film-makers] have ignored the fact that our audiences, especially people in the country-side, cannot possibly cope with a film like this.[16]

In reading the script – the barest of bones on which to hang a movie – one becomes fully aware of the central role played by cinematography and art design (the latter directed by He Qun). With dialogue held to a minimum, as in many an early Chinese film (*Street Angel* of 1937 provides a good comparison), characterization and setting establish its essence. Unspoken gesture, even reticence itself, together with private passages embedded in song, become all the more poignant and re-vealing. The role of landscape – mountains, water, sky – takes on heightened importance. Yet these remain suggestive signifiers, indicative rather than declarative. The resulting ambiguity is critical to the deep effect of the film and to the differentiation of that effect on different viewers. Of this ambiguity, Bonnie McDougall has written:

The multiple associations developed by these images gave the film a quality of open-endedness that was so unusual in Chinese film that it needed to be defended . . . [The] fact that it has meant so many different things to so many different kinds of people is also a testimony, to Western eyes at least, to the artistic subtlety and philosophical depth of the film, just as its appeal to audiences unconscious of or uninterested in the film's political messages is testimony to its cinematic skill . . . Corresponding to the indeterminate-ness of the imagery, the film can be interpreted as being 'about' a range of subjects; again, this was a feature that pleased some, puzzled many more, and irritated most of the authorities.[17]

Chen Kaige has said unequivocally, 'The aim of the film is to explore our national character.'[18] But in a state-managed film studio, such a subjective critique required the camouflage of restraint and indirec-tion.[19] The basic plot of *Yellow Earth*, therefore, is left so understated as to seem almost pointless to a cultural outsider. The tale is simple. A People's Liberation Army soldier, Gu Qing, comes to the people to gather peasant tunes so that he can re-write them for propaganda purposes, providing them with new socialist lyrics (illus. 9). He speaks

9 *Yellow Earth*. Gu Qing is introduced as song-gatherer to the wedding guests.

10 *Yellow Earth*. Cuiqiao looks.

11 *Yellow Earth*. Cuiqiao last seen, challenging the Yellow River and history itself.

to them of a new lifestyle, one of mutual help and lessened oppression. But he never comes to understand them, while their repeated grunts of collective politeness lack any true assent, understanding, or evident potential for taking revolutionary responsibility, and they mostly go on living their lives unchanged by him. A young girl, Cuiqiao, seeks to join him but is thwarted by him; then pursuing an independent course, she apparently loses her life (illus. 10, 11). Only this, with little elaboration. Taken at face value, this is little more than an extended vignette. Like the figures themselves, gaunt and introspective, the film and its political critique remain closed to the casual viewer and must be examined intratextually, prised open and scrutinized historically, to divulge its meaning.

What stands between Gu Qing and the people, between the people and change, lies in the remoteness of each, in the peasants' unshakable fatalism, in the soldier's dispassionate manner, as reliant on Communist rhetoric and bureaucracy as the peasants are on their traditions, as smug and unquestioning about the revolutionary change he intends for the peasants as the peasants are that nothing will or can change. (The name Gu, translatable as 'The Overseer', seems well selected, but this would-be leader of peasants doesn't even quite know how to guide a plough and must be 'roughly' corrected by Cuiqiao's father.)[20] When the soldier asks why young girls must suffer so,[21] the father responds with the classic Chinese reply – *ming*, Fate: it's determined (illus. 12). And he speaks to the soldier prosaically of gendered relationships dependent not on love but on food, its availability and absence at the family table: 'Meat and wine friends, rice and wheat spouses . . . Where's love when there's no food?'[22] When the soldier speaks to him of replacing forced marriage by spousal choice and advocates the education of women, the father rejects this, saying, 'How can that be? We farmers have rules' (illus. 13). But the plot is laced with irony and leads to tragedy: when the soldier finally wins an unintended convert, the young Cuiqiao who seeks to follow him in order to escape an arranged and unwanted marriage, the soldier demurs in terms that mirror the father's own intransigence (illus. 14).

We officials are bound by official regulations; it would have to be approved by the leadership . . . We officials need these regulations to conquer the land.[23]

This, of course, reminds the audience of all those things that haven't changed since the Communists become China's new emperors and bureaucrats.

The soldier vows to come back for her some time later – by April (illus. 15) – but fails to keep that promise. And when he finally returns, it is too late to matter. Having encountered her ideologically but failing to engage her adequately as an individual, to access the details of her life, to perceive the personal depths of her suffering, her desperation and her haste, Gu Qing leaves the audience to wonder how he can save the masses if he cannot save this one poor soul. He is a rhetorician, not a man of action, unable to deliver on utopian promises. His treatment of Cuiqiao, while intended to offset the traditional inequities of her peasant community, turns out to be yet another line of gendered circumscription. That this failure is mutual, as much the result of Cuiqiao's own reticent acquiescence as of Gu Qing's aloofness, seems ironically to cast this

12 *Yellow Earth*. Why must the young girls suffer? 'It's Fate.'

13 *Yellow Earth*. The peasants are bound by tradition . . .

14 *Yellow Earth* . . . and the Communists are bound by authority.

15 *Yellow Earth*. Gu Qing promises to return by April.

mismatch between the peasant girl and the soldier, between the people and the PLA, in the large and immutable form that the peasants themselves know best: fate, sad fate. It is a tale cast as fiction but already told, tragically and irreversibly, by history itself. Through cinematic form and dramatic structure, this presentation is inscribed in terms of national destiny.

The tradition of government tune-gathering among the people goes back to the *Book of Odes*, which was collated by Zhou-period governments from lyrics and texts of the tenth to sixth centuries BC, and edited and interpreted by Confucius himself, among others. The dual function of monitoring popular sentiment and rewriting such texts in order to educate the masses to the satisfaction of their lords must also have been an ancient tradition. In his study of this conversion from folk song to Confucian 'allegory', Haun Saussy writes: 'Poetry tattles on society – a society formed (in part) by the canons of its poetry. The work of art, it seems, gets lost and found between its two functions of documenting mores and changing them.'[24] This practice was brought back to life in modern times, and it forms the basis of one of the brightest Maoist-era propaganda films, the musical *Third Sister Liu* (*Liu Sanjie*, 1961; illus. 16), whose eighth-century heroine, anachronistically and reflexively, intones the nascent aspirations of the people,

> Whatever sentiment is in the mind suppressed
> Erupts like fire in songs from the breast.
> Mountain songs are like springs so clear,
> Sung in vales and jungles everywhere.
> They rush and roar like floods unfurled
> Breaking all dykes, inundating the world . . .
> If songs are not sung, sorrow will spread.
> If roads are not walked upon, weeds will grow.
> If steel knives are not sharpened, rust will erode them.
> If heads are not held high, backs will bend.[25]

The gathering of songs (*cai feng*), their conversion into history and of history into allegory for contemporary use – a fundamental Confucian practice revived in the Maoist era – parallels the degree to which Confucian theory itself was culled in the 1950s and early 60s for 'heritable' traits (*jicheng yichan*), making the past serve the present. Kam Louie's re-evaluation of this latter phenomenon, *Inheriting Tradition*, asserts:

Taking the pre-Cultural Revolution period as a whole, it was quite evident that nearly all contributors to the discussion agreed that Kongzi's [Confucius'] educational thinking should be inherited in the new socialist society . . . On the whole, the interpretations of Kongzi's ethics and educational thought were less damning than the May Fourth ones.[26]

Ironically, it is in the post-Mao era that this Confucian/Communist practice of 'reflective history' (*yingshe*), this forcing of history into a contemporary mold, has received the greatest criticism.[27] Appropriation lies at the heart of this tradition with perhaps not a little deception, taking songs from the peasants, altering them, and returning them to the people as their own. In the case of *Yellow Earth*, however, this tradition is appropriated *from* the government and the practice held up for critical scrutiny. Yet at the same time, *Yellow Earth* utilizes and further perpetuates that practice, in its own way.

In *Yellow Earth*, almost all of the songs are about marriage and target the feudalistic practice of forced marriage and child brides (see illus. 19). Arranged marriage was a frequent target of May Fourth and Communist propaganda from the 1920s on, including the early participation of Mao Zedong, whose own first marriage at about age fourteen was arranged

不是仙家不是神

16 *Third Sister Liu*. Revolutionary musician Liu Sanjie sings: 'I'm not an immortal, I'm not a goddess.'

(with an illiterate peasant girl six years his senior)[28] and who in 1919 directed some of his earliest political tracts against the practice.[29] Arranged marriage, then, becomes the film's central trope on the backwardness of traditional society. The lyrics of the hired entertainer at the impoverished wedding scene with which the film opens (illus. 17, see illus. 8).

> Pairs of ivory chopsticks // are set out on the table,
> The sieved wine from the silver pot // is poured with a golden ladle . . .

describe a ceremony far removed from that one actually taking place, and his characterization of the marriage,

> Paired off in twos // carp swim in the rills,
> Paired off in twos // goats leap in the hills,
> Paired off in twos // pigs root in the trough,
> Fortune smiled // as they pledged their troth . . .

follows with scant credibility.[30] This song, then, initiates the audience into a sceptical mode. For the peasants *in* the film, such lyrics may briefly form a poor substitute *for* reality, but for the audience they arouse a suspicion about rhetoric that soon extends to Gu Qing's own lyric endeavours.

Pairs of carp swim in the stream

I'd like to say what is on my mind, but I don't know how

I want a good husband, not a bed-wetter

17 *Yellow Earth*. The wedding singer: 'Pairs of ivory chopsticks // are set out on the table . . . Paired off in twos // carp swim in the rills.'

18 *Yellow Earth*. Cuiqiao sings to herself what she can't tell to others.

19 *Yellow Earth*. Hanhan sings.

Song-gatherer Gu Qing finds, at first, that the peasant family he has been assigned to won't sing for him. But once they do, their tunes turn out to be quite different from that of the entertainer, far less of fantasy and more of harsh reality. The central figure of the film, the adolescent peasant girl Cuiqiao, sings only to herself as she works (illus. 18), often late at night. Her songs all lament her impending marriage at the age of fourteen. Only gradually does she share her songs and her predicament with the guest. Her younger brother Hanhan (literally,'the Mute') is slow to speak or to sing, but when he does at last he offers a crude, earthy parody of childhood marriage, about a bridegroom so young that he still pees in his bed (illus. 19). The soldier laughs good-naturedly at this song but his laughter is a measure of his distance from the peasants, for whom this irony is far more grim than humorous.

The father's song is also slow to come ('I'm not happy and not sad,' he says at one point, so 'why should I sing now?'), but when the soldier is due to leave he offers the grimmest tune of all, a ceremonious recitation on the fate of women, stereotype enclosing historical reality:

> The first hour // of First Month strikes.
> Big bright eyes // two shining lights.
> Curving eyebrows // Two arched bows.
> All adore her // wherever she goes.
> Betrothed at thirteen // at fourteen a wife,
> At fifteen a widow // for the rest of her life.
> Three loud cries // on all ears fell.
> Three low cries // she jumps into the well.[31]

The watery fate of this Chinese bride will be played out on many levels in *Yellow Earth*, as it had been countless times before in Chinese history.

Motherless, Cuiqiao is about to be married off at the age of fourteen. Her resistance to this marriage has already earned her a thrashing by her father and cannot be accommodated: her betrothal money has already been spent or promised, in part to provide for her dead mother's funeral, the rest set aside for her younger brother Hanhan's wedding. In this way, she's earned back the cost of her childhood upkeep, and having used up her value in her own family she will soon be dismissed to serve some other. Once 'abandoned' by Gu Qing, Cuiqiao is married off to a much older husband who is shown to the audience only as a darkened hand reaching out to grasp her – the director's ready dismissal of forced marriage as a devilish institution, although too easy a melodramatic stroke for many Western critics.[32] Perhaps to accentuate the gap between peasants' rooted helplessness and the Party's feverish rhetoric, that grim bridal scene is immediately juxtaposed with a view of a PLA troupe of waist-drummers performing enthusiastically before Gu Qing at the Communists' Yan'an headquarters (illus. 20). She suffers while they celebrate. The film then returns to Cuiqiao by the banks of the Yellow River, described in the director's script notes as

now dressed as a married woman. Already all trace of her former gentleness has disappeared. Her expression is confused, dull, blank, as if she could easily be startled. Her married life can be known by the grief and fear contained deep within her eyes.[33]

There by the riverbank, Cuiqiao tells her brother, 'I'm suffering, I can't wait any longer,' and desperate to flee her new marriage, she now determines to find the better life that solder Gu Qing had described. Striking out on her own in the dead of night, she seeks to cross the Yellow River, and she does so with a song taught her by Gu Qing, evidently appropriated from some peasant tune. But she pays for this transgression with her life, a victim of the Yellow River's life-giving waters, and she dies with Gu Qing's military song on her lips (see illus. 11). As her boat disappears from view, her song is interrupted most tellingly –

> The hammer, the sickle // and the scythe,
> For workers and peasants // shall build a new life.
> The piebald cock // flies over the wall.
> The Communist . . .

– leaving unsung the words '. . . Party will save us all'.[34]

Cuiqiao's death, drowned as she fails to navigate from one culture to another, from ancient tradition to modernity, is a disturbing omen of unfortunate things to come for the Chinese people. Although she dies with her hopes intact, her faith comes to nothing. Cinematically, as Gu Qing first appeared like a speck on the land, so Cuiqiao is last seen as a speck upon the water. Read as allegory, the implication drawn from Gu Qing's inability to save her from this fate is that the lives of these peasants, unchanged for thousands of years, lie beyond the reach of the soldier, of the PLA bureaucracy, and of the impending Communist

20 *Yellow Earth*. At Yan'an, the waist-drummers dance.

21 *Yellow Earth*. The Three Obediences and the Four Virtues.

Revolution. The yellow earth and the Yellow River, rather than the red revolution, will ultimately control the lives of these Chinese people.[35]

Bonnie McDougall writes that in China and among sinologists, *Yellow Earth* has been seen more in terms of the father and son, less in terms of the daughter.[36] Esther Yau has effectively 'unbraided' the different 'strands' within the film, representing the differing interests first of the father, then Cuiqiao, next of the soldier Gu Qing, and finally of brother Hanhan.[37] Yet the plot of *Yellow Earth* turns on the young girl, whom Chen Kaige has described as 'the hope of our whole people',[38] and much of the film is filtered through Cuiqiao's feminine perceptions, her acculturated passivity and the futile gesture of her flight. The audience watches her watch her own oncoming fate. That fate is inscribed as female and tragic. Cuiqiao is first seen at a village wedding, an event which clarifies and circumscribes her own destiny as she watches by a doorway on which is written the Confucian code of behaviour for women, 'The Three Obediences and the Four Virtues' (*san cong si de*; illus. 21).[39] Her eyes are filled with a sad curiosity as if she knows already, however dimly, the victim's role that lies ahead. A symbolic victim of this film, she represents the suffering of all Chinese people, and she's all the more a symbol for being young, scarcely into her adolescence, as well as for being poor. In a Chinese idiom, one might parody this as 'The Three Vulnerabilities' – poor, young, and female.

As was the case in so many pre-1949 films in the 'May Fourth tradition' which *Yellow Earth* calls upon, the Chinese nation has been equated with the female gender through their mutual victimization. From the 1984 perspective, however, there is no singular villain: no foreign imperialism, no petty-capitalism with its radical division of rich and poor, not even the old feudalistic economy of landlords and peasants. Now, the too-bureaucratic PLA has had its chance to perform the saviour role and the too-reticent peasantry its chance to be saved; but salvation is nowhere at hand. If there is villainy now, it is collective. But perhaps there is only fate, inescapable as gender and engendered as female.

In the timeless peasant world of *Yellow Earth*, the earth is sexualized and all things derive from that: 'Poor as it was,' says Chen Kaige of the yellow earth, 'it nurtured our Chinese race, it has the warmth of a mother, it gives us strength and hope.'[40] In this world, men work the soil, women provide water. *Yang* and *yin*, simple, essentialist. The father is a widow. For him, the earth is his daily mate (see illus. 12). He sexualizes it as he furrows the soil and urges on his ox with a repeated 'How the fuck can we sow, hoi hoi hoi hoi . . . How the fuck can we sow, hoi hoi hoi hoi.'[41] He's a disciplined farmer and a stern parent. Like his farming father, brother Hanhan is linked to the land as a shepherd, a roamer of the hills, clad in sheepskins and dirt (see illus. 19). In the coupled world of *yang* and *yin*, gender shifts with context. The earth is female in relation to sky and mother to the man, but earth is male in relation to water. In contrast to father and son, Cuiqiao, the daughter of tradition, is linked to water, to the great Yellow River, as waterbearer for the family (see illus. 6, 18).[42] Daily she fetches water, descending from her homestead to the deep Yellow River valley, three miles distant, then ascending the steep mountainside to bear the precious liquid home. The remainder of her time she spends about the family's cave-dwelling, sewing and cooking, coming outdoors mainly to bring liquid nourishment to the fields at lunch time – a brothy millet gruel. Gu Qing roams the landscape as a nation-builder; Cuiqiao, try as she might to overturn tradition, cannot escape from water.

Cuiqiao's misery is private: repressed longing more than actual rebellion, committed to songs sung only to herself –

> Sixth month on the river // the ice has not yet thawed.
> It's my own father forcing me // towards the wedding board.
> Of all the five grains // the green pea is the roundest.
> Of all us poor folk // daughters are the saddest.
> Daughters are the saddest, o daughter o.
> Pigeons fly high above // one with the other,
> The one I long for // is my own dear mother.[43]

Deprived of a mother, or of any female companionship, she is also deprived of a sympathetic understanding except that from the cinematic audience. Her reluctance to wed can readily be understood by a modern audience, Chinese as well as Western. In an arranged marriage, when the match is poor with husband or mother-in-law, the alternatives open to the wife are few. Mao Zedong, in the articles already noted, identified China's high female suicide rate with arranged, loveless marriage and modern studies bear out the continuing linkage to oppressive female conditions.[44] And yet, not every young girl resisted marriage. Why Cuiqiao resisted so is not explored or explained psychologically in the film. Her personality is too internalized and opaque to provide an explanation. Her response is not ideological either, and as her rebelliousness lay less in personality than in plot, it is defined more by the larger, allegorical issue of China's fate than by her own individuality. Her rising desperation preceded the solder Gu Qing and his revolutionary message and was not simply triggered by his arrival or his rhetoric. Yet if her rejection of the normal was there before him, a proper alternative was lacking, and so it is Gu Qing himself, a gentle but detached embodiment of socialist virtues, who awakens Cuiqiao's active response. Gu arouses her hopes and feelings with his rhetoric, with his song of flight and freedom –

> . . . The piebald cock // flies over the wall,
> The Communist Party // shall save us all.[45]

Gu Qing arrives to the film's initial wedding scene – that of another village daughter but portending Cuiqiao's own – and he reveals through his frowns at the end of the ceremony his ideological distance from their customs. From that moment on, this sublimated ideologue is a rival to the arranged marriage-partner of Cuiqiao. His focal opposition to marital arrangement makes it so. Thus, a confluence of interests emerges – Cuiqiao's unwanted marriage, Gu Qing's ideological opposition to unfree marriage customs – and with it, a special kind of courtship. However subdued she may seem, Cuiqiao progresses from hopeless to hopeful, from withdrawn to assertive, as expressed by the young actress Xue Bai through sensitive and subtle changes in poise and countenance – in the rate at which she pumps the bellows at the family hearth (see illus. 35), in the slow trudge of her feet en route to and from the river which later becomes a happy patter. To what degree does Gu Qing himself, then or later, become the object of her response? (see illus. 15). In form, is this a romance? A seduction? Is Cuiqiao responding only to the message, or also to the messenger? Though a Western audience might anticipate the possibility of sexual liaison, a Chinese audience knows better. But romance is not out of the question.[46]

The near-formlessness of *Yellow Earth* encourages a mode of shifting appropriation that is associative rather than specifically referential. The verses about which much of the film is structured inevitably call to mind the *Odes* and their own manner of historical appropriation, but other traditions also pertain. Rubie Watson, for example, has studied the bridal songs of Hong Kong's New Territories, 'a series of laments (literally "crying songs", *kuga*) that punctuated their ritual journey from daughters to wives'.[47] While improvisational and heartfelt, these songs are taught by older women and memorized by the bride, who sings them not only to express her own sorrow at leaving her parents and friends behind but to ritually assert that the filial rupture about to transpire comes not from her own lack of piety but from society's exogamic demands upon her. In doing so, she effectively reasserts her virtue and demonstrates her capacity to shift her noble allegiance from family to in-laws. 'Through her mournful and often bitter songs, each bride at once disrupts and reunites the fragile communities of women that endure but yet with every bridal leave-taking are violated.'[48]

Thus, whatever her personal sense of loss and anxiety, she does not so much create an oppositional concept of filial piety as refashion the more public Confucianized image.[49] There is perhaps some equivalence to this in the Ansai district of Shaanbei, where the folksongs collected by *Yellow Earth*'s film-makers originated, a regional song type identified at the outset of the film as *xintianyou*.[50] This may raise the question of how much Cuiqiao's lament is refashioning her social obligations and how much it is oppositional. Her actions – her flight from marriage and the community – seem to provide an answer. And yet her last act before departing, urging Hanhan to console and care for their father, suggest a nobility, a social purpose to her revolutionary spirit, and her intention to 'refashion' things in a larger social sense.

Chen Kaige has described *Yellow Earth* as 'very sexual', a notion that might scarcely occur to most Western viewers and which when offered might strike them as peculiar or even perverse.[51] Although the issue of childhood betrothal rests somewhere near the core of its plot, Cuiqiao's husband appears only instaneously, shown as nothing more than a darkened hand removing her bridal hood, and her flight from this unwanted match leads both Cuiqiao and her audience away from sexual libido into the tight embrace of liberationist politics. So, just what Chen means by 'very sexual', and what is sexual or romantic about *Yellow Earth*, demands interpretation.

Another poetic tradition comes readily to mind in considering Cuiqiao's 'flight' and the 'romantic' form of *Yellow Earth*, that of China's first famous balladeer, the exiled and frustrated politician-poet from the state of Chu, the high minister Qu Yuan (328–278 BC). As it had done throughout two millennia of traditional Chinese culture, the Qu Yuan literary tradition 'has served the modern Chinese as a medium for grappling with problems in the transformation of twentieth-century Chinese society . . . a forum for discourse, a stage for dramatically posing and answering questions, for expressing dilemmas'.[52] For centuries a Confucian model of loyalty to the state, Qu Yuan became for many Maoist intellectuals before the Cultural Revolution a proto-revolutionary reformer and man of the people, sometimes 'the very source of China's revolutionary romantic tradition', and even something of a 'mythic alter ego for Mao Tse-tung', whose poems invoked Qu Yuan's precedent.[53] As China's national poet, his death commemorated annually as China's Dragon Boat Festival national holiday, Qu Yuan provides the prototype for the transfigurative analogue between political lament and sexual romance.

'When Qu Yuan was banished, / He wandered along the river's banks, or walked at the marsh's edge, chanting as he went.'[54] Thus began an ancient poem, written about Qu Yuan not long after his death. Qu Yuan's 'chants' or romantic laments (sao), like many of the Confucian Odes, were apparently modelled on romantic folksongs, which in some cases had already been appropriated for secondary purposes – 'shamanic' purposes – before being heard by Qu Yuan in the exotic territory to which he was banished. In the Nine Songs attributed to Qu Yuan, a shaman or shamaness ritually poses as a solicitous, seductive lover, wooing a deity of the opposite gender pursued in shamanic flight, including one song dedicated to the Lord of the Yellow River (illus. 22).[55] So Qu Yuan, writing (adapting) songs intended for the ear of his unfaithful king, poses as the poser, sings twice-borrowed love songs with the intent of winning back the heart of his king and being recalled to his ministerial post. Lord and vassal become male and female, lover and suitor. These chants begin spectacularly, with shamanical spirits soaring aloft and end tragically, with them falling out of the skies:

> Open wide the door of heaven!
> On a black cloud I ride in splendour,
> Bidding the whirlwind drive before me,
> Causing the rainstorm to lay the dust . . .

> I am no longer near him, fast growing a stranger.
> He drives his dragon chariot with thunder of wheels;
> High up he rides, careening heavenwards.
> But I stand where I am, twisting a spray of cassia:
> The longing for him pains my heart.
> It pains my heart, but what can I do?[56]

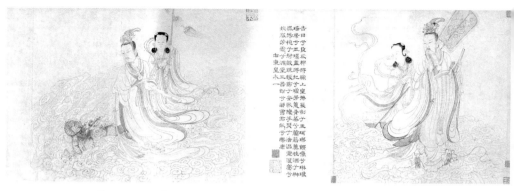

22 Zhang Wu, *The Nine Songs*, 1360, section from a handscroll, ink on paper. Cleveland Museum of Art (purchase from the J. H. Wade Fund).

The two deities illustrated here are Tai Yi, God of the East (right), and the Lord Among Clouds.

Notably, in song as in real life, Qu Yuan fails in his quest and his failure ends in suicide by drowning.

This well-known material suggests how far back in time one can trace the high literary tradition in China of appropriating female identity in the pursuit of masculine political ends. As early as the Han dynasty, poets had begun to combine elements of the *Odes* with gendered elements of Qu Yuan in political allegories whose indirect reference contemporary critics understood as designed to skirt possible political difficulties; by the Tang period, it was common to locate one's contemporary criticism in the Han.[57]

Like Qu Yuan's verses, to which parallels can be drawn, *Yellow Earth* effects the dual equation of politics with shamanical transformation and shamanic magic with mystic romance. The analogue with Qu Yuan is not cast as a one-for-one set of parallels – there is plenty of slippage – but *Yellow Earth* is drawn on similar themes. Bound to one earthly site as an exile, Qu Yuan bounds skywards in song, wooing celestial deities, but proclaiming as his subtext a Confucian-like loyalty; *Yellow Earth*'s cast of peasants are earth-bound by fate, but as two of them rise to the secular faith of Communism, Gu Qing the socialist deity is wooed with increasing enthusiasm by Cuiqiao the shamanic aspirant. Not all of this is lodged in patently sexual terms: Cuiqiao may be of an age to marry, but *Yellow Earth* is not that earthy. Gender and marriage are among the film's concerns, but they are only its means; its ends are transcendentally political, the putative reform of tradition *by* social-ism, and the mating of Cuiqiao to Gu Qing is a sublimated wedding of dreams. What the film, through them, proposes and then disposes of is a wedding of people and Party. And yet, while sexual romance is not the

34

evident substance of this tale, and might even be viewed as a distorted reading, the plot is cast and the tension of the film is captured in romantic form.[58]

The first time Cuiqiao sings[59] with Gu Qing near, she does so to solicit his intervention, raising her voice for him to hear that she needs someone to turn to, that she would brave any hardship to avoid her arranged marriage:

> . . . The embroidered purse // is round and neat,
> As long as I don't marry // hardship is sweet.
> Up on the window-sill // the cock lies sleeping.
> Who can I turn to // when I get a beating,
> When I get a beating, o daughter o.

The next time she sings, still alone, Gu Qing has become the subject of her tune, and her lament now is her inability to approach him openly. Her song is now populated with traditional images of romantic mates: ducks and geese in pairs and swimming freely, expressing her longing; poplars and willows lining the riverbank, the tropes for elegant lovers in many a traditional poem.

> Ducks float along the river // and geese swim.
> The Official doesn't know // that I, Cuiqiao, can sing.
> Poplars and willows // eighteen in a row.
> Cuiqiao longs to speak // but how she doesn't know.
> She doesn't know, o daughter o.[60]

By the time Cuiqiao finally sings openly for Gu Qing, he's already rejected her entreaties to take her along. She sings now of the Eighth Route Army that she hopes to join ('Should the Eighth Route Army // only bid me prepare, / I'll discard my red [wedding] shoes // and straw sandals wear'). But Gu Qing himself is very much in this song, in which she sounds praises for his masculinity, as the Communist cock, prepared to fly off beyond her reach. As a gauge of *Yellow Earth*'s engagement with appropriation as both theme and form, this image refers back to Gu's socialist song, which in turn derived from Cuiqiao's own 'sleeping cock' on the window-sill. Cuiqiao casts herself as a dutiful female, a spinner of cotton, and in semi-erotic terms as a loyal would-be spouse, through the time-honoured trope on the feminine beauty of tender willow branches:

> The piebald cock // stands by the tree,
> From the Communist Party // comes a man who's free
> Choosing one horse from many // one beats the rest.
> Comparing you with the others // our Official's the best, Yi-ai-yo! . . .
> Two ounces of cotton // are spun into a skein.

I'm afraid that from now on // I'll never see you again,
Never see you again.
The wind has dropped // but willow tips sway,
For your return // I long night and day.
As soon as I hear // our Official return,
Two holes in the window // shall my meagre eyes burn.
Larks crossing the river // won't fall to the bottom,
For the rest of my life // you'll not be forgotten . . .

By the conclusion of this song, Gu Qing is no longer in earshot and her hopes for herself and her fellow poor are dashed, beyond the reach of the Party propaganda – much like a Qu Yuan lament, with Qu Yuan's shaman come crashing out of the sky:

Onions can't root // in bare stony ground.
When can we poor folk // turn our fate round,
Turn our fate round?!
Behind the cloud // the sun dips low.
My lips can't speak // my heart's sorrow.
Green grass and cow dung // can't put out a fire,
Folk songs can't save me // poor Cuiqiao
Poor Cuiqiao, o daughter o.[61]

Cuiqiao rebels against her fate, but she cannot escape. In the end, what she pursues in her desperate futility is not the messenger but the message, not the person of Gu Qing but the idealized world of liberated women he has described to her. She 'murmurs' to Hanhan, 'No! I'm not looking for brother Gu, I'm going to cross the river. The Eighth Route Army lies east of the river. . .'[62] All along, that alternative remains ill-considered, in need of further definition. Cuiqiao does not understand her impulse or its directive and does not answer Hanhan's plea to re-consider her intention to cross the river. Spurned by Gu Qing as Qu Yuan was spurned by the gods, she drowns as Qu Yuan had drowned, with Gu Qing's song on her lips.

Although he aroused Cuiqiao emotionally, Gu Qing was never himself aroused. He never shared her longing. The viewer is obliged to ponder in retrospection Gu Qing's peculiar lack of emotion – for therein lies his failure to connect with Cuiqiao, or its equivalent in Chen Kaige's time, the Party's rupture with the People. The ideological enthusiasm of Gu Qing's Eighth Route Army song is contrasted starkly with the personal sentimentality of Cuiqiao's lyrics. Why is he prepared to intervene with words and ideas yet unable to succeed with deeds? Through what mismatch of cool intellectuality (his) and native reticence (hers) do they fail to communicate her compelling need, and why the inadequacy of his response? Like Qu Yuan's deity on high, Gu Qing 'soars serenely . . . careening heavenwards', while Cuiqiao is left earthbound and vulnerable.[63] On this inadequate romance of would-be god and all-too human worshipper, this challenged pairing of Party and peasant, of lofty goals and harsh realities, turns the plot of *Yellow Earth*, with ordinary life held in the balance.

The nature of Cuiqiao's death has been questioned. Film critic Shao Mujun regarded it as a suicide, as it was indeed intended to be in Ke Lan's original story.[64] According to McDougall (who herself calls it 'half-suicidal'),[65]

Deng Baochen also raises and answers some other questions on the plausibility of Cuiqiao's story. Why didn't she wait for daylight to cross the river in safety? Because her absence would be discovered at daybreak and her husband's family would set off in pursuit. Why did Gu Qing refuse to take her with him when she asked? Because it was not a Liberated area and it would have created a bad impression for Gu Qing to carry off even a reluctantly betrothed woman (in a Liberated area, a woman could not be betrothed against her will).[66]

Others have even insisted that it remains uncertain whether she actually died or not, for indeed her death is only implied and not depicted. Modern Chinese audiences – at least those still attuned to the certain success assured by socialist realism – are said to have sighed on departure from the theatre, 'If only he'd taken her with him it would have been all right!'[67] Why, then, the need for Cuiqiao to die? A clarifying word from Cuiqiao and everything might have been different. The situation seems manipulative and melodramatic.[68]

But there's much more to it than that. Reminded of her father's ominous song, 'Three low cries // she jumps into the well', one might reiterate the true, and truistic, answer for this: 'Fate.' And yet, why is this fated? To this one might respond, because *Yellow Earth* is not really about Cuiqiao, who merely gives a determined form to something much larger. Like Qu Yuan's shamanical ode, which provides a trope on Qu Yuan's own political demise, this film is a trope on something that the film-makers wished to cast as already, indisputably having taken place, namely the failure of Mao's party to bond enduringly with the people and achieve its declared goals. As the shamans in Qu Yuan's *Nine Songs* repeatedly suffer the experience of mere mortality in pursuit of all-powerful divinities, the irreversibility of Cuiqiao's death seals the modern breach between Party and people. That this failure is a tragedy of epic proportions is reified by the very form Chen Kaige chose for it, an ancient form whose familiarity defines the content – that of women's suffering, timeless and endless.

To return now to the image with which this essay began, like many a muted moment in *Yellow Earth*, the inchoate image of a jar in a pool of water, recurring three times during the prayer ceremony, obliges patient contemplation, revealing its significance slowly and, even then, only partially (see illus. 1–3). Examples abound in China's traditional visual arts of complex dialogue, often political in nature, carried on in the disguised forms of landscape and landscape elements, or of various symbolic flowers and animals, and even of styles functioning as coded socio-political stances. Bada Shanren, a seventeenth-century artist of royal blood, transformed moon and melon into a lament that the kind of revolt launched centuries earlier against the Mongols was not about to recur in his own time, when the Manchus had conquered China and driven his kinsmen from the throne (illus. 23).[69] Once-lovely willow trees, prematurely stripped of their beauty, were painted by Bada's contemporary, Gong Xian, to portray the destruction of his own budding political career by the Manchu invasion (illus. 24).[70] Similarly, for painters of that generation, the spare style of the fourteenth-century artist Ni Zan, who lived and suffered during the reign of the Mongols and their downfall, was used to represent native loyalism, though the eccentric Ni Zan was probably far less concerned with loyalist politics than with simply being left alone.[71] Through such imagery, Chinese intellectuals managed to devise critiques of government that were too dangerous to express in any less cryptic terms.

Like many traditional Chinese paintings, the image of this submerged vessel in *Yellow Earth* is a cipher for something other than itself, its proper reading esoteric, potentially subversive, intended for a limited and, ultimately, élite audience. The image unmistakably harks back to the last water seen, the Yellow River at the time of Cuiqiao's failed crossing. And it substitutes for the sight so significantly withheld at that time, the sinking of her frail boat, as the jar, with its attached red fabric, descends slowly, fills with water, and bubbles rise pathetically to the surface. It is this image which stitches together the final two scenes of the film: the young girl Cuiqiao drowning while paddling away from this ancient culture (see illus. 11); the horde of peasant men, led by the old and refusing to budge from past ways, praying before a phallic stele to an impotent dragon king who fails to respond (see illus. 4, 5). The image of this jar is associated with traditional female qualities: a hollow vessel, a passive receptacle for that which comes its way, virtuous if filled with virtue, otherwise not.[72] Here it is associated with water, also *yin* or female, recalling Cuiqiao's role as water-bearer for the family (see illus. 6, 18), and reminiscent of traditional female sacrifice, oppressively linking her drowning and the submergence of her dreams

23 Bada Shanren, *Moon and Melon*, 1689, hanging scroll, ink on paper. Arthur M. Sackler Museum, Harvard University Art Museums, Cambridge, MA (Gift of Earl Morse).

Bada Shanren (1626–1705) was a member of the Ming royal family, eighteen years old when the dynasty was overthrown by Manchu invaders. His next three decades were spent as a priest, much of the time in hiding with his true identity disguised. His paintings and poetry were similarly disguised. This one combines melons, which had been used to symbolize loyalty to a fallen regime since the time of the Duke of Dongling, Shao Ping, who retired at the fall of the Qin to grow melons outside the capital city walls. The moon, for Bada, was taken to represent rebellion through the reference to mooncakes, which at the end of the Yuan dynasty were used by rebels to identify each other. The inscribed poem (translated here by Richard Barnhart) laments, some forty-five years after the Manchu invasion, that it is too late for this rebellion to ripen:

A Ming cake seen from one side,
The moon, so round when the melons rise.
Everyone points to the mooncakes,
But hope that the melons will ripen is a
    fool's dream.

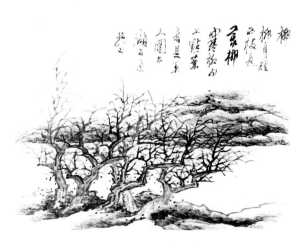

24 Gong Xian, *Wintry Willows*, 1680s, leaf from an instructional album, ink on paper. Location unknown; published as *Gong Banqian shoutu huagao* (Shanghai, 1935).

A loyalist to the fallen Ming dynasty, Gong Xian reversed the usual depiction of willows as elegant beauties, which had often signified women of the gay quarters (see illus. 169), painting them as shorn of their beauty in order to portray his own fall from political grace after the Manchu conquest of China in 1644.

39

to the onslaught of drought upon the land.[73] This linkage is a reminder of the contrasts and ironies, the reversals and perversities of *yang* and *yin* in traditional China and its culture of appropriation: the Yellow River as China's hope and China's sorrow, Chinese women as China's hope and China's hopelessness.

The link between shamanical rain-making and ritualized female drowning is an ancient one. Confucianists opposed it strenuously, but without great success. Its best-remembered opponent, the local magistrate Ximen Bao (425–387 BC), from the state of Wei, a town known as Ye, was made famous three centuries later by the imperial historian Sima Qian, in a narrative which may be paraphrased as follows:

On his arrival, Ximen Bao convened the town elders to inquire what the people suffered from, and the elders answered: 'Their suffering comes from the marriage of the Lord of the Yellow River, *He Bo*, and from this comes their poverty . . . When the Three Seniors and their officers collect the annual taxes from the people, they gather up several millions of their money, and they use two-to-three hundred thousand of this for the marriage of the Yellow River Lord. They divide the remainder with the *wu* and *zhu* shamans and depart. At that time, the *wu* are travelling about seeking a lovely (*hao*) unmarried maiden, saying it is for the River Lord's marriage. Once a bride has been selected, they bathe her, supervise the making of new clothing of silk and satin, have her fast in isolation and have a hall for fasting prepared. By the river, a tent is spread out in which she is placed and oxen and wine are ceremonially prepared for her consumption, all over a period of ten days or more. Then she is made up, and she is then ordered on to something like a bride's bed, and this is set afloat upon the river. At first, this floats some tens of *li*. But then it sinks. The families who have lovely daughters all fear that the great *wu* and *zhu* shamans will select theirs for the Lord of the River and so many of them snatch up their daughters and flee far away. And therefore the city is increasingly depopulated and emptied, and the resultant poverty has gone on for a long time now.

Ximen Bao requested to be present the next time a bride was set sailing. On that occasion, he requested ceremoniously to confirm whether the bride was truly lovely and not ugly and then – on what the reader may understand as a Confucian pretext – he announced that she was *not* lovely to a stunned audience of the Three Elders, the *wu* and *zhu* shamans, and the patriarchs. This Confucian official ordered the chief shaman – *not* a man at all but a 70-year-old *da wuyu*, a senior 'shamaness' or 'witch' with a following of ten female acolytes in plain-woven silken gowns – to 'report to the River Lord that we will strive harder in seeking a lovely girl and will send her to him later'. Then – before a gawking crowd of two or three thousand spectators – he commanded the officers to throw her into the (Yellow) River. As the *wuyu* failed unsurprisingly to 'return', Ximen Bao had three disciples thrown in one by one to help out. Failing their return, before a now horror-stricken audience, he turned to the Three Elders, the *wu* and

everyone else kneels down. The so-called 'trigram' is a small octagonal wooden block called 'the Eight Trigrams'. Inscribed on its surface are the various phrases: 'On the third day rain will be adequate'; 'Pilgrims hurry back home'; 'The people are not sincere in their hearts'; 'Prosperous harvest in the five valleys'; 'Go and gather, and rain shall increase'; 'Verbal intent is unclear'; 'Wind is harmonious and rain favorable'; 'Great good fortune going far'. After the elder offers a prayer, he casts the divining block down. They wait for the block to come to a halt and if the phrase on top reads, 'Go and gather, and rain shall increase,' the elder then hollers out loudly: 'The Dragon King wants to come out of the mountain and pray for rain – aye!' Ranks to pray for rain immediately take form, and the diviner [*yinyang shi*] takes up a 'jar of holy-water' [*shengshui ping*] in the shape of a bottle-gourd, and the assembly lifts up the Dragon King Tower [*Longwang Lou*] in the shape of a sedan-chair. This Dragon King Tower is made of wood and holds inside an image or tablet representing the Dragon King. The elder cries out: 'Horsemen, let's go with the Dragon King!' The horsemen, with 'rain-circle' woven wreaths [*bianzhi de yuquan*] made from willow branches on their heads, then lift up the Dragon King building. There is no pattern to the route they take, as they rush down to the riverbank, going up and down, left and right, in abrupt fashion. Once they arrive at the riverbank, the Dragon King Tower is [carried in] a circle on the ground and then the diviner puts on a rain-prayer banner embroidered with a blue-green dragon and white clouds, places the jar of holy-water in the river and watches to see whether or not it fills with water. If the jar doesn't fill up, the leader of the troops must then bow and kowtow repeatedly, and then consult the divining block again. If the top face of the block reads 'Verbal intent is unclear', the leader then responds: 'Verbal intent is unclear, the divination is a good divination; the humble people cannot comprehend the divination block . . .' If it reads 'The people are not sincere in their hearts', the leader then responds: 'The stars in the sky have not been bright for many months, and many of the people on the earth below are not open in their hearts; the hills in the mountains are high and roads uneven, many are the fish in the river and the water is not clear; vast in number are the people and many are un-settled; there are more than enough good people and exceedingly few bad people . . . At the same time, the diviner prays for water with the 'holy-water jar'. If they still cannot raise the water with prayer, the leader then commands everyone to kneel down and sing in loud voices facing the sky. He sings one phrase: 'Old man dragon spirit, hurry up and come down!. . .' and everyone sings in response: 'May a cool breeze and light rain save . . . the hill . . . people!' They sing again and again until the 'holy-water jar' finally through prayer fills up with water; only then does the diviner race from village to village holding tightly to the 'holy-water jar' filled with river water. Everyone follows closely behind the 'holy-water jar'; no one wants the rain water collected by prayer to be lost on the way. It is said that after they have gone through this laborious and devout invocation through prayer, the dragon-spirited old man [*Longshen Laoweng*] will then be able to make a great display of compassion and send down life-saving rainfall.[82]

This knowledge, perhaps not available to many Chinese urban audiences or critics, allows us better to understand the course of events in this scene, posed as a question, and their relationship to the conclusion of the film, presented as an answer – or as close to an answer as a film steeped in ambiguity and indirection will permit.[83]

Chen Kaige described Cuiqiao as 'the hope of our whole people',[84] and *Yellow Earth* has treated her as a vessel of hope, placed her in another vessel of hope to cross the Yellow River, and sunk her to the bottom. The film then juxtaposes this with the magical jar of the rain ceremony – one more vessel of hope, each of these vessels engendered as female. The sinking of the jar denotes the success of the ceremony and triggers the rush of peasants at the end, filled with hope. But is it real hope, any more real than the hope which launched Cuiqiao in the previous scene and took her life? Any more real than the hope with which Qu Yuan's shamanic figures begin their journeys, before their fall from grace? This implement of 'hope' provides the bridge to the last moments of the film and the 'hope' posed by the apparent return of Gu Qing.

Though often treated as modern, avant-garde, the visual style of *Yellow Earth* is in many ways as old as China's age-old landscape arts and constantly works against soldier Gu Qing's modernist agenda. Following the film's opening credits and historical commentary – conspicuously written in China's archaic clerical script so as to reinforce the timelessness of place and social condition that the film describes (illus. 25) – *Yellow Earth* begins with a landscape setting that stages Gu's arrival, a vast embodiment of the eternal Chinese essence which he sets out to transform according to a modern, socialist agenda (illus. 26, 27). The lateral panning motion of the camera reflects, imitates mechanically, the viewing of an antique Chinese painted handscroll (illustration 28, which depicts this region of China as seen nearly one thousand years ago). The camera's sideways movement describes an endless expanse of nature and facilitates optical travel through it: travel always marked as a temporary passage through nature's permanent vista.[85] This lateral motion contrasts with Gu Qing's actual arrival (illus. 29), shown as movement in (or out of) depth, designated as an even-more-momentary pause in the temporary phenomenon of travel through the unchanging realm of landscape. This is a device that frequently appears in traditional landscape paintings, often framed by the eye-stopping details of human habitation (illus. 30).[86] As Gu Qing arrives (beneath a moon that must signify, somehow, his forthcoming encounter with Cuiqiao), the camera stops; but as with the handscroll, so too with the cinematic format, we realize the impermanence of the pause.[87] Gu Qing is dwarfed

几位八路軍的文
艺工作者結队而来.
又少散开吞,他们想
寻找陕北民歌的源

*Artists of the Communist Eighth Route
Army came to collect folk songs*

25 *Yellow Earth.*
Opening credits, in
archaic clerical
script, signal the
persistence of
Chinese tradition.

by this landscape setting. Overall his stay is brief, and along with his socialist ideology and rhetoric it is measured by the vastness in scale and the slowly changing clock of the natural world. So Gu's presence occupies the moment but from the outset is questioned as to its duration and lasting effect. Expressed through the traditional imagery of silent yellow landscape, the entire film is bracketed by the opening questions – does he bring real hope? can he provide lasting change? – and by the cinematic reply at its conclusion, when Gu is not there.

In its interior scenes, set in the family cave deep within the yellow earth, the film works towards this conclusion in an equally traditional fashion. Rather than exploiting the modern techniques of cinema with mobile shots and countershots, cinematographer Zhang Yimou uses static camerawork to achieve a slow, steady characterization of individuals. This a philosophical exploration, more like traditional Chinese figure painting than a modern action film. In cramped and darkened interiors, set with minimal detail, neither activity nor dialogue holds sway. For long periods, silence reigns supreme; conversation is brief, leaving the few words uttered to be long contemplated, slowly savoured during unspoken passages of time. Figures dwell deep within themselves with firmly held poses, dominating or receding by virtue of age, social status and moral qualities. Position, posture and gesture communicate as much as words, figural details readable and revealing, very much as in a traditional Chinese painting.

In the early painting *Xiao Yi Steals the Orchid Pavilion Manuscript*, after a seventh-century design (illus. 31), the protagonist bears down on his intended victim from an elevated position, with a fierce stare, a forward lean of the shoulders, hidden hands and well-planted feet, while his hapless rival sits helplessly, with one hand open and a dumb-

26, 27 *Yellow Earth*. The film begins: the yellow land . . . and a mysterious wild-pear tree.

28 Attrib. Guo Xi, *Autumn in the River Valley*, mid-11th century, section from a handscroll, ink and colour on silk. Freer Gallery of Art, Smithsonian Institution, Washington, DC.

founded look upon his face – the visual design leaves no doubt about the narrative outcome. *Yellow Earth* applies related visual principles to its own figures. When Gu Qing and Cuiqiao's father first meet, Gu immediately presses an exchange of views on child marriage and the rights of women – the target issue for the film's ideological exploration, synecdoche for the larger encounter between revolutionary force and traditional inertia. Seated on the family *kang*, the two are placed at the same height (illus. 32): two 'middle figures', neither heroes nor villains, matched as moral equals. Gu Qing leans forward, smiling and gracious (illus. 33) but visibly naïve to the difficulty of his task in engaging the old man (who tells Gu Qing he's forty-seven but according to the director's notes 'looks at least sixty'). Implacably, the father engages Gu as much with silence as with words, often avoiding his questions with a mere grunt, and with lowered eyes refusing to 'see' Gu's challenge (illus. 34). In the background, even when she is in the foreground, Cuiqiao listens in silence, excluded from the conversation by age and by gender. Yet her attentive response is signalled by the rate of her

29 *Yellow Earth*. Beneath a full moon, Gu Qing arrives.

pumping the bellows at the hearth, and the audience is encouraged to
listen through her (illus. 35). Gu, and the audience, realize painfully
that it is the old man who must be budged in his ways if China is
to change, and he is not moved. The result, visually and textually, is a
stand-off, one that embodies *Yellow Earth*'s daring assertion of Communism's failure to fulfill its rhetorical mission. The reference, the
return, to a traditional mode of figural depiction once vilified by Maoist
cultural workers reinforces the essence of the film's theme by map-
ping it on to a site in the history of visual style, charting visuality as
ideology through the persistent survival of this artistic tradition despite
Communism's persistent efforts to eliminate it.[88]

Just as it is true to the particulars and patterns of traditional Chinese
rural life, *Yellow Earth* is also true to the character and values of traditional Chinese art. In the final scene, Gu Qing returns to the village, to
the scene of the rain ceremony, but he has arrived far too late to be of
help to Cuiqiao and goes unnoticed by the villagers in their ecological
distress, as they turn to their Dragon King for relief. Only brother
Hanhan, converted to the soldier's cause, runs against the crowd of
peasants to get to him. At this point, it is he who represents the indeterminate future of agrarian China.[89] Strikingly, visually, with hands

30 Xia Gui, *Pure and Remote Views of Rivers and Mountains, c.* 1200, section
from a handscroll, ink on paper. National Palace Museum, Taipei.

This section of the scroll shows travellers arriving at a temple, their transverse
motion, perpendicular to the painting surface, indicating a stopping point in the
viewing of the scroll, with architectural detail intended to fix the viewer's attention.
Here they will perhaps stay for the night before travelling on, moving laterally along
the scroll toward the left.

31 Attrib. Yan Liben (d. 673), *Xiao Yi Steals the Orchid Pavilion Manuscript,* mid-
7th century, section from a handscroll, ink and colour on silk. National Palace
Museum, Taipei.

This painting depicts the effort of the 7th-century scholar-official Xiao Yi (right) to
gain by ruse a famous calligraphic scroll which the emperor has commanded by edict
for the imperial collection but which its owner, the Buddhist priest Biancai (left), has
refused to relinquish and hidden away. Even in this historic moment of heightened
confrontation, actual physical combat is avoided and mental engagement is all
important. But the superior position of the noble scholar and his inevitable victory
over the wily priest are revealed in physical terms by his elevated position, his determined look and concealed hands, his well-planted feet and ready, forward-leaning
posture; the priest is lower down, with head and hand outstretched in a quizzical
gesture, caught off-guard and vulnerable. This suggestive mode of visualizing dominant and subordinate figures is firmly rooted in the Chinese painting tradition.

raised in desperation as he bobs up and down amidst the waves of peasants flowing in the opposite direction, he seems to be drowning on dry land (illus. 36, 37). Whether Hanhan's struggle to reach Gu Qing is intended to match Cuiqiao's own fatality, her futility, or instead is meant as an open question for future history to determine – will they conjoin or not? – is one of the final ambiguities of this film. But as Gu Qing is shown coming over the hill to meet him, replicating his arrival in the opening moments of the film, his putative return is repeated over and over again for our focused consideration, three times in all, like the three-fold depiction of the water jar (illus. 38). This frame-for-frame repetition is surrealistic and contrary to the cinematic naturalness found elsewhere throughout the film. Gu approaches yet remains far away, tiny and silent, and he never arrives. Cuiqiao's younger brother struggles towards him, shouting, 'Save Our People', but the people, the masses, rush away in the opposite direction. And then at the fourth repetition, at the last moment of the film and to the ironic accompaniment of *his* song, Gu Qing is *not* there, he has disappeared (illus. 39). The camera pans down to the parched and barren yellow earth until it entirely fills the frame, rising up and enduring alone, unchanged by the peasants' prayers for rain, unchanged by the brief appearance of this modern man.

This chapter began with an assertion about the 'allusiveness' and 'ambivalence' of *Yellow Earth* and the jar of holy-water as an exemplification of this. It ended with assertions that appear less ambivalent than allusive. Now I would like to revert to the former mode, to assert the obvious: that what I have provided is just one possible reading of the film text. While no conflicting reading of this jar of holy-water has been published, multiple interpretations of many other elements in

32, 33 *Yellow Earth*. In the cave-dwelling, seated as equals on the kang, Gu Qing and the father discuss the status of women. Gu leans forward to engage . . .

The world must change.
The south has changed

34, 35 . . . while the father remains dark, unfathomable, resistant . . . and Cuiqiao, excluded from conversation, listens intently.

36, 37 *Yellow Earth*. Hanhan at the rain ceremony . . . drowning on dry land.

this rain ceremony have already been gathered in the collation *Hua shuo Huang tudi* and in Bonnie McDougall's volume. From the latter:

> By placing the rain prayer at the end, followed only by shots of the barren yellow earth [and Gu Qing's putative return], the film-makers open up the possibility of several interpretations. The most obvious message is that peasant vigour as represented by Yenan is still a limited phenomenon, poised against the enormous weight of traditional fatalism. Another reading, commonly adopted by the film's supporters [in China], is that the latent energy shown by the peasants in the rain prayer is in itself a sign of hope: it only awaits proper organization to be transformed into a positive force for change; the film shows respect for their unrealized aspirations and admiration for the beauty of the rituals that they create in their desperation.[90] A third interpretation is hinted at in the juxtaposition of similar wording in the peasant's rain prayer and Gu Qing's song as sung by the disembodied voice of the dead Cuiqiao: the peasants invoke an outside force (the Dragon King/the Communist Party) to appear as their saviour. In this reading, peasant superstition will not be overcome by the Yenan spirit but merely transferred, with the active encouragement of the Party, to the Yenan leadership.[91]

These multiple readings force an acknowledgement that perhaps *all* readings are overreadings and that *Yellow Earth* is indeed, in any final accounting, ambivalent and ambiguous. The jar of holy-water, an empty receptacle and signifier of the female gender, of the passivity and victimization of the peasantry, of Cuiqiao, of hope and the vagaries of hope, of shamanic practices and the persistence of traditional superstition, and of the traditionalism of *Yellow Earth*'s visual style, is in the end just a jar of holy-water. Seven seconds in an 86-minute film. And it raises the question of whether the ambiguity of this film is a means or an end.

38, 39 *Yellow Earth*. Gu Qing returns . . . but in the end, he's not there.

This can be dealt with in a number of ways. One of them would be to consider its function in the context of contemporary Chinese film censorship. If the film-makers *wanted* to offer the political critique that I among others have outlined, how better (or how else) to do this than through indirect means which the censorial system would not notice, could choose to ignore, or would have ample means to deny as representing the presence of dissidence in the material approved under their auspices. Another way would be to address the ambivalence of this film in terms of the ambivalence of the film-maker's generation toward Maoism – mightily aware of radical failures, but in light of the faithless pursuit of materialism which has followed in its wake, nostalgic for the hope that Maoism once embodied and the sense of common purpose that he inspired. Such feelings don't allow for an outright dismissal of Communism as a failure, deferring instead to the attitude that socialism 'hasn't succeeded *yet*'. From this perspective, an identity might be established between the film-makers and PLA soldier Gu Qing, a 'middle figure' not lacking for lofty, romantic ideals but for the realistic means of achieving them. In that regard, the film-makers' stance also parallels that of post-Cultural Revolutionary mainland scholarship, which has demoted Qu Yuan from his role as Maoist proto-revolutionary hero and more realistically 'absorbed [him] into the great forces of history'.[92] Since Gu Qing's failed rhetorical mission of song-gathering derives from Mao's 1942 'Yan'an forum' injunctions – to 'start by studying the language of the masses'[93]– and since their own film-making remains rooted in this practice, they have further problematized their own contemporary efforts.

Still another approach, focused on the director as film-maker, might locate this work within the Daoistic orientation and essential conservatism of director Chen Kaige. This has been done before and is readily supported.[94] A fourth would be to note an equally conservative source for such practice in traditional Confucian behaviour and the indirectness of Confucian rhetoric. The Confucian statesman, theoretically, never told a superior what to do but vaguely suggested the desired alternative. Confucius and his followers didn't appropriate the folk songs of the *Odes* merely for the sake of literary rape and pillage nor simply as a means of class control, but rather because of their need for an appropriative means to an allusive end: a suitably irrelevant text provided deniability to speaker and listener alike in their exchange of indirect rhetoric, saving face and preserving safety in a distinctly unequal relationship. The behaviour of the modern Chinese social critic in the face of state censorship is hardly different than that of the statesman under imperial rule, and many of the same strategies are employed, with or without an awareness of the historical precedent.

Some of these issues will come up for detailed discussion in later chapters. Fortunately, as multiple allusions appear and ambiguities emerge in *Yellow Earth*, we aren't obliged to choose between all the referential alternatives that audience and critics might observe. In one sense or another, they all pertain. They all help to explain. The conditions of such analysis, from the facilitation of multiple viewpoints other than the film-makers' own to the emphasis on the richly signifying capacity of such passing details as the jar of holy-water, may seem beholden to the world of academic post-modernism. In fact, they depend upon and grow right out of the Chinese tradition itself, indirect and layered with alternative meanings like those created and exploited by Chinese artists, writers and politicians since ancient times – a native-bred 'semiotics' that matured in Chinese art and literature long before the Western term was invented.[95] It is this fact that allows *Yellow Earth* to seem avant-garde, post-modern, by contemporary Chinese standards, at the same time as it joins the ranks of traditional Chinese art.

2 Ruins of a Sorghum Field, Eclipse of a Nation: *Red Sorghum* on Page and Screen

My thinking about culture begins the moment it is in ruins.
– Chen Kaige[1]

Throughout their history, Chinese film studios have retained writers far more for the purpose of adapting previously published literature than for creating original scripts. In the 1920s, '30s and '40s, emerging in Westernized Shanghai from the novelty-medium of 'peep shows', serious film borrowed not only the content but the prestige of literature in a culture that profoundly venerated written text. This new genre was referred to as *yingxi*, 'shadow theatre' or 'filmed drama' which emphasized spoken text rather than visuality – staged dialogue captured through a relatively static photography (long shots, long takes) that modern critics distinguish from true 'cinema' (as characterized by mobile camerawork and dynamic film editing).[2] Not until the rise of 'Fifth Generation' film did cinematography begin significantly to amplify textuality. But even now, the tradition of literary adaptation continues virtually unabated.

In the process of adapting text, predictably, plots are condensed, narration and rumination give way to action, the concrete supplants the abstract. And yet, while such changes may constitute a generic necessity, they are often matched by changes of opportunity, altering both style and purpose to suit the politics of the day, the taste of the film-makers, and the constraints imposed by censorship. In the 1950s, films like *Family* (1956), *New Year's Sacrifice* (1956), and *The Lin Family Shop* (1959) – all of which began with visual tributes to the original texts and their authors – redirected 1920s–30s left-leaning 'May Fourth' style literature towards new, Communist Party ends.[3] Reversing this direction a generation later, in *Yellow Earth*, director Chen Kaige and colleagues took a propagandist 'essay' scripted as a 'landscape of flowers, flowing water and birdsong in the valleys'[4] and turned it into a profound elegy for Chinese socialism, set in a desiccated land lacking birds, flowers and hope.[5] In the film *Judou* (see illus. 249–51, 254), many of the fundamental changes made by director Zhang Yimou[6] to Liu Heng's original novella, *Fuxi fuxi*,[7] exemplify the transformation of Chinese literary text into filmscript, turning complex characters into melodramatic silhouettes and allowing for an allegorical political critique to emerge. All such changes result in something far different

53

from a 'filmed novel', describing instead a highly dynamic mode of adapting literature to film such as has been prevalent not only in the 'Fifth Generation' but among preceding generations as well.[8]

Unfortunately, there has been virtually no analysis to date of the transformation of Chinese literature into film. In such inquiry, a major factor that must sooner or later come into play is the role of government censorship and the unequal scrutiny given to diverse artistic media. Throughout the arts in general, as I have written elsewhere,

The Communist system of censorship bears little relationship to the popular image of hard-fisted bureaucrats who know only politics and little of art, and who are readily identifiable by artists as outsiders and enemy intruders. In fact, art censorship as the suppression of completed works of art scarcely exists in socialist China. Rather, the entire system is conceived of as benign and couched in terms of education, helping artists to understand what is expected of them so they might avoid anything that could cause trouble. The goal is to create compliance and thereby to avoid forcible intervention.[9]

The result I have dubbed a 'do-it-yourself system', administered through the obligatory participation of qualifying artists in various media-based associations. Organized under government auspices at the local, provincial, and national levels, these associations are united nationally into the All-China Federation of Literary and Art Circles under the direct control of the Communist Party and its Propaganda Department. Membership in the various artists' associations is carefully screened according to factors that include political background as well as more purely artistic qualification. With Propaganda Depart- ment commissars ever-present to promulgate central directives and monitor the correct response, members take on responsibility for running their own associations within the confines of external expectations. Based on their unequal potential to reach and affect the public, arts such as painting, literature, and film are prioritized by Chinese authorities.

Movies are virtually all produced in state-run film studios,[10] involve massive amounts of capital and labour, and reach a broad audience. Along with television and radio, they are judged to have the greatest capacity for sowing dissent and receive the most intensive scrutiny from the hardest of China's censors. Equally critical to a film's fate, post-production, is the state-run China Film Distribution Corporation which retains tight control on the availability of films to movie houses. In the past decade, for the first time, 'art workers' like painters and sculptors have gained the ability to operate independently of their associations if they are prepared to forego the possibility of public exhibitions, teaching positions, and other forms of state support. Similarly, independent literary publishers have sprouted up by the hundreds. But this kind of independence is scarcely available for film-makers. Layer upon layer of negotiated self-censorship is required before, during, and after shooting a film, generating art by committee(s), and requiring of film-makers subtlety and subterfuge in the formulation of any dissenting social critique. All the more allusive and indirect for this negotiation, any such filmed critique is all the more likely to miss its public target, to facilitate a cooptive and sterilizing interpretation by hostile critics or public authorities, to justify reduced internal distribution, and to be effectively neutralized by the design of the system. For all these reasons, film is a far more constrained medium than literature.[11]

Cinematographer and director Zhang Yimou has lamented the effect of all this on film:

In China today, novels surpass the level of films tremendously. This is because each year thousands of new novels and short stories are published, and no one can keep up with them, especially the government censors. Not even their subordinates in their offices can keep up, so they just give up trying. That's why good novels get through the system, and that's why Chinese writers look down on film-makers.[12]

But Zhang has also done more than merely lament. He and various 'Fifth Generation' film-makers have set out to challenge this system, both indirectly and directly, negotiating a variety of works to completion which have rivaled dissident literature in their effect. Although relying in part on screen image and cinematic structure, on visual rhetoric and reference, to convey past the censor and impart to the audience what they dared not include as spoken text, various of these films have at least temporarily been banned from internal distribution after completion. Such films include Zhang's *Judou*, *Raise the Red Lantern*, *To Live*, *Shanghai Triad* and *Keep Cool*, Chen Kaige's *Big Parade*, *Life on a String*, *Farewell My Concubine* and *Temptress Moon*, Tian Zhuangzhuang's *Blue Kite*, and Mi Jiashan's *The Trouble-Shooters*, among others. One film to avoid such a ban, though no less controversial – it took moderate Party Secretary Zhao Ziyang's personal approval to spare it the fate of the others – was *Red Sorghum*.[13]

For Zhang Yimou's directorial début, the film *Red Sorghum* was adapted from the first two parts of a much longer novel by Mo Yan. A spiritual offshoot of the Soviet writer Mikhail Sholokhov's hard-bitten magic-realism, Mo's novel is as intensely visual in its text as any film could be in its imagery.[14] In 1987, as the first 'Fifth Generation' film to star the now-famous performers Gong Li and Jiang Wen, *Red Sorghum* also became the first and only 'Fifth Generation' film to top the Chinese annual popularity charts. It is the fictional story of a social libertine and

The groom is so eager.
He can no longer wait

40 *Red Sorghum*. Grandma inside the bridal palanquin, Grandpa leads the sedan-bearers in giving her a furious, traditional shaking.

wartime heroine, the narrator's grandmother Dai Fenglian, known as Jiu'er, 'Little Nine' or 'Ninth Child', a name with suitably masculine overtones in Chinese numerology.[15] Set during the war against Japan, these two characteristics, gender liberation (her fight against feudal standards) and patriotic leadership (her resistance against the Japanese), are paralleled, with economic enlightenment thrown in for good measure. Her sexual liberation comes first: in succession, she resists the consummation of marriage to a leprous husband; welcomes the sexual encounter of her bridal sedan-bearer (the narrator's grandfather; illus. 40), who had thwarted the efforts of another would-be rapist along her bridal route; denounces her own father for having married her off to this leper in return for a donkey; overthrows her lover, the sedan-bearer, and then receives him back on her own terms. Her economic liberation comes second, as she takes over management of the red sorghum winery from her murdered husband and establishes an equality of ownership among all the workers (illus. 41). Later on, it is no surprise when she, rather than the men-folk, raises the banner of resistance against the bestiality of the Japanese invaders (illus. 42). One may question why it takes a male to initiate her sexual liberation, or why she ends up like a house-wife delivering food (fistcakes and wine) to the men at the time of her heroic demise, but these are lesser notes. The fact is, throughout *Red Sorghum*, while Granddad has the passion, she has the purpose.[16]

Throughout the tale, the rebellion of Jiu'er finds a metaphor in the locally grown red sorghum, which grows as wild and natural as she does, which nourishes and protects the peasants, produces the red wine which gives them their vitality and serves as a healing medicine, in whose fields she procreates with abandon, whose trampling down by command of the Japanese to build their military roadways equates with their brutal domination of China, and whose fields she reddens with the blood of battle. 'I didn't realize until I'd grown up,' writes Mo Yan,

that Northeast Gaomi Township is easily the most beautiful and most repulsive, most unusual and most common, most sacred and most corrupt, most heroic and most bastardly, hardest-drinking and hardest-loving place in the world. The people of my father's generation who lived there ate sorghum out of preference, planting as much of it as they could. In the late autumn, during the eighth lunar month, vast stretches of red sorghum shimmered like a sea of blood. Tall and dense, it reeked of glory; cold and graceful, it promised enchantment; passionate and loving, it was tumultuous.[17]

Throughout much of its length, the film glows with the colour red – pink in its few happy moments, fiery red or blood red when the temperature heats up. Jiu'er herself is the fiercest, reddest soul of all. Unlike *Yellow Earth*'s Cuiqiao, she's hardly a child bride and more than a match for her two mates, two facts that may stretch credibility sociologically but which, with Gu Changwei's bold cinematography and Zhang Yimou's taut directorial management, contribute to a mythic story-telling effect. To the shock (and fascination) of Chinese audiences, *Red Sorghum* substituted a realistically brutal visualization for the artificially staged pseudo-toughness of socialist film-making.

41 *Red Sorghum*. Economic revolutionary, Grandma proclaims the winery a working commune.

42 *Red Sorghum*. Political heroine Jiu'er plans the attack.

Skinhead Granddad is a phallic creature – body and head all one – who seizes the woman he wants and marks territory like a wild animal, pissing on what he claims as his own and battling all those who dare to cross his line, whether Chinese bandits or Japanese invaders (illus. 46). He appears as some minor version of the theatre's great power figures, mythic heroes often misalloyed with brutal, morally flawed, and sometimes even villainous qualities, playing to audiences both awed by their highly impulsive behaviour and prepared – for what else can such impulse lead to? – to see the downfall of 'great' men (see illus. 43, 90).[18] Traditionally, the 'high arts' of China (meaning painting, not stage drama) celebrated reason, not body and brawn, and only alien sources – traditional Indian/Central Asian and modern Western – inspired such a physical display. So even an icon of Chinese art like Ren Xiong's self-portrait, from the 1850s, with its remarkable display of body, which drew from both traditional Buddhist and Western sources and which announced the arrival of a new modernity, came with a strong dose of modern cynicism and functioned as the self-portrayal of a kind of rebel-hero (illus. 44). Though cast as a 'timeless' rural primitive, Granddad shares strongly in that modern attitude. In the art of our own time, Granddad's physicality corresponds to a thoroughly contemporary code of matter over mind, the modern loss of philosophical bearings, given form in Fang Lijun's postmodern skinhead thugs-without-a-cause (illus. 51).

From the modest vantage-point of traditional Chinese painting, when we catch a rare glimpse of a Chinese woman riding through the countryside on the back of a donkey, we cannot help but wonder what she is doing out there and where she is headed (illus. 52). If she is at all well-off, she is further at risk as a woman out of doors, physically as well as socially, and the rarity of such exposure conveys the urgency of her transit to safety from one walled-in enclosure to another. No wonder the young males in the background of this painted scene – the ones who constitute this threat – gawk in near disbelief. The sense of risk is inherent – it is inherited – in *Red Sorghum*. Jiu'er, after having spent her first three nights of marriage resisting with a pair of sharpened scissors the advances of her leprous husband, returns for a customary visit to her father's home. She rides her father's newly-gotten donkey which, as she protests, was the meagre price of her hand in marriage (illus. 45). Along the way, as she travels through the wild sorghum field, rhythmically, sensuously pulsating in the wind, she is met forcibly by the man who three days earlier had borne her bridal sedan to her husband's home and saved her from the hands of a rapist thug encountered along the way (illus. 46).

43 Shang Xi, *Guan Yu Capturing his Enemy Pang De*, mid-15th century, hanging scroll, ink and colour on silk. Palace Museum, Beijing.

In traditional Chinese imagery, such boldness of melodramatic form is found primarily in folk art and religious imagery but here has been brought to court art. The popular 3rd-century military figure Guan Yu, sanctified after his death as the fierce God of War, sits in a dramatic pose as he decides what justice to meet out to his captured sworn-enemy Pang De, who fearlessly scorns anything less than a death sentence. Guan has him beheaded but buried with honours. This painting proclaims the standard for stern court discipline which characterized much of the Ming period. Venerated at court by the military founders of the Ming dynasty, Guan Yu is shown here in heroic pose, with glorious costume and flowing beard. The convulsive form of the nearly nude Pang De (resistant to the stakes to which he is bound by hair and foot), the torrent of water rushing forth from the background (rather like a stage prop, suggesting the flood that facilitated Pang De's capture), the pines that seem to ripple with divine wind, the forward thrust of stone stairs leading up to Guan Yu's altar-like throne, and the military attendants dramatically posed in charismatically-rippled drapery – all these are carried out in a court painting with a stylized boldness derived from popular taste and possibly from the theatre itself.

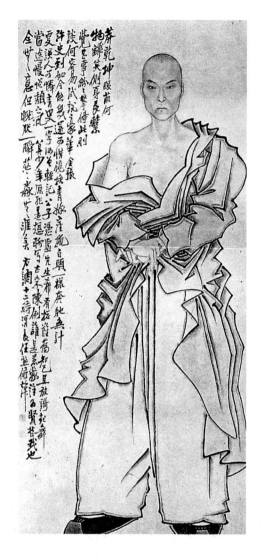

44 Ren Xiong, *Self-Portrait*, 1850s, hanging scroll, ink and colour on paper. Palace Museum, Beijing.

This unusual work – the artist portrayed as cultural iconoclast – provides something of a prototype for *Red Sorghum*'s rebel-hero, Yu Zhan'ao ('Granddad'). In it, Ren Xiong draws on two 'Western' sources: traditional Buddhist arts and European oil painting. In Buddhist painting, the semi-draped figure was common, part of the Indian heritage: rather than making a spectacle of the body, exposure was a revelation of human nature, physical frailty, and one's inevitable mortality. Chan Buddhist paintings often combined drapery done in rough brushwork with greater detail for heads and hands, as seen here with considerable exaggeration of the contrast. European art, whose impact was most pronounced in the commercial port of Shanghai where Ren Xiong worked at this time, contributed to the shading of the body, the detailed realization of the facial features, and to the unusually direct engagement of subject with audience. Ren Xiong's self-portrait, immodestly life-sized, transforms the old and assimilates it into the new, exemplifying late imperial China's turn to 'modernity.' But for Ren, modernity had brought only poverty, social frustration, and a short, tragic career. Ren's self-portrayal – in its bold physicality, its unflinching encounter with the audience, and its calligraphic inscription – set forth his profound discontent with this age of transition, a time when traditional standards of style and patterns of patronage had been discarded and even the heroes of the past offered no effective guidance. His inscription begins (in James Cahill's translation): 'With the world in turmoil, what lies ahead of me? I smile and bow and go around flattering people in hope of making connections; but what do I know of affairs? In the great confusion, what is there to hold on to and rely on?' The artist stands here, bold and defiant, like some martial artist from a Chan Buddhist or Daoist temple, ready to go down fighting like a rebel rather than submit passively to the confusion of his times.

45–50 *Red Sorghum*. Newly wed, Grandma rides a donkey back to her father's house. In an unexpected encounter in the sorghum, as Grandpa lifts his hood . . . Grandma goes from shock . . . to swoon . . . ending with *Red Sorghum*'s famous 'rape' scene. Like a saint, Grandma enters and leaves the sorghum field in a halo of sunlight, prelude to the solar eclipse at the end of the film.

The question of whether or not what follows next in *Red Sorghum*'s famous 'rape scene' is really a rape has been discussed frequently by critics. Aware of the irreconcilability of various critical viewpoints about the women in this and other films, Ann Kaplan frames the issue like this:

Would a Chinese audience read the sex scene . . . as a rape? How is rape conceptualised in China? Does the definition of rape vary from culture to culture? Is rape acceptable as a representation but not socially? Are we driven to an undesirable relativism in such cross-cultural comparisons? . . . One wonders if Chinese scholars need to learn how to talk about film in one way for an American audience, in another way for a Chinese audience.[19]

This is a fair set of academic questions, yet we need not approach Zhang Yimou's scene with any great diffidence, for *Red Sorghum* is no

51 Fang Lijun, *Group Two No. 5*, 1992, oil on canvas. Private collection. Jiang Wen as 'Granddad' set a model for the so-called 'cynical realist' paintings of the post-Tian'an Men era. In an age when art seems sorely challenged by political authority, Fang Lijun's many presentations of coarse and leering skinheads seem to return the challenge, to confront authority through art. At the same time, like the rebellious hero of Mo Yan's novel and Zhang Yimou's film, they also mark the loss of public idealism in post-Maoist China.

52 Zhao Gan, *Early Snow Along the River*, mid-10th century, detail from a hand-scroll, ink and colour on silk. National Palace Museum, Taipei.

Rashomon. Jiu'er clearly initiated this enticement in the earlier scene with coy looks and the intentional exposure of her foot to her sedan-bearer, just after he has saved her, and when she runs from him it is only because he is hooded and unrecognizable (just like the would-be rapist he spared her from). As he removes his hood, she swoons (illus. 48). In the book, the author Mo Yan is clear as could be on the matter, writing:

A muscular arm swept her off and carried her into the sorghum field. Grandma fought halfheartedly. She really didn't feel like struggling. Certain individuals become great leaders in an instant; Grandma unlocked the mysteries of life in three days. She even wrapped her arms around his neck to make it easier for him to carry her. Sorghum leaves rustled . . . Grandma and Granddad exchanged their love surrounded by the vitality of the sorghum field: two unbridled souls, refusing to knuckle under to worldly conventions, were fused together more closely than their ecstatic bodies.[20]

A film is not a book and a script may depart significantly from an original text.[21] But here, in the film as in the book, once Granddad removes his hood for Grandma to recognize her pursuer, her flight is ended, her passion clearly lit, and a train of events is set in place that guides her life along a wholly new trajectory.

Just as she rode into this scene surrounded by a natural halo (illus. 50), at the conclusion, back on her donkey, a transformed Grandma rides off into a beatific glow of sunlight. To understand this event as a rape, as some have insisted,[22] is to place one's own agenda ahead of Mo Yan's, for he clearly presents Jiu'er as rebel, bold and proud, every bit the match for her men, advancing from one rebellion to another, from sexual to economic to political. To deny her sexual willingness at this critical moment stands in the way of understanding what the film and the book are really all about.

To extract the events which shape the trajectory of *Red Sorghum*, which link book and film and best define their difference, it will be useful first to turn towards a concept that has hitherto played little role in Chinese art-historical and cinematic studies: the theme of ruins.[23] What is meant by 'ruins' – that reference to things fallen down but not yet disappeared, persistent parts significant chiefly for their reference to the impersistence of the whole; what Chinese nomenclature or terminology this Latinate word appropriately refers to; from what aesthetic foundations any Chinese equivalent arises, and how this differs from the post-medieval aesthetic on which the modern Western understanding of 'ruins' is typically derived: these are all matters for an initial stage of investigation. Perhaps it is never quite clear when in its decline a physical object qualifies for the label 'ruin', its purpose replaced by some contemplative function related to something more evanescent than either the physical ruin or the original object itself. Perhaps we more or less know a 'ruin' when we see one. But *Red Sorghum* presents dimensions of both physical and cultural ruination, and with that comes the question of by what standard do we measure the ruination of a whole culture.

In considering ruins, Western style, Rose Macaulay's memorable phrase 'the pleasure of ruins' comes readily to mind, with the challenge to determine what, if anything, makes a fallen-down edifice pleasurable (illus. 53, 54).[24] In a comparison with the post-Renaissance West, the critical ingredients suggest the following:

First: The leisure of an educated observer, something that Chinese culture supplied equally well;

Second: The capacity for and love of travel, also common to China's educated observers;

Third: Plenty of wrecked architectural objects – and here differences start to emerge, particularly considering the relative scarcity of stone-built architecture in China and the readiness with which the elements of China's timber-built, modular architecture were replaced and renewed and whole buildings disassembled, reconstructed, salvaged, and even moved from place to place. In China, the wreckage of ancient buildings was not simply left strewn about for leisured travellers to view and contemplate. Though ruins were celebrated in poetry in the poetic genre known as *huaigu*, 'cherishing' or 'lamenting the past',[25] architectural ruins were very rarely celebrated in painting[26] and such pedigreed architecture as the Jiangnan region's 'Ming' gardens was regularly rebuilt, updated in style, and often expanded throughout the Qing and Republican periods and again after the depredations of the Cultural Revolution, as were still earlier sites like Sichuan's Three Su's Shrine (originally eleventh century, in Meishan) and the Du Fu Thatched Hall (questionably dated back to the eighth century, in Chengdu);

Fourth: A profound appreciation for the historical past, and how could the Chinese be outdone here? But a cultural separation from that past, as of an eighteenth-century Anglican from the ruins of papal times or Roman times in England, or from the ruins of faraway Rome itself – an identity *separate* from the distant past and from its alien, exoticized cultures – was something that was lacking from the experience of Chinese scholars, who were steeped in all the trappings of the world's longest-surviving unbroken cultural tradition, and for whom each past barbarian assault or internal decline could still be felt as a part of, or an analogue to, the threats and blows and decay of the culture of their own time;

53 Caspar David Friedrich, *Cloister Cemetery in the Snow*, 1817–19, oil on canvas. Formerly National Gallery, Berlin (destroyed 1945).

The near-destruction of this cloister, embraced by a natural framework of rugged, ancient trees that echo its form and translate it from the man-made into the God-created, and wrapped in the silent purity of new-fallen snow, enhances the transcendental aura and romantic pietism of Friedrich's work. The communal experience of these monks in sharing this otherworldly ruin is marked by their marching in silent pairs.

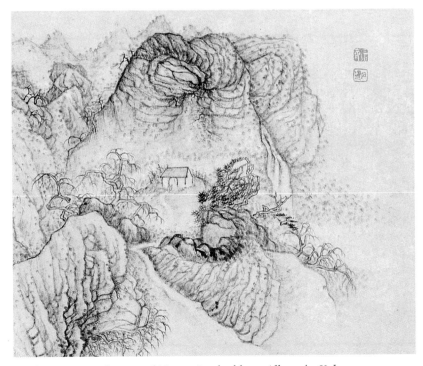

54 Shitao, *Hut at the Foot of Mountains*, leaf from *Album for Yulao*, c. 1690, ink and colour on paper. C. C. Wang Family Collections, New York.

Many of the natural elements here are similar to those in Friedrich's work – combining to provide a shared, spiritual experience for those present. But while aged, twisted, and gnarled, the trees and hills display a boundless vitality, defying death and ruination. Nature is cast as the comprehensible form of spiritual essence rather than a transient signifier of the transcendent hereafter.

Fifth: An attitude that in the ravages of time, or through the human destructiveness which a sufficient passage of time will inevitably bring to bear, is made visible the hand of a benign creator – the evanescence of the material pointing comfortably towards the permanence of the immaterial and a welcome abode for the soul. How different this was from the Chinese, for most of whom the mysterious darkness beyond this world seemed totally ineffable, or worse, called forth an absolute dread, and for whom merely to speak of ruins (as to speak of death) might seem threatening enough to silence the viewer of ruins and drive him away from the view. As a rule, in a society concerned with spiritual pollution and its strenuous avoidance, to restore and renew was a cultural imperative. Heaven's own way was to destroy and renew; history was a repeated cycle of decline and re-establishment. So while the notion of ruin could not be hidden away and supplied an important impetus to reconcile oneself with nature, it rarely led to aesthetic appreciation.[27]

That 'the Chinese' attitude towards ruins called forth not some elegiac pleasure steeped in religious aspiration but rather a melancholic contemplation on the unkind nature of Fate is a broad and essentializing but nonetheless supportable generalization upon which these comments about Chinese cinema are based. Although warfare's massive destructive force is by no means newly experienced in twentieth-century China and is richly recorded in Chinese historical and poetic literature, only with an infusion of a 'modern' sensibility in which such ruins actually began to shape identity and provoked new explorations into political conscious-ness do we find a visual art form that regularly invokes ruination; and this we could scarcely call a celebration of ruins but rather a culturally-pained public acknowledgement of humiliation as a prod to (re)action and revitalization (illus. 55). Before relating this to *Red Sorghum*, I would like to look at another film to establish the point.

Wu Yigong's *Cheng nan jiu shi* (1982; literally, *Old Tales from the Southern Part of the City* but known in English as *My Memories of Old Beijing*) was perhaps the first film of the Deng Xiaoping's 'Second Liberation' era to earn some measure of international acclaim.[28] Like *Yellow Earth*, the much better-known film that it helped usher in, *Memories of Old Beijing* is structured around an innocent and power-less yet strong-willed young girl. Through the eyes of Lin Yingzi the audience watches a parade of stories about ordinary people's sufferings. First comes Xiuzhen (illus. 56), a delusional neighbour who went 'crazy' several years earlier when her radical student-lover was arrested and possibly executed by Nationalist troops and their illegitimate infant daughter, Guizi, was given away or simply abandoned at the city gate. Avoided by all, the outcast Xiuzhen is befriended only by the open-hearted Yingzi, despite the warnings of her parents to keep her distance.

55 Li Hua, *Fleeing Refugees*, c. 1939, woodblock print. Lu Xun Memorial, Shanghai.
The site is the ruins of Shanghai after the Japanese bombing campaign which accompanied their seizure of Manchuria in early 1931. The print not only depicts the victims but locates the cause in the class division between rich and poor that led to China's weakness in the face of Japanese and Western imperialism: the poorly-clad peasant widow and semi-orphaned children, shown in black, flee on foot, in contrast with the wealthy comprador being carried away in a litter. The Western-influenced architecture, a monument to the intrusions of China's imperialist enemies, stands here as part of the indictment of those who have dismembered China, rather than being celebrated or mourned.

(Xiuzhen confusedly treats Yingzi as a substitute daughter.) At the same time, we meet Yingzi's young playmate, Niu'er (illus. 57), abused by her adoptive parents and apparently being trained by them to become a street or cabaret musician, like a monkey on a rope. Eventually, these two victims are brought together with the help of Yingzi, who recognizes Niu'er as none other than Xiuzhen's long-missing daughter. Reunited, mother and child run off to freedom only to be killed immediately, run down by the very train on which they seek escape from their heartless neighbours.

Yingzi's family moves at once to another home. 'The past is past. You'll gradually forget about it,' she remembers her father saying (illus. 58). But death seems to follow her relentlessly. The next episode echoes the first in the film. Set in the ruins of a haunted courtyard just around the corner from Yingzi's home, we're reminded of her haunted and emotionally ravaged neighbour Xiuzhen and left to wonder if it isn't Xiuzhen's ghost that's followed her. In the privacy of this abandoned yard she encounters an unnamed thief who steals in order to put his impoverished younger brother through school. He hides his stolen treasure – the key to his brother's future and to his own fate – amid the

56 *My Memories of Old Beijing*. Xiuzhen reaches out to Yingzi.

57 *My Memories of Old Beijing*. Lin Yingzi and Niu'er/Guizi.

rubble and ruins of someone else's past. To the innocent Yingzi, a friend to all, he reveals his shameful secret, expecting her condemnation. But non-judgementally, she replies, 'Can you tell the difference between the sea and the sky? . . . I can't tell the sea from the sky, and I can't tell good people from bad people' (illus. 59). Ironically, it is through the innocent Yingzi's own unwitting actions that he is caught and executed (illus. 60).

Though these and subsequent episodes might seem unrelated, they gradually bring tragedy closer and closer to home, beginning with strangers and then with friends, leading next to her nursemaid's family and then finally to her father, a scholar known for protecting radical students like Xiuzhen's lover. This final death brings an end to the cycle as the family remnant returns to their native home in Taiwan and Yingzi's childhood is forcibly brought to an end.

My Memories of Old Beijing is based on three of five semi-autobiographical tales by Taiwan author Lin Haiyin, first published in 1960.[29] Like her young Lin Yingzi, Lin Haiyin grew up not in Beijing, as it is called throughout the film, but in the dilapidated *former* capital, Beiping, as the book names it, stripping the site of its political authority. It is on that impoverished stage that Yingzi's tales of innocent friendships and human ruin are set. These remembered relics of a distant past are retained only in the mind of the Taiwanese narrator, for whom time and distance provide a perspective on original events as a material ruin does of an original monument: what were once mere artifacts to the innocent child become the design of cultural history to the adult. The important truth is embodied in the thief's response to Yingzi's comment that 'she can't tell the difference': 'But one day,' he replies, 'you will.' Collectively, as translated into film, this remembered human ruin comprises an elegy to China's pre-Communist culture, condemned by its own lack of humane feelings and dearth of sympathy for the plight of ordinary citizens. It was a time when honest friendship threatened betrayal and death. But in the hands of 'Fourth Generation' director Wu Yigong, preoccupied with his own time and place, these twenty-year-old tales seem also to analogize the recently concluded Cultural Revolution, that frenzied decade whose frontal assault on humanitarian sentiment stripped Maoism of much of its original authority.[30]

58 *My Memories of Old Beijing*. 'The past is past. You'll gradually forget about it.' Yingzi's family moves their home but can't escape fate.

59 *My Memories of Old Beijing.* Little Yingzi and her criminal companion: 'I can't tell the sea from the sky, and I can't tell good people from bad people.'

60 *My Memories of Old Beijing.* Paraded off to his fate, the arrested robber stares at Yingzi: does either one of them realize that she unwittingly led to his capture?

While *Memories of Old Beijing* might not initially seem to be an essay on ruins, it instructs us well on three aspects of the topic: first that the concept of 'ruins' need not be limited to the aesthetic products of human creativity (toppled architecture, fragmented stelae, whatever) but ought to include humans themselves, who are after all the *first* ingredient in any definition of culture and are just as vulnerable to decay and destruction. Secondly, it focuses our awareness on the central, mediational role of memory and contemplation in valorizing any 'ruin' as being something more than a mere wreck, unworthy of appreciation and as something that lofts our awareness to a higher level through the consideration of things *in time*. Thirdly, it reifies cinema as an equivalent to other media – to architecture, most obviously – as a creative vehicle for objectifying ruins and for contemplating Heaven's ruinous ways. With architecture, only belatedly does time enhance its erosion with value, but cinema can create a ready-made ruin and speed the audience directly to its contemplative essence. Even the memory itself may be in ruins, but in those relics which persist in memory, through their linkage of past experience with the physical present, lies an understanding of the enduring human condition. Essential to the viewing of ruins is the process of mental reconstruction. Young Yingzi, alone among her peers, understands these figures not as crazy people, not as common criminals, not even as mere victims, but rather as friends, precisely because she looks past the ruins of these figures to view them as they once were, as whole people.

If *Memories of Old Beijing* is cast in terms of human debris, *Red Sorghum*, a brawling celebration of the natural, primitive vitality of the Chinese people, is negotiated through the 'architecture' of nature.[31] In the film, the sorghum is ruined twice, three times in the novel. Each ruin is a marker of primary significance. The first occurs when Jiu'er and Yu Zhan'ao, the bride and the marital sedan-bearer, the narrator's Grandma and Granddad, first make love and conceive his father (see illus. 49). This time, the ruination is small in scale and hardly understood as such until compared with the later, more disastrous ruins. Illicit love this is, for Grandmother has just been wed to a wealthy leper, whom Granddad will then murder, and the encounter seems to start out as a scene of rape, he chasing her through the sorghum. But it ends as a moment of sexual and spiritual liberation, on a natural bed that Grandpa has trampled out of the vintage sorghum: a Heavenly circle built on the ground, upon which are united body and soul. It is here that Grandma and Granddad, as already quoted, 'exchanged their love surrounded by the vitality of the sorghum field: two unbridled souls, refusing to knuckle under to worldly conventions, were fused together more closely than their ecstatic bodies'.[32] Here, Grandma embraces her own human nature and from this liberation will go on to others. Rising from this small patch of ruined crop, in which the restraints of feudal custom are cast aside, the couple goes on to tumultuous marriage and to the production of a red sorghum wine that becomes famous throughout the region.

The next ruination of the sorghum that takes place is a trampling of the fields to build a military roadway for invading Japanese troops. Carried out by an unarmed army of Chinese peasants, marched before the guns of the enemy and united by the Japanese as they could never manage to unite against them, this destruction gives form to the brutal

61 *Red Sorghum*. Marched before Japanese guns, the villagers trample down the sorghum fields to produce a military roadway.

domination of China by the invaders. It is here in the ruined temple of red sorghum that the Japanese' most horrible sacrilege is carried out, the brutal live flaying of wine-plant manager Luohan (illus. 62). And it is here, where she was first sexually liberated years earlier, that Grandma becomes politically emancipated, where her ire and imagination combine to plot the act of revenge for this desecration that brings the film to an end with the assassination of a Japanese general (see illus. 42). Here, the grains of sorghum become the grapes of wrath and with this vintage comes an undaunted trampling down of enemy soldiers. But with this trampling comes Grandma's own demise in a hail of bullets and an infernal flame (illus. 63, 64).

The film ends, Grandma a fallen martyr, but the book goes on. And on. Unseen in the film, Grandmother's vengeance provokes a Japanese reprisal that pitilessly destroys the very town she lived in, that reduces

62 *Red Sorghum*. The brutal flaying of Luohan by the Japanese.

63, 64 *Red Sorghum*. Unafraid to fight, Grandpa leads the assassination charge against the Japanese general . . . which leaves Grandma a martyred hero.

the landscape to a bleak ruin populated mostly by packs of wild dogs that live off human flesh (the dogs symbolic, perhaps, by their coded colours as battling Nationalists, Communists, and warlords); and the destruction doesn't end until after the Japanese war and the civil war give way to 'peace', Communism, and the third ruination of the sorghum. Despite all this violence, it is the heroism of Jiu'er's rebellion that the narrator, her grandson, holds up for highest praise, because of a still worse fate that lies ahead, after the dogs are slaughtered, after the Japanese are gone and civilization is restored.

Ironically, it is the third and most complete destruction of the sorghum, omitted from the film, which gives Mo Yan's story its central meaning, a sprawling novel written as if to host a single paragraph, like a church erected to hoist a steeple – and this message is withheld from the reader until the last paragraphs. Despite the evident flouting of socialist-realist style in both book and film, the declarative meaning of the story is absent from the film, having been reserved in the book until the next to last page, where even there it is couched exclusively in symbolic terms, in the imagery of sorghum and its ruin:

[A] variety brought in from Hainan Island, the lush green sorghum now covering the rich black soil of Northeast Gaomi Township is all hybrid. The sorghum that looked like a sea of blood, whose praises I have sung over and over, has been drowned in a raging flood of revolution and no longer exists, replaced by short-stalked, thick-stemmed, broad-leafed plants covered by a white powder and topped by beards as long as dogs' tails. High-yield, with a bitter, astringent taste, it is the source of rampant constipation. With the exception of cadres above the rank of branch secretary, all the villagers' faces are the color of rusty iron. How I loathe hybrid sorghum.[33]

Hybrid sorghum: that unnatural, cross-bred product of China and Communism. Here, finally, we see that the greatest villain of all is Communism and Communist bureaucratism, which brought peace by imposing its own dogmatic order but sapped the vital nature of the rural Chinese. To Mo Yan, in the earlier decades of this century, no matter how cruel the world of the Chinese, there were at least heroes like Grandma and Granddad, not just passive followers and pathetic victims of authority, but a band of hearty people with blood in their veins, lust in their pants, and the courage to rebel. Now all that is gone, weeded out by socialist planners and faceless bureaucrats.

From this point we can look back on the three-fold ruination of the sorghum as established by Mo Yan. The first occasion was but suggestive, perhaps even more a prefiguration than a genuine ruin, small in scale, clearing the way for a private breeding ground, a sacred habitat screened from human view but linked to the great circle of Heaven. Bred here was a genuinely Nietszchean order of human inspiration. The second ruin was purely destructive, public and vast in scale. The Hegelian contradiction between the liberated spirit of the first ruin and the alien threat behind the second remains unresolved in a battle in the sorghum fields that results in the death of both the foreign general and the Chinese avenger. With these first two ruins woven into one narrative site,[34] the field now awaits its culminating outcome: will the Chinese succumb to alien suppression or rise to avenge the avenger? In Mo Yan's telling, the third destruction is absolute, and it, too, is brought about by an invading alien force – Marxism. This ruin dooms the liberationist hopes of the first ruin and exceeds in magnitude the disaster of the second. Although total, its horror is muffled by totalitarian repression. It seems all but irreversible, though Mo concludes his epic with a charge to the young to bring back one 'stalk of pure-red sorghum'.[35]

This charge – in effect, for a future generation to bring back the past –

confirms the mythic nature of the author's conception. His preference for a mythologized past – a time of primitive 'vitality' [36] ('They killed, they looted, and they defended their country in a valiant, stirring ballet') [37] – to a modernity lacking 'soul', [38] reverses both evolutionary and revolutionary formulations of the present ('Surrounded by progress, I feel a nagging sense of our species' regression'), [39] and it contrasts with *Yellow Earth's* problematizing of past and present alike. As the vanguard of an emerging artistic movement, its fabulations remind one of American Southern literature, which offers a similar conversion of moral ruin into bygone virtue and which 'took on seriousness and grandeur only when . . . its writers were forced to look back upon a past that was irretrievable and forward to a future that seemed intolerable'. [40] Of course, in China this was hardly new. The distant past was always the seat of highest virtue, and one need look no farther back than *Lights of Ten-Thousand Homes* (from 1948, moments before the Communist Revolution), with its apotheosis of rural integrity and the extended family system, to find an immediate cinematic predecessor.

The truncation of Mo Yan's epic novel by film-maker Zhang Yimou is understandable in cinematic terms, where a 90-minute limit entails compression and compromise. Moreover, Mo Yan writes with a harsh spectacularity that one scarcely encounters in film and perhaps would prefer not to. [41] But the film's omission of the terminal 'ruin' described here and of what might seem to be the fundamental thrust of the novel requires some special consideration of compromise negotiated not only with the film medium but also with the conditions of censorship and self-censorship. Nowhere in the film do we experience the inability of the Chinese, too busy in the book brawling with themselves, to come together against the Japanese and protect their sorghum – that is, their culture. Mo Yan writes of this timeless Chinese Bonnie and Clyde:

They abandoned themselves to pleasure, living an existence of moral degeneracy and fickle passions. Granddad had become a bandit by then; he coveted not riches, but a life of vengeance and countervengeance, a never-ending cycle of cruelty that turned a decent commoner into a blackhearted, ruthless bandit with great skills and courage to match.

– and he provides some demented psychological dimensions to match. [42] But the film, instead, converts these Chinese into mere innocents: Granddad's murder of Grandma's leprous husband is glossed over and left ambiguous ('It's never been determined who did it,' the narrator/grandson tells us); Granddad's and Grandmother's numerous brawls and mutual infidelities are ignored, while Second Grandma – Jiu'er's rival – doesn't exist; father, a fifteen-year-old gun-toting fighter throughout the book, becomes an innocent bare-bottomed tot in the film; Luohan's adultery with Jiu'er is omitted; whereas in the book Luohan has rather foolishly earned at least some measure of Japanese recrimination,[43] the film converts him into a Communist and has him singled out for no other particular reason to be skinned alive by the Japanese before the assembled Chinese. But ironically, if overtly 'sanitized' of Mo Yan's bitter commentary on Communism, Zhang Yimou's film has also washed away Mo Yan's profound, debilitating pessimism about China's ruined culture, focusing on its latent vigor and posing a more determined threat to China's entrenched establishment than Mo Yan has to offer.

Like *Yellow Earth* and its jar of 'holy-water', discussed in the previous essay, Zhang Yimou's *Red Sorghum* ends not with dialogue, explanation, and resolution but with a singularly telling visual image that sets forth an ambiguous range of possibilities requiring interpretation, allows for alternative critical explanations, and perhaps expresses authorial ambivalence. Unlike the subliminal, almost unnoticeable, exposure of such imagery in *Yellow Earth*, this image helps to draw the film to a spectacular close and lingers, retinally, long after its ending. But ironically, as with *Yellow Earth*'s jar of holy-water (see illus. 1–3), this potent image has nowhere generated comment, interpretation, or controversy in all the critical literature about *Red Sorghum*. Set forth like an apparition after the death of Jiu'er, this is the image of a celestial eclipse (illus. 65): a profoundly inauspicious event in traditional Chinese culture, particularly in the case of a solar eclipse like this one when *yin* (the moon, female, the masses) overcomes the sun (the ruler, the patriarch, *yang*).

At the outset of her book, *When the Moon Waxes Red*, Trinh Minh-ha recognizes the political analogue of eclipse imagery: 'Politics waxes and

65 *Red Sorghum*. Solar eclipse spells revolution.

76

wanes, and like a lunar eclipse, it vanishes only to return rejuvenating itself as it reaches its full intensity.'[44] Of course, the moon doesn't really go anywhere, and then neither does politics; they only change in appearance, in intensity. But once in a while, the moon or the sun does vanish, and in a society governed by *natural* order, celestial events were Heaven's own commentary on the conduct of politics. In *Red Sorghum*, this eclipse occurs virtually without comment;[45] like the holy-water jar in *Yellow Earth*, it is a visual rather than a textual assertion. But the image is not self-sufficient, and in order to appreciate it as the censors and critics apparently have not, one must account for its referencing of tradition and text. To take a classical treatment of the subject as typical, the poem 'Tenth Month Eclipse' from the *Odes* was understood by Zhou dynasty commentators as forecasting specifically the impending ruin of Zhou:

> At their [celestial] conjunction in the tenth month,
> On the first day of the moon, the day *xin mao*,
> The sun was eclipsed [literally, 'eaten'],
> A very evil omen . . .
> The sun and moon announce evil,
> Not keeping to their proper paths.
> All through the kingdom there is no proper government,
> Because the good are not employed.
> For the moon to be eclipsed
> Is but an ordinary matter.
> Now that the sun has been eclipsed –
> How bad this is!
> Grandly flashes the thundered lighting.
> There is a want of rest, a want of good.
> The streams all bubble up and overflow.
> The crags on the hill-tops fall down.
> High banks become valleys;
> Deep valleys become hills.
> Alas for the men of this time!
> How does (the king) not stop this thing?. . .[46]

The poem goes on to establish its own reading of the metaphor, the eclipse being likened to officials 'acting out of season', and to give the purpose of the metaphor, decrying those officials' discordant behaviour. The narrator of the poem is himself an official who proclaims his loyalty to the ruler, but clearly the eclipse – like the rulers' failure to rid the government of bad, *yin*, officials, who mask his countenance – betokens dynastic upheaval and revolution.[47]

As an analogue rather than a linear reference, the climactic eclipse in *Red Sorghum* can support multiple readings. One understanding of this image might be as a natural counterpart of the unexpected ruin that Jiu'er's rebellion has brought, a pathetic fallacy indicating the vastness of the destructive metaphor, not unlike Mo Yan's dismal conclusion. Another, not inconsistent with the first, is a gendered identification of the eclipsing moon with the rebellious female Jiu'er, rising up against her Japanese overlords (first preparations for the attack take place at night beneath the rising moon), a cosmic inscription of her bold revolution, the female/'weak'/'backwards' Chinese peasantry overcoming the male/'strong'/imperialist Japanese, and an ominous sign not merely of the invaders' offence against Heaven and earth but also of Heaven's resonant, sympathetic, and determined response. Moreover, as a cyclical, recurrent event, the eclipse could be seen to link this event and this moment to other times and takes us from the historical setting of the film[48] to the present tense of its creation, into its own social context and the immediate subject of its commentary – in other words, to other rebellions yet to come.

The book ends with Grandma long dead and Second Grandma buried in a tomb surrounded by the hopelessness of hybrid green sorghum. The film spares us this despair. Peculiarly, in the film the sorghum is always green, never shown in its autumn hue except once: at the end, as the eclipse turns the sorghum red, recalling the red vitality of marriage, birth, death, and all those acts of valiant resistance in between, it transforms a bloody military horror and China's black despair into new hope for China's future. The film ends not with hybrid green and not in spiritual darkness, but in revolutionary red with the darkening and return of the eclipsing sun. The film has – necessarily, in the light of film censorship – been purged of the book's subtle but nonetheless notable criticism of the Party (via hybrid sorghum) except for a brief and doubly-subtle reference to the book itself.[49] But it comes heavily equipped with its own subversive message, buried deep like the homemade land mines that rock the end of the film.

In the book, the spiritual centre is the sorghum and the deepest cut is its desecration under Communist rule. Long before the end of the novel, the heroine is dead and the reader is forced to go on and on, pained with the sense of her loss. In print, Jiu'er's rebellious spirit is remembered and celebrated, but hope is never rekindled. On screen, however, it is the defiant female Jiu'er who occupies the spiritual centre. When Jiu'er dies her rebelliousness survives her, symbolized in part by her son urging her spirit to safety.[50] From the best-selling book, the film audience already knows what the battle is about in modern terms: the issue is not the past but the present, not Japanese but Chinese. The strutting Japanese are but a foil for Communist hegemonists. In Zhang's

Red Sorghum, it is the people – without the Party, without the PLA – that rise up against the Japanese, and they could very well rise up again. And as the unruly Chinese peasants have been shown to be a worthy adversary for the organized force of the Japanese, they can also be expected to be able when the next time for battle comes. Whereas Mo Yan's book implodes at the end, Zhang Yimou's film explodes, and the eclipse leaves us to wonder, when is the next explosion? If the ruins of Tian'an Men, three years later, provided a tragic or inconclusive answer to this question, it was not the final answer, for Zhang Yimou's ever-subversive eclipse measures cycles of ruin and renewal which continue without end. Not ironically but with a logic that derives from Heaven's own rounds, for ruin and regeneration are its Way, the celestial spectacle that witnesses both Jiu'er's success and her failure seems designed to calibrate both the rebellion and demise of her own bold, unwashed generation and the predictable upheaval of the present well-washed but spiritually fettered generation.

From 1984 on, the films negotiated in terms of the ruins of Mao's state socialism are many. Yet these terms vary from film to film, and this diversity helps place *Red Sorghum* in cinematic perspective. In *Yellow Earth*, the traditional rural culture once slated for demolition by the Communist wrecking ball is seen as persisting for the very same reason that socialist ideals failed to provide a viable alternative, namely the strict adherence to inflexible rules. So socialism itself is left in ruins, revealed as nothing more than the empty rhetoric of a better life, while traditional culture, though socially flawed, lives on. Embodying this ruin, caught in the middle and crushed, or rather drowned, is the young heroine of the film, unable to navigate from one system to the other, though she represented in the words of director Chen Kaige 'the hope of our whole people'.[51] The mere impotence of the Communist Party in *Yellow Earth* contrasts with Communism's devastating effect as seen in Chen's own later work, *Farewell My Concubine*, which chronicles (partly literal, partly allegorical) the brutal havoc wreaked on China's artistic traditions by the political tyrannies of this century (see illus. 112). And as a socio-economic critique, *Yellow Earth* has not held up well over time. It portrayed China as a rusticated, immovable dragon when today's chief fear is that China, economically unleashed and without direction, is simply moving too fast, like a dragon run amok, with a massive movement of rural peasants to China's urban centres representing the largest human migration in world history. Of course, it is too soon to know, as Asia's 'little dragons' come crashing down from the skies, as the gap between rich and poor in China yawns wider and wider, and as China undertakes the massively risky Three Gorges Dam project.

It also is perhaps too soon to evaluate how well the critique of Huang Jianxin's *Black Cannon Incident* of 1985 will hold up. Here is a satire on China's efforts to modernize while still labouring under the heavy hand of Party bureaucratism. In this savvy spoof of *film noir* mysteries, the pursuit of a political crime that never took place leads inexorably towards the ruin of a single, massive piece of industrial machinery, symbolizing the notion that China is building for itself an industrial disaster. The Party's ageing corporate commissars are held responsible for perpetuating a distrust of intellectuals and a hopelessly anachronistic political paranoia that spells doom for China's industrial efforts to catch up, while the set designer provides a mocking array of clocks and timetables as a constant reminder that time is running out for basic change in China (see illus. 197).

The continuing inability of China to change its ways and climb out of the ruins of its past is located in its authoritarian mode of education by Chen Kaige's *King of the Children* (1987). Based on a short story by Chen's literary friend Ah Cheng,[52] this gentle film follows the brief career of a young teacher at the end of the Cultural Revolution who is sacked for teaching his students to think for themselves rather than to memorize revolutionary texts. A philosophical musing on the role of language in establishing and maintaining power, it poses the conundrum of how to teach independence so that the teacher's power cannot be abused (see illus. 238). Looking back on the film, Chen wrote,

Many would say the Cultural Revolution has destroyed Chinese culture since numerous cultural relics were destroyed. However . . . from their blind worship of the leader/emperor figure to the total desecration and condemnation of individual rights . . . [these] are mere repetitions of tradition. Repetition is a characteristic of Chinese traditional culture.[53]

Chen concludes that so ruinous is the traditional role of rote repetition in Chinese society, the only solution is to destroy all vestiges of tradition in order to build a totally new foundation

. . . what is embedded in the film is my judgment on traditional culture. The burning of the wasted mountains at the end of the film is a metaphor of my attitude towards traditional values. 'Don't copy anything [quoting here his own film character], not even the dictionary'. . .

seeming, ironically, as iconoclastic as the Red Guards themselves (see illus. 235).[54]

The experience which led Chen Kaige to this conclusion was thrust upon him as a youth during the Cultural Revolution, like many of his peers sent down to the countryside, often to peripheral areas of China populated by ethnic minorities.[55] It was precisely this physical and cultural remove that provided a comparative perspective on the dominant Han culture of China, leading many to reconsider China's age-old chauvinist assertion of superiority, deeply inscribed in both Confucian and Marxian doctrines.[56] 'Fourth Generation' female director Zhang Nuanxin's *Sacrificed Youth* (1985),[57] set among the Dai of Xishuangbana, is perhaps the leading example of a film in which youth looks back on the ruinous ways of the Cultural Revolution to conclude (rightly or otherwise) that only from the arrogance of the dominant Han culture could such destructiveness erupt and that the real lessons of life were to be learned from China's peaceful ethnic minorities. Dai natives have long been cast romantically as smiling children in the socialist Chinese family (illus. 66).[58] In the unreal world of literature and image, not only do these and other minorities function as cement for the entire multi-ethnic polity, always under centrifugal stress, more importantly they fix the 'Han' majority's greater proximity to socialist ideals by their own greater distance from them.[59] Here they are cast as peaceable,

66 Cheng Shifa, *A Joyous Occasion for the Dai Tribesmen*, 1960, hanging scroll, ink and colour on paper. Guangzhou Art Gallery.

sexy forest folks, simple but in many ways wiser than the Han. They know their woodlands and their fields and they remain benignly aloof from the struggles of the Cultural Revolution. The Dai distinguish themselves by their pursuit of beauty and the openness of their sexual expression, leaving the young Han protagonist, Li Chun (Achun) (illus. 67), who has been sent down to live among them, to wonder as she gazes upon a lovely lotus pond,

I had been taught, beauty lies with the inconspicuous. I used to wash a shirt again and again to make it look old. It had never occurred to me a girl should make herself look charming. . .

Later, she laments, 'Isn't it better to speak out one's feelings? Unlike us Hans, always beating about the bush.'

Sacrificed Youth validates Stevan Harrell's assertions about civilizing projects, that 'In no case can we understand the entire project by looking from the perspective of only one side', that the staging ground of such projects is the entire zone of interactivity in both cultures, and that the impact may be felt as much by the colonizers as by the colonized.[60] The dominant culture is shown as having made few inroads, and even the Cultural Revolution has made little impact other than requiring the natives to calculate labour in terms of work-points and to have a few Han visitors laid on them, like Li Chun and Ren Jia – outsiders as childlike and quaint to the natives as the natives are quaint to them. Achun, nevertheless, soon adopts the tight-fitting native clothing, which she then parades before the other Chinese as a kind of reverse sophisticate (illus. 68). Indirectly, literally unspoken, by reappropriating the minority voice and the natural honesty of these ethnic 'children', *Sacrificed Youth* targets the emotional blockage of Han voices, and with that, the dishonesty of regulated dialogue within Han political society. As Achun engages the culture, her description of Granny Ya goes from 'witch' to 'caring'. But she is able to penetrate only partly into this other world. She remains unable to pursue a fulfilling relationship with either of her suitors, her Dai 'Elder Brother' and her fellow Han, Ren Jia. Over her head in the relationships she has blundered into, Achun's confusion about native expectations of her ultimately obliges her to flee the village.

At the end of the film, after the Cultural Revolution has subsided, Li Chun (now equipped with a modern education and dressed in modern clothing) returns to re-establish ties, only to discover that Ren Jia and his entire village have been destroyed in a massive mudslide, silencing them for ever.[61] This destructive apotheosis of the re-romanticized native life transmutes Li Chun's experience into a kind of ethnic 'Peach

67, 68 *Sacrificed Youth*. Modest city girl, Achun watches native girls bathe semi-nude . . . then she herself is absorbed into the hybrid space between.

69 *Horse Thief*. Horse thief Norbu carries a mock-skeleton in a shamanical exorcism.

Blossom Spring', leaving the repatriated traveller no return to her mystic experience and no exit from her own native Han culture. Perhaps with some implication that minority cultures cannot for long retain their integrity in the face of Han cultural hegemonism, the effect is to loft Achun's beloved Dai to the status of an experiential ruin, pleasurably isolated in memory beyond the reach of modern realities, while lamenting the persistent Han as a living wreck of a culture. It is ironic, though, and revealing that this effect can only be envisioned by appropriating – cinematically ruining – the healthy native culture so as to transport some of its sensibility back into the emptiness of Han values.

This collapsed cultural chauvinism has a political parallel in director Tian Zhuangzhuang's *Horse Thief* (also 1985). Tracing the life and death of Tibetan horseman Norbu, whose thieving ways are a challenge to reconcile with his devout Buddhism and gentle, loving parenthood, Tian produced an intentionally opaque picture of Tibetan behaviour that left virtually all critics nonplussed (illus. 69). To them, Tian Zhuangzhuang replied,

I'm talking about distancing; you're talking about identification . . . I didn't set out to give the biography of a horse thief. If I had, I'd have gone about it another way, beginning with horse theft during the grandfather's generation . . . What you would like is to understand more of the details and to clarify each specific point. That's normal . . . These [Tibetan] customs are the major obstacles the Chinese audience confronts. They would pose no problem for most native Tibetans.[62]

In short, Tian seems to be saying to his own Han people, if you can't understand this film, it's because you can't understand Tibet; and since you can't understand Tibet then how can you lay claim to its being

Chinese? Thus, in film terms, just as *Sacrificed Youth* despoils Han cultural superiority, *Horse Thief* lays waste the Han fiction of China's multi-ethnic political integrity. Tian uses film deconstructively, not just to document but to make happen. But *Horse Thief* is said to have sold only six or seven prints.[63] Tian's assertion in a 1986 interview with Yang Ping that 'I shot *Horse Thief* for audiences of the next century to watch', served only to enrage authorities.[64] And perhaps unintentionally, for those Chinese disposed to look disparagingly on Tibetans and their culture, *Horse Thief* may only have helped to confirm that negative view.

Tian Zhuangzhuang and others, beginning in 1988, applied this kind of ethnographic approach to another Chinese subgroup: China's own urban youth. Tian's *Rock 'n' Roll Kids* (illus. 70), though often misread as an entertainment film, as the director taking a commercial break, is actually an anthropological study brought home, looking at China's youngsters and telling their parents, did I say you don't understand Tibet? – you can't even understand your own children, so how can you

70 *Rock 'n' Roll Kids*. Shifting values – break-dancing before the image of Tian'an Men.

claim *them*? *Transmigration* (or *Samsara*, 1988), by *Black Cannon Incident* director Huang Jianxin from a short novel by Wang Shuo, is perhaps the most chilling study of China's modern urban youth, especially the sons and daughters of the élite and the would-be leaders of the next generation, betrayed by the Red Guard experience, alienated by the downfall of Maoism's unifying credo, and corrupted by the corruption of their parents. The film's central figure, Shi Ba, is the orphaned son of a high party official and the inheritor of wealth and self-indulgence. At first, he loves art, beauty, and money, surveyed efficiently by the film's cold, mod style. But he holds affection for no one, not for his beautiful and devoted wife and increasingly, as his narcissism fails him, not even for himself (illus. 71). Keeping the audience at arm's length with the lack of any sympathetic characters, what this film coldly surveys is not a ruin but a wreck.

Shi Ba's youthful identity is like that of Deng's New China. His parental orphanage is China's cultural orphanage. Neither he nor China have a past to guide them. The Cultural Revolution denounced and sullied all previous culture, and it in turn was repudiated. With this double destruction, the past retains no value, offers no lineage, provides no direction. It never appears, in fact, doesn't really exist: in *Transmigration*, as in *Rock 'n' Roll Kids*, there is scarcely an adult in view. If parental culture in any way lies 'in ruins', it is not a ruin that can be venerated or appreciated or lamented; all that is left is a site, the ruin having disappeared, swept off-site and now 'forgotten' or ignored. On

71 *Transmigration*. Shi Ba's self-sacrificing wife declares, 'You only love yourself' – but he doesn't.

the battlefield of ideology, Shi Ba's elders demolished each other and vanished. Collectivism vanquished, this barren soil now *must* grow a post-ideological individual. But Shi Ba is constructed as *the dilemma* of China's new identity formation: this young and developing ego, though free to be anything, without the parentage to nourish it, the models to guide it, the society within which to develop a sense of obligation, where can it find the values to become anything of value?

Beginning and ending with mechanical images of mobility that identify modernity with alienation and suggest the turning of the Buddhist wheel of life that plunges us headlong into the future – escalators, speeding trains, modern superhighways – *Transmigration* leaves the Chinese past far behind, that rural past of *Yellow Earth* and *Red Sorghum*, and leaves the Chinese audience to wonder where it is headed. In 'transmigration', in *samsara*, everything is interconnected. So Shi Ba's drive to isolate himself – perhaps in order to define himself – can only prove to be self-destructive. It leads first to a crippling encounter with a gang of monied racketeers – the new economic order disfiguring him as it has China – then to a spoiled marriage, and finally to his demise. In the penultimate scene, young but no longer youthful, Shi Ba, with his cane (of all things), traces his shadow upon the wall, an exaggerated distortion of his own lack of revolutionary stature, grotesque and hollow (illus. 72). And then, having come face to face with his own emptiness, from a balcony high over the city, beneath a frightening, blood-red moon that reflects his own negativity even as it mockingly symbolizes immortality, he drops to his death (illus. 73).

With *Transmigration*'s suicidal last scene, we are encouraged to remember earlier engagements of man and moon, earlier reflections on the fleeting nature of life, on self and selflessness, as a historical measure of modern alienation. No finer example of this exists than the Ming painter Shen Zhou's revealing self-portrait in painting and poetry, from his sixtieth year, contemplating the mid-autumn moon at that time of the year when the calendar cycles from *yang* to *yin*, a celebration in which the Chinese reaffirm the bonds of human friendship through the agency of nature (illus. 75). On that night, friends everywhere watch the same moon, at the same time; however far removed, they are together. In Shen Zhou's handscroll, the moon is brought low, down to eye level, where he and his intimate companions can toast it almost as if it were one of them. And in his accompanying poem, the ageing master asks knowingly,

> . . . How many mid-autumns can an old man have?
> He knows this passing light cannot be held.
> Time changes men; it does not change the moon.
> The old moon and young men are poles apart.

How dull is youth; it knows not this.
Every year, it sees the moon and every year is glad.
But old men have eyes and see this same return
And we, we are full of memory . . .[65]

Like Shi Ba, Shen Zhou is quite prepared to die. But unlike Shi Ba, he is linked to the past and bound to nature by a sympathy shared with his contemporaries; wisdom, not cold vacuity, prepares him for his future demise, for a dignifying passage from self into selflessness. What Shi Ba lacks is the warm fluid of nostalgia coursing through his veins, and the coldness of his life leaves no one to mourn his degraded death. He represents an entire generation: blind to life's unifying circularity (transmigrational history), its faith in both traditional and messianic communality crushed, and now adrift, alone, and unfulfilled in its passage to modern individualism. In a scene halfway through the film, Shi Ba visits Beijing's National Gallery where the surrounding modern images reflect his own anomie and facilitate his developing paranoia (illus. 74). Shen Zhou and the harmonious ideals of the past are conspicuous by their absence.[66]

As the film ends, with an unanswered questioning of its own cynicism, we are told (in an insert title) about Shi Ba's child, born six months later 'in a black room',[67] which leads us to think about the transmigration from the socialist father of Shi Ba to the faithless Shi Ba to the uncertain future of this fatherless offspring. This birth notice is set, ironically, to the background marching music of Communist China's youth anthem, 'Song of the Young Pioneers'.[68] Perhaps *Transmigration*, with its exaggeratedly impersonal characters, personalizes the sense of China's cultural wreckage more than any other film, portraying a society constructed without a past and without parentage,

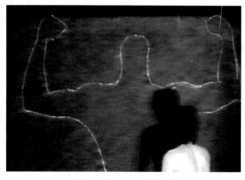

72 *Transmigration*. Shi Ba takes the measure of desire, image and true self.

73 *Transmigration*. Death comes to the emotionally-lifeless Shi Ba.

74 *Transmigration*. Shi Ba's paranoid fantasies come to life in a gallery of modern art.

without historical pride or generational obligation, with nothing more than a mass of uprooted, drifting, selfish selves. In shifting attention from the cultural collective to the individual psychology of loss in this generation's experience of alienation, *Transmigration* reveals the predicament of a self divorced from society, of a people without community, of a society divorced from its own past. Defined by lack and absence, *Transmigration* makes clear the social need which has given rise to the recent revival of Mao not as ideologue but as a cultural icon signifying (*not* filling) a cultural void. As a prominent painter of Mao-as-cult-figure, Yu Youhan, has said of China's tormented relationship with its own past, 'When we reject Mao, we reject a piece of ourselves' (illus. 76).[69] Or as elaborated by Chinese avant-garde patron Chang Tsong-zung (Johnson Chang): 'It's like an unhappy childhood. You cannot dwell on it all the time and impose it on others, but if you disown it completely, you will be an artificial or incomplete person.'[70]

Numerous other films have lodged their critique of modern China in grim allegorical tales of China's failed social architecture, both Marxist and post-Marxist. Xie Fei's *Woman from the Lake of Scented Souls* (1992), contrasting one woman's economic modernization with her old-fashioned persecution of her daughter-in-law, looks at the ruinous state of women's liberation in contemporary China and the age-old complicity of Chinese women in perpetuating their own social predicament (see illus. 158). Zhang Yimou's *Story of Qiu Ju* (1992) is a satire on the legal reforms, or pseudo-reforms, of the post-Mao era. Its heroine, a slow-witted but unbudgably honest peasant woman engaged in the

75 Shen Zhou, *Gazing at the Mid-Autumn Moon*, c. 1486, handscroll, ink and colour on paper. Museum of Fine Arts, Boston.

76 Yu Youhan, *Chairman Mao in Discussion with the Peasants of Shaoshan*, 1991, oil on canvas. Private collection.

Here Mao's friendliness toward the people is remembered with a combination of affection and satire. Based on a well-known photograph of Mao's 1959 trip back to his own home village, the smiles are exaggerated as in billboard advertisement. The canvas is strewn with wallpaper-like flowers reminiscent both of the floating lotus that decorated ancient Buddhist illustrations of deities and of Mao's own 'hundred flowers', his catch-phrase for political openness – as unrealistic in this depiction as the autocratic Chairman's own 'liberality' and yet not without a longing for the way things might have been. Ironically, at the same time as it satirizes Maoist visual propaganda, Yu Youhan's work embodies the pop-nostalgia for this universal father figure that set in by the early 1990s together with the increasing cynicism about Mao's successors.

pursuit of simple justice, reveals that the daily disposition of civil law remains much as it always has: opaque, bureaucratically ensnarled, and ever-tilted in favour of the state and its functionaries. The new legal scheme, it suggests, is a built-ruin (see illus. 117). More recently, film-maker Zhou Xiaowen's satirical *Ermo* (1994) wags the shaggy-dog tale of another slow-witted but fiercely determined peasant woman, a lowly noodle-maker who sets her heart on owning the biggest television set in her village (illus. 77, 78). An urban critique of China's post-socialist infatuation with consumerism and capital formation, *Ermo*'s excess and her success are used to mock the spiritual emptiness of post-Mao

77 *Ermo*. The noodle-seller.

78 *Ermo*. Staring modernity in the face and wanting it, badly. Ermo (centre, rear) gazes at the television she's determined to buy, orders the shop-keeper to turn it off so it won't be worn out by the time she can afford it. By the end of the film, however, it is Ermo who is worn out.

China's commercial goals as the wreckage of China's once-lofty ideals. Ermo's unwitting desire is for freedom from poverty and rural isolation but her pursuit of modernity in a box, earned with her feet and her blood, enslaves her body and soul. The young and sexually-charged Ermo contrasts with her ageing, impotent husband, the former village chief, now a signature for the displacement of the Maoist old guard in China's pursuit of economic 'progress' and its growing social inequities. He argues for the old values, for putting her profits into another room for their house, but he is unable to thwart the entry of the box into the home and its introduction of ruinous Western values into the family. 'In China,' says director Zhou Xiaowen, 'money was once a synonym for filth. Now money has become a god. But will [this god] be able to satisfy his people?'[71]

These cinematic views of China's cultural ruination are grim, portraying a society whose cultural architecture is in a shambles, whose virtues lay strewn about while only her worst traditional features remain standing. Yet these films also pose an art-historical question that ranges far beyond their own specific context, that goes to the issue of what kind of context produces good art. Even a ruined polity and a tattered social fabric do not equate with the ruination of an *artistic* culture. Art, after all, lives symbiotically, not parasitically, within its culture, preserving as it transforms, defying time as it defines and is defined by its times, refusing ruination as it provides the stuff of ruins.[72] However deteriorated the cultural context which generated these films – and which, in turn, is critiqued by them – this group of films represents the most extraordinary burst of fine film-making and arguably the most striking florescence of visual art in twentieth-century China. Of course, we don't know how long this 'golden era' will last (or whether it might already now be past – for some, it ended prematurely, with the appearance of *Red Sorghum*).[73] But thinking broadly, we may reflect that the heyday of many great cultural moments in China corresponded with ages of political and social decline or military subjugation – as in the periods that produced Wang Xizhi and Gu Kaizhi (of the fourth century), the splashed ink painters (of the late eighth and late thirteenth centuries), and the eras of Ni Zan and Bada Shanren (the fourteenth and seventeenth centuries). To many a historian's dismay, there seems to be no direct or simple correlation between political health and cultural prosperity in Chinese history, nor even the inverse, and at most only some tentative correlation between certain particular characteristics. It could be argued then, at best, that today's cultural complexity and the decline of central political authority have combined to permit, if not produce, all this cinematic creativity, aroused by chaos and nurtured by the spirit of dissent. Zhang Yimou himself understands this: 'Art dies in freedom and lives in oppression.'[74] Yet it must also be acknowledged that this film-making era may now be over, a golden age now lying in its own ruins, the victim (more than anything else) of the continuing conditions of internal cultural repression.

Still, not all the fine films of this era are wrapped in such negativity, and even among the ones which view today's landscape as a cultural wasteland are those which send forth the call to come admire the ruins or repair the foundations left by China's modern collapse. Directed by Wu Tianming – who as Xi'an Film Studio head administrator made possible such pioneering films as *Horse Thief, Black Cannon Incident, King of the Children, Red Sorghum,* and *Judou – Old Well* (1987) begins with a

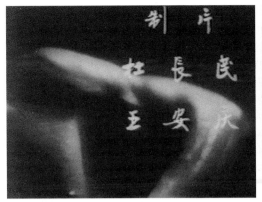 

79, 80 *Old Well*. Opening credits, an old-fashioned faith that hard labour . . . can lead to a cultural rebirth.

production credits sequence focused closely on the hard work of survival and the labour of rebirth (illus. 79, 80). Like *Yellow Earth*, *Old Well* deals with drought in north China. But whereas *Yellow Earth* ends with a futile pursuit of rain by a swarm of peasant men, unresponsive to the Communist Party's calls for modernization, praying superstitiously to an impotent dragon king, *Old Well* provides a much more temperate message: in the end, hard work, education, and community spirit bring in the water and assure the survival of a healthy, co-operative culture. One film looks to the Heavens and documents the futility of hope for change; the other digs into the earth and (as Eugene Wang has observed) brings life out of the womb of a well (illus. 80).[75] Both films end with a meditation on time and history: *Yellow Earth* measures the transience and brevity of the socialist experiment, and no trace even of its ruins remain at the end as the film credits roll across the screen (see illus. 39); while *Old Well*, in its deeply moving last moments, throws no credit to socialism but instead casts the final success of a northern community's epic efforts in the traditionally hallowed form of a Chinese stone stele, not an object of worship (see illus. 4) but an historical record of the first success among the many failed efforts and the many lives laid waste in the process of digging one dry well after another (illus. 81, 82). This form gives hope and heroic measure to human effort and persistence. To achieve their success, the determined heroes of the film had to overcome history itself and a history of failure signified in the film by the ruins of two earlier stelae, one of them cast to the bottom of a dry well, another used as the base-stone for a human latrine. And so we know, ironically, that even the stele with which the film ends will itself some day, somewhere lie in ruins and that the survival effort will require constant renewal, pitting human beings in a timeless struggle against the corrosive effects of historical time itself.[76]

The Trouble-Shooters (1988), directed by Mi Jiashan with a script by Mi and Wang Shuo, takes an up-beat, satiric view of survival in the postmodern ruins of Chinese socialism. It follows the creative exploits of a group of young entrepreneurs who set up a company, called T-T-T (offering to 'take on your worries, take on your troubles, take on your responsibilities'), to help solve any kind of problem you might have in coping with the social uncertainties and chaos of this brave new world. In its most remarkable scene, a young and probably untalented writer who can't figure out how to gain recognition for his work has come to T-T-T, which decides to solve his problem more directly than by working on his skills and instead goes straight to the question of audience recognition. They arrange for an elaborate writers' award ceremony, full of famous literary celebrities, at which the failed poet becomes the chief honoree. A huge bash is staged and high-priced tickets are sold for the occasion, which features a fashion-show kind of walk-on with models, female body-builders, and break-dancers, plus characters in Chinese opera costumes, PLA soldiers, Guomindang officers, warlords, public security officials, and so forth (illus. 83). Filmed in a year of hope, 1988, just before Tian'an Men, this is more than mere silliness: it provides a wonderful analogue to the breaking down not only of traditional values and modern ideologies alike but to the demise of the age-old barriers between people and classes which all of these conflicting values and hateful ideologies have long enforced.

By the end, this social menagerie is all dancing together to a high-spirited song of hope for the future, cavorting with the greatest of

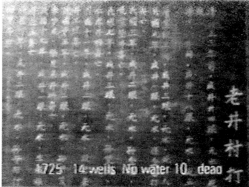

81, 82 *Old Well.* Commemorating centuries of effort and hardship with a stone . . . '1725: 14 wells, no water, 10 dead . . .'

83 *The Trouble-Shooters*. Bridging ancient rifts between the old society and new, a turn-of-the-century landlord dances with a bikini-clad model.

84 *The Trouble-Shooters*. 'That's great!' exults the poet.

pleasures on the ruins of the past. Celebrated here is the demise of a cultural prison, built with a flawed architecture, collapsed of its own faulty design, allowing the prisoners to run free. In the awards scene that follows, the difference between film satire and ridiculous modern reality is totally blurred, deconstruction deconstructed, and when the young writer for whom this event is staged discovers that he's been fooled, that all the famous literary figures were just paid stand-ins, he declares, 'Really? That's great!' (illus. 84) – embracing, in other words, the ascendancy of art over reality, the triumph of future dreams over past ruins and present disenchantment.

3 A Farewell to Arts: Allegory Goes to the Movies

If you don't study the *Odes*, you will have no means by which to communicate.
– *Analects*[1]

It's not an epic. It's a personal story about a few individuals.
– Chen Kaige, on *Farewell My Concubine*[2]

Yellow Earth, for all its significance, is a little story, or hardly a 'story' at all; *Red Sorghum*, in its cinematic form, is but a fragment of Mo Yan's sprawling story, its 'point' concealed and compressed into a few final moments of the film. *Farewell My Concubine*, by contrast, is a massive epic that carries us through much of the twentieth century, from the early nationalist period, through the Japanese occupation, the return of the Nationalists and their capitulation to the Communists, through the Cultural Revolution and its aftermath. Among Chinese films, it's been recommended, appropriately, for that oft-given '*Gone With the Wind* award'.[3] In it are all the classic themes rolled into one: arts and entertainment, war and social upheaval, love, jealousy, betrayal, and revenge. Marking Chen Kaige's first major success since he had teamed with Zhang Yimou to produce *Yellow Earth*, it lost Hollywood's Academy Award for best foreign film to a little Spanish sex farce, which somehow seems appropriate for a tragedy of its magnificent stature.[4] Produced in 1993 when the emotional turbulence of Tian'an Men was still fresh, it bitterly recalls that event through its critique of the unending, vice-like grip of revolutionary politics in earlier decades. Twice, the film was banned and unbanned in China, where it won no awards. *Farewell*'s twists and turns defy summary, but one character stands at the core of the film, a complex character divided twice-over into two parts: the little boy Douzi, given up by his prostitute mother to a training school for young actors (illus. 85), and the man he grows up to be, the famed female impersonator, Cheng Dieyi – boy and man, male and 'female' (illus. 86).

The first part of the movie reads like a Chinese adaptation of Charles Dickens. At Master Guan's opera school, when mistakes are made, the young students are punished so they will get it right the next time. When they get it right, they are punished so they'll not forget and do it wrong later on (illus. 87). The discipline by which these youngsters master the crafts of acting, singing, martial arts, costuming, and so on is little short of sheer torture (illus. 88). But the particular torture held out

85 *Farewell My Concubine.*
Master Guan rejects Douzi's
mother, equating the
theatre with prostitution.

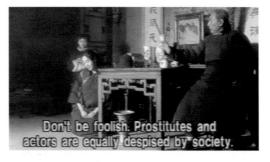

86 *Farewell My Concubine.*
Beautiful Cheng Dieyi.

Don't be foolish. Prostitutes and
actors are equally despised by society.

for Little Douzi is that of being remade from a boy into a girl. In time,
as the adult Dieyi (literally, 'clothed as a butterfly'), he becomes more
perfect, more desirable than any woman. The film derives from a novel
by Hong Kong's popular female writer, Li Pik-wah or Lilian Lee, with
many literary passages hard to translate into graphic medium:

A *dan* [impersonator] has to be even more feminine than a woman. In real
life, a woman's charms are enough, but something else is needed for the
stage. It takes a man to understand what other men desire.[5]

Dieyi's fervent admirers were deluded, however. It wasn't him they loved –
it was the idea of him. Men loved him as a woman; women loved him as a
man. Nobody knew who he really was.[6]

Little Douzi's sexual conversion does not come easy. Time and again,
he flubs the telling operatic line, 'I am by nature a girl' (illus. 89), and
each time he is beaten worse than before, until finally he becomes that
girl. Once he does, his attachment to his art is nothing less than 100 per
cent. And with this sexual transformation, there comes a kind of deconstruction of the notion of a gendered reality. If Douzi, a boy, can be a girl

87 *Farewell My Concubine*. Hand outstretched, Shitou is told: 'This is so you'll remember to do as well the next time.'

88 *Farewell My Concubine*. Hands roped to the wall, legs forced apart by bricks, young Douzi becomes a student of the theatre.

in the minds of his audience, then in his own mind he can become the very woman whose role he plays on stage; and if he can do this, then he can transcend time and history; and if he can transcend time and history, then he can avoid compromise with the repeated intrusions of political tyranny, and his art can transcend the tyranny which politics holds over culture. In the course of the story, Dieyi, the man-woman, plays out his role without regard for the political waves that wash over China: attached only to his art and not to politics, he performs for the nationalists, he performs for the Japanese, he performs for the Communists, insisting only on perfection in his role. He refuses to adapt his style to the new Communist aesthetics. And of course, time and again he pays a heavy price. He is tried by the Nationalists for playing to the Japanese. And he is brutalized by Communist Red Guards, and denounced under pressure by his lifelong friend and stage partner, Duan Xiaolou, for his political infidelities and sexual transgressions.

In a structured sense, Dieyi's doom was certain; to read again from the novel:

After all, life is just a play. Or an opera. It would be easier for all of us if we could watch only the highlights. Instead, we must endure convoluted plot twists and excruciating moments of suspense. We sit in the dark, threatened

89 *Farewell My Concubine*. Young Douzi not yet reconstructed, still clinging to his gender.

by vague menaces. Of course, those of us in the audience can always walk out; but the players have no choice. Once the curtain goes up they have to perform the play from beginning to end. They have nowhere to hide.[7]

Of course, it was in real life that Dieyi had nowhere to hide, because once he was converted from male to female, he was no actor – for him, the stage became the real thing and the theatre became his only real life. His difficulty lay in coping with the unreality of life offstage.

The adult Dieyi had been doomed from the moment that Little Douzi was wedded to his female role. From that time on, he became one with the historical figure he was to perform for the rest of his life, the royal concubine Yu Ji. Yu Ji's lover was Xiang Yu, the King of Chu (illus. 90), the greatest man of his time, but fated – by flaws in his personality – to lose on the battlefield to Liu Bang, who founded the Han dynasty in 206 BC (illus. 91). As Xiang Yu approaches his fate, he tries to set his horse free, but his horse is loyal and won't go. He tries to set his concubine Yu Ji free, but Yu Ji stealthily draws the sword from Xiang Yu's scabbard and commits suicide. At the moment the child actor Douzi becomes a girl, he becomes Yu Ji, and as Yu Ji gave her life in loyalty to the King of Chu, the adult actor Cheng Dieyi must some day give his life out of loyalty to traditional Chinese theatre. The film ends with this suicide, with the complete merger of life and art (see illus. 114).[8]

90 *Farewell My Concubine*. The King of Chu.

91 Anonymous, *The Feast at Hongmen*, c. 50 BC, mural from Luoyang tomb no. 61.

This poorly preserved Han-period tomb painting presents a pivotal event in the founding of the Han dynasty, closely following the historical text of Ban Gu's *Han shu*. An early example of historical illustration, it already reveals in prototypical form some of the 'classic' staging devices common to both painting and the theatre. The 'central' figures of the textual narrative, contenders for the throne of China, kneel at the middle of the painting. The right figure of this pair, Xiang Yu, known as the 'King of Chu' in the opera *Farewell My Concubine*, at this point has victory within his grasp. On his left, his rival Liu Bang, responding to an invitation he couldn't refuse, attends a showdown banquet rather like a restaurant scene from *The Godfather*. Xiang Yu's henchmen move in from the far left, plotting to assassinate Liu Bang while performing a mid-dinner sword dance: the grimacing villainous cousin, Xiang Zhuang, with sword in hand, and next to him, the evil advisor Fan Zeng. From the right, the quick-witted Fan Kuai, swashbuckling star of this scene, enters the tent from out of doors to foil that attempt, with a dashing tip of his hat as he joins the fray. This is pure melodrama. (The bear near the centre of this painting is a tomb guardian figure, extraneous to the painted narrative.) Rescued from this critical encounter, Liu Bang will go on to eventual battlefield victory over Xiang Yu, while Fan Kuai, up until now his lowly charioteer, will rise to become minister of state. The symmetrical framing of the central figures by their lesser agents, as used in this painting, became a classic convention of Chinese figure painting, used for centuries to come: see illustrations 3 (now lacking an original figure on the right), 103, 130.

The sexual conversion of Douzi is prefigured early in the film when he is first brought to the opera school by his prostitute mother and rejected by the master for his physical deformity of an extra, sixth finger. Here, in order to secure his admission, his mother slices off the finger with a carving knife. One need not confuse digits with other parts to appreciate the significance of this mutilation as the first step in the painful, forcible remoulding of the natural boy to make a female star of the stage.[9]

The scene in *Farewell* where Little Douzi is consecrated in his female role has as its prelude one in which he runs away from the theatre school with a friend and both run smack into a real theatre. There for the first time they see a live performance of the art they have been suffering to learn. As the magnificence of what they see brings tears to their eyes, Little Douzi beams beatifically, while the other boy exclaims, 'What does it take to become a star? How many beatings does it take?' Now of their own free will they rush back to their school, Douzi to a ferocious beating, his friend to death by his own hand. Immediately following this suicide comes Douzi's beatification as a creature of the stage. This scene, one of the finest in all Chinese film-making, takes merely two minutes and twenty seconds, but it is dense and complicated, and challenging to fathom at a single viewing. It is set before the shrine of the school, whose offertory altars and ancestral images (including Yi Su as the patron god of opera singers) transform Douzi's sexual conversion from profane into sacred (illus. 92). It is accompanied by the headmaster explaining for the first time the inner meaning of the opera *Farewell My Concubine* to the pupils, who have been learning it by rote memory for years (illus. 95). As he expounds, the camera pans sideways along the line of boys, as if moving along a Chinese handscroll (although in the 'wrong' direction, left to right) (illus. 93, 94). A nearby temple bell begins tolling, which proves to be a death knell accompaniment to the battlefield story, set long ago and far away. Douzi now is shown close-up, in the shrine, fixed and focused compared to the handscroll motion, as if being offered up sacrificially, like fruits on the ritual altar that frames him (illus. 96). In the back-ground, we begin to hear sounds from the past, horrific cries from Xiang Yu's last battle. 'No matter how resourceful you are,' says the master, describing the King of Chu, 'you can't fight fate' (illus. 97), and as the camera returns to Douzi (illus. 98), we know it is his fate that we're hearing about, inseparable from that of Concubine Yu Ji and her unflinching loyalty. The camera then cuts from Douzi to a painted handscroll illustrating Yu Ji's suicide (scrolling now in the 'proper' direction; illus. 99). The master then takes a chair, as if he were him-self the King of Chu ascending a throne and flanked by his followers (illus. 100; see illus. 103), and he tells them that they all have a respon-sibility for their own fate – that is, not to change their fate but to learn how to deal with it. At this, Douzi, whose fate lies in the balance, first takes on the responsibility of being his own master, beating himself into bloody submission (illus. 101). Finally, as we watch this self-inflicted discipline, we begin to hear voiced-over from the *next* scene – out of the future, yet already radically determined by *this* scene – a rehearsal set by the lakeside, a chorus of boys chanting the King of Chu's final words of self-encouragement as he faces his certain doom (illus. 102).

The opera
"Farewell My Concubine"_

_the Chu warriors fled
in a great panic.

No matter how resourceful
you are, you can't fight fate.

_that each person is responsible
for his or her own fate.

"I am so strong
I can uproot the mountains_"

Like much of *Farewell* cinematically, this scene may seem very un-Chinese. For those who hold up American film as the standard for modern Chinese films to aim for, this movie, this scene – with its ever-mobile camerawork, its rich coloration, and its multilayered sounds and images – reached an historic threshold, as *Red Sorghum* had done earlier. With Gu Changwei's photography and Pei Xiaonian's film editing, this work compares in sophistication to Francis Ford Coppola's *The Godfather* (Part I, 1982) in its climactic moments – another dark film about the corruption of profession and the inescapable bonds of 'family'. In *The Godfather*, Michael Corleone becomes godfather to his nephew in a cathedral setting while, simultaneously, five arranged murders are

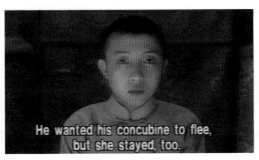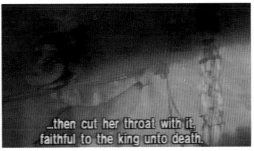

92–102 *Farewell My Concubine*. Young Douzi's theatrical initiation.

carried out elsewhere which make him the godfather, interlacing with mingled sights and sounds the sacred and the sacrilegious, the community of god and the families of crime, and the blood-centred rituals of each.[10] In each case, a distinctively cinematic reality is created, unlike what any one person can actually see and hear in linear time and only like what one might conjoin in imagination or stitch together as experienced insight.

And yet this cinematic style is no more indebted to Hollywood than it is to depictions of political heroes who, just like the King of Chu, populated the traditional Chinese stage and numerous painted scrolls. Like *Farewell My Concubine*, most such paintings were glamorous,

103 Anonymous, *Breaking the Balustrade*, mid-12th century, detail from a hanging scroll, ink and colour on silk. National Palace Museum, Taipei.

This historical narrative depicts the Han emperor Chengdi holding audience with his courtiers in a garden setting. He serves as the political arbiter and central pivot in the clash of figures around him. Indicating the corruption of the times, in the early first century BC, the emperor is closely surrounded by lackeys (including a eunuch and two women, none of them legitimate participants in court politics). Loyal and honest courtiers, farther removed at a respectful distance, plead and demand that the truth be heard about his henchmen. Though royal guards prepare to remove the more outspoken of the two, the famous social upstart Zhu Yun, the emperor pivots away from his inner circle and towards the politically and spatially isolated pair, setting a memorable precedent for his readiness to entertain criticism. This painting was probably commissioned as a 'recruitment theme' by an early Southern Song dynasty emperor, Gaozong or Xiaozong, publicly advertising a policy of intended imperial toleration toward even the most brutally honest advice and advisors at court. Its narrative devices of gesture, posture, and placement, which clearly signal the virtues of flaws of each character, are closely related to staging in traditional Chinese theatre.

brightly coloured and crisply delineated works (*gongbi*), produced for court and temple (see illus. 43; illus. 103). And like *Farewell*, they are dramatic renderings of narrative text, layered with literary and visual reference and imbued with the potential for coded meanings and interpretation. Likewise, the issues considered in this film are thoroughly traditional, from the impact of the past on the present, to the encounter with one's fate, to the status of entertainers and role of entertainment in Chinese society.

With this scene, then, Douzi has been initiated into the theatre, wedded to his role, but the consummation of this marriage lies in the next major, bloody scenes, where he fails his line one more time: 'I am by nature a boy' (see illus. 89). It is now for his childhood friend and life-long stage partner, Shitou (called Xiaolou as an adult), to ream out Douzi's mouth with a long-stemmed phallic pipe (illus. 104).[11] This is Douzi's final mutilation. And no sooner does Douzi at last complete his lines successfully ('I am by nature a girl') than he is ravaged backstage afterwards, ritually 'deflowered', by a pedophilic patron. In the film, this assault comes with the prior acquiescence of Master Guan, whom the stage manager informs that 'the concubine will have to die one way or the other'. In the book, this patron – Master Ni, a former Qing dynasty official, a eunuch who envies Douzi's physical perfection – reminds Little Douzi of Yu Ji's loyalty to the king in order to compel Douzi's sexual compliance:

'Who does Yu Ji die for?' he asked smoothly.
    'She dies for the General.'

104 *Farewell My Concubine*. With pipe in hand, Shitou orders Douzi: 'Open your mouth.'

Master Ni was pleased by this response . . . he was beginning to feel aroused.

'That's correct. Yu Ji is a woman, frail and weak, and yet she shines with integrity. She is so loyal that she dies for her lover . . .'[12]

This fulfils the logic of his marriage to theatre via sexual conversion and prepares him for his off-stage homosexual life. Later, the adult Dieyi – Douzi, grown up – will play Yu Ji to his homosexual lover, another great opera patron, Yuan Shiqing,[13] who similarly assumes the role of the King of Chu in order to assume sexual authority over Dieyi (illus. 105). As Yuan first watches Dieyi perform, it is the stage manager who characterizes Dieyi's fluid identity, both theatrical and sexual, saying, 'You judge . . . has he not blurred the distinction between theatre and life . . . male and female?' (illus. 106).

From this point on, Douzi's critical lines are perfect. Perfect, that is, until the end of the film when Douzi and Shitou recapitulate their relationship and restore their partnership. Then, as the ageing Dieyi, he fails his lines again – perhaps in order to correct them, to repurify himself – and then through death, becoming Yu Ji and using the king's sword to slit her/his throat, he demonstrates undying loyalty to his stage partner, to the King of Chu, and to the theatre (see illus. 113).

In the scene from *The Godfather*, mentioned earlier, the cathedral setting provides an ironic analogue for what the murder scenes are *not*, and yet each site transfigures and distorts the other, elevating a crime

105 *Farewell My Concubine*. Gay Dieyi, following his sexual ravishment by opera patron Yuan Shiqing.

106

106 *Farewell My Concubine.* At the theatre, arch-patron Yuan Shiqing watches Dieyi for the first time, with stage manager Na by his side.

film into a work of overarching allegorical significance. Similarly, in the convoluted tale of *Farewell to My Concubine*, a broader signification is indicated that requires a reading of the film as allegory.

The most fundamental aspect of allegory, of course, is that things do not say what they mean (in Quintilian's antique formulation, 'It indicates one thing with the words, another with the sense'),[14] establishing the necessity of interpretation and an inconclusive diversity of possible explanations. Asked once to comment on *Farewell My Concubine*, director Chen Kaige resisted describing it in allegorical breadth and said of it only that 'It's not an epic. It's a personal story about a few individuals.'[15] On other occasions, he has noted his own relation to these individuals. Chen Kaige, described as forever working day and night at film, too focused to sustain a family life, has said of Cheng Dieyi, 'To a great extent, I identify with Cheng Dieyi; he's a great master of Beijing Opera, but an idiot in life. He often confuses the real world with the world on stage. Someone like him is very lonely as he goes on the stage.'[16] And of the climactic struggle session in which Xiaolou betrays Dieyi only to have Dieyi exact revenge on Xiaolou's wife, Juxian, Chen has confessed to having modelled this on a moment at the outset of the Cultural Revolution:

You know what happened between my father and me. You know, I just denounced my father, just as you saw it in my film *Farewell to My Concubine* . . . There is a big enigma in my heart, and not only in my heart. We cannot forget, even if we try very hard to forget. Spiritually we are living in that period. That's the point.[17]

For Jianying Zha, writing counter to some other gender-oriented interpretations of *Farewell My Concubine*, homosexuality 'was not his movie's central subject – betrayal was . . . if one must pick out a central theme, then betrayal it is: an artist's betrayal of another, one man's betrayal of art'.[18] This would make art the subject of betrayal but not the central subject of the film; it does not, of itself, render the form of the film as allegorical. But Zha has taken this interpretation one step further, writing that 'Perhaps, then, the film itself can be seen as an allegory of the partnership and rivalry of Chen [Kaige] and Zhang [Yimou]' – implying an allegorical significance brought to the tale by Chen Kaige, possibly accounting for his selection of the subject, expanding himself metaphorically on Lilian Lee's novelization.[19] If anything, *this* view of a post-facto reading of Lee's book points to the individuality of allegorical understanding and the multiplicity of *other* possible views.

The question of whether Chinese culture, literature in particular, has ever produced a form equivalent to Western 'allegory' (translated into Chinese today as *yuyan*, or 'lodged words') is a prickly matter, already much discussed by literary theorists. Technically, the matter has been said to be ontological, cosmology-dependent. Since 'Western' language is based on a dualistic view of the world (a real-ideal paradigm in the case of pagan antiquity, a sacred-secular dichotomy in Christian times), it allows for Quintilian's paradigm. But as the 'Chinese view' instead is said to be monadic (inner and outer realms, mental and material, being merely *manifestations* of the same thing), some scholars – undaunted by the essentialism of this East–West distinction – have asserted that the 'impossibility of a Chinese allegory becomes situated . . . in the very logic of sameness and difference that provides the means of telling a metaphor from a synecdoche'.[20] For Pauline Yu, '. . . the seamless connection between the individual and the world [which] enables the [Chinese] poem simultaneously to reveal feelings, to provide an index of governmental stability, and serve as a didactic tool' permits synec-doche (the part represented by the whole) but not metaphor (something standing for something else) or allegory (generally understood as 'continuous metaphor').[21] Haun Saussy, however, in his survey of this matter, contextualized around the long history of the Confucian engagement with the *Odes*, objects that such a view 'leads directly to a hypercategorical':

Metaphor and fiction, instead of being dismissed or bracketed as constructs of Western ontology, have now been promoted (as categories) to the status of realities.[22]

The matter is more than 'merely academic', and its significance is lodged in the classical Chinese uses of allusion in court rhetoric, leading us back in time from *Yellow Earth* to origins in the most ancient anthology of Chinese literature, the *Book of Odes*, and to the Confucian uses and abuses to which these *Odes* were historically subjected. Allegorical interpretations of popular poetry as moral pieces were established early on, on whatever questionable grounds, for use in facilitating the indirectness and deftly negotiated nature of court rhetoric, of liege speaking to lord with the utmost deference and caution. So integral did the allegorical recitation of the *Odes* become to court performance – discretion in the face of danger – that Confucius, who lived in as dangerous a time as any and who played as large a role as anyone in editing the form and function of these poems, taught his students, 'If you don't study the *Odes*, you will have no means by which to communicate'.[23] Model interpretations were taken as dogma until the late nineteenth century. The real 'problem' of allegory in Chinese literary tradition is not the appropriateness of the term but rather the hardened attitudes toward it resulting from its historical overuse.

With the influence of Western ideas and modernization at the end of the Qing dynasty, a backlash set in against 'abusive' allegorical interpretations that remains today as a powerful reactionary force, demanding instead 'original' readings of the poems as popular songs pertinent to folk, and not as court matters. This converted the *Book of Odes* '(again?) into the anthology of unrelated poems that, for centuries, it had not been',[24] valued for their aesthetic naturalness rather than their diplomatic use. And yet, with the rising interest in contextualized readings, a backlash has now set in against the backlash, and historical allegory and its study are back in favour. In Chinese visual arts, paintings which (like the *Odes*) used open-ended genres – famous encounters between figures, certain flowers and animals, landscapes and landscape elements, and even certain styles to code socio-political stances – have been decoded in modern times and used to explain to a contemporary audience China's artistic modes of expressing laudatory or dissident attitudes (see illus. 23, 24, 43, 103, 189).[25]

The pervasive control of public speech and constraints on political thought that led to such literary subtlety and indirection, and to such 'abuse' of original texts, is not exclusively old or new. Rather, it unites the past with the present. It is a topic dealt with directly in Hong Kong writer Lilian Lee's book, the fictionalization of a condition that, ironically, is reified by the necessary absence of this conversation from the film:

The two friends retired to Xiaolou's house after the show. Xiaolou pulled up a chair and sat down with Dieyi. He had a lot on his mind.

'Juxian, pour us some tea. Serving the People is thirsty work.'

Juxian snorted derisively.

'I spent my entire day with a group of women, taking care of other people's children and cleaning up after other people's messes. I'm tired, too. We were *really* serving the People!'

'Who were you looking after?'

'Our worker and soldier comrades,' she replied sarcastically.

'I thought they also served the People. They can't be the People.'

'Well, who are the People?'

Dieyi began to recite a list of different types of people.

'We singers aren't the People. Women aren't the People. Workers and soldiers aren't the People. Nobody is the People, but everybody seems to be serving the People. Who are the People? Who's left?'

'Chairman Mao?'

Juxian clapped her hands over Xiaolou's mouth as fast as she could.

'Are you out of your mind? Are you trying to get yourself killed?'

Xiaolou broke away from her.

'I'm just having a quiet conversation in the privacy of my own home. What is there to be afraid of?'

But fear had become contagious, like a lingering flu nobody could shake. Politics was a matter of life and death, and people learned not to discuss certain subjects if they could help it. Even a silkworm sealed inside its cocoon would have been wary of uttering a sound. Despite its high-minded goals, the revolution was crude in its methods; but people had no choice but to go along with Party policy.[26]

It is this reality, the translation of the varying historical degrees of Chinese imperial despotism into the censorial conditions of China in 1993, that defines the continuing *need* for allegory.

The course of allegory in Chinese history closely paralleled that in the West, falling from grace in the nineteenth century – for 'appending moral tags to otherwise innocent tales', as Poe accused Hawthorne of doing,[27] allowing first for the rise of a romantic theory of arts unfettered by historical content and later for a modernist art-for-art's-sake. But allegory has begun to recover its status in 'postmodern' times. In contemporary China as in the West, allegory's 'hopeless confusion of all aesthetic mediums and stylistic categories', its 'appropriation, site-specificity, impermanence, accumulation, discursivity, hybridization', its drawing 'nourishment from melancholy', its simultaneous interest in historical revivalism and attraction to 'the fragmentary, the imperfect, the incomplete – an affinity which finds its most comprehensive expression in the ruin', and finally that 'atomizing, disjunctive principle which lies at the heart of allegory', all appeal to the post-modern/ post-socialist sense of subjectivized reality.[28] As with deconstructive discourse, allegory stimulates 'reading' but allows no *particular* reading, distributing authorship among the audience. As such, it remains the best rhetorical antidote to the intended ideological monopoly of totalitarian government. In this context, the weakness of allegory – the uncertainty of how to read it – becomes a strength, leaving 'a margin of error, a residue of logical tension that prevents the closure of the deconstructive discourse',[29] and undermines cultural hegemony. As Hungarian critic Miklós Haraszti put it, 'You do not need much theoretical training to realize that there can be no "real" reality when there are many realities.'[30] Allegory, therefore, by any name, is a well-conditioned cultural response that no politically sensitive Chinese artist, visual or textual, modern or traditional in period, has needed to think too much about in order to use. It is as well established as the cosmological monadism that permits some to argue its very non-existence. Its impetus taken from the need to negotiate from a position of inferior authority, with the voice of a supplicant, it may be thought of contextually as a mode of self-censorship, conditioned by native circumstances into a classical perfection.

One striking fact of Chinese cinema history is that no major film has ever been made directly *about* the world of the film-makers.[31] China still has no *Sunset Boulevard*, no equivalent to Robert Altman's *The Player*, no life-imitating-art documentary like *Hearts of Darkness: A Film-maker's Apocalypse*. The tight rein kept on the film industry by China's government agents has long made such films all but impossible. But films about other sectors of China's entertainment world – opera, street musicians, and prostitutes – are both possible and increasingly common substitutes for films about film. It is natural, therefore, to read in *Farewell My Concubine* a reflexive comment on the relationship between film and state.

Like an old refrain, in films about entertainers from *Street Angel* (1937) to Tian Zhuangzhuang's *Street Players* (1991, adapted from Lao She's novel), we are reminded that in China, actors (like fallen women) have always been the lowest of the low, the ninth and last of the professional grades, or what Maoists liked to call 'the stinking ninth' (illus. 107, 108). Both films, set in the Republican era, feature young, adoptive sisters, purchased as slaves and forced into the twin halves of China's traditional 'entertainment' industry, the older a prostitute, the younger a cabaret musician. *Street Players* is punctuated with lines like, 'What is a street performer? For ages, he's just been a servant of the rich and powerful . . . That's fate.' And, 'If [prostitution] is degrading, isn't our work [street music] degrading too?' (illus. 108). And, 'It's hard to change

107 *Street Angel*. Angel Yun approached by a street customer.

attitudes that have been passed down through the ages.' To the daughter's question, 'What will we do? Can't we do something else?' the father (a far kinder figure in this tale than in *Street Angel*) has no word of response. This same reading runs through *Farewell My Concubine* as a consistent strand in the narrative, set forth in the very first episode of the film. Little Douzi's prostitute mother brings him to the opera training school but he is at first rejected for the deformity of his hand. Not to be denied, she offers her body to the director: 'You can do anything you'd like,' she tempts him. But he won't stoop to the bait. 'Don't be foolish,' he replies. 'Prostitutes and actors are equally despised by society' (see illus. 85). The importance of this theme to *Farewell* is set forth emphatically in the first lines of the book, which proclaim: 'Prostitutes have no heart; actors have no morals. So people say.' Among immoral actors, the most immoral are the men who play the roles of women.

In traditional Chinese parlance, art as a whole is gendered as female, referred to as literary or *wen* and classed with civil matters, in contrast to military and political matters, or *wu*. Art is *yin*; politics is *yang* or male. In addition to broadening the meaning of 'female', Cheng Dieyi's

108 *Street Players.*
'If that [prostitution] is degrading, isn't our work [street music] degrading too?'

transsexual female has been appropriated – analogized, allegorized, broadened – to represent the arts, threatened and oppressed by the revolutionary politics of his time. Dieyi's efforts to survive as a female in a century of unbridled militancy represent the life-or-death struggle in modern times of everything civil, cultural, and artistic from China's historic tradition.

The values of the film centre on Dieyi, but the plot revolves around his stagemate Duan Xiaolou (Shitou grown up), who plays the male lead as King of Chu, and around the rivalry for Duan's affections between Dieyi and Duan's female lover, the former prostitute – hence, actress – Juxian (illus. 109). A natural beauty but a powerhouse to boot, Juxian (actress Gong Li, working with Chen Kaige for the first time) is a hardy rival to the effeminate Dieyi (performed by Leslie Cheung; illus. 110). Yet her interests lie strictly in securing Xiaolou's affections for herself, in completing the passage from prostitute-outcast to normal wife and mother. This reverses the role of Dieyi's mother, who abandoned him in order to remain a prostitute, and it brings her into direct conflict with Dieyi and his transsexual relationship with Xiaolou; for Dieyi (Douzi), having taken Xiaolou as his mother-substitute and accommodated him with a gender change (playing Yu Ji to his Xiang Yu), Xiaolou's potential abandonment of him in favour of Juxian threatens to repeat his mother's desertion. This layering of identities fuels the psychic tensions inherent within this unstable love triangle, and these tensions in turn parallel those between theatre, private life, and ideological politics. For Juxian, as for the others, revolutionary politics repeatedly stands in the way of attaining her ideals. The appearance of a fourth member, a child, might have changed the equation, but Juxian loses her only pregnancy during a fight in the theatre in which Xiaolou defends artistic standards against an unruly troop of Nationalist soldiers ('Even the Japanese didn't do this sort of thing,' says Xiaolou, who unlike Dieyi had refused to perform for the invaders, and the fight

109 *Farewell My Concubine*. The prostitute Juxian with clients at the House of Flowers, 'a theatre of another kind . . . a stage for illusion'.

110 *Farewell My Concubine*. A tough Juxian glowering over the passive-aggressive Dieyi.

breaks out). A second, desperate attempt to conceive is both stimulated by and interrupted by the outbreak of the Cultural Revolution. Her failure to bear Xiaolou a child limits Juxian's feminine authority, while assuring the perpetuation of this forever-unstable triangular relationship and helping to maintain Dieyi's centrality within it.[32]

Despite Juxian, Dieyi and Xiaolou always return to each other, and thus to their triangle. What finally and irretrievably destroys this complex relationship is not Juxian, not some bilateral sexuality, but politics: Communist politics. This disruptive, outside force is personified by a child from a younger and very different generation – Xiaosi. An abandoned baby, 'adopted' impulsively by the child Dieyi in the moments following his initial sexual molestation, Xiaosi seems intended as a replacement for Dieyi's lost innocence, but he fails badly in that; he also appears as a perverse substitute for the child that Juxian couldn't bear Xiaolou.[33] Brought up in the theatre but distinguished by his eventual rejection of traditional discipline and *esprit de corps*, as a malcontent in his own realm Xiaosi embraces 'the politics of the working people'. An unabashed opportunist, when the opportunity arises, he drives the politically disgraced Dieyi from the stage and takes his place. Urged on by Juxian's concerns for her husband's political safety, Xiaolou agrees to perform opposite Xiaosi, the new Concubine. But before long, with the arrival of the Cultural Revolution, the young Xiaosi turns yet another allegorical corner and leads the charge against the old theatre. Pathetically, then, it is the spoiled character of Xiaosi, denouncing his seniors, who performs as director Chen Kaige's *alter ego* and provides the public *mea culpa* for Chen's own youthful misdeeds of that era.[34] In the theatre of politics, as the Cultural Revolution turns friend against friend and lover against lover, both females pay the price for their gender: the natural female Juxian censured by Dieyi for having been a prostitute, and (as Xiaosi listens ecstatically; illus. 111). the unnatural female Dieyi condemned by Xiaolou for the unspeakable crime of having played the female role not just on stage but also with his offstage lover, Yuan Shiqing (illus. 112).

111 *Farewell My Concubine.* Xiaosi in ecstasy as Xiaolou reveals Dieyi's homosexuality to Red Guards. As director Chen Kaige himself had done, the child condemns the parent. The Red Guard crowd chants, 'Sweep away all cow demons and snake spirits!'

112 *Farewell My Concubine.* Scarcely able to voice the words, Xiaolou denounces Dieyi's homosexuality to the Red Guards.

Before it's all over, both 'females' have followed their gendered fate to its logical conclusion: suicide.[35] But there is a critical difference between these two deaths. Juxian, after having been denounced to Red Guards by Dieyi as a prostitute, is publicly renounced by Xiaolou in a misconceived effort to protect her from his own damaged reputation. This devastating abandonment prevents Juxian from attaining even in death the dignity that Dieyi finally achieves. She, alone having betrayed no one but shocked by the betrayal of others, hangs herself, in her bridal clothing.[36] Dieyi's suicide, more than a decade later, reunites his life on and off the stage, the ultimate expression both of his personal love for Xiaolou and of his professional loyalty – through Xiaolou as the King of Chu – to the theatre (illus. 114). But it was Dieyi, in the heat of politics, whose unbottled jealousy brings down Juxian, and in the wake of that comes Xiaolou's renunciation of her and her death. In words uttered before their Red Guard interrogators, Dieyi had cried: 'Do you think this disaster just falls from the sky? No. We have come step by step towards this fate. It is retribution.' He had learned by the time of his death that art, politics, and private/sexual life *could not* be isolated, however pure his artistic ideals. And so, compounding the tragedy of Dieyi's suicide must have been his own awareness of its futility. Even his suicide could not provide full retribution for his role in Juxian's death. What, then, is this futile gesture itself, if not art itself?

One of *Farewell*'s most fundamental metaphors (extended into allegory) lies in this: Xiaolou, as the King of Chu, need only be loyal – indeed, *is* only loyal – to himself. He is his own political end, internalized, whereas the object of Dieyi's loyalty, or the Concubine's, is external. This helps define Xiaolou's politics (typically self-serving and only occasionally capable of matching his on-stage heroics with boldness in the face of real-life complexities) and Dieyi's lack of politics (forever placing art ahead of self, and thus unifying his on-stage and off-stage personas). Xiaolou won't perform for the art-loving Japanese when personally insulted by a soldier, while Dieyi risks doing so for the sake of art; later on, Xiaolou bows to 'art'-hating Communist standards in order to preserve himself and Juxian when Dieyi, again for the sake of art, will not.

As a play within a play, *Farewell My Concubine* allows for the doubling and tripling of metaphors, the ancient past (Yu Ji's Han dynasty) marking the fictional past (the film's setting, from 1929 to the late 1970s), the fictional past marking *the present*, the post-Mao, post-Tian'an Men era. The latter – too dangerous to critique in the present – is indicated not with words but by the sense of words. There are minor occasions when this diachronic overlay is all too evident, as when the

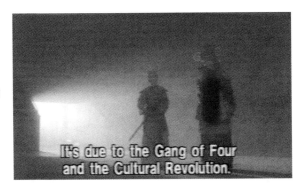

113 *Farewell My Concubine*. As the film begins, a stammering Cheng Dieyi unconvincingly blames the Gang of Four for all China's woes.

Communist troops are about to enter Beijing in 1948 and stage manager Na proclaims, 'The Han King is about to enter the city,' equating Liu Bang, conqueror of the King of Chu, with Chairman Mao, who becomes the destroyer of Duan Xiaolou. But the primary example of this is represented by the entire first scene (illus. 113), which introduces the audience to Xiaolou and Dieyi in the fictional 'present' tense (labelled 1977, the first year after the Cultural Revolution, though we are encouraged to regard this as the true present, 1993), as the pair are reunited in costume for the last time:

Voice offstage: I'm a great fan of both of you.
Xiaolou: Is that so?
Voice offstage: It's been over twenty years since you've performed together, hasn't it?
Xiaolou, stuttering: Uh, ah, twenty-one years.
Dieyi, correcting him: Twenty-two.
Xiaolou: Yes, yes, twenty-two years.
Xiaolou, again: And it's been ten since we last saw each other.
Dieyi: Eleven. Eleven years.
Xiaolou, stuttering: That's right, eleven years. Yes.
Voice offstage: It's due to the Gang of Four and the Cultural Revolution.
Dieyi, hesitantly, insincerely: Isn't everything . . . due to the Gang of Four?
Voice offstage: Things are better now.
Dieyi and Xiaolou turn to look at each other in disbelief.
Dieyi, slowly, insincerely: That's for sure. Everything's fine now.
Xiaolou: Uh, ah, yes, yes.

The words say everything is fine; the foolish stutter says that all is not so fine.

More importantly, while the words tell us that the horrors of this play-within-a-play are now past history, the stutter and the patent insincerity tell us that the past is still present, that this post-Mao moment is really post-Tian'an Men. We take the stutter and the insincerity as cues seeking our attention, and we are led to believe in them as reminders of the continuing *need* to conceal. As in *The Godfather*, it is an irony which alerts us to metaphor: in this case, not only are the figures metaphorical (the King of Chu as Xiaolou, and so forth) but so too is time itself (Han as modern as Maoist, as post-Maoist), with time extending metaphors into allegory. Following this prologue, the story is presented in flashback until it leads forward to this stage reunion again and ends in Dieyi's suicide (illus. 114). The narrative bracket created by this costume reunion at the beginning and end of the tale is as ironic as the stutter itself: rather than delineating a boundary between 'fiction' and 'reality', like a frame separating a painting from its surroundings, it reminds us of the original intention of a painting's frame, which is not to visually segregate art *from* non-art but physically *to attach* the painting to the wall, art *to* non-art. This cinematic bracket is still a frame, calling attention to the edge where 'opposites' normally meet, but its primary intention here instead is to displace that norm, declaring itself not a boundary but joinery.[37] The concept is not new but common to classic Chinese opera, where figures often first appear to help set the stage historically, for the audience's

114 *Farewell My Concubine*. A suicidal conclusion: 'My king, quickly give me your precious sword.'

115 *Farewell My Concubine.* 'I deserve it!' The adult Duan Xiaolou receiving a beating from his old master.

benefit, and at the end acclaim the outcome or proclaim the moral of the tale.[38] In 'classic' Chinese painting, too, a pictorial realization of this principle, expanded to include the audience as part of the bracketing and suggesting the seamlessness of viewers and viewed, reality and image, is found in numerous Han through Song-period figure paintings (e.g., see illus. 91, 130).

The politically inclined might readily find in this tale a critique of the Communist regime for its failure to save the lowly, the social victims on whom its rise to power was founded, destroying them instead with an ancient, unreconstructed sexual loathing. Rather than healing China's ancient social and cultural divisions, the Communist Party here is indicted for continuing to exploit these conflicts for its own narrow, political purposes. With sexuality and arts being conflated analogically, *Farewell*'s critique need not be narrowly focused on transgressive sexuality or homophobia. Film-making itself, in China, has often seemed to the film-maker a form of prostitution. The shockingly harsh treatment of children by their teachers throughout the first portion of the film analogizes the unequal relationship of film-makers to the state, just as it does the unequal relationship between prostitutes and society. Years later, the beating that Dieyi and Xiaolou absorb from their master *as adults* seems to lament that once a whore, always a whore (illus. 115).

In his *History of the Principles of Chinese Literature*, Wang Jinling writes, 'When the great officers of the feudal states "chanted poems to suggest their thoughts," they were *using* the *Odes*, and because they were using them, their only concern was to communicate their views through the poems; they were not about to analyze the thought processes that had led to their chanting, or to explain all the reasons why this or that poem fit the occasion.'[39] The art of usage, or of rhetoric, not the art of poetry, was their concern. On this missing poetics, Haun Saussy comments, 'Again and again the exchange-value of the poems [their applied, analogical function] is shown as essential, and their intrinsic value [that is, their original intent and aesthetic value] is passed over in silence.'[40] Although Chen Kaige's *Farewell My Concubine* engages in a similar analogic, it represents quite a different aesthetic situation. *Farewell* not only uses the fictionalized subject of art and artists for a political critique of cultural politics (which may render the term 'extended metonymy' even more appropriate than allegory),[41] it simultaneously advances its own art – film art – to advance artistry in opposition to politics. Its internal contradiction is that through its narrative it laments the end of art, bids it farewell (while bidding farewell to Dieyi, to Concubine Yu, to virtue, and so on), yet in its own cinematic style, in its artistic success, it demonstrates full well that historically there was no such end to fine art.

In its own way, Zhang Yimou's *Story of Qiu Ju* (1992)[42] also bids farewell to art – it adopts an intentionally 'artless' style in order to speak with the voice not of creative fiction but of a documented reality. But its intention is *also* to create a fiction, for the reality it 'documents' is a purposely disguised unreality, a reality that will be ultimately unmasked as the Untruth. Its internal contradiction is that this 'artlessness' is no less artful than the arty melodrama of *Farewell My Concubine*.

That the two directors Chen and Zhang seem to have switched stylistic persona at this moment (1992) has already been observed.[43] Chen's *Yellow Earth* (1984), for all that seemed new about it, was something of a throwback to the pessimism of the pre-socialist era, to the 'naturalistic' film values of that period, less dependent on camera than on character, and to the still-older aesthetic of understatement of the Chinese scholarly tradition. Zhang Yimou's *Red Sorghum* (1987), by contrast, prized action and emotion over intellect. Zhang preserved and glamorized the melodramatic form and vengeful violence of Communist era theatre, making his violence more shockingly graphic, adding sex to the violence and violence to the sex. Through subsequent films like *The Big Parade* and *King of the Children* (Chen, 1985, 1987), *Judou* and *Raise the Red Lantern* (Zhang, 1990, 1991), the two filmmakers remained true to their distinctively different forms of understatement and overstatement. Then, as suddenly as Chen had come forth with the suave style, epic dimensions, and melodramatic plot of *Farewell My Concubine*, Zhang had produced in *Qiu Ju* a piece of seeming naturalness, a 'human interest' story about a peasant woman of no particular account and her encounters with the law in its current state of post-Maoist 'reform'. Its title figure, Qiu Ju, serves as a kind of modern Don Quixote tilting with undersized weaponry against the hypocrisy of the contemporary judicial system, questing for justice in an all-male world of authority where legal absolutism, despite its many masks, prevails today as much as it always has. Zhang reveals the authorities ironically, as seemingly benign creatures who individually assist Qiu Ju along every step of the way while assuring collectively, systematically, that she will never succeed in her quest. The film rests its critique, therefore, not on 'aberrant' moments like the Cultural Revolution or Tian'an Men nor on aberrant individuals leading others astray but on the whole system in its best accounting.

Adapted from a short story by Chen Yuanbin, an author self-described as interested in plots 'woven around legal themes',[44] the themes of this cinematic parable involve China's recent policies on economic enterprise (the so-called 'individual responsibility' system) and the installation of a judicial code that, in theory at least, allows individuals restitution against government abuse. Such issues as China's spottily enforced one-child policy also crop up. Before the film has begun, Qiu Ju's family has tried to build a new drying shed for the chilli peppers they raise, so that they can expand their level of production. The village chief refuses them permission to do so for the economically baffling reason that this is land meant for growing peppers, not for drying them. An argument ensues, and Qiu Ju's husband, Wan Shanqing, undoubt-edly resentful that the chief has three children when everyone else is only allowed one, insults the chief for having nothing but girls – 'You only raise hens' is the way he puts it. The way the chief puts it, then, is to kick Qiu Ju's husband in the crotch. So the film begins with a trip to the doctor, but pretty soon it becomes an odyssey in pursuit of justice, each step of the journey taking us higher up the judiciary ladder.

It is Qiu Ju who leads this crusade, first with her (now emasculated) husband's support, later without it ('You take orders from your wife?' he is teased): first relying on newly instituted mechanisms of media-tion, later initiating a suit under the new laws permitting citizens to challenge their public officials. Qiu Ju's odyssey begins at the village Public Security Bureau, then moves on to the big city, where she appeals to higher levels of mediation at the district Bureau and then at the city Bureau. Failing these, she is introduced to the Western notion of litigation, totally confusing to her, and with the help of a lawyer, she takes her suit to court. In the process we get a profile, a cross-section, of the local and regional justice system. At every stage of appeal, Qiu Ju is rebuffed, only to be encouraged by the authorities to try again at a higher level (illus. 116, 118). Each time, she is offered a dollar settle-ment, but she refuses it, wanting instead a formal clarification on the limits to which a public official can go in his exercise of authority (illus.

116 *Qiu Ju*. 'Take your case to court,' the city Public Security Bureau chief urges Qiu Ju.

117 *Qiu Ju*. Qiu Ju to the local head of Public Security seeking clarification.

117).[45] Every step up the ladder further alienates her from her family and her family from the community, though a surprising civility between the combatant families prevails throughout (credit due to the chief's wife). In the end, Qiu Ju wins her case, but only after her persistence has subjected her family to much local ridicule, after she and the village chief have patched up their personal enmity, and on a technicality.

Pregnant throughout her social journey, Qiu Ju bears a son just before the end of the film, a son the chief never had – accomplished with the timely intervention of the chief himself after her labour goes badly. When she subsequently wins her case on an overlooked detail (the husband's groin just doesn't seem to count but a rib, it turns out, was cracked in the beating and that counts), then its punitive terms make her feel like she's lost. Chief Wang is jailed for fifteen days. Qiu Ju, distressed by the outcome, never gets the clarification of official authority that she pursued so compulsively, suggesting that 'the system' knows all too well how to provide punishment but not how to engender humane engagement or conceptualize its own limits.

This systematic legal appraisal does not sound much like the stuff of entertainment, and certainly not like the basis of high or wry comedy (illus. 118). After the drama of works like *Red Sorghum*, *Judou*, and *Raise the Red Lantern*, Zhang Yimou's *Qiu Ju* seems to have left American audiences and critics disappointed, not because they couldn't absorb its lessons in Chinese law but perhaps because they missed the ironic tone, lodged in small, comic moments, that animates the film.[46] One such moment: the village chief has been willing to pay Qiu Ju for medical damages but not to admit that he's wrong. The Public Security Officer backs him up on this: 'The Chief is obstinate,' he says, 'but he's the Chief. Don't make him lose face . . . He'll pay. That means you're

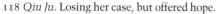

118 *Qiu Ju*. Losing her case, but offered hope.

119 *Qiu Ju*. Village chief and dog: 'Bitch!' – a comment addressed to whom?

right and he's wrong. That way he'll apologize. All right?' And so, the chief has offered Qiu Ju 200 yuan, but he's thrown it at her feet: 'Bow your head and pick them up,' he sneers, like an official of ancient times, demanding that she kowtow to imperial authority. 'You'll bow your head to me twenty times. Then we'll be even.' Qiu Ju replies, 'I'll decide when we'll be even!' and walks away. The chief resists picking the money up, leaving his dog to nose around in it – as only a dog would, we're left to believe. Later, the chief is forced by Qiu Ju's unshakable obstinacy to become more contrite and this time he politely hands the money to Qiu Ju's injured husband, who delivers it to her. But now it's Qiu Ju's turn to throw it down. She does, and this time the dog grabs the money; the chief snatches it back from the beast, shouting 'You bitch' at what looks on screen to be the dog but is clearly intended for Qiu Ju's ears (illus. 119).

Actually, Qiu Ju isn't bitchy, though the story comes to us tightly framed by the patriarchal perspective she has challenged: Qiu Ju is more of a stubborn mule, too inflexible and perhaps a little too dim-witted to give up in her futile quest. She's driven by intuition, not understanding; she's innocent, not wise. She's semi-literate, at best, and much of the time is given to grunts of assent and semi-understanding. She's a naïve mark for all the knowing men around her. Unable to write out her own complaint to the district office, she approaches a streetside scribe who leads her on in search of a good fee. In a piece of satire written at the expense of modern China's impotent intellectuals, this dottering old scribe asks, 'How strongly do you want it worded? If it's worded mildly, your opponent saves face and can back down if necessary. But a merciless complaint letter would leave him no way out. He'd be cornered . . . I've helped over a dozen people win their cases. Like you, they wanted mild letters. I've also written six merciless ones. The result? Two were shot. The four others got life sentences. I only asked for twenty yuan. That's not so expensive' (illus. 120). She utters a few gullible grunts and pays the price, but she loses her appeal nonetheless. Before long, she's exhausted all the levels of mediation and has been introduced to the notion of civil law and a lawyer. She hires the lawyer, but as she leaves his office she confesses, 'I still don't get it. We pay him money and he'll get us an apology? Then we wasted all our time before!'

Qiu Ju is like a reverse shaggy dog story. Like the little case that no one can understand the point of but goes all the way to the Supreme Court, it's a little story with a big message. Contextually, the film is shot through with a humor that an urban(e) Chinese audience wouldn't miss. The very idea of Gong Li, *Red Sorghum*'s glamorous leading lady, playing a dowdy, puffed-up, pregnant peasant, her toes pointed out, her knees turned in, and leaning as far back as she can to avoid toppling forward is ironic at least, or a comic sight for an already well-primed audience; try to imagine which glamorous American comedian of manners could pull this off and the once-glamorous Gong Li seems here at her best. When Qiu Ju goes to the big city to plead her case, she's immediately ripped off by a taxi driver; and when a hotelier warns her that she's an easy target, get some city clothes, she buys a new jacket

120 *Qiu Ju*. 'Two were shot,' brags this street scribe of his well-composed petitions.

then pulls it on right over her old one, layering up as only a peasant would do. Most laughable, from a social perspective, is the repeated image of Chinese officialdom treating this semi-literate, pesty, obstinate woman with the most constant, delicate deference – turning down every appeal, as one might expect, but then confessing, 'We might have made a mistake' and urging her to appeal, to find a lawyer, to challenge the government.

The date of this movie, it should be pointed out, was 1991–2, Zhang's first film after the disastrous attempt of China's student movement to challenge their government at Tian'an Men Square. In its aftermath, show trials were in progress. All this 'humour', then, is not a frivolity but a necessity, a strategic distraction. Needless to say, a frank critique of Chinese justice could not be brought but perhaps a small, well-disguised cinematic jibe could be managed. At the time, Zhang's two most recent movies were already banned in China. For most of its small American audience, this particular portrayal of officialdom may have meant nothing special. For a more critical American audience, it seemed a bit peculiar: why was this bold, rebellious director passing so light on Chinese officialdom? But for the Chinese audience, Qiu Ju was preposterous and therefore taken as a joke, the parody of an 'exhausted' genre of films – of a whole generation of film in which the government's notion of 'justice' always won in the end. John Cawelti has written of recent American film,

Generic exhaustion is a common phenomenon in the history of culture. One can almost make out a lifecycle characteristic of genres as they move from an initial period of articulation and discovery, through a phase of conscious self-awareness on the part of both creators and audiences, to a time when the generic patterns have become so well-known that people become tired of their predictability. It is at this point that parodic and satiric treatments proliferate and new genres gradually arise.[47]

In the Chinese case, however, the rise of parodic allegory which Qiu Ju represents comes less from the natural conclusion of a slow ageing process than from a sudden and radical transformation of the political culture dictating audience perspective. This transformation, for the first time in the Communist era, drove a wedge between audience and authorities. And in a place and time where inappropriate criticism of the government was nearly impossible and could have cost Zhang what was left of his directing career, this audience understood the indirectness of it all and made Qiu Ju the Hundred Flowers' most popular film of the year. Every time a Public Security Director offered this dirty peon a ride in his sedan, or she heard an appraisal that she just couldn't lose her case because then the people wouldn't believe in this new law that

121, 122 *Qiu Ju*. Qiu Ju and sister-in-law Meizi with presents that the city Public Security Bureau chief won't accept . . . but others will.

allowed them to sue the government, or she decided she just couldn't sue a high official because he'd been *so* nice to her, the savvy audience could respond in sarcastic accord with something like an American 'You bet!' In one scene, Qiu Ju and her sister-in-law, having no idea about city customs, stew for a while about what to buy as a 'gift' for the city director of the Public Security Bureau, to win his sympathy in the case and help assure the right outcome, and they finally settle on oranges and a gaudily coloured black-velvet painting (illus. 121). But the director refuses the gifts that Qiu Ju offers, so lofty are China's official standards. 'You bet,' we can hear the audience saying one more time, and sure enough, Zhang Yimou is right there with them: several scenes later, as Qiu Ju sits outside the Bureau waiting for the director's return, for a split second we see three officials just like him sauntering by, each one carrying just the kind of gift the director had earlier said 'no' to (illus. 122) – not something an American audience could easily notice, quicker perhaps than the censor's eye, but a good laugh for anyone lucky enough to catch it.

There is another reason, however, why this film left the wrong impression with many foreigners while hitting just the spot with the Chinese audience: its quasi-documentary style. From *Yellow Earth* on, 'Fifth Generation' films were defined by the rejection of socialist realist 'fakery', by their new visual naturalness. In *Qiu Ju*, Zhang Yimou deliberately took this tendency to the limit. In his own words, while filming was still in process:

The characters are played by real people: peasants, policemen, judge, and so on. We used only four professional actors . . . Fifty percent of the film was shot secretly; people didn't see the cameras . . . The cameras were hidden from view, and tiny microphones were attached to people's clothing. Like the marketplace scene, we just shot. We got there at 5:00 a.m. and climbed onto the roof to hide the mike. We're editing with a 35-1 proportion [of film shot to film used]. Most Chinese films are 4 to 1 because studios can't afford to use up that much film . . . We can get away with 35 to 1 because we're shooting 16 mm, not 35 mm. This way the price comes out about the same. Later we'll take the film to Japan and transfer it to 35 mm.[48]

The result was a film in which everything looks just like it really happened. Even the local Shaanxi dialect was strictly observed, so hard to understand that most of China saw it with subtitles.

The city scenes are all done in industrial bluish-grey (illus. 123); in the rural scenes, it's all orange-brown (illus. 124). The city scenes all look like they were taken with security cameras, the compression of figures and vehicles exaggerated by the snoopy long-range lens. The rural scenes, on the other hand, are compressed by the tightness of humble indoor settings, the camera shooting so close-up that there's often only room for one major figure on frame at a time. They are crowded by a mass of domestic detail, by secondary figures passing in

123 *Qiu Ju*. Street scene – the image of China's material well-being.

124 *Qiu Ju.* In the village chief's home, rural interiors convey the texture of rural intimacy. The chief's twin daughters can be seen in the middle-ground.

front of the camera, cutting off our view with a hip or a steaming bowl of soup. Trying to follow the dialogue, the camera weaves its way through the throng of extended family members, as if looking for who spoke last.

I called this 'quasi-documentary'. Really, it is pseudo-documentary, because it's made with the intent to deceive, or perhaps to pseudo-deceive. Irony is its goal and the fundamental artistic basis of its achievement. But also ironically, as the public laughed, the authorities likewise found it very nice. Liking to think of themselves as the good guys, all the public security officers who played in the film put on a demonstration of their best behaviour for the camera, and later, when they became the audience, they saw themselves in the movie as the good cops they want to be. Perhaps they didn't laugh because like the American audience they failed to catch the irony of it all – Qiu Ju 'wins' but she doesn't win, she *can't* win – taking the parody for the real thing; or if they did get it, they could at least send forth the film with their own benign interpretation of it, coopting the director's intended message as so often happens with the Chinese propaganda machine. And so instead of being added to a growing list of banned Zhang Yimou films, *Qiu Ju* was released at the behest of Li Ruihuan, head of the Communist Party's Propaganda Department – timed just right for a renewed liberalization push by Deng Xiaoping. And with it, Zhang's two previously banned films, *Judou* and *Raise the Red Lantern* (see illus. 249, 259), were at last unbanned.[49]

Some Western critics thought Zhang Yimou had sold out in order to achieve this result. Paul Pickowicz, for example, wrote that *Qiu Ju* 'portrayed China's feared Public Security forces in a surprisingly favourable light' so that Zhang 'was even allowed to win a couple of highly coveted domestic film awards'; and he derided Zhang Yimou as a 'quasi-dissident film-maker' and a 'highly privileged insider'.[50] But Zhang Yimou, and his Chinese audience, certainly had the last laugh. Lest there be any doubt of Zhang's political intentions, here are his own words:

This is a very ordinary story that happens all the time in China. One never knows who to talk to, what to do, where to go. Most problems are not so bad to start with, they only become so because of the workings of the bureaucratic system and the ordeals you have to go through. In China, you have to try twenty times, spend years in order to solve the most minor problems. Officials don't make any mistakes really, but in the end, there's never any answer. To request that something be done is the beginning of democracy. With this film, I wanted to say that every Chinese – and not only the peasants – should do the same thing: to fight for their right and discover themselves in the process.[51]

A comparison with one of China's most famous paintings can hardly be resisted, Zhang Zeduan's *Qingming Festival* scroll of the twelfth century, as close to a 'filmic' document as anything in China before the nineteenth century (illus. 123, 125). This can be told as a tale of two cities, or of the two Zhangs – Zhang Yimou and Zhang Zeduan – and in many regards it is the same tale for both tell a story of what isn't. Zhang Yimou takes us from countryside to Xi'an in his odyssey about a liberalization that exists only on paper. Zhang Zeduan, one of the emperor's atelier painters, leads us out of the countryside and through the capital city to portray China at peace, just as the ruler would like it to be seen; but at that moment, the court was poised on the verge of bankruptcy and beyond the Great Wall a horde of Jurched Tartars was massing, soon after to loot and burn the Song capital at Kaifeng, to carry the emperor off into captivity and put an end to native rule in north China. Art historians have long assumed that the boisterous but civilized scenes of this scroll were actually depicted in the years just before that onslaught, when China's vulnerability should have been sensed but was not. Recently, suggestions have been made that this painting was actually done after the fact, as a kind of nostalgia piece once the Jurched Tartars had ruined everything. Either way, it is a deceptive view, as is Zhang Yimou's.

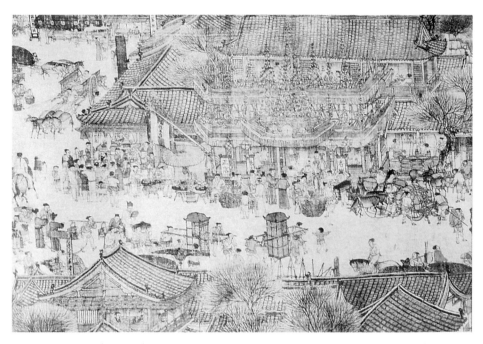

125 Zhang Zeduan, *Going Up River at Qingming Festival Time*, early 12th century, section from a handscroll, ink and colour on silk. Palace Museum, Beijing.

But one great difference underlies the two: Zhang Zeduan would have liked to believe in his deceptive construction, while Zhang Yimou could be said to be satirizing and deconstructing the deception of his own time. He has said that he's never once met a film censor face to face,[52] but he knows they're no fools. Between film-maker and film censor is played a cat-and-mouse game, with the mouse determined to find out just what it can get away with. In *The Story of Qiu Ju*, Zhang Yimou is not only interested in getting the cheese, he's actually filming the cat. Moreover, he's using the cat's own film, or at least the cat's own filmic process – surveillance technology – creating a compelling appearance of reality out of sheer visual rhetoric. But the film's appearance is deceiving, an extended metaphor, precisely, for what it is *not*. An awareness of the artist's ironic intention – Gong Li dressed up as a peasant, Public Security officials paying their polite respects to the camera – distances us from the film and shows us instead that in place of what initially appears to be a wholly 'transparent' film, this view of the Chinese legal system is really a classic example, in postmodern terms, of the Other returning the gaze, or in feminist terms, the observed as fetishized female stripping the male voyeur of his masculinity. Rey Chow is certainly right that Zhang Yimou's films are about film,[53] at least in part. But while *Qiu Ju* comes to us from a man's point of view, this too has been deconstructed by the film. Hardly another 'masculinist' 'Fifth Generation' film, as some critics might have it, it is the *deficiencies* of the traditional 'masculine' view that *The Story of Qiu Ju* is really all about.

4 The Veil of Tradition: Victims, Warriors and the Female Analogy

What do you think of marriage?
– Qiao Xiaoyu, in *Army Nurse*

What I want to express is the Chinese people's oppression and confinement, which has been going on for thousands of years. Women express this more clearly on their bodies because they bear a heavier burden than men.
– Zhang Yimou[1]

Fredric Jameson, in a set of statements about 'national allegory' now more notorious than merely notable, has claimed that

Third World texts, even those narratives which are seemingly private and invested with a properly libidinal dynamic – necessarily project a political dimension in the form of national allegory: *the story of the private individual destiny is always an allegory of the embattled situation of the public third-world culture and society. . .* [T]he telling of the individual story and the individual experience cannot but ultimately involve the whole laborious telling of the experience of the collectivity itself.[2]

Taken out of context, as they are here and typically are elsewhere, these passages seem inflammatory, condescending and narrowly circumscribing of third-world culture; though to the contrary, in context, it is industrialized first-world culture that Jameson understands as circumscribed and as lacking a collective dimension.[3] But whether in or out of context, 'necessarily' and 'always' are unyielding, deterministic words. As the films discussed in this volume have been selected primarily on the basis of their providing commentary on issues of Chinese national concern, Jameson can only, if arbitrarily, seem right if applied to them. Other films, a different selection, might well leave him in a different light, though that is not our concern here. But at least for the films being thought of here, more often than not, the narrative metaphor carried by these films' dominant females is one of national allegory (as in *Yellow Earth, Red Sorghum, Qiu Ju*, or by a female impersonator in *Farewell My Concubine*). Ironically, some of those least comfortable with Jameson's assertion seem nonetheless to acknowledge the appropriateness of his general principle to this set of 'Fifth Generation' films, getting greater discomfort, one would think, from those film-makers who conform to Jameson's stereotype than from Jameson himself.

The issue with Jameson's formulation of 'national allegory' might rest largely with the defining of 'national' but for the complicating view of the term 'allegory' formulated long ago by Walter Benjamin and conveyed more recently to the analysis of these films by some of his followers (positioned, in large part, as Jameson critics), Benjamin's view being that 'Allegory . . . means precisely the non-existence of what it presents.'[4] This position, unless itself taken 'metaphorically', conflates allegory (representation of the other, therefore self-modifying) with irony (representation of the opposite, therefore self-denying) and treats the ironical exception as a rule. Applying Benjamin's definition, which is perhaps more appropriate to the studied irony of *Qiu Ju* than to the studied ambivalence of *Yellow Earth*, leads to a binary view of these two films and numerous others: if the subject is female, then the allegory must not be *about* gender but *about* something else . . . like nation. It does not *include* gender. The negative critique of these films that emerges from this logic is that while repeatedly portraying the traditional injustice meted out to females in China, their real concern lies only with China's national predicament, and they really *are not* about female liberation. Their female leads are seen as just being borrowed and used, as women have so often been used in the past: appropriated, sexualized, primitivized, exoticized, and sacrificed, while 'the genuine complexities of Chinese society' are avoided.[5] Feminist critic Rey Chow on film-maker Zhang Yimou:

[His] women's sufferings reveal a larger human *nature* that has been unjustly chained and that seeks to be liberated; they are a kind of wronged, maligned, exploited *noble savage* whose innocence must be redeemed . . . His films do not change the mundane nature of the stories but enlarge the possibilities of our enjoyment of precisely these unspeakable, at times pornographic fantasies that are, shall we say, a culture's 'shame'.[6]

Rey Chow also provides this distinctive characterization of Zhang Yimou's appropriative system, in which already appropriated women are now appropriated for something else – liberation politics at one level, but beyond that, film as a 'narcissist' end in itself:

Zhang is building one semiotic system on another, in such a manner as always to bracket the denotative meaning of the 'raw' first level of signification . . . What is displayed [in his films] is not so much woman or even feudal China per se as the act of displaying, of making visible. What Zhang 'fetishizes' is primarily cinematography itself. If we speak of a narcissism here, it is a repeated playing with 'the self' that is the visuality intrinsic to film. *This* play *is* the sexuality of Zhang's works . . . Accordingly the seduction of Zhang's films – the appeal of his visual ethnography – is that they keep crossing boundaries and shifting into new spheres of circulation. The wish to 'liberate' Chinese women, which seems to be the 'content,' shifts into the liberation of 'China,' which shifts into the liberation of the 'image' of China on films, which shifts into the liberation of 'China' on film in the international culture market, and so on.[7]

This cinematic appropriation is regarded by Lydia Liu as being part of, one axis of, the multidimensional extension of modern state hegemony:

The category of women, like that of class, has long been exploited by the hegemonic discourse of the state of China, one that posits the equality between men and women by depriving the latter of *their* difference (and not the other way around!). In the emancipatory discourse of the state, which always subsumes women under the national agenda, women's liberation means little more than equal opportunity to participate in public labor.[8]

How cinematic masculinism relates to contemporary Chinese imperialism is formulated in this way by Rey Chow:

Preoccupied only with China's 'victimization' and 'marginalization' vis-a-vis the *West*, contemporary Chinese intellectuals, in particular many of those from the People's Republic, specialize in cultivating the form of primitive passion that is sinocentrism or Chinese chauvinism. In spite of their consciously declared rebellious intentions, this primitive passion unites these intellectuals with the ongoing fantasies of their authoritarian government, fantasies that continue to fuel a political and rhetorical orthodoxy, and currently a seemingly unimpeded economic growth, in the name of some original, unique 'Chinese' difference.[9]

This posited extension of the modern geopolitical realm into the sexual, female narratives appropriated as a wedge for the reassertion of Chinese nationalism (seen in these commentaries as 'male'), has historical dimensions but tends to be discussed only in the present tense. The appropriation of female imagery and female situations for political ends has been common throughout much of Chinese cultural history – for so long, in effect, that it has become a part of the language, with an acquired history in rhetoric. Exemplary of this fact, the allegorical assignment of political and moral intention to the folk songs in the *Odes* by élite scholars from Confucius' time on was so commonly accepted at face value throughout Chinese history that the claim of the twelfth-century philosopher Zhu Xi to the contrary – i.e., that much of this literature was actually, of all things, romantic ('poems of lust and elopement', in the words of Zhu's pupil, Wang Bo)[10] – was questioned in modern times by one of China's greatest political appropriators, Mao Zedong himself, and treated by Mao as a half-truth at best.[11]

An extensive account of traditional female appropriation, which has yet to be written, might begin with such well-known tales as that of Lady Cai Wenji. This well-educated only child of the famous statesman-scholar-musician Cai Yong was kidnapped in waning days of the Han period by northern nomads and forcibly married to a Xiongnu chieftain, an event that came to symbolize all of China in her moment of weakness: woman as the weakened nation, in need of rescue (illus. 126).

The story of Lady Wenji has regularly been trotted out in times of Chinese military insufficiency, appearing in paintings from the mid-twelfth century on[12] and recycled on the theatrical stage as recently as 1979 when China went ill-prepared into battle against Vietnam. A somewhat similar story is told of the court beauty Wang Zhaojun or Mingfei, negotiated away as a tribute bride to a barbarian chieftain because of a moral rectitude which her emperor failed until too late to recognize (illus. 127). Whereas the Wenji trope seems to have indicated the entire Chinese nation, Zhaojun more readily suggested the individual scholar-politician whose talents had gone un- or under-recognized, female as male.

Many were the female themes that pointed to the opposite gender, to the individual male politician frustrated in his career. And many times their lead women remain unnamed, adding to the sense of 'female' powerlessness and by implication to the depths of male frustration. When the ninth-century poet-politician Bo Juyi was exiled, he transformed his private lament into the famous, doleful lyrics of a jilted lover, a female musician he claimed to have met while boating in the moonlight. Banished from the *yang* world of active male politicians, exiled to the passive world of *yin*, Bo himself was, one might say, 'rendered female', politically castrated. So there was no need for him to be shy about relations with 'another' woman, and no need for a go-between for those whom peripheralization and suffering had already joined together. The poem's central lines read, 'We, together, banished to the ends of the earth / Meet, and then what does it matter whether we were acquainted before?'[13] Romantic only in form, this encounter obliterates gender and transcends sexual romance to proclaim a bond of intimacy between *all* those who suffer (illus. 128, 129).

Many of Bo Juyi's late-Tang peers created similar poetic images of unnamed women – vulnerable, misunderstood, neglected – while really writing of themselves. Unlike the melodramatic narratives of Wenji and Wang Zhaojun, some of these poems were as purposefully lacking in drama as their signifying women were shy of name, the better to represent their authorial male politicians' sense of entrapment. The ninth-century poet Li He, after his short-lived political hopes were reduced to dust, once projected his dejection and malaise on to a fading court beauty whose own life has been drained of purpose. In a late morning scene, having laid about until the mid-morning springtime breeze annoyingly wakens her, she ties up her hair in 'eighteen tiresome knots' and with that, runs out of steam. Ponderously 'measur[ing] her steps in the cloudy skirt, as a goose walks on sand', she expends all her energy only to get nowhere at all – just like Li He's ever-so-slow-motion

126 Anonymous, *Encampment by a Stream*, early 13th century, leaf from the album *Wenji's Captivity in Mongolia and Her Return to China* (originally a hand-scroll, formerly attributed to Chen Juzhong), ink and colour on silk. Museum of Fine Arts, Boston (Denman Waldo Ross Collection).

In the early 3rd century, as the borderlands of China fell increasingly prey to marauding nomads, the daughter of one of China's famed statesmen-scholars, Cai Yong, was carried off, married to a nomad chieftain, and became mother of two of his children before being ransomed back to China the following decade. On her return, Lady Cai Wenji – having abandoned her sons, for which many later moral critics never forgave her – wrote of her sufferings in eighteen verses (*Eighteen Songs of a Nomad Flute*) that then became the subject of imitations in verse and illustrations in painting. One scene – from a group of four, all that now remains of the oldest extant illustration set – is depicted here. This scene accompanies the fifth lament in Liu Shang's 8th-century imitation of Lady Cai's original, which reads (in Robert Rorex' translation),

> I sleep by water and sit on grass;
> The wind that blows from China tears my clothing to pieces.
> I clean my hair with mutton fat, but it is seldom combed.
> The collar of my lambskin robe is buttoned on the left;
> The fox lapels and badger sleeves are rank-smelling.
> By day I wear these clothes, by night I sleep in them.
> The felt screens are constantly being moved, since there is no fixed abode;
> How long my days and nights – they never seem to pass.

127 Attrib. Gong Suran, *Mingfei Crossing the Border*, early 12th century, section from a handscroll, ink on paper. Osaka Municipal Museum.

When Han emperor Yuan Di, in the mid-1st century BC, ordered portraits of all his courtesans, all except Wang Zhaojun (or Mingfei) bribed the court artist, who in turn portrayed her as the ugliest of all. When the emperor came to give away a tributary bride to a Xiongnu chieftain, he gave the 'ugliest' – too late, he realized his mistake and had the artist executed. This painting shows the beautiful consort en route to what today is Mongolian territory, where her tomb is still preserved. So intertwined is this historic tale pictorially with that of Lady Cai Wenji, that another version of the work (by an unknown artist surnamed Zhang, now in the Jilin Provincial Museum and possibly an earlier version than this), is entitled *Wenji's Return to China*. The depiction is striking for the dignified poise of the noble Zhaojun, a traditional ideal based on the acceptance of fate as the proper mode for preserving one's virtue.

128 Qiu Ying, *Saying Farewell at Xunyang*, early 16th century, detail from a handscroll, ink and colour on paper. The Nelson-Atkins Museum of Art, Kansas City, MO (Purchase: Nelson Trust).

Bo Juyi's 9th-century poem became a popular subject for painting in the 16th century. Qiu Ying's early rendition of this theme incorporates a variety of standard conventions, including the male traveller's horse, the boats of the exiled parties, and the water and moon of the reclusive female musician.

129 Peng Xiancheng, *The Lute Song*, 1987, hanging scroll, ink and colour on paper. Private collection, USA.

Peng Xiancheng's work, from 1987 when the Cultural Revolution was still fresh in memory, documents its persistence into our own time in the service of a widespread audience brought together by the shared experience of victimization. More important, it documents the persistence of rhetoric: here, as alive today as when it was composed in the early 9th century, Tang poet Bo Juyi's central couplet, singled out for inscription on Peng's painting, proclaims the unity of all people joined by unhappy circumstance. Victims need no other go-between: as these poetic lines put it, 'We, together, banished to the ends of the earth/Meet, and then what does it matter whether we were acquainted before?'

130 Zhou Fang, style of, *Ladies Playing Double-Sixes*, late 8th century, handscroll, ink and colour on silk. Freer Gallery of Art, Smithsonian Institution, Washington, DC.

Serving figures entering from the right and the left focus attention – and visual tension – on the seated figures in the centre of the painting, while the two attendants behind them establish an implied relationship with the viewing audience to achieve the same effect. This four-sided framing device engages the audience to participate in the 'reality' of the painting. Its origins are so old (see illus. 91) and its practice so common that long after this painting had been divided into two frag- mentary works by the removal of the two first figures (on the right) and housed in two museums (the Freer Gallery and the Museum of Fine Arts, Boston) it became easy to recognize their common origin and eventually reunite them. The famous Xiao Yi scroll (see illustration 31, shown only partially here) is similarly missing its opening figure, a fact confirmed by extant copies.

131 Cover photograph from *Newsweek*, 19 May 1997, captioned 'model at a Hong Kong fashion show'. This photograph of a Hong Kong model blindfolded by a mainland Chinese flag (appropriated by *Newsweek* from a recent Hong Kong fashion show) conflates several images in the Western viewer's mind: justice, female, with balance-scales in hand, and traditionally shown blind to represent her neutrality; or that same blindfold, ironically, signifying the obstruction of justice or blindness to injustice; and the victim blindfolded, unjustly set before a firing squad.

poem itself and just like his gone-nowhere career.[14] A marital pawn in the diplomatic exchange between families, where *could* such a court lady ever go? Or for that matter, where could a failed scholar-official, a political pawn like Li He go? This era of widespread political disaffection gave rise to a somewhat equivalent genre in painting, steeped in psychological realism, of court ladies well beyond their prime and weighted down physically as if enervated by some inner, spiritual languor. In the well-known *Ladies Playing Double-Sixes*, done in the late eighth century style of Zhou Fang, whatever the keen but narrowly-focused intelligence present at this gaming table, whatever the fleeting drama of a competitive move well made, these painted court ladies are less a celebration of domestic sport than a study of boredom within the inner chambers (illus. 130). Here, too, such boredom must have appealed to those under-utilized scholars who might gaze into such paintings as if into a mirror.

These examples of neglected women, both lyric and painted, whether beautiful victims or over-the-hill dowagers, all present the perceptions of men, and they all represent men. Or they might represent 'all men', at a time when all men lived in a weakened, threatened nation, in a time of *yin*. The subject is vast; their presence here is meant simply to introduce the Chinese tradition of using women to talk about other things, an age-old tradition that persists as a powerful force in modern Chinese imagery (illus. 131). Wayne Wang's recent film, the allegorical *Chinese Box* (1998), fits squarely into this gender mould, as does the historically derived but cinematically derivative *Red Cherry* (dir. Ye Ying), China's most popular film of 1995.[15]

The importance in recent film of the appropriated female subject is openly touted by the directors themselves. 'What I want to express,' Zhang Yimou claims, 'is the Chinese people's oppression and confinement, which has been going on for thousands of years. Women express this more clearly on their bodies because they bear a heavier burden than men.'[16] Scarcely the creation of the film-makers themselves, their use of it is part of their dialogue with and about the past. It is part of the Chinese terms of dialogue. This heritage neither excuses nor condemns the modern practice of appropriation. But it frames the matter quite differently than a narrow view of recent film alone will provide, and its mere presence is not sufficient to perpetuate the past itself. This *can* serve as a language of change and liberation. Whether or not it does, it is part of *the* language, the common parlance of China. As counterpart of the now-commonplace realization that language constitutes part of the message must be the reservation that to impose one linguistic system or one rhetorical tradition on another, as some critiques of these films and film-makers have risked doing, is to primitivize the Chinese language, to orientalize the culture, and to engage in a form of academic chauvinism.

The notion that these film-makers' use of women lies in some 'narcissistic' interest in producing good cinema and is, therefore, exploitative is hard to sustain. The gender critique of these films' appropriative use of women as unconcerned with female liberation and, *prima facie*, misogynistic needs to be examined on the basis of the cinematic record, as it will be later in this essay. It has seemed to me that this body of film-making has devised many inventive strategies for using old rhetorical forms to new ideological ends, including redesigning gender appropriation so as to promote gender liberation.

Looking at another dimension of this issue, one needs to consider the derivation of much of Chinese rhetorical practice from analogical formulations and the reliance of analogy on strategies of appropriation. One unintended outcome of a construction of gender appropriation that doesn't account for rhetorical tradition is to prejudice the critique against the analogical mode of reasoning which this rhetoric serves. By contrast, a historical interest leads one to appreciate the whole strategy of appropriative analogic which prevails throughout so much of Chinese rhetoric and which bridges old and new. A critique of Chinese cinematic gender appropriation lacking a knowledge of the old privileges the contemporary, and seems to proceed from Eurocentric values, whereas an historical or art-historical pursuit is guided by the regard for native traditions and their persistence in contemporary formulations.

In appreciation of this persistence, I would assert: to analogize is to appropriate. The films discussed throughout this book are steeped in forms of allegorical analogic, framed references in a rhetorical tradition that links the time of Confucius and Qu Yuan to that of Chen Kaige and Zhang Yimou. Their appropriative use of women closely parallels, as a rhetorical phenomenon, the commandeering of landscape subject matter by traditional Chinese painters as a device for expressing a broad range of personal and public concerns.[17] Examined historically, I no more consider this body of film to be anti-female than I consider Bada Shanren or Gong Xian to have been anti-ecological (see illus. 23, 24).[18] In China, to appropriate has been considered a skill and, at its best, a fine art. And in a very valid sense, *all* artistic representation is appropriation, though that's another story.

Academic critiques of the female in recent Chinese film are no more uniform than the films themselves, with writers like Rey Chow and Esther Yau, Bonnie McDougall and Eugene Wang taking a number of different approaches and arriving at a range of different observations. Esther Yau, to cite one example, has written of *Yellow Earth* as 'subtle and complex in its enumeration of sympathy for women' and concludes (very much in keeping with traditional values) that

It frustrates if one looks for phallocentric (or feminist, for that matter) obsessions within an appropriatable space, and it satisfies if one lets the sense of endlessness/emptiness take care of one's desire (i.e., a passage without narrative hold). In these instances, one sees an image without becoming its captive.[19]

For Lydia Liu, on the other hand, the 'rape' scene in *Red Sorghum* (see illus. 49)[20] represents the construction of male fantasy and deceptively minimizes female concerns:

In such a signifying practice [as this rape], the female body is ultimately displaced by nationalism, whose discourse denies the specificity of female experience by giving larger symbolic meanings to the signifier of rape: namely, China itself is being violated by the Japanese rapist. Since the nation itself is at stake, the crime of rape does not acquire meaning until it is committed by foreign intruders.[21]

Eugene Wang, different from both Yau and Liu in his approach to gender in China, understands this scene, Jiu'er's ready participation in it, and the raw sexuality (by Chinese film standards) of *Red Sorghum* not simply as masculinist fantasy but rather as a symbolic study in the liberating force of female sexuality:

Red Sorghum, despite its predominant male presence, articulates an all-embracing female subjectivity which . . . destroys the distinguishing line between female sexuality and maternity . . . The film, ostensibly about the uninhibited manners of masculinity, is, however, ironically and structurally contained or cocooned in a discourse about the maternal.[22]

He suggests that in contrast to the Western critique of *Red Sorghum*'s Jiu'er as weak and passive victim, the 'attributes [that Chinese] detractors find *lacking* are mostly feminine restraint, introversion, refinement, and so forth'.[23] Reading traditional male Chinese culture ironically, reading it as essentially feminine, 'favoring femininity over masculinity'[24] –

As the aspired-to stillness and passivity have touches of femininity, femininity itself becomes a condition highly aspired to. Instead of being afflicted by castration anxiety, the problematic of the lack is quite reversed in the Chinese cultural context. It is the man who lacks.[25]

– Eugene Wang describes the violence of *Red Sorghum* as 'pushed to extremes to jolt the audience out of their cowardice and insensitivity', 'out of their self-delusion about a tranquil feminine utopia, and out of their collective and private insensitivity to all kinds of massive social horror'.[26] Of China's sexually repressive society, he writes, '*Red Sorghum* is fundamentally a liberation of repressed collective desire,' liberating not merely individuals and not primarily males, in Western libidinous terms, but of all alike – the whole *culture* – through the very denial of distinction between male and female desire.[27]

Wang's reading is by no means unsympathetic to feminist theory nor does it divorce sexuality from politics, but it opens the way for a challenge to any culturally vague application to China of Laura Mulvey's 'gaze' theorems, as borrowed by her from Lacanian psychoanalysis and applied to Western cinema.[28] Per Mulvey, Western screen logic maintains,

Whenever the movie screen holds a particularly effective image of terror, little boys and grown men make it a point of honor to look, while little girls and grown women cover their eyes or hide behind the shoulders of their dates.[29]

But in *Red Sorghum*, when Luohan is skinned alive by the Japanese (see illus. 62), it is the heroine Jiu'er who hides the eyes of her son while she stares unblinking (illus. 132, 133), just as earlier in the film she stared (enticingly even) at her two would-be rapists. Similarly, in *Farewell My Concubine*, Juxian stares in disbelief at the unravelling of her male companions during a Cultural Revolution struggle session, then rushes forth herself into the turmoil to rescue from the fire a treasured sword (illus. 134, 135).[30] Jiu'er, Juxian, Judou (see illus. 256), Qiu Ju (see illus. 117), and *Yellow Earth*'s Cuiqiao (see illus. 110), each in their own way, refuses to blink in their defiance of male authority.

The drowning of Cuiqiao in *Yellow Earth*, the deaths of Jiu'er in *Red Sorghum*, of Judou, of Coral in *Raise the Red Lantern*, and of Juxian in *Farewell My Concubine* are all, of course, troubling (see illus. 11, 64, 249), raising questions that reach beyond the confines of their own tales. Though scarcely different in kind from the earlier deaths of Mingfeng in *Family* and Yun in *Street Angel* (see illus. 107, 260), they are said to have ratcheted victimization up to a degree that raises the spectre of sadistic indulgence. Rey Chow has written of Chen Kaige's films that, 'Instead of being placed in the social symbolic, women in Chen's films are thus the primitives of utopia, which means, literally, that they are *nowhere*' and 'Women seldom appear and when they do, they are usually sacrificed.'[31] This issue of 'sacrifice' has been linked to female transgression, to what happens 'when the woman looks', as Judou does, as Cuiqiao does, as Qiu Ju does, a popular notion in Western film theory. Derived from Mulvey's writing on the male 'gaze', it asserts the unacceptability in film as in social reality of a returned female gaze, of an assertive female role, of a positive role for female desire:

132 *Red Sorghum*. At Luohan's flaying, Jiu'er hides her son's eyes . . .

. . . the woman's look . . . offers at least a potentially subversive recognition of the power and potency of a non-phallic sexuality. Precisely because this look is so threatening to male power, it is violently punished.[32]

Thus, Cuiqiao and the others, appropriated into the victims' role as females, have been seen as punished because they are female – transgressive, castrating females. And so, by this logic, their cinematic appropriation has been proved degrading to their gender. Intentionally, this focuses on the part rather than the whole, privileging the women instead of appreciating the synecdochic nature of the allusion. An alternative view is that these women represent suffering of which they are but a part, and they are 'sacrificed' not for a neo-Freudian logic, not because they are libidinous women, but because of China's suffering in which they share, and because of their traditional place in Chinese rhetoric, the conventional foundations on which these films build their modern twists of form.

Rather than simply being victims, in the traditional sense, these women gaze back: they defy their oppressors, they challenge the audience to identify where it stands ideologically toward them and their fate, and they fall in the line of battle just as do the men because they have had the courage to place themselves there. They die as many heroes die, because they had something worth dying for, because their cause was unfulfilled, and so that others might be inspired to follow their resistance to injustice (see illus. 42). Of course, heroism has its own emotional logic: among China's favourite Western literary heroines, Emma Bovary dies, Nora Helmer does not; closer to home, a somewhat transgressive Cuiqiao dies, while an even more transgressive Qiu Ju does not. These women fall with no greater frequency, or clearer logic,

133 . . . while she stares unflinching.

than do their critically overlooked male counterparts. The many males 'sacrificed' for the sake of a cinematic moral include Yang Tianqing in *Judou*, the nameless thief in *My Memories of Old Beijing*, Ren Jia in *Sacrificed Youth*, Luohan and a host of unnamed others in *Red Sorghum*, Norbu the horse thief, Shi Ba in *Transmigration*, Sun Wangcai in *Old Well*, Li Huiquan in *Black Snow*, Cheng Dieyi in *Farewell My Concubine*, among others (see illus. 60, 62, 69, 73, 114, 254). 'Crazy' Qin in *Hibiscus Town* (see illus. 178) is as badly victimized and as blatantly appropriated as any cinematic female ever was to represent the suffering Chinese masses (and to designate their mode of coping with suffering). Moreover, any equation of women simply as victims and any equation of victims simply as women, defined in neo-Freudian terms by 'lack', mislocates the issues of victimization and resistance within some rather ordinary or stereotypic definitions of 'women' and 'men' rather than closer to the margins, where challenging and/or 'masculinized' women play across from passive and emasculated, emotionally blocked or disfigured males: among the women, Cuiqiao in *Yellow Earth*, Madame Zhou in *Black Cannon Incident*, Jiu'er in *Red Sorghum*, Li Guoxiang in *Hibiscus Town*, Laidi in *King of the Children*, Judou, Xiang Ersao in *Woman From the Lake of Scented Souls*, Qiu Ju, Juxian in *Farewell My Concubine*, Ermo (see illus. 15, 49, 77, 110, 117, 157, 177, 228, 237, 251); and among the men, Zhao Shuxin in *Black Cannon Incident*, Qin Shutian, 'Autumn Snake' Wang, and Gu Yanshan in *Hibiscus Town*, Lao Gar in *King of the Children*, Shi Ba in *Transmigration*, Yang Jinshan and Yang Tianqing in *Judou*, Dieyi in *Farewell My Concubine*, Yu Zhongliang in *Temptress Moon*, Qiu Ju's husband, Ermo's husband (see illus. 72, 105, 183, 186, 200, 238, 250,

134 *Farewell My Concubine*. At the struggle session, as Xiaolou and Dieyi exchange betrayals, Juxian looks on in disbelief . . .

255, 265). It is through figures on the margin, through roles like those listed here, that the most interesting cinematic discourse about change (or the failure to change) in China has taken place.[33]

It seems well worth emphasizing that despite the diverse responses these intentionally provocative films have generated among critics, revealing a variety of different critical agendas and diverse priorities, these critical authors retain some common ground. On the one hand, Eugene Wang's view of China's feminized male values seems logically to subvert the Lacanian focus on castration anxiety; and this seems contrary to Rey Chow, who writes,

. . . it is clear that Zhang [Yimou]'s films do not depart at all from the politics of the polarization of male gaze versus female body that was problematized by Laura Mulvey's influential essay 'Visual Pleasure and Narrative Cinema'. On the contrary, Zhang's films provide a demonstration, from the perspective of a non-Western culture, of Mulvey's incisive observation of what in many ways is still the predominant heterosexual problematic.[34]

On the other hand, Eugene Wang defines this (in traditional Chinese terms) as a matter of appropriation, similar to what we have already seen enacted in historical dimensions through the medium of painting (illus. 128–30), suggesting that China's traditional feminization of men merely constructs a different form of the contradiction:

It does not follow, however, that the femininity complex relieves women of their inferiority, nor is the curse of the 'lack' lifted from woman as her place is elevated. What happens is that men usurp women's proper space so that women are pushed aside, marginalised, expelled, suspended, bracketed, and

146

135 . . . then boldly rushes forth to seize the precious sword that Xiaolou and Dieyi no longer dare to claim.

exiled into the realm of the imaginary to become icons and absences. . . . Thus men not so much speak for women as stand in their place to speak, thereby replacing women's linguistic space, usurping their world of consciousness, and denying women of their right to speak.[35]

Moreover, Wang writes of the

danger that the audience will temporarily bracket the political, racial and historical significance of the scene for vicarious sado-masochistic pleasure. Even if the jolting effect exists, its cinematic elaboration may work in conspiracy with the audience's secret visual pleasure. In this way, the film encourages an insensitivity as well as discouraging it.[36]

As a kind of corollary to this, at the same time as she disparages their means, Rey Chow acknowledges Chen Kaige's and Zhang Yimou's cinematic powers and higher motives; for example, while considering the focal moment of *Judou* where Judou turns to Tianqing (her nephew by marriage, her fellow victim, her voyeuristic abuser, her own lover-to-be and partner in social rebellion) to expose her brutalized beauty,[37] she writes,

Judou's 'turn' thus amounts to an exposition of what we might call *the brutality of the cliché and the brutality of convention* . . . she turns the eroticism of the spectacle into a deliberate *demonstration* of and against the patriarchal order that crushes her.[38]

What is one to make of films that risk encouraging traditional insensitivities at the same time as they dare to discourage them, of films that engage in the very modes of patriarchal spectacle they hope to crush? The contradictions between critics, the *internal* contradictions of some individual critics, seem directly responsive to the ambiguous nature of the films, the ambivalence of the film-makers, to the film-making tradition and to Chinese tradition itself. Considering the appropriative character of allegory, Craig Owens has written both of 'the unavoidable necessity of participating in the very activity that is being denounced *precisely in order to denounce it*', as is characteristic of these films, and of the deconstructive interpreter's risk of falling into the very same trap:

There is thus a danger inherent in deconstruction: unable to avoid the very errors it exposes, it will continue to perform what it denounces as impossible and will, in the end, affirm what it set out to deny.[39]

There is perhaps no way out of this quandary and no need, critically, to travel lesser routes, all of which lead deceptively away from the essential irreconcilability of the matter. One is left to wonder whether lament or critical protest over the appropriative use of women as victims might not reify and perpetuate that role, quite contrary to the critics' intent, adding *yet another* layer of female victimization rather than rendering the stereotype old-fashioned and obsolete.

Rather than tossing a blanket condemnation of female appropriation over all of this allegorical cinema, as has sometimes been done, such films deserve to be examined individually with an eye to the diverse usage of allegory and irony which allows them to express indirectly or unvoiced what otherwise, in China, they might not be allowed to express at all. The considerable diversity from film to film of thematic roles, models and messages conveyed by gendered means does not easily support a generic charge of 'abusiveness' in the sense of these films *simply* continuing the traditional Chinese 'abuse' of women. Beyond a 'subtle and complex . . . sympathy for women', as Esther Yau has put it, these films provide a revealing critique of the larger cultural conditions in a society where nothing, analogically, lacks for gender and where gender, ironically, is not always what it seems to be.

In the analogic of China, when the larger cultural conditions have been addressed, then so too have the smaller. Ann Anagnost writes of *Qiu Ju* as part of

the tradition of elite male narrators' using female characters as a displacement of their own desire rather than exploring gendered subjectivities for their own sake. Gender is used here as a commentary on the effects of power more generally and not just on gendered relations of power.[40]

And yet, addressing the general *through* the particular, through the exemplary, through the analogue, is not so much male as it is Chinese, and *any* Chinese rhetorician would be left to wonder, with gender effectively used to draw a more general truth that embraces gender along with various other imaginable particulars, why would one prefer to deal with gender 'for its own sake'? Why deal 'just' with it? Why privilege individual 'subjectivities'? Nowhere is this kind of analogic better applied than in Chen Yuanbin's ironic Chinese title for *Qiu Ju, Wan jia susong*, which can be translated with equal accuracy either more narrowly as 'The Wan Family's Litigation' or more inclusively (punning on the name Wan, or ten thousand, everyone) as 'Ten Thousand Families' Litigations': one family represents all.

Issues of gender are scarcely independent of place. Women in the West are engaged especially in the struggle for equal opportunity with men in the work place. But Chinese women are more likely to rally for gender difference. For them, entry into the work force came historically not as an individual opportunity but rather as a public obligation, defined and obliged by socialist authority. Labouring for the Communist Party and the socialist state has left little room for gender differentiation, for individuation, sexuality, and personal gratification. Ding Xiaoqi's translator, Cathy Silber, writes of China before the mid-1980s that 'Women were masculinized, but everybody was emasculated . . . Love and revolution did not mix.'[41] And so, Chinese feminists have been described as typically less concerned with workplace inequities (though there's no lack of that in China) than with how to preserve their distinctive womanhood in a society that has forced its women into the workplace, turning its women into men and everyone into the 'cogs and wheels' of state machinery. Chris Berry observed in 1988 that the notion of a 'women's cinema' was still highly problematic in China, and that

Western women may well be equally surprised at the main concerns of [Chinese] women's films and women film makers . . . Particularly prominent are not issues of equality in the broad social sphere but the reassertion of difference and the valuation of the personal. This quite often manifests itself in ways which seem strange to Western feminists. For example, the film *Sacrificed Youth* gives very positive connotations to self-adornment and making oneself attractive to the opposite sex, connecting this to the process of self-discovery and self-awareness that for many Western women has involved rejection of the very same thing.[42]

With concepts of feminism differently developed in the West than in China, it is not surprising that some Western critics and academicians tend to perceive both more 'masculinism' and more feminism in Chinese films than do the film-makers themselves. While interviewer Dai Jinhua presents director Huang Shuqin's *Woman, Demon, Human* (1988) as 'a woman's film (*nüxing dianying*)',[43] Huang herself asserts, '"Feminism" is a notion I had never thought of back then,' and 'I had never made a strictly woman's film, nor did I have any intention then of making one either.'[44] When Dai presents the film *Oh, Cradle!*, on which Huang worked, as coming 'from a feminist point of view' and as representing 'a turning point in the transformation of images of women', Huang responds: 'I haven't thought about it at all. I never related the movie to women's issues or viewed it from a masculine or feminine perspective.'[45] Similarly, of her female peers, she notes that in China, 'most women directors do not do women's films'.[46]

Huang Shuqin laments the persistence of male dominance from pre-Maoist to Maoist to post-Maoist times: '. . . during the Cultural Revolution, men wanted women to be masculinized. In commercial society, however, men want women to be feminized. In terms of male power, however, they are basically the same.'[47] She pronounces that 'Ultimately, the whole point of art is rebellion . . . women must rebel against the whole society – against men's society, that is.'[48] But she also tends to put her concerns in a comparative perspective, recalling that '. . . when I went to France, it struck me that the status of Chinese women is quite adequate; compared to the situation of French women, we measure up.'[49] And she observes that the difficulty of reconciling the creative life with one's private life (a central theme of Huang's *Woman, Demon, Human*) is 'the same for both men and women'.[50] She repeatedly parries her interviewers' questions about encountering problems working with male scriptwriters or male cinematographers – 'Never. I've always gotten along well with my team members' – and then concludes, 'I usually put males in charge of the different divisions. That's because I have encountered some female workers who were too indirect in expressing themselves, narrow-minded, troublesome, and prone to jealousy.'[51] Hu Mei, female director of *Army Nurse* (1985), similarly compares the mostly-female crew of that film with the with largely male crew of her subsequent film, *Far from War* (1987), complaining that in the former,

They were always squabbling about this and that, and telling on each other. I could barely make the movie, I was so busy dealing with that sort of thing. This had happened at home, the kid was that, and I don't know what. It was ridiculous. It's much easier working with men. Work is work, and there's nothing else involved. They go play football in the breaks. There's none of that complaining about each other. I don't know if women are like that all over the world, but it's very common in China. I asked the leaders to do their very best to assign men to work with me this time. Really.[52]

The point of all this is simple, though the reality it points to most decidedly is not simple: such comments describe a world, a woman's world, and women film-makers' views of a world that is half-a-world apart from the West, from Western film, and from Western film theory. That world is the socio-cultural matrix from which emerge the nationalist critiques presented in films from *Yellow Earth* and *Red Sorghum* to the two films highlighted in this chapter, *Army Nurse* and *Woman From the Lake of Scented Souls*, and against which any academic critiques of these cinematic critiques must be gauged. Not only do these films build upon an ancient language of analogical appropriation, they also work with – or against – a film heritage that engaged intensely in gender appropriation during both the Republican period and the Maoist era.

Despite the intent of the May Fourth Movement to liberate women and break new social ground, most films made in the spirit of that movement, in the 1930s and 40s, spoke a language of pessimism and maintained considerable continuity with premodern Chinese traditions. In many of these films, whatever their primary pitch, women were featured as victims and seemed to stand for all the weak of China as well as for China itself, the so-called '*weak man* of Asia' (representing the weakest of 'men' as woman). A prize example of 'May Fourth style' melodrama is the much-loved film *Street Angel* (1937), distinguished by its deeply-shaded photography and the brilliance of its performances. The film's two female leads are sisters, purchased as bond-servants and forced by their adoptive 'parents' to earn their keep as entertainers: the younger sister a cabaret musician (performed by the young Zhou Xuan, who later became China's leading cabaret artist), the older sister a prostitute. Together with the younger sister's boyfriend, a street musician (Little Chen, in a legendary performance by Zhao Dan), these entertainers are introduced as the 'lower depths' of Shanghai society and through them is revealed the perversity of China's social stratification in both its traditional 'feudalistic' and its modern bourgeois phases (illus. 136, 230). The prostitute-sister – the 'street angel' – is the more abject of the two, dour and totally without hope for herself, an inequity within an inequity (see illus. 107). At best, she can only hope for and help her younger sister. Typical of left-leaning, non-Communist intellectual expression, *Street Angel* offered deep sympathy for those on the social margin but, as often noted, articulated no political agenda, envisioned no alternative social system that would relieve the misery of their times – an escape, but to what? – and inspired little optimism for the future.

Despite their obvious victimization, these women are scarcely passive, identical victims and nothing more, and a good part of the film is given to their rebellion. The younger sister, Hong, has been promised in

136 *Street Angel*. The tragi-comic trio, musician Hong, prostitute Yun, and boy-friend Chen.

marriage to a Shanghai gangster and no escape seems possible other than suicide. Elder sister Yun convinces the younger Hong to avoid her fate by eloping with Chen, a particularly noble gesture since (as the most challenging feature of the film) the otherwise likeable Chen cannot find gratitude or sympathy within himself for this lowly prostitute until tragedy finally strikes. Though they are all tracked down by thugs and Hong's promised gangster-husband, Yun points the way to Hong's escape and remains behind to confront the pursuers. For this bold transgression, Yun pays with her life, but with it she earns the others' freedom and, finally, their respect. And although Yun has pointed the way, the film ends by her deathbed, unready to envision the future as anything better than an escape into still lower depths.[53]

Other films of the Republican era could easily be singled out to demonstrate the diversity of female roles. *Lights of Ten-Thousand Homes* (1948) describes the transition from traditional to modern kinship values by recent rural immigrants to Shanghai. The happy adjustment to urban modernity made by Mr Hu Zhiqing is suddenly transformed into a social morass when his entire country-bumpkin family decides to follow his footsteps and arrives at his doorstep (illus. 137). Coincidentally, this occurs just as his childhood friend and current boss, tycoon Qian Jianru, determines to close his factory in order to speculate in gold and has Hu fired. The unemployed Hu and boss Qian may represent core conflict in the public economy, but they are paralleled and even peripheralized by core conflict in the social sector, represented by the varied solutions set forth by the women: Hu's mother, who helped raise Qian and thus expects support for her son as a matter of old-fashioned community obligation; and Hu's wife, chic and urbane, who negotiates the matter directly with Qian in pragmatic, business-like terms but without the experience to know when she is being duped. Neither woman is a lie-down victim – indeed, Hu's mother attacks Qian with her cane in a traditionally-spirited effort to batter him into a sense of shame (illus. 138). But they fail, each in their own way, before the unmitigated callousness of Qian – whose name translates, literally, as 'money [used to cut] like a sword' – and their differences split the family apart.

Mr Hu is the passive one, simply unable to cope with wife and mother being in different camps, and he winds up a victimized, hospitalized amnesiac. Hu's recovery and return home coincides with a final resolution to this family melodrama: the reconciliation of mother and daughter-in-law and elevation of the mother, an extended-family living on rural family values in a Shanghai apartment. Though *Lights* valorized classic melodrama's happy ending, in reality neither Mr Hu nor the women in his life, mother and wife, had any viable alternative to past practice by which to contend with their increasingly bleak economic future.

After the Communist victory, China supposedly 'stood up' and its women were empowered to 'hold up half of the sky'. In films of this era, beginning with *Three Women* (1949), we find the women raised in stature, former victims now cast as avengers, symbolizing progress

137 *Lights of Ten-Thousand Homes.* Within a single family, the collision of city and countryside.

138 *Lights of Ten-Thousand Homes.* A 'traditional' peasant-class approach to straightening out wayward behaviour: Hu Zhiqing's mother takes after Qian Jianru (on right, with hat) with a cane.

through Marxist class struggle. Whereas Republican period film plots identified conflict but preferred the pursuit of harmony, Maoist era film-making embraced conflict and insisted on the success of its pursuits. Colour film swept away the gloom of May Fourth-inspired cinema and glossy images captured the bright hopes of Maoist modernity. But victims, female victims, still abound. Typical of Cultural Revolution production under Jiang Qing's stewardship is the filmed ballet *The White-Haired Girl* (1972), the story of Xi'er, who is seized by an evil landlord in payment for her poor father's debt. She escapes, but several years of living in the wilderness turns her hair white like a ghost's (illus. 139). As expected, in a society founded on the righting of old wrongs, she exacts her revenge, something denied of pre-Communist period film victims, although when it comes to actually pulling the trigger, it still takes a boyfriend to do the job. In *Three Women*, gender mattered; soon after, gender was subsumed by class, but women were still featured.

The four films highlighted in the previous essays, from the post-Mao era, each featured women in political roles, each followed older and newer traditions in doing so. In *Yellow Earth*, with its post-socialist reassessment of the Communist government, its ideals and its failures, played out through a sublimated sexuality, we saw a post-Maoist reversion to the standard pre-Maoist theme of woman as hapless victim, representing the whole nation (see illus. 121). *Red Sorghum* shows woman as rebel, as she had been in the Maoist era but now as a call for a new post-socialist rebelliousness: social, sexual, economic and political (see illus. 42). *Qiu Ju* presents a female embodiment of justice crusading through the imperfect Chinese justice system (see illus. 117), while *Farewell My Concubine*, from a novel by a woman writer, offers

139, 140 *The White-Haired Girl.* Xi'er in a classic revolutionary pose . . . but the boyfriend still wields the gun.

a deconstruction of the female gender and with it comes a challenge to the Communist view of art and culture (see illus. 86). In each, woman is more means than end: two additional films now provide the opportunity to consider whether female appropriation is strictly a function of male authorship, whether there is any real alternative to the appropriative role of women and whether women differ in this regard from men. *Army Nurse*, the only one of these films both by a female author and a woman director, is about the relation of women to society and society's expectations of them, suggesting that women's needs are distinct from those of men and from those of society as a whole, and lamenting that these needs have been trampled by the revolution. *Woman From the Lake of Scented Souls* is about women's relation to women, suggesting darkly that once they are liberated to be themselves, women may prove to be not terribly different from men.

Previous essays here have considered films with woman as victim, woman as rebel, woman as crusader, and 'woman' as art. But so far, we have not considered a film made by a woman, nor have we witnessed a representation of woman simply *as* woman – if there truly is such a thing. When *Army Nurse* scriptwriter Ding Xiaoqi was nine years old, her parents – both musicians – were sent down to the countryside and she 'grew up more or less alone in an apartment full of books'.[54] Eventually graduating from the People's Liberation Army Art Academy, she became a lyricist for the PLA Naval Song and Dance Troupe –

the aim was to produce some lyrics to do with nurses; how much they did for the revolution, that sort of thing . . . 'The flowers are opening, and the Party has opened its meeting, the whole motherland is in bloom.'

– and she began writing in her own free time ('The officers in charge of me were always asking me why I was writing this stuff and pointing out that it had nothing to do with my work . . . Of course, I couldn't tell them I'd been writing a novella or what it was about').[55]

Ding's collaborator on *Army Nurse*, director Hu Mei, also came from a musical family, her father the conductor of the central symphony orchestra of the People's Liberation Army. During the Cultural Revolution her parents were arrested. Her grandfather, a painter, died of fright when seized for questioning. At the age of ten, 'I was struck dumb. . . My parents were locked up and under guard, but we had our school principal locked up and under guard. I saw half her hair being chopped off, and I was there as a little Red Guard representative when they beat her to death in the women's toilets. I was scared because I knew my parents were being beaten up, too.'[56] Hu Mei eventually made her way into acting and then into directing. She graduated from the Beijing Film Academy with the 'Fifth Generation' class of 1982, a classmate of directing majors Chen Kaige and Tian Zhuangzhuang and cinematographers Gu Changwei and Zhang Yimou. After graduation, Hu Mei was assigned to a position with the August First Film Studio, the film studio of the People's Liberation Army, in Beijing. Based on Ding Xiaoqi's script, 'Nüer lou' (literally, 'The Women's Quarters' or 'Maidenhome'), *Army Nurse* was co-directed by Hu Mei and older director Li Xiaojun. ('He's an honest, nice guy,' says Ding Xiaoqi of Li Xiaojun, 'but an idiot. Hu Mei – you know she's a tough cookie – muscled her way in and later gave Li Xiaojun the boot.')[57] The film was released with the first batch of 'Fifth Generation' films in 1985. Only later was Ding's script (Kang Liwen was given shared credit) converted by her into a much-altered short story. In temperament – quiet and slow-moving, plain and under-stated – the film compares with *Yellow Earth*. Both centre on an adolescent girl's formative attachment to a military man. But in *Yellow Earth*, the attachment is sublimated into the political whereas in *Army Nurse* the political is disguised within the repressed romantic. Produced in the army's own film studio, subjected to military as well as Film Bureau scrutiny, *Army Nurse* (like *Yellow Earth*) restrains its emotions carefully but shades them sensitively, embeds its ideas in images, and steps away from unneeded confrontation.

Army Nurse specifically raises the issue of Chinese socialism's impact on women, but as with *Yellow Earth*'s Cuiqiao, its women seem to stand for the fate of all Chinese, women and men alike, if not for the Chinese nation itself. Like *Yellow Earth*, whose central gender issue was the traditional contracted marriage of child brides, *Army Nurse* further reminds us that the concerns, definitions, and agendas of women and feminism are by no means the same in every country and culture. *Army Nurse* is the film equivalent of 'scar' or 'wound' literature (*shanghen wenxue*), a genre of self-expression which emerged soon after the death of Mao, spilling forth the sorrows, the remorse over shattered dreams of the Cultural Revolution decade. A literary concept first, it soon spread into painting (illus. 141) and finally emerged in the complex medium of film with works like *The Legend of Tianyun Mountain* (dir. Xie Jin, 1980; see illus. 173) and *Evening Rain* (dir. Wu Yigong, 1980). *Army Nurse* explores one talented and fairly successful young woman's conflict between public duty and her own personal needs during that decade, the story of Qiao Xiaoyu.

In this story, in 1968, two years into the Cultural Revolution, Qiao Xiaoyu was packed off by her parents at the tender age of fourteen to work in Army Hospital 547 in the cold, remote north-east province of

Jilin. From the opening moments, she problematizes this supreme moment of revolutionary fervour with her own uncertain hesitancy. 'I didn't know what to say or do,' she tells us, voiced-over. 'Should I cry or should I smile? In the end I think I smiled, but I'm sure it looked awful.' 'How different from going to Granny's,' she adds, as if to remind us of Mao's famous phrase, 'A revolution is not a dinner party.' En route, as her fellow comrades wave their Little Red Books and swagger politically, she stands aside and joins a stranger in quiet, new-found sisterhood. Dedicated and bright (and sensitively performed by Xu Ye), the shy Xiaoyu eventually becomes a model worker.

Four years pass before Comrade Qiao encounters a patient, Ding Zhu, who arouses the unprofessional side of her being (illus. 142). Eighteen years old now, she is stirred but ashamed. In her nursing duties, she eyes him with the innocence of a lamb and tries to keep her distance. (In a voice-over, we hear from her that 'At that time, I was only a grown-up child. I hadn't even thought about love. But he . . . he quietly walked in front of me.') Ding Zhu is more than a pair of seductive eyes: compassionate and dedicated, he is a good soldier who shows Xiaoyu that responsibility is more than just carrying out assigned duties. He helps her become a better nurse. Their physical encounter is brief and so chaste it would scarcely qualify as a sexual encounter in America; but initiated by a girl, narrated by a woman, and representing a whole culture so starved for personal affection after ten paranoid years of destroying all internal enemies, the brief ten seconds when army nurse touches military patient became one of the most emotionally charged moments in modern Chinese cinema (illus. 143–5).

Then, emotionally inexperienced, denied any natural preparation for romantic life, Xiaoyu has no idea how to handle her adolescent longing for Ding, and after ten short seconds she represses it and lets it slip away. When the soldier, who apparently was no better prepared for romance than she, later writes to confess his feelings for her ('When I first saw you, I always hoped to see you . . .'), she is baffled and confused and with trembling hands destroys his letter, flushing it down a toilet in fear that she might respond emotionally to it (illus. 146). The audience may be wishing for romance to bloom, but this was still a moment when only one love was proper: the all-embracing love for the Party Chairman, the 'bright red sun in the hearts of the people'.

Xiaoyu's kindly political supervisor, Commissar Lu (illus. 147), notes her recent moodiness after Ding Zhu's departure. As we wonder just how much this Party know-it-all really knows, he reminds her that moods are not a good thing, and he tells her: 'As a girl, be careful about your private life. Put work and study first. Devote yourself to duty,

141 Gao Yi, *I Love the Oil Fields*, *c.*1980, oil on canvas. China Art Gallery, Beijing.

The two figures shown here are young 'rusticated' urban intellectuals (*zhiqing*), sent down to the countryside for re-education during the Cultural Revolution. But gone from their hearts is the enthusiasm (or pseudo-enthusiasm of the title), genuinely experienced at the outset of the Cultural Revolution by many of the participants and replaced at the end of that 'chaotic decade' by irony and bitterness. Allowed only the love of Mao, Motherland, and their daily labours, and not of each other, the longing and lacking suggested in this painting stand for a full ten years of missed education, family, friends, and the experience of youth.

understand? . . . Write more frequent thought reports. Try to join the Party as soon as you can.' In the book, he adds, 'When the time comes, even if *you're* not thinking about marriage, the leaders and the Party will be thinking about you.'[58] Unfortunately for Xiaoyu, the time never comes; and even worse, though her soldier boy is gone, his memory just won't fade away. Her continuing success as a public servant is constantly played out against this lost opportunity, which stirs deep in her soul and blocks her ability to attach to any other man. She is finally matched with a would-be mate (yet another military model, he calls himself 'a model late marrier'), Tu Jianli (illus. 148). Tu is a kindly but somewhat stiffened mannequin who looks like he's just stepped out of a Maoist-era film – personal character replaced by cliché. As a cultural relic, he is a generation older than the virtuous but self-possessed and seductively

142 *Army Nurse*. Ding Zhu, at his parting from Qiao Xiaoyu.

'cool' Ding Zhu. Tu arranges a position for Xiaoyu in a modern urban hospital, one he condescendingly calls 'worthy' of her abilities. But after her arrival, in her inability to differentiate her personal from her professional needs, his comment that 'Your mountain hospital can't compare' only serves to evoke memories (a visual flashback) of Ding Zhu in what now looms in retrospect as their rustic 'utopia', and she abandons Tu Jianli on their wedding night. With neither of them prepared for marriage, and never having shared a wedding bed (conspicuously shown unruffled), Xiaoyu returns to serve her rural hospital. That service which once dominated her youth now becomes her entire adulthood.

In its understated way, *Army Nurse* refuses to draw any explicit conclusions about complex social matters, relying instead on the implications of a truncated plot narrative, working through intuition rather than reason and on partially revealed intimacies rather than rhetorical drama. Vagueness and the crafting of non-essential aspects to satisfy the Army's censorial demands were critical to the very survival of this

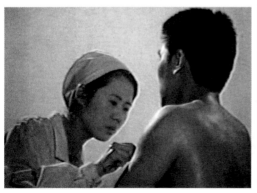

cinema project. Originally, there were three men in Xiaoyu's film life, beginning before her army induction with a teenage boyfriend who was jettisoned after the first cut.[59] 'In China,' says Ding Xiaoqi, 'they don't think teenagers should know anything about love. One of the leaders in the studio said, "A teenager and she knew about love? What a kid!" Actually, I told them I was in love already when I four years old in kindergarten . . . Anyway, I figured that if Maomao had to go, OK.'[60] Ding says,

. . . back then I was very aware that I had to set her up as a heroine first . . . We told August First [the PLA film studio] that Qiao Xiaoyu was a heroine, a woman who had contributed to the revolution for many, many years. That was the only way we could get them to agree to let us make the film. In making the film, we could return to the intentions of the original story: the effect of being in the military for a long stretch and the oppression of sexuality in the military. We could only put in a little bit of that, of course. We didn't dare deal with it too directly.[61]

According to Hu Mei, the resulting indirectness split the Chinese audience by gender:

Many men said, 'How can she be like this? She doesn't want this one and she doesn't want that one. She's bullying men!' They felt this woman absolutely didn't sacrifice herself for the people, that she didn't make a contribution to society, and all that. 'She's a nurse, she's got a job, why is she always having affairs?' Older women all tended to think it was a good movie.[62]

Disagreement also surrounds the cause for Xiaoyu's abandoning her new marriage and returning to the old hospital. Chris Berry concludes that '. . . in deciding not to marry the man her friends have fixed her up with at the end of the film, she is asserting her desire to stay alone rather than give in to the social pressure that is insisting on her

143–5 *Army Nurse*. Qiao Xiaoyu prepares to treat Ding Zhu's wound . . . is overcome by her feelings for him . . . until Ding Zhu reluctantly pleads with her to 'hurry up'.

146 *Army Nurse.*
Xiaoyu tears up Ding
Zhu's letter.

marriage'.[63] Director Hu Mei, on the other hand, acknowledges the censorial necessity of presenting the Army with the image of a model worker rising above personal interests, but in the end she says, 'Of course she may have gone back because of her work, but that could hardly be the case.' To her author – who now becomes privileged to define the central message of the film – Xiaoyu's 'reason' is neither one of renewed professional dedication nor narcissistic indulgence but instead one of on-going self-denial, the conversion of oppression into internalized repression. Ding Xiaoqi again:

... after getting a letter from him, she flushes it away in panic before she even gets to read it properly. She's not just afraid that someone will find out; she's even afraid herself to see what is in it. I felt that was a crucial scene because it shows how Xiaoyu oppresses herself to the point where she throws one's love down the toilet.[64]

When Xiaoyu forsakes marriage for public duty, *Army Nurse*'s intention is to show that what has been denied is just what is most needed: intimacy, attention to the personal psyche, family. Indeed, it is just these things that *Army Nurse* attends to most closely as film, with its unusual (for that time and place) close-up shots and voiced-over disclosure of what its subjects seem to think and feel but are actually unable in their lives to express to others. Of the envelope that she retained after flushing away Ding Zhu's letter, Xiaoyu as narrator tells us what she could never bring herself to tell to him, that 'Over time, the address became a song in my mind.' In another voice-over that was eventually cut from the scene where the young soldier takes his farewell, Xiaoyu asks: 'What is a shadow? I really don't understand. Sometimes I really want to grab it, but I can't get hold of it at all. When I want to grab hold of it, it goes far away, and when I want to get rid of it, it insists on following me.'[65] The immediate concerns of *Army Nurse* are so simple

– women sitting about, talking about jobs and families, gossiping about male patients – and its story line so unremarkable that it's rather like a soap opera without any bubbles. The hospital gossip among friends informs Xiaoyu that Ding Zhu is the son of a pilot, that his name is written with an unusual character combining 'man' and 'fly' and meaning 'to soar', that

He doesn't like to talk. But there's something in his eyes. He looks proud and aloof. As though he looks down on other people . . .

and that 'his teeth are so even'. Xiaoyu's hospital friendships (illus. 149) constitute an exception to Ann Kaplan's assertion that 'Missing from [Chinese women's] films . . . are images of female-female bonding of the kind that would rival heterosexual priorities.'[66] These female friends are scarcely ideal types. Su Menghong is personally ambitious, and through her foreknowledge of a college opening that the girls can all compete for ('the chance of a lifetime') she gains unfair advantage (which Xiaoyu refuses to share) and thus blocks Xiaoyu's only opportunity to leave this remote childhood exile. Spoiled Li Lingling is largely dependent on her family connections. Li Yamei is mischievous and irreverent, a sharp-tongued (and sometimes foul-mouthed) comic who finds Lingling and the others 'so stuck up'. Menghong offers them all the off-coloured advice: 'You learn from me how to deal with these men. Don't give them an inch! Otherwise, everything'll be upside down!'

At least from Xiaoyu's vantage, these women have a degree of control over their lives that she cannot manage to gain for herself. And yet, the forces that bind them together always prove stronger than the desires which drive them apart and for much of the film they constitute a platonic family in place of the erotic one that is denied them. Menghong, despite her betrayal of Xiaoyu, remains friends with her over the years

147 *Army Nurse*. Commissar Lu, representing the Party, described by Xiaoyu as a 'good man'.

148 *Army Nurse*. Tu Jianli says to an unimpressed Xiaoyu, 'They say I'm a model late marrier.'

and introduces Xiaoyu to her would-be husband, Tu Jianli. When Xiaoyu, already set up but still greatly uncertain about the prospect, asks, 'What do you think of marriage?' (illus. 150), Mengong responds, 'That's something you should ask yourself,' and she tells her, 'Really, Xiaoyu, I understand you. Just like you understood me back then.' Yamei adds, 'Marriage is an important thing. For a woman, everything ends at marriage.' For Yamei, Xiaoyu's marriage spells the end of this extended sisterhood.

The major promontories of this subtle film – the spoken question, 'What do you think of marriage?' and the unspoken one, 'What do you think of love?' – rise only slightly above the level topography of this intentionally unspectacular landscape. Its romantic heroine, Xiaoyu, is no beauty, though in time she may come to *seem* beautiful. So lacking in the sophisticated cinematics of a later film like *Farewell My Concubine*, *Army Nurse* could scarcely hold its own against a traditional Chinese melodrama, let alone against Hollywood's imports. The film's static camerawork is undistinguished, yet it is wholly appropriate to the unassuming nature of the content: this is not an uncommon story but one that has occurred millions of times over. That commonality is both part of its point and is made the central basis of its style. Its flashback structure and voiced-over narrative, which take us into Xiaoyu's most private thoughts, might be dismissed in America as uncinematic, retarditaire, or just plain corny, but in 1985 in China they provided a new subjectivity, a doorway into individualized personality, that made *Army Nurse* seem more avant-garde than old-fashioned.

One scene from *Army Nurse*, the emotional exchange between Xiaoyu and the patient, Ding Zhu, has become legendary in 'Fifth Generation' film. Dressing Ding Zhu's wound, Xiaoyu first yields to her personal desire then yields to his self-restraint and reaffirms her social obligation

149 *Army Nurse*. Xiaoyu and her better-adjusted friends, Yamei and Menghong.

150 *Army Nurse.*
Xiaoyu understates
the theme of the film:
what do women really
need?

What do you think of marriage?

– a brief moment which restructures her whole life (see illus. 144). The
soundtrack helps to shape the scene: the mundane background hammer-
ing of a workman, formerly seen repairing a window, and the call of an
army bugle are worked into this romantic fantasy – are they real or
imagined? this is left ambiguous – and they play a part in the urgent
feelings and mental disrepair of this young army nurse: an aural transformation of military discipline into that very same sexuality which
the military, as the leading model for society as a whole, has tried to
suppress. Contemporary studies of Chinese film are illustrated wholly
by publicity stills, photographs that differ – often considerably – from
what actually appears in the films themselves. The still photograph
used to depict the two main figures in this notorious erotic 'moment'
shows both of the figures' faces (illus. 151), yet the actual film footage
from this shot shows only Xiaoyu's face, with the solider's face cut at
the chin. The actual footage produces a significantly different effect,
unequally revealing the two characters and centring the subjectivity on
the army nurse alone. It is, after all, her story, her romantic life, which
the soldier is prevented by the Party from wholly entering. The soldier's
entire face is shown only after he interrupts her reverie – accompanied
by the camera crossing the 180° line, which transforms him from the
body of desire into the voice of denial (see illus. 145).[67]

   Like so many things called 'avant-garde' in China, *Army Nurse* is old-
fashioned by international measures, but then this is not surprising:
since everything 'old' had been under assault in the radical decade of
the Cultural Revolution, the revival of the old became part of China's
'radically new' in the late 1970s and early 1980s. The cinematic values
of *Army Nurse* are true to an ancient code of 'naturalism' (*ziran*), a core
value of traditional Chinese painting and calligraphy – artistic expression through bland understatement and uncompromising sincerity,

with little regard for popular appeal – a subdued aesthetic which makes many a fine Chinese painting so hard for American museum-goers to appreciate at first sight. Superficially, initially, Xiaoyu (like the film itself) is as plain as an old tree (illus. 153). But like many an old tree from classic Chinese painting, one learns to treasure it deeply, to discover its beauty hidden deep inside (illus. 152). In traditional China, such a comparison could only be made between a tree and a male scholar. But the artistry of this film demasculinizes that virtue and lets us appreciate woman for something other than her superficial film beauty. Just as the movie does, Xiaoyu remains compelling and credible for her basic sensibility, and she exemplifies 'woman' in terms of that sensibility. But while this sensibility guides us to an understanding of Xiaoyu's social predicament, it isn't sufficient to protect her from it: a good woman, she's *too* sensible, too compromising, too giving of herself to ever achieve what's right for her personally. Society, the state, takes all that she can give and then asks for more.

What society took from Qiao Xiaoyu was neither simply fabricated by Ding Xiaoqi nor unduly melodramatized by Hu Mei. Rather, the character 'Xiaoyu' emerged from actual interviews of military nurses quite like herself. Ding Xiaoqi describes this bluntly, and it doesn't take a psychologist to recognize how such childhood deprivation shapes an individual, or a marriage, or a whole culture:

I met many women soldiers there. Many of them were similar to Qiao Xiaoyu, the main character in the novella. One woman told me directly she'd known her husband for three or four years, but from the time they'd been introduced to the time they married, they'd only spent a total of about one hour together. The person who introduced them was there the whole time. She was thirty then. She'd joined up when she was fourteen, and she hadn't left that mountain valley since then . . . She told me she hated her husband. When I asked her why, she said, 'He sticks it right in the minute he sees me.' There was no lovemaking process. The minute he met her it was onto the bed, off with their pants, down to it, and then it was all over. They had nothing to say to each other. She was terribly upset. Her husband had been a soldier since he was a teenager, and so neither of them had ever had any education about relationships or sex. Holding, touching, loving; he didn't know anything about any of that.[68]

It is one of the gracious features of *Army Nurse*, however, that Xiaoyu's would-have-been lovers are both as repressed as she is and gentle to a fault, unwilling and unable to further either their own personal needs or hers. Males and females suffer alike and perhaps equally from their internalized 'marriage to the Chairman'. This even includes Xiaoyu's kindly if misguided Commissar Lu, of whom Ding Xiaoqi says,

151 *Army Nurse,*
publicity photograph.

152 Wu Zhen, *Old Fisherman,*
1342, hanging scroll, ink on
silk. National Palace
Museum, Taipei.

153 *Army Nurse.*
Qiao Xiaoyu, unable
to find words for the
parting Ding Zhu.

. . . if you remember the political commissar who introduces a boyfriend to her and tries to get her married, well, he was sexually repressed himself. Why else would he constrain those women in so many ways and not let them get involved with men? I didn't dare to write about any of that . . . Of course, he wouldn't see that he was sexually repressed himself, but that's the truth.[69]

This is a truth that Commissar Lu himself seems to know, exclaiming to Xiaoyu in his later years, 'People! We're all afraid of emotions.'

   Ann Kaplan has written of this equalization of suffering, this blending of gender, as avoiding the real issue of gender differentiation:

. . . one could see Chinese women as working their way through a modernist phase in their assertion of subjectivity. But there seems to be some guilt about the assertion of a specifically *female* subjectivity, *female* desire: this I read from Hu Mei's rather abrupt outlining of an allegorical reading for her and other female directors' films about female desire. We see in operation, again, the difficulty for the Chinese of confronting difference (here specifically sexual difference) head on. Hu Mei got concerned about an analysis that seemed to separate males from females – to emphasize specifically *female* frustrations and repressions – and she resorted to an analysis that would apply to *all* the Chinese, that would reassert the collective.[70]

But Hu Mei and Ding Xiaoqi are not experiencing guilt. Production within China's censorial system, obligatory constraints within the margins of a cultural hegemony: that is what constrains *Army Nurse* and defines its *realpolitik*. What Ding Xiaoqi (the primary author of this story) *has* addressed herself to in the above statements is the interactive social dynamic that stands in the way of any one-sided, any one-gendered solution to Chinese women's problems. Kaplan, despite her previously expressed reservations, concurs:

. . . the gaze is often more mutual [in Chinese cinema] than in American films – men's desire imaged as equally frustrated and impossible as that of women; but, further, the entire signifying of sexual relations may stand in as a metaphor (or analogue) for the broader political/social/intellectual frustration of both genders . . . State communism, in demanding male submission to the Law of the Father with little possibility for obtaining at least some parity with the Father position (as in free-enterprise capitalism), may produce men psychically damaged in deeper ways even than women.[71]

Commissar Lu, while paternal, is no obvious villain (see illus. 147). He watches Xiaoyu lose her opportunity for college but gains for her a place in nursing school. He maintains the standards that deny her a relationship with Ding Zhu but he helps arrange her marriage to Tu Jianli. The tragedy, of course, is that Jianli is no Ding Zhu and that these alternatives are alternatives to free choice. But rather than demonizing individuals or gender, *Army Nurse* examines attitudes and consequences and poses the question, 'What is possible?' Commissar Lu has more than a match for his ideological rectitude in the hospital matron who at the start of the film welcomes Xiaoyu and the other young girls to their new state of discipline by admonishing patients listening to Beijing opera rather than reading Mao in study sessions, 'Aren't you ashamed! Revolution requires discipline. You'd have us in total disorder.' Before the end of the film, it is Xiaoyu as hospital matron administering a different standard of discipline to a younger generation steeped in a different ethic – advantaged, outspoken, and spoiled to a degree once impossible. 'I think we live to be happy,' one of her young charges complains. 'All this field rescue! It's boring! Besides, my husband lives in the city. I always speak my mind. Criticize me or punish me if you want. If someone wants to be a nun let them! I don't.' Xiaoyu, denied a childhood, denied a free voice and a husband, and now denied the heavy hand of past authority, responds as a member of a now-lost generation, 'You can quit studying. You can even leave. But I won't let you slander our hospital.' Ironically, and with nuance, while examining the tortuous route from social oppression to internal repression, *Army Nurse* still offers praise for that discipline which comes from within and it still draws a line against social irresponsibility.

Once again, in the best Chinese fashion, analogy rules the film: in *Army Nurse*, repressed sexuality, the oppressive military state, and the censorship of film may all be substituted interchangeably, one for the other. All of these elements appeared on stage together as Ding Xiaoqi repeatedly wrote and rewrote her script and as Hu Mei cut and recut their film to ease it past studio officials. The early childhood love affair was cut from the film, just as it would have been cut from real life; a nude love scene with the husband became, several transformations later, an unconsummated marriage. As the authorities progressively denuded the film-maker's art, Ding and Hu progressively clothed the message of their film. The film's own repression is Xiaoyu's repression. As Xiaoyu could not possess or become possessed by Ding Zhu, so Hu Mei could not retain possession of *Army Nurse*: 'In the end,' she says, 'It was not my work.'[72] So when Ding Xiaoqi (who emigrated to Australia in 1989 after witnessing the Tian'an Men 'episode' firsthand) says, 'The whole Party is all about sexual repression! Party discipline is about repressing personal feelings, including sex . . . their aim is to repress all of that so that you will become obedient,' we are advised of the universality of what Xiaoyu's individual sexual repression stands for.[73] The universality of that meaning – and the meaning of that universality, that interweaving of all strands – is that women's issues *cannot* appear in isolation. Everything in China, by analogy and in fact, appropriates everything else.

Like *Army Nurse*, *Woman From the Lake of Scented Souls* is imbued with a female sensibility, but it leads in a very different direction. *Army Nurse* suggests that despite social(ist) efforts to equate men with women, their social needs are hardly the same; *Scented Souls* suggests that in their social behaviour, in their perception and response to fundamental social goals, women and men may not be all that different. In *Army Nurse*, the central unit of Chinese social values, the family, is conspicuous by its absence, suppressed in favour of state unity; in *Scented Souls*, the family is back, but what a family!

Co-winner of the 1993 Berlin Film Festival Golden Bear Award for best film,[74] *Lake of Scented Souls* was scripted and directed in 1992 by Xie Fei from a short story by Zhou Daxin, *Sesame Oil Workshop by the Side of Scented Souls' Lake*[75] – an ungainly title, but its juxtaposition of semi-modern industry and timeless landscape analogize the central tension of the narrative: changing economic values and unchanging social mores. The setting is a rural village in central China (identified in the book as the Nanyang area of Hebei province) whose lakeside scenery provides much of the languid beauty of *Scented Souls*. But like the lives in the film, the lake is a vessel for unhappy souls, named for two young women, one rich and one poor, who drowned themselves there in a past century presumably for reasons of love but never made clear. The audience is left to consider the parallel between them and the central figure of *Scented Souls*, Mrs Xiang Ersao, an economically liberated woman whose grand public success masks a deeply troubled private life.

154 *Woman From the Lake of Scented Souls.* 'I'll beat you to death!' In the world of Scented Souls, men struggle to retain the upper hand. Here Xiang Ersao's husband has just discovered her use of birth-control pills.

155 *Woman From the Lake of Scented Souls.* In the world of business, Mrs Xiang is the boss.

Xiang Ersao is a battered wife whose husband is lazy and lame and into the new vogue for Hong Kong pornographic movies followed nightly by forced sex (illus. 154). But in this land of romantic lotus, Ersao is no delicate bloom, and in all other regards she dominates the family (illus. 155): she runs the most successful shop in the village, named after herself, and produces prize-winning sesame oil; she handles the family's finances and its social affairs, and she orders her husband about like a child; she even has a long-running love affair with her company truck driver, Mr Ren, about whom the audience is given enough clues to realize that he is the father of Mrs Xiang's young daughter (see illus. 160).

Given depth of character but a determinedly opaque personality in performance by China's most distinguished actress, Siqin Gaowa, Mrs Xiang is a tough and manipulative woman. But here's where the trouble begins: in her toughness, our heroine deals with the question, 'Why can't a woman be more like a man?' and provides the answer, 'She can.' Xiang Ersao can do anything a man can do, including persecuting other women. This is played out through the arranged marriage of her son, an epileptic and otherwise dimwitted lad, Dunzi, for whom Mrs Xiang insists on securing a bride of the very best vintage, imagining that this might cure his illness (illus. 156).

A master manipulator, Mrs Xiang uses her newfound wealth to procure a beautiful young mate, Huanhuan (see illus. 162), from the family of a neighbouring village whose economic straits she exploits to the fullest. That this marriage is illegal, given Dunzi's epilepsy, has been made clear to Mrs Xiang but is callously brushed aside as of no

156 *Woman From the Lake of Scented Souls*. Oblivious to the tragic realities of the situation, Dunzi is made up for his wedding.

consequence (the deeper issue of justice in policy toward the handi-capped is not considered). In addition, Mrs Xiang has cleverly ferreted away Huanhuan's intended husband, Jinhai, an employee of her sesame oil factory whom she posts far off in the district capital with the allure of making him wealthy there (illus. 157), while she goes about finan-cially seducing Huanhuan's impoverished mother. Huanhuan also offers the prospect of being a wholly subservient daughter-in-law, unlike another marriage prospect whom Mrs Xiang has previously rejected out of hand as all-too-modern and self-assertive (in other words, too much like herself). Before long, Huanhuan is doing the household chores and serving the meals while Mrs Xiang sits at the family table, so that even a foreign audience can readily see the benefits for the Chinese mother-in-law of a well-arranged marriage.

As the evidence piles up from the day of the wedding on of her son's sexual mistreatment of the young bride, Mrs Xiang turns a blind eye, explaining to the daughter-in-law her familial obligations from a tradi-tional, patriarchal point of view. But there's no patriarch-to-be in this family, for the son can only bite and punch his bride in bed, while love and sexual intercourse are beyond his limited capacities. Huanhuan's troubles unfold parallel to those of Mrs Xiang, though we learn much less about the girl behind the troubles than we do about the older woman. Ironically, the young girl discovers and responds to her mother-in-law's woes before the reverse is true. But then, by the time the older woman has put two-plus-two together, recognized her own battered condition in that of the daughter-in-law, and offered an annulment with even the dowry for a new marriage, it's entirely too late. The young girl, robbed of her innocence and reputation, sobs in the moonlight by the side of the lake of scented souls, 'Who would want me now? Who would want me now?' and the film ends (illus. 158).

'Fourth Generation' director Xie Fei, best known for *Girl from Hunan* (1985; illus. 159), gives his films a visual delicacy and sensibility of content that has misled many of my students into thinking he was a woman.[76] The foremost visual cues of *Scented Souls* are all *yin*, female, associated with water and mist, night-time and the moon. The Lake of Scented Souls provides a watery backdrop for much of the film, including its opening and closing moments, when the lake is shrouded in *yin* mists. From the start, the lake's fertilizing waters provide the basis for marriage rituals mimicked by young children and adolescents, for the conveyance of the bride Huanhuan to the family home, and for secret trysting early in the film by Huanhuan with her true love, Jinhai, and by Xiang Ersao with Mr Ren. By daylight, the lake's pink lotus play in scenes of romance and innocence. The lake's blue moonlit colour suffuses the many scenes of extramarital intimacy and marital violence in darkened, rippling tones, as if the characters were underwater,

157 *Woman From the Lake of Scented Souls.* Xiang Ersao sets the trap for the un-witting Jinhai: 'If you accept the job, you must commit to staying several years.'

drowning (illus. 158 and 160). One of the film's opening scenes links these two contrary scenarios. As a band of scantily-clad youngsters participate in a mock marriage, bearing their lotus-carrying 'bride' to her groom, they chant, 'Thinking about getting married? What's so great about getting married?' (illus. 161). Their words innocently contradict their actions but foreshadow (despite the brilliance of the sunlit scene) the darker sexual behaviour and disillusionment of adults. Dunzi, even more childish than the children and stimulated by this pervasive and precocious sexuality, offers a lotus to Huanhuan while a girlfriend mocks her that she's about to be stolen away from Jinhai (illus. 162). Jinhai looks on with a naiveté that matches Dunzi's, unable to imagine that this taunt describes a future reality (illus. 163). By the end of this encounter, Dunzi is seen molesting Huanhuan for the first

158 *Woman From the Lake of Scented Souls*. At the film's end, Xiang Ersao and a disconsolate Huanhuan by the side of the lake.

159 *Girl From Hunan.* Child bride Xiaoxiao married to an infant husband.

160 *Woman From the Lake of Scented Souls*. Xiang Ersao and Mr Ren trysting in the blue moonlit lotus fields.

time, grabbing at her in public (much as his mother will grab her legally) and childishly babbling, 'I want a wife! I want a wife!' while Jinhai, when needed, is nowhere to be seen (illus. 164). Provocative in its physicality, this scene foretells much of what lies ahead, at the same time – by casting the action on to mere children – as it predicts that this cycle will be re-enacted again and again. The film will end tragically near this very same lakeside spot.

On viewing women and water together, any Chinese audience, whether in an educated, literary way or in a more folkloric manner, will anticipate the role that water might play as either a mirror of beauty or for the darker possibilities hidden below its surface. As personified water deities, women often ruled the waves, celebrated in verse and image like the Luo River Goddess and the paired Goddesses of the Xiang River. But many such deities, it is understood today, may have been the unhappy spirits of drowned victims involved in female sacrifice, young girls given in local rituals as 'brides' to pacify male river gods.[77] Others may have been romantic love suicides (nobly following the decease of husbands, or consummating transgressive romantic situations) or victims of no-love situations (avoiding or escaping unacceptable arranged matches), while still others represented punishment for female sexual transgression (as in Xie Fei's *Girl from Hunan*).[78] The historic legacy of female drowning informs a variety of contemporary

161–4 *Woman From the Lake of Scented Souls.* As children participate in mock sexuality in the lake's fertilizing waters . . . Dunzi is aroused to romance . . .with the naive Jinhai's fiancé . . . and quickly proceeds from romance to violence.

films, from *Yellow Earth* to Xie Jin's recent *Opium War* (1997), as well as older text-based films like *Family* and even the original text of *Raise the Red Lantern* (where the film's substitution for female drowning in a well by hanging in an upper story has been decried as an unrealistic alteration of the novella).[79]

Ironically, though once polluted by double suicide, the lake's pure waters are the basis for the modern-day success of the Xiang family's superb sesame oil. Mrs Xiang's surname is the same as that of the lake, 'scent' or 'fragrance', formally linking these two *yin* bodies. It is, furthermore, a homophone (pronounced identically but written with a different character) for the Xiang River, a classic name in the history of drowning. In ancient times before the first of China's political dynasties, upon the death of the legendary sage-emperor Shun, his two wives (daughters of the previous sage-ruler, Yao) in loyalty drowned themselves in the Xiang River and came to be regarded as the divine spirits of that river and the great Dongting ('Cave Palace') Lake which the Xiang fills. The statesman-poet conflates his identity with the Xiang goddesses in two of the famous 'Nine Songs', traditionally attributed to the authorship of Qu Yuan. And in 277 BC, Qu Yuan, in loyalty to his fallen state of Chu, similarly drowned himself in the Xiang or its tributary river, the Miluo (a real piece of female appropriation, one might say, and of life imitating art).[80] The title of the film, then, if these Xiang waters are related, points not just to the local lake and not just to the personal struggle lodged within Xiang Ersao's own soul but beyond, to the rhetorical sources of social lamentation in Chinese history.

The blue colour scheme of *yin*-gendered lake territory contrasts with the earthen colours that dominate the public sector and male zones of activity (illus. 155). *Yang* colours are used for the shop where Mrs Xiang

176

surpasses the men of her town at their own business. This is also incorporated into Dunzi's name, meaning a mound of earth or a block – earth in contrast to water, signifying male patriarchy and its permanence, but suggestion as well to the son's clodlike mental inertness. Punctuated with celebratory *yang*-red is the large public wedding of Dunzi, where Mrs. Xiang's basest achievement is publicly celebrated (illus. 156). That the husband, named Lü ('Limpy') Ershu and physically lame, doesn't think much better than he walks and can behave no more humanely than his mentally and morally deficient son is a somatic condemnation of traditional male sexual behavior. The naïve Jinhai, easily duped by the promise of riches (his name means 'Sea of Gold'), further contributes to the way in which these menfolk (as in many of the films already discussed) are reduced to mere ciphers, either vacillating, misguided, and cowardly, or else impossible brutes, or some combination of the two. Arguably, though one can hardly speak up for the social ills they embody, it is they, much more than the women, who have been stereotyped and primitivized by their textual and cinematic creators. But the distinctive function of *Scented Souls* is to extend this embodiment to the other gender.

For all its sensitivity and understanding of woman's lot, the emphasis of *Scented Souls* is the reverse of *Army Nurse*. In *Army Nurse*, a woman's task may be the same as a man's but her needs and sensibilities are genetically quite different. *Scented Souls* is more like *Farewell My Concubine* in showing the gender barrier as permeable through behaviour and personality. In *Farewell*, the gender-bent Dieyi is more feminine than the toughened prostitute, Juxian. But while the mechanism of Dieyi's theatric transsexuality may be dismissed as atypical, in *Scented Souls* the agency for altering gendered behaviour is increasingly widespread if

165 *Woman From the Lake of Scented Souls.* Xiang Ersao grieves by the water's edge.

not yet universally available: namely, modern economic opportunity. Perhaps for Qiao Xiaoyu in *Army Nurse*, becoming a professional at the age of fourteen, a cog in the wheel of state, was no golden opportunity but rather an obligation imposed upon a whole generation. But Xiang Ersao, like Juxian, is tough; she's a bright and savvy woman hell-bent on achieving her own economic liberation in the post-Mao era. Whether this is psychic compensation for her sexual slavery, we can only surmise, for Xiang's psychology is buried from view. But she cuts deals with the Japanese, observes the Japanese working woman's manners, discovers how they play the game of extramarital relationships, figures out how to expand her household operation into a small company, and shrewdly plans for the next generation. Representing a resurgent petit-capitalism in China, Xiang Ersao joins a host of predecessors engaged through the centuries in Chinese home industries, spinning and weaving thread, pushing against the limits of economic utility imposed on women by Confucian strictures (illus. 166),[81] together with a host of semi-independent operators, female musicians and courtesans from China's traditional 'entertainment industry' (see illus. 128), hardly appreciated in their own time as economic 'modernists' as they purchased their 'independence' through the oldest institutions of sexual dependency. We might imagine that the question for all these women, as for Mrs Xiang, was how does increased economic independence affect their lives as women and wives?

It is only when she discovers her bond with another woman, Huan-huan – or rather their shared bondage – that the toughest question of the film is planted: which should come first, economic or social liberation? Should women transcend their gender identity, or should they stop to help each other? Unspoken but projected throughout this film is the fact that traditional Chinese women's *un*liberation has been built on centuries of female complicity – mothers binding daughters' feet, mothers-in-law dominating their daughters-in-law in order to compensate for their own years of servitude and to assure the patriarchal succession. Significantly, the daughter-in-law Huanhuan's name refers to encirclement and can be thought of equally in terms of being entrapped by the mother and son – that is, by a male–female collusion – and as the linkage of female victims from one generation to the next. How each generation of women helps to replicate the tyranny which they themselves have suffered lies at the heart of this exploration. Mrs Xiang herself, as she confesses to her Japanese counterpart, was sold to her in-laws at the age of seven and nearly committed suicide early in her own marriage. Only her mother-in-law's counsel of patience saved her – so that she might now pass on this miserable legacy to her own daughter-in-law. This film ends with no answer to the question, will economic liberation bring women's liberation or will it just turn women into men?

Like the other films discussed here, *Scented Souls* is both about women *and* about China, and in this case about the tension between China's economic fate and its troubled social condition. The contrasting economic status of Xiang Lake's historic female suicides, one rich, one poor, suggests gender rather than class as the dominant factor in determining the fate of women, though poverty obviously lends a hand. The fact that the details of these suicides remain undisclosed and shrouded in myth is a testament to the deep internalization of female suffering and to how well-protected patriarchal control remains. And while contrasted to this, Mrs Xiang's economic success and her gendered failures are in numerous ways directly linked.

At the same time as Mrs Xiang discovers modern manufacturing with the help of Japanese patrons, she discovers that in modern countries like Japan, extra-marital affairs like her own are more or less commonplace and discreetly accepted, rather than deep, dark and fearful secrets like her own. On finding out that her Japanese patron, Miss Shinyo Sadako, is both employee and (scarcely disguised) mistress to her boss,

166 Attrib. Liang Kai, *Sericulture*, Southern Song dynasty, early 13th century, section from a handscroll, ink and colour on paper. Cleveland Museum of Art (John L. Severance Fund).

her initial response is to seize that kind of sexual 'liberty' for herself – she immediately goes to phone her own Mr Ren. But fatefully, she's stymied at that moment by his absence. And by the next time they tryst, she has come to question whether she's anything more than his sexual plaything: 'You've taken me for your concubine indeed!' Xiang Ersao has discovered, it would seem, that she may be an economic 'modern' and an effective manipulator in the public realm, but she's been nothing more than exploited in her private life. Socially, she may be but a mere 'primitive' by Japanese standards but what, on the economic stage, is the role of gender? Whether employee, as Miss Sadako is, or employer, as Mrs Xiang is to Mr Ren, both women are just women, socially peripheralized and sexually disadvantaged. The ensuing argument leads, at her next meeting with Mr Ren, to a parting of ways after an affair of more than twenty years. Whether or not she comprehends that her empty, vicious marriage was the stimulus for her illicit affair, her previously impregnable self-confidence is shattered and she is at last forced to contemplate her extension of this abuse to the next generation.

Perhaps she has become more advanced – more 'modern', or perhaps more post-modern – than Miss Sadako by discovering the asymmetry between economic liberation and sexual victimization. But the discovery only marks the beginning of a painful process. Mrs Xiang progresses from emotionally unstrung to physically weakened, just as her greatest business success emerges in the form of an award by the county governor himself. Instead of celebrating, or even managing a diplomatic smile to those congratulating her, in a scene that risks becoming maudlin, she then rows off alone deep into the sesame-growing marsh-lands, if not considering suicide then at least to wail together with the tormented souls of Xiang Lake (illus. 165). Here, like some analogue in shape and season found in the ancient *Odes* or lodged in some old painting, sesame plants in pale autumn yellow, desiccated forms in a desiccated light, thrashed by the autumn wind, resonate with Xiang's own withering emotions. And here *Scented Souls* extends a history of romantic images attached to the lakeshores: the ageing female musician riding the waves in a painted boat, singing a saddened song, with the spectre of drowning never far away (see illus. 128); the courtesan longing for her lover, gazing from an upper storey by the water's edge (illustration 168, a seventeenth-century scroll actually painted by a famous courtesan on just such an occasion); and hosts of paintings about lovers, musicians, courtesans, and prostitutes, coded by some combination of water, moon, willow, and Chinese lute (the *pipa*) (illus. 169).[82] The women in such romantic works, no matter what their actual period, were frequently visualized in the manner of the seventh to ninth centuries, a period now thought of as a historical high-water mark in the relative power-status of Chinese women and whose paintings set a 'classic' standard in defining the mature female figure. That the actress Siqin Gaowa, who looks every bit like a mature lady of the Tang, was chosen for the weighty, matriarchal role in *Scented Souls*, rather than some younger ingénue, credits the film-makers' understanding and respect for this deeply-etched traditional image of the powerful female figure (illus. 157, 170).

Like an Ibsen drama, *Scented Souls* raises questions that only society, not the story itself, can answer. And so it is left unclear just how well Xiang Ersao understands these problems or from just what motivation she seeks to extricate herself from them. Their shared, internalized misery is the tightest bond between women in this film, and its persistence is the mark of their failure to unite in opposition to it. Rather than the outspoken mother directly admitting to complicity in her daughter-in-law's misery, it is the submissive Huanhuan who builds the first bond by acknowledging the mother's suffering. Up to this point, Mrs Xiang has remained the skilled manipulator, though her social fabric has come unravelled with the failure of her relationship with Mr Ren. *Scented Soul's* penultimate scene begins with the return of Huanhuan's original fiancé Jinhai, now travelling down Mrs Xiang's road to economic opportunity, calculating only his financial gain and not his personal loss. He comes bearing presents out of gratitude for all, including one for Huanhuan. Huanhuan is there and isolated glances are exchanged, but the two who might still be in love can no longer speak to each other. One might expect that at that moment, for the first time, it would enter Jinhai's senses just how totally suckered he has been, but he's largely unable to engage that reality. Mrs Xiang expertly dismisses him before he can make anything of it, though not without responding to the pathos of these glances with her own empathic sigh.

But Huanhuan is not so easily dismissed. In this part of the scene, we see the two sides of Mrs Xiang: manipulative and scheming, yet vulnerable and pained by what she is slowly and painfully discovering. Previously when the daughter had learned of her mother-in-law's battles with her husband and his suspicions of her marital infidelity with Mr Ren, Mrs Xiang in a stereotypical mother-in-law way had threatened to 'rip your mouth out' if Huanhuan ever spoke of the matter. Now, as only the two women remain, it is the younger woman who attempts to inspire some mutual understanding, in a process filled with ethical compromises and carried out with subtle detail. Huanhuan raises the subject of marriage to Mrs Xiang in an indirect way, making a request to attend a wedding in the village. Mrs Xiang's slow response leaves time for the audience to question, what replication or permutation of the Chinese marriage pattern will be played out there, for Huanhuan to witness and liken to or contrast with her own marriage? Yet since this wedding is never to be seen in the film, its partners never known, it remains a mirror that can only image Huanhuan's own marriage, held up to the mother-in-law who fashioned it. To Xiang Ersao, perhaps, is also revealed an image of her own wedding to a brutal husband, perhaps even some reflection of her non-marriage to Mr Ren, or an in-depth glimpse of history itself. Out of 'kindness', by her own unkind standard, Ersao responds guardedly, cryptically, to the request, that she will 'take into account' Huanhuan's silence on 'that matter' (in other words, Huanhuan's not having spoken of Xiang's battles with her husband and her tryst with Mr Ren). This may sound callous and crude, but it acknowledges Mrs Xiang's need for help and understanding in her own wreck of a marriage. We never hear Xiang's final answer, but something larger is in the offing. Building towards some mutual dependency and sympathy, daughter offers mother what mother should be able to offer her daughter: 'Mother,' says Huanhuan, 'I know you've been feeling much pain.' On film, as she waits for Xiang's reply to her request, as these words of understanding are spoken and until they sink in, Huanhuan appears backlit as a shadow on a semi-transparent fabric placed between the two women (illus. 167). As her words begin to break down the veil of ancestral tradition that has hung between them, Huanhuan lowers this screen and they are able to see each other in a new light. Earlier, the glances Xiang Ersao had cast toward Huanhuan betrayed some possible growing sensitivity but her tears seemed less for Huanhuan than for herself. It is for Huanhuan, no longer intimidated, to openly first address the other, and as Huanhuan returns to her filial chores (this is community building, not rebellion), Mrs Xiang cranes her neck in that direction. She says nothing but betrays her growing sympathy for the daughter whose misery she has caused.

Like the most critical scenes in the film, this encounter is set against the backdrop of water, that lake of haunted lovers, body of *yin* vitality and victimization which continually gives question to the image: what is woman? what will she be? The questions flow like water. Is matriarchy separable from patriarchy? Can the tragic spell of the lake, of China's past, be broken? The answers might be lodged in the fate of Xiang Ersao's love-child, the daughter Zhi'er – but probably not. Though Ersao (uneducated and largely illiterate) nurtures the hope of providing Zhi'er an education and her real father ('Uncle' Ren) promises the money for it, by the end of the film, Mr Ren is gone and Zhi'er is left with a 'father' whose attitude is clear enough: 'Why do you let Zhi'er go to school,' he grunts. 'She'll be a member of another family. No need to go to school.' Possibly, the problem of women's unity is no smaller than the historical Chinese system of exogamy.

Deng Xiaoping's notion of 'socialism with a Chinese face' implies in a most un-Marxian fashion that the socio-cultural superstructure can be uncoupled from its economic base, that China can undergo a so-called 'second revolution' economically while retaining its traditional 'Chineseness'. The question that *Scented Souls* asks, by way of its female analogy, is not whether China *can* do this (in Marxian terms or otherwise) but whether it *should*. At the same time, while concluding that the social character of China *is* as much in need of a revolution as China's economy, it does not make clear any belief that this *can* be done.

Scented Souls was made in 1992, as three years of harsh censorship gave way to increased cultural liberalization, but the memories and doubts raised by Tian'an Men remained strong and specific. Any film about family suggests a possible analogy to the state and *Scented Souls* is no exception – the state, after all, is modelled on the Chinese family. In Xiang Ersao's family, everyone collaborates to assure its preservation, rulers and ruled alike, male and female, old and young. Just like the state, this family is somewhat dysfunctional but still unified, sometimes cruel in its maintenance of authority and in the pragmatic in the victimization of its own members. By and large, victims within the family are submissive and self-sacrificing, and if need be they are ready to betray one another individually rather than rebel against the collective family authority. Illicit affairs, like subversive thoughts, remain concealed rather than bursting out into the open. Moreover, those outside the family (analogous to China's neighbours) do not become

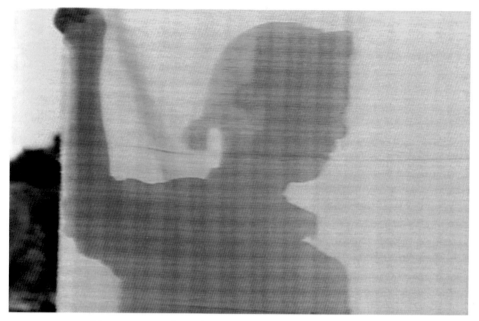

167 *Woman From the Lake of Scented Souls.* Huanhuan, separated from her mother-in-law by a veil of tradition.

involved in internal matters, in Huanhuan's behalf. The marital go-between, Auntie Wu, plays the co-conspirator, aware but tolerant of all the legal and moral abuses concocted by Mrs Xiang at Huanhuan's expense. The villagers see little harm in Dunzi's antics and only laugh off the all-too-visible suggestions of his marital abuse.

But this family greatest problem lies in its troubled patriarchal succession. It is in this behalf that Mrs Xiang has, in the traditional fashion, betrayed her own gender, lining up a good mate for Dunzi, and yet in the end all this proves to be for naught. Dunzi's idiocy hasn't stood in the way of his investiture but he can't produce *the next* generation. It is only when Xiang Ersao accepts this cold reality that she releases Huanhuan from her ties to the family. Whether this failure spells the end of the familial line, one can only speculate, for other alternatives have been pursued – unspoken – throughout the film. A change in the line of succession to assure the preservation of this dynasty has long been pursued by Mrs Xiang's husband. Like old man Yang in *Judou* (illus. 250), he hasn't merely indulged in sex and the abuse of his wife for the sheer pleasure of it; he wants a competent male heir: a replacement for Dunzi. For him, pornography has not been a modern end to narcissistic gratification but a traditional means,

168 Liu Yin, *Misty Willows at the Moon Dike*, 1643, handscroll, ink and colour on paper. Palace Museum, Beijing.

169 Ma Kui, *Leaving the Willow Bank*, early 13th century, fan painting, ink and colour on silk. National Palace Museum, Taipei, Taiwan.

The theme of a scholar-gentleman leaving the 'gay quarters' is indicated exclusively but unmistakably through symbolic visual devices – willow bank, water, and moon – an image common to both poetry and painting.

170 Attrib. Gu Hongzhong, *Night Revels of Minister Han Xizai*, mid-10th century, detail from a handscroll, ink and colour on silk. Palace Museum, Beijing.

The facial features of a Tang-type beauty are as well rounded as her lute. In this famous depiction of lurid partying by high ranking members of the Southern Tang court, the unusual gaze and counter-gaze make clear the lascivious intent. The painting illustrates the ancient Chinese conflation of professional entertainment – music and theatre – with prostitution.

a stimulus to sexual arousal and fruitful procreation. He makes us aware that the violence of this family-state model derives not from perversity, pure and simple, but from the need for family-state preservation and reminds us that this tradition of violence is as much internally directed as it is externally meted out.

Perhaps some political parallels become visible in this. Outbursts of Communist Party violence, like the 'ten chaotic years' of the Cultural Revolution or like that at Tian'an Men, have all been an overflow of violence *within* the Party. Such violence is endemic in family and state alike, made so by the structure of male kinship, by exogamy and the reduced status of wives. The family and the Party analogize each other, and the lingering message of the film is that almost fifty years after 'Liberation', this their behavior has yet to change.

Throughout much of the film, as her husband has harboured one great wish, Mrs Xiang has had one great secret: though she can hardly withhold her body from her husband in his sometimes violent pursuit of a better Dunzi, she can withhold her fertility – by taking the pill (supplied, it is suggested visually, by Mr Ren). So her economic independence has bred a sexual counterpart, freedom from reproduction. She is only superficially available to her husband, her generative energy, like her feminine psyche, buried deep within and far beyond his reach. So far, she has withheld another child from him, and she voices fears of breeding another Dunzi, generating a succession of miscreant males (a voice which makes her husband wonder, is not his one healthy child – a daughter, not a successor – someone else's child). Perhaps, deep down, Ersao even wants to end this patriarchy, once all her efforts to save this male succession through Dunzi's line have come to naught. Yet how far Xiang Ersao has come towards this end of dynastic suicide remains unclear at the end of the film, and any question of what lies ahead lingers on as a haunting uncertainty. Xiang Ersao's reproductive rebellion, discovered by her husband toward the end of the film (illus. 154) but never resolved, could change the entire patriarchal equation.

All the films discussed to this point reveal the diverse treatment of women in the cinema that has come forth with the increased intellectual freedom, and despite continuing intellectual constraints, of recent years. There is no simple view of what woman is or should be, from victim to warrior, representing herself or representing something else, and no singular way of viewing the issue of gender appropriation. Other films and other female leads might have been selected to trace other paths, but films like these continue to refine the definitions and enrich the characterizations of women as they appear in Chinese cinema. That these women can signify so much – that they are analogized and appropriated in so many ways while still retaining a central significance in their own right – results from contemporary cinema's having built on and continuing to develop China's age-old but seemingly ageless rhetorical tradition of women in art and literature.

5 The Force of Labels: Melodrama in the Postmodern Era

Zilu asked, 'If the Prince of Wei called on you to carry out his administration for him, what would you set out to do first?' The Master said, 'It would be the rectification of names [*zheng ming*] . . . If names are not correct, then speech does not accord; if speech does not accord, then affairs cannot be properly carried out; if affairs are not carried out, then rites and music do not flourish, and if these do not flourish then punishments are not just; if punishments are not just, then people have no means whereby to regulate their activities.'
– *The Analects*[1]

The name [*ming*] that can be named is not the eternal name.
– *Daode jing*[2]

In the world of Chinese film, Xie Jin is an unparalleled phenomenon, an institution unto himself. In 1961, his *Red Detachment of Women* won China's first Hundred Flowers award for the most popular feature film, while two decades later his *Legend of Tianyun Mountain* (1980) won the film industry's first Golden Rooster awards for best film, director, script, cinematography, and art design.[3] Six times during the 1980s the most popular film of the year was directed by Xie Jin. In the 1990s, he even formed his own film company, the Xie Jin Hengtong Corporation. In 1997, when the impending death of Deng Xiaoping and the transfer of Hong Kong to mainland jurisdiction led to the tightest restrictions on film production in years, his film *The Opium War* was produced on a monster budget by Chinese standards (a record US\$12,000,000, reportedly with considerable private backing by high public officials), opening to a widespread Chinese release on the date of Hong Kong's return, 1 July.[4] Not shy about his preeminence in a system that is predisposed towards art by committee, Xie Jin has said, 'I am not too uncomfortable with the designation of *auteur*, though other directors don't like it. I choose my own materials, even though I don't write the scripts myself. I pour my feelings, my thoughts, my interpretations into my films.'[5]

In the absence of any clear-cut equivalent to Western genres (the musical, the screwball comedy, the western, science fiction, the horror film, *film noir*, etc.), mainland critics of the 1980s and 90s have frequently described Chinese film in terms of four basic modes: *the propaganda or education film* (a holdover from the Maoist era, somewhat modernized in style and mellowed tone from the fervour and ideological fixity of those years); *the entertainment film* (officially justified in the post-Mao era in terms of reward for the hard-working masses, nonetheless remote from Party principles and officially denounced again in 1989, but still the most common and profitable film genre);[6] *the 'art film'* (antagonistic to the Party, typically engaged in a search for cultural roots and only occasionally 'non-political', most notably attached as an adjective to 'Fifth Generation' film-makers but not simply theirs alone); and *the 'Xie Jin model'* (seen as a synthesis of the first two or sometimes all three of the above).[7]

Born in 1923, Xie Jin is identified in Chinese critical parlance as a 'Third Generation' director. But his films – approximately thirty, dating back to 1951 – stretch across five decades, and a more accurate characterization might be that he rises above generation. In the 1950s and early 60s, working within the framework of propaganda film, Xie Jin managed to make his figures more emotionally powerful, more visually compelling, and more popular than the others. In the post-Cultural Revolution decade, he established a style which seems drawn from all the film-making strands of his generation and woven into a kind of grand synthesis – political criticism cast in entertaining yet patriotic tones – that has proved enormously satisfying to the Chinese

"Now! ... *That* should clear up a few things around here!"

171, 172 Gary Larson, 'Now! . . . That should clear up a few things around here!' and *The Names We Give Dogs*, 1988 and 1991, cartoons. THE FAR SIDE © 1999 FARWORKS, INC. Used by permission. All rights reserved.

The control of labels as the prerogative of those in power is virtually universal, and everywhere subject to ridicule. Here we see the equivalent of Confucian and Daoist attitudes toward 'the rectification of names' set forth in modern dress.

audience. While this 'Xie Jin model' is often critiqued as a combination of two film modes, political films made entertaining, his most supportive critics also credit his cinematic artistry, refusing to cede the territory of 'art film' to 'Fifth Generation' film-makers, who often publicly reject Xie Jin's patriotic melodrama.

However one classifies this complicated director or judges the 'Xie Jin model' (which some critics feel unduly credits one man for the achievements of a whole cinematic generation), the critical term most firmly attached to his cinematic style is 'melodramatic'. Xie Jin himself would not quibble over this. His dramatic flair has certainly kept the Chinese audience on his side. And while melodrama, in China as in the West, is often belittled as artificial and vulgar, unrealistic and unrevealing, it is scarcely lacking of merit or shy a strong theoretic defence. The 'Xie Jin model' in many ways parallels definitions of melodrama and can be characterized as follows. It is more oriented to plot than to character development, more concerned with 'what' than 'how'. Characters are stereotyped and clearly distinguished between good and bad. Dramatic and visual styles are bold, exaggerated but blended with realistic elements to establish their credibility with the audience. Entertainment value is provided out of 'respect' for the 'interests' of the audience. Emotions run high, suspense alternating with relaxation, tensions carefully orchestrated as the struggle between good and evil is played out. The audience, through its emotional engagement, is provided catharsis, for which the film-makers claim high ground as attending to the 'needs' of the people.

In these films, the personality types are matched to socio-political roles, and characters are followed in terms of visible plot but not tracked in terms of psychological development. They are 'hollow' stereotypes, 'concrete' on the outside only, and not so by some crude or cultural neglect of 'personality' but rather by conscious design. This hollowness locates the meaning in the situation and the action, not in the subtleties of individual persona. Rather than ignoring personality, this construct lodges personality less in the characters portrayed and more in the audience. It is left for the audience to fill in the characters' inner lives with their own imagination, to provide personal meaning, to insinuate themselves and establish a personal identification in their own way. The film audience is thereby engaged in 'spiritual' terms and reminded of the 'indefiniteness' of the inner realm. This approach to audience engagement runs through such seemingly disparate visual traditions as the conventionalized painted figures of China's local operatic traditions, the popular puppet theatres whose characters remain but a shadow on the curtain, and the more theatrical modes of figure painting (see illus. 43). As a corollary, 'art films' have been critiqued from a socialist perspective for filling in all too much of the psychological territory of the characters, becoming too definite in their psychological descriptions, and so particularizing their characters as to deny their audience an interactive role. Such 'concreteness' forecloses the audience's potential 'pleasure of being co-film-makers'.[8]

The notion of melodrama, with its long history in the West, begins with etymological roots in Greek drama accompanied by chorus; is given modern form, still sometimes accompanied by dramatic music, on the French theatrical stage in the time of Rousseau, who may be responsible for the term's present usage;[9] and is later manifested in literature, theatre, and film by qualities of sustained emotionality, exaggeration of action and rhetoric, stereotyping of characters and situations, strenuous moral assertion and unambiguous polarization of good and evil, and ideological grounding in collective socio-political economies more than in metaphysical fate (the latter merely contextualizing the former).[10] The appropriateness of the term 'melodrama' to Chinese film has been debated. Despite certain reservations about this appropriateness, mentioned later, I would add the following supportive note here: for 'melodrama', modern Chinese critics simply write 'drama' (ju), not distinguishing drama from melodrama. One might argue that they feel no need to distinguish the two since in the traditional Chinese theatre and in so much of Chinese film, drama is melodrama. In further support of this, the character ju itself has a second reading that means 'acute, severe, intense', and that is certainly an apt description of most Chinese drama. This leads to the questions not only of how Chinese melodrama (if that is what we agree to call it) relates to modern Western form, but also of how contemporary Chinese film melodrama relates to traditional Chinese theatrics.

As for the first of these questions, several primary characteristics recommend the cross-cultural application of the term 'melodrama' to Chinese film, whether of the Republican period, the Maoist era, or the current age of ideological reorientation.

1. **The absence in melodrama of any subtle or ambiguous 'middle ground' in the struggle between good and evil, right and wrong.** From the sharp conflict of heroes and villains in traditional Chinese opera, to the juxtaposition of villains and villainized in Republican period film, to the formal proscription in Maoist aesthetics of the appearance of 'middle characters', the dramatic arts in China have typically reserved little room for moral uncertainty or nuance. The stereotyping of characters and cases in melodrama comports well with an analogical mode of reasoning, based on the matching of clearly understood figure types and moral situations. This also

fits well within the Hegelian mode of historical reference, with its formal regimen of antagonisms, contradictions, and resolutions.

2. **The timeliness of melodrama's social function in China's modern century of unending definition and redefinition of values and goals.** In China, melodrama effectively 'seeks' (in the words of Paul Pickowicz) 'to put an insecure and troubled mass audience in touch with the essential conflict between good and evil that is being played out just below the surface of daily life'[11] in a time of rapidly changing values, just as it did for the post-Revolutionary French bourgeoisie in whose presence modern melodrama took on its classical form.[12]

3. **The ready inscription of melodrama's connotative history on to the Chinese concern with family life.** In Paul Pickowicz's account, 'The petty conflicts of daily family life may seem trivial, the audience is constantly warned, but they are actually a manifestation of profound life-and-death struggles that confront the human community. The melodramatic mode is hostile to realism and naturalism because these modes of representation do not allow the narrative to "break through" to the plane on which moral polarities are visibly at war.'[13] Nick Browne writes that Chinese films are 'almost inevitably' concerned with 'continuity and conflict that turn on the relation among the self, the family, the workplace, and the state', and that 'the most complex and compelling popular film form that embodies the negotiation between the traditional ethical system and the new state ideology [and] articulates the range and force of the emotional contradictions between them' is melodrama.[14] On the Chinese stage and in Chinese film, as in their Western counterparts, the 'interiorization and personalization of what are primarily ideological conflicts' frequently turn on 'the abuse of aristocratic privilege', 'a thoroughly corrupt yet seemingly omnipotent social class (made up of feudal princes and petty state functionaries)', star-crossed lovers and situations of rape and forced marriage, and at least a prefiguration of 'the struggle of a morally and emotionally emancipated bourgeois consciousness against the remnants of feudalism'.[15] Out of the family comes allegory, and to this may be added one further ingredient pervasive in both allegory[16] and melodrama: melancholy.

4. **The timeliness of melodrama as an emergent subject for cultural analysis, particularly in popular culture and third world cultures, contemporaneous with the advent of Chinese film as an academic theme, subjected to all the tools and trends of post-modern inquiry.** As Wimal Dissanayake writes: 'Until very recent times, the term melodrama was used pejoratively to typify inferior works of art that subscribed to an aesthetic of hyperbole, and which were given to sensationalism and the crude manipulation of the audiences' emotions . . . However, the past fifteen years or so has seen a distinct rehabilitation of the term . . . Melodrama is now primarily employed not as a term of derogation or disparagement but as a neutral term that characterizes certain genres of film.'[17] She adds, 'In most Asian

societies melodrama has a distinguished history considerably different from its history in the West and is intimately linked to myth, ritual, religious practices, and ceremonies . . . Although there is no term for melodrama in the classical vocabularies, Asian scholars and critics of cinema are increasingly using this Western term to effect finer discriminations.'[18]

As director, Xie Jin has always been ready and able to apply the skills of the trade to produce a highly emotional response. 'When The *Legend of Tianyun Mountain* was first released,' he says, 'the audience was moved to tears. When the film ended, a lot of spectators didn't rise. They just sat there and wept. The same is true of *Garlands at the Foot of the Mountain*. These films were a means to a necessary release. This is the ideal response to which I aspire. The film which can generate genuine feeling is, to me, the ideal film.' It is 'the response' that Xie Jin aspires to, using a theatrical form that (in Western definition) has traditionally 'refused to understand social change in other than private contexts and emotional terms', with a 'healthy distrust of intellectualization and abstract theory – insisting that other structures of experience (those of suffering, for instance) are more in keeping with reality'.[19] Of these two landmark films, *Tianyun Mountain* (1980) was the first that dared to deal with the still-sensitive injustices of the anti-Rightist movement, while *Garlands* (1983) was the first to deal critically with China's disastrous border war with Vietnam (illus. 173, 174).[20] But as with most Western melodrama, despite the emotional response generated by these films, it can be argued that neither of these films aspired to alleviate the 'ignorance of the properly social and political dimensions of these [events] and their causality'.[21] Instead it could be maintained that – according to the same Chinese socialist aesthetic principles that prefer the stereotype to the psychologically delineated character, fabricating a 'concrete' exterior with a 'hollow' interior – Xie's method provides the opportunity and stimulates the individual members of the audience to engage in their own private discourse and render their own silent verdicts on these matters. Of this semi-transgressive phenomenon – individual verdicts privately rendered but not pronounced in public – more will be said later. Xie certainly knows his Chinese audience, and while he may not offer as much pure escape as today's entertainment films do, in most of his films his dramatic skills provide a cathartic release for deeply-lodged emotional wounds. 'I like my films to touch my audience, to cause an emotional impact . . . By their nature, my films represent a reflection of what I, as a film artist, have seen, known, understood, assimilated, and subsequently described. That is a part of my function. I have an obligation to my audience that I must respect.'[22]

173 *Legend of Tianyun Mountain.* Song Wei, in the foreground, confronts her husband, a high Party official, having discovered his corrupt opportunism in politically destroying her original fiancé in order to seize her for himself.

174 *Garlands at the Foot of the Mountain.* Soldiers turn angrily as they hear that their fallen colleague will be denied burial honours for a technical infraction of military code.

Longer ago than many of today's film-makers can first remember, Xie Jin was busy producing government propaganda in a film era whose greatest product was wooden art (*Accusation*, 1951; *Woman Basketball Player No. 5*, 1957). *Red Detachment of Women* (1960) and *Stage Sisters* (1964) are among his best-known works from the pre-Cultural-Revolution years; the former became China's first Hundred Flowers award film but *Stage Sisters* was severely criticized during the early years of the Cultural Revolution – characters and environment, it was suggested, rather than class and class struggle, had dictated the plot – and Xie Jin was badly persecuted, making no more films until nine years later when he filmed Jiang Qing's model opera *On the Docks* with Xie Tieli. Following his return to film direction in a somewhat freer era, his negative experience of the Cultural Revolution provided Xie the personal motivation and the emotional ammunition for much of his melodrama. Xie himself writes,

My films at their best are melancholic. They reflect the painful experience the Chinese people went through over the past ten or twenty years. It's because of what happened then that there is an implicit sadness about all recent Chinese films. These films are all reflections of that terrible period . . . The time of the ten chaotic years is difficult to clarify because this was such a rare experience. People of other countries have never experienced a 'cultural revolution,' the kind of experience we have gone through here. It's rare. I would add this, too: If there will ever be a 'Shakespeare' in China, he is going to emerge from works about this era.[23]

In a culture dominated by Party, nearly everything Chinese becomes tinged with politics both in content and style. Yet after China's overdose of cultural confrontation under Mao and Jiang Qing, even Xie came to look on this as a burden. 'The most serious problem Chinese film has to overcome,' he has said, 'is its political purposes, the politically heavy messages it is forced to carry, and its formulation . . . I am not concerned with politics.'[24] Of course, whatever his claims, Xie remains an establishment figure at the pinnacle of the film industry, a wholly political creature, and his films remain densely political: *The Legend of Tianyun Mountain*, about the failure to rehabilitate a loyal Party member wrongly denounced in the anti-Rightist campaign, two hours and seven minutes saturated with ideological dialogue; *Garlands at the Foot of the Mountain*, laying China's Vietnam débâcle at the foot of privilege and favouritism in the upper ranks of the People's Liberation Army; and *Hibiscus Town* (1986), about the abuses and distortions of socialist values during the Cultural Revolution and, at the same time, an economic polemic in behalf of individual entrepreneurship (illus. 175).

As much as anything else, it is the heavy political load of these films that has prevented their reaching an American audience. Xie Jin's professed lack of political 'concern', however, must not be read as some disingenuous claim of political disinterest *per se*, but rather as an active interest in ending the succession of factional, fratricidal political movements that have intruded upon, abused and disrupted socialist culture and cultural production since the mid-1950s. Xie's interest lies in assuring that there *is* such a thing in socialist China as a 'private' domain and the establishment of individual rights. A master propagandist, Xie Jin has mastered the skill of staking out a carefully measured distance

175 *Hibiscus Town.*
Ideologue Li Guoxiang
(right) sets the trap
for the industrious
Hu Yuyin.

from the Party line and from the government policies that support him.

For Xie Jin, disavowing politics (meaning *abusive* politics) is intended also to disavow old-fashioned political styles (meaning *clumsy* propaganda). In China, he says,

characters are too often stereotypes and the plots are formulas . . . [In the United States, in the early 1980s,] I saw several films which I thought were heavily political, but the difference is in how the political message was being conveyed, explicitly or implicitly. I think you should hide the political message behind rich portrayals of characters and an interesting story. The political message should be wrapped up.[25]

Abuse may be opposed and clumsiness may be rejected in his films. But the politics and propaganda remain; and so, too, does melodrama, the form in which his message comes wrapped. Ironically, while much has been made of the 'Fifth Generation's' rejection of Party mythology and its abandonment of Party-sponsored styles, beginning with *One and Eight* and *Yellow Earth* in 1984, it was Xie Jin's melodramatic *Tianyun Mountain* and *Garlands at the Foot of the Mountain* that initiated the cinematic critiques first of the Party and then of the PLA. And yet, for most critics, Xie remains an establishment figure and his films remain establishment films. For all the social complexity of Xie Jin's films, their dense cinematic texture and emotional range,[26] many critics disapprove Xie Jin's 'cater[ing] to audience desires',[27] his melodramatic appeal through sentimentality which satisfies rather than challenges and disturbs. Ironically, his most severe critics are as much in disagreement with each other as they are with Xie Jin himself. Possibly, the degree to which they seem to contradict not only each other but even their *own* assertions may stem, unseen, from internal contradictions hidden within Xie Jin's own work, or between Xie's ideology and the style of his works.

Paul Pickowicz has observed the frankness of Xie Jin's political criticism and his aim at virtually sacrosanct targets:

Whereas most scar literature dwelled on the abuses people suffered during the Cultural Revolution and heaped blame on the Gang of Four for the sorry condition of China in the late 1970s, *The Legend of Tianyun Mountain* said almost nothing about the Cultural Revolution. The underlying assumption of the film was that the difficulties that continued to plague China in the 1980s had their origins in the 1950s, especially during the time of the anti-Rightist movement of 1957 . . . The film complained that those who stressed the destructiveness of the Gang of Four were missing the point.[28]

And yet, despite his highly visible critique of mass movements engineered by Mao and Deng,[29] critics have repeatedly depicted Xie as lacking in courage and political direction, pursuing his own popularity and a formalist art instead. For example, the critic Li Jie:

Xie Jin is a rare and talented director. We are sorry to see that for various reasons, both subjective and objective, his talent has been brought lopsidedly into play, and a kind of psychological structure we call Xie Jin's model has been formulated. This model, unfortunately, cannot be characterized as a specific artistic style, but rather a model that panders to all kinds of tastes. Whenever we view Xie Jin's films, we feel uneasy, for we realize that this talented director nods from behind his screen in whatever direction will gain enthusiastic albeit blind cheers and applause. Such pandering tells us that Xie Jin's film-making is more a process in which he caters to audience desires than one in which he makes artistic explorations.[30]

For Shao Mujun, such 'pandering' and 'catering' is understood in pragmatic terms as necessary caution. Shao counts Xie Jin more cunning than bold, linking him to 'Fifth Generation' film-makers by their mutual recognition of the limits on artistic freedom and their response to political realities by indirect and referential means:

The following might be thought an unusual opinion, but in a certain sense, the film which established the basic pattern for New Chinese Cinema was Xie Jin's *The Legend of Tianyun Mountain* . . . *Tianyun Mountain* can be regarded as a model for New Chinese Cinema because, first, it strenuously avoids crossing the dividing line between what may and what may not be permitted; and second, given that precondition, it presents certain non-political ideas (either moral or cultural) as a protective screen.[31]

Of course, Shao was aware of *Tianyun Mountain*'s being banned for a time precisely for its 'crossing the dividing line', so that what is important here – and peculiar – is his inability to credit Xie, and Xie's melodramatic form, with the degree of boldness attributed by others to 'Fifth Generation' film and film-makers.

Xie Jin's values embrace a partial reversion to pre-Revolutionary values, seeking some common ground on which traditional values and socialist ideology can arrive at an accommodation. It is this pursuit of a middle ground, of a more benign socialism, through an artistic form that traditionally has no middle ground, which has opened him to criticism from both left and right, even making it hard to tell sometimes which direction is which. In 1986, as the initial achievements of the 'Fifth Generation' film-makers were first becoming apparent, and as Xie Jin was about to release *Hibiscus Town*, he was targeted as a backwards-looking 'Confucianist' in Shanghai's propagandist cultural journal *Wenhui Bao*. At what appeared to be the possible onset of a new ideological campaign, Zhu Dake wrote:

As in any models of popular culture, the moral code of Xie Jin is always arranged in a regular pattern. 'The good wronged,' 'the discovery of values,' 'morality changed by persuasion,' and 'the ultimate triumph of good over evil' are the four principal topics . . . The symbol of Xie Jin's *Ru* [Confucian] principle is his representation of women. They are amiable, kind, industrious, and [therefore, critically] intolerable. They follow 'the three obediences and the four virtues' and are fully self-sacrificing. Their characteristics, the accumulation of standard images of women from the old days, are nothing other than the products of a patriarchal culture. Women, entirely dependent upon men, are used to discover and approve male values and to make men happy. Those small houses and yards filled with local color silently reveal the willful longing for the agrarian life in which men plough the fields and women sew the clothes. The comfortable family of the Middle Ages is the highest stage of human happiness. Consequently, the destruction of the family is the ultimate tragedy.[32]

In this, Zhu Dake equates Xie's melodrama with conservatism, patriarchy, and Confucian feudalism. But Zhu's argument is weakened by the fact that all three female leads in *Tianyun Mountain*, far from sewing clothes, were professionals, activists, and ultimately defied both political and marital authority to defend their personal perceptions of moral rectitude.

It has been suggested that Zhu Dake's *Wenhui bao* article represented an attack from the left, the author serving as a surrogate for the Party against an all too popular film director who had gone too far before and who it was feared was about to do so again in his forthcoming filming of the novel, *Hibiscus Town*.[33] If so, it would be ironic that Xie was charged by 'the left' for using those very tools and values that Party propaganda was historically wedded to: 'the good wronged', 'morality changed by persuasion', the 'triumph of good over evil'. These, of course, are the cornerstones of socialist realist melodrama. Zhu Dake didn't stop there in his assault on melodrama, writing that 'Anyone with a bit of common sense will quickly discover that these obsolete aesthetic ethics designed to manipulate emotions have much in common with the dissemination of religion in the Middle Ages . . . Xie Jin provides his audience with a magnificent moral fairy tale in which all social contradictions are resolved.'[34]

Although sufficient motivation for an attack on Xie Jin could be found on the left, Xie Jin's opposition lay all around, and indeed the design of Zhu Dake's critique seems to point in other directions. On top of the short-lived *Wenhui bao* affair came the 'New Cinema's' frontal rejection of Xie Jin's model, the subject of the final essay in this book. In Paul Pickowicz's accounting,

To use the words of Shao Mujun, [Xie's films] 'arouse emotions.' But it is exactly for this reason that Xie Jin has been attacked so vigorously by younger film-makers who insist that it is time to move beyond sensational, melodramatic representation.[35]

Moreover, a number Western film scholars with their own critical agendas seem also to have arrived at a similar rejection of Xie Jin's popular melodrama. Pickowicz, speaking for himself, writes disparagingly of (Xie's) melodrama:

Life is just not as simple as it appears in Xie Jin's films. One does not learn much about how the system 'really' works by viewing films like *Hibiscus Town* . . . The melodramatic mode provides easy and comforting answers to difficult and complex questions. It offers moral clarity at a time when nothing seems clear. But by personalizing evil, the film leaves the impression that everything would be fine if only the 'evil' people were removed from power and replaced by people of 'virtue' . . . The problem with Xie Jin's popular melodramas is that they are hostages of a genre that severely limits the imagination.[36]

Whose imagination is limited, Pickowicz does not say, nor does he acknowledge that to 'personalize' with historical examples is the age-old Chinese means of providing moral and political instruction (see illus. 103). Neither does Pickowicz deal with Xie Jin's numerous departures from melodramatic norms, sometimes leaving crises unresolved (as most melodrama tends *not* to do), sometimes leaving evil powers in place, and frequently tempering heroic drama with a dash of bitter realism. At the same time, far from denying the power of Xie Jin's melodramas with the Chinese audience, Pickowicz acknowledges that it is Xie Jin's mastery of the melodramatic form that breeds the fear of him by illiberal elements in the Party:

The young film-makers are interested in subtlety, nuance, and ambiguity, and this is why Western scholars are attracted by their works. Xie Jin is interested in the confrontation between clear moral absolutes. Western observers prefer Fifth Generation directors, but the undeniable fact is that they have practically no audience in China. That is why the authorities never felt politically threatened by them. Xie Jin, the veteran melodramatist who sees the Chinese world in basic Manichaean terms of darkness and light, is the one who has the audience . . . It is for this reason that Xie Jin, a veteran party member himself, is so disliked and distrusted by such Party elders as Deng Liqun and Hu Qiaomu.[37]

All told, while Xie Jin's cinematic eclecticism has pleased a large Chinese audience, it seems to have pleased few critics, East or West, who distrust Xie's popular success and want his artistry justified by some courtship of the unpopular, who want to see him become more artistically 'challenging', each critic tugging this celebrity artist in a different direction. The 'Fifth Generation', rejecting the emotional 'excess' of his works, remains unimpressed by Xie Jin's measured departure from the standard structures and the bright outcomes required of socialist melodrama. And they are unimpressed by Xie's criticism of the army and the government in films like *Garlands at the Foot of the Mountain* and *Hibiscus Town* because they remain unsympathetic to the moderate ideology of these films. Xie's willingness to accommodate the present regime seems to rankle many writers, just as his challenges to this regime must have rankled Party cadres. Unable to agree on a common point of assault on his politics, what many of Xie Jin's politically diverse critics *have* agreed on as a common target is his particular brand of melodrama. The more popular the Xie Jin model became with the public, the more vocal was the rejection of his 'melodrama' by various sectors of his critics. 'I don't feel comfortable with melodrama,' Chen Kaige has said, 'because I don't like emotional excess. I could never make a film like Xie Jin's *Hibiscus Town* . . .'[38]

Evaluating this, we find ourself in the clutches of history, looking back over various distinct moments in the definition and redefinition of melodrama, at the inconsistencies of its aesthetic embrace or disdainful rejection by critics, at modulations in the handling of its formal structure, at questions about its uncertain cultural domain. One of the signifying features that will take on critical importance here is that of melodramatic resolution: the denouement. With French theatre as his model, Peter Brooks asserts that one of the necessities of melodrama is its 'final reward of virtue':

Melodrama is less directly interested in the reassertion of the numinous for its own sake than in its ethical corollaries. Melodrama starts from and expresses the anxiety brought by a frightening new world in which the traditional patterns of moral order no longer provide the necessary social glue. It plays out the force of that anxiety with the apparent triumph of villainy, and it dissipates it with the eventual victory of virtue.[39]

This is the 'classic' Western model, which accords as well with the socialist model. In this incarnation,

Evil will first be articulated and recognized, then the sign of virtue will begin to overcome its repression. By the end of the play, desire has achieved its satisfaction. No shadow dwells, and the universe bathes in the full, bright lighting of moral manichaeism.[40]

On the other hand, in contrast to this set order, Thomas Elsaesser suggests the possibility of charting an intellectual history through the changing features of melodramatic rupture and resolution:

. . . there seems a radical ambiguity attached to the melodrama, which holds even more for the film melodrama. Depending on whether the emphasis fell on the odyssey of suffering or the happy ending, on the place and context of rupture . . . that is to say, depending on what dramatic mileage was got out of the heroine's perils before the ending . . . melodrama would appear to function either subversively or as escapism – categories that are always relative to the given historical and social context.[41]

Relatively, then, he proceeds to generalize about these melodramatic parameters according to time and place. 'Whereas [in France] the pre-revolutionary melodramas had often ended tragically, those of the Restoration had happy endings; they reconciled the suffering individual to his or her social position by affirming an "open" society where everything was possible.'[42] Similarly, America's young and optimistic democracy favoured 'virtue triumphant', some positive turn-of-fate inevitably emerging to allow for a more secular resolution of crisis in the here-and-now. But in Catholic countries such as Spain and Mexico, a more pessimistic impulse generated instead sublimated 'themes of atonement and redemption'.[43]

Thus, the question of affirming or denying the applicability of 'melo-drama' by some set standard may be elevated into a contextualized evaluation of its varied character, and reception, over time and place and across internal cultural boundaries. In China, most Republican period films (like so much of the May Fourth literature it was indebted to) indulged deeply in melodramatic modes of emotionality, characterization and visuality while remaining essentially pessimistic, unsuccessful in their resolution of crises, naming the enemy but failing to pose any adequate device for his overthrow and leaving it uncertain whether he would ever be vanquished. Lacking the common but (arguably) not mandatory ingredient of a happy ending – innocence persecuted *but what?* virtue rewarded? – protagonists (and audiences) were driven towards a projected future resolution, if any at all, or if not, then towards a spiritual salvation. In contrast to the salvation-through-happy-coincidence of a Chinese film like *String of Pearls* (1934), borrowed from Guy de Maupassant's short story *The Necklace*, the pessimism and melancholic irresolution of Chinese 'family melo-dramas' like *Plunder of Peach and Plum* (1934), *The Goddess* (1934), and *Street Angel* (1937) attached most Republican period film to grim endings that reflected and sublimated rather than reformed their actual place and time.

The alienation of such 'left-liberal' films from the 'modernity' of their day contrasts this May Fourth film era with the later polemical certitudes of Maoist melodrama, produced in the heyday of Maoist modernism, in the 1950s, 60s, and early 70s, by China's centrally controlled, socially progressive film industry. With Hegelianism to rationalize an economy of optimism and Maoism to fiercely enforce it, the intensity of struggle was itself sufficient to valorize a Communist aesthetic rooted in modern melodrama, home grown under the name of 'revolutionary romanticism'. As Mao Zedong proclaimed at Yan'an in 1942,

... the people are not satisfied with life alone and demand literature and art as well. Why? Because, while both are beautiful, life as reflected in works of literature and art can and ought to be on a higher plane, more intense, more concentrated ... nearer the ideal, and therefore more univer-sal than actual everyday life. Revolutionary literature and art should create a variety of characters out of real life and help the masses to propel history forward.[44]

To deprive the masses of the positive resolution they are capable of and deserve was branded as 'oppositional'. Writing of France in terms that describes Mao's China just as well, Peter Brooks has described revolution *as* melodrama –

The Revolution attempts to sacralize law itself, the Republic as the institu-tion of morality. Yet it necessarily produces melodrama instead, incessant struggle against enemies, without and within, branded as villains, suborners of morality, who must be confronted and expunged, over and over, to assure the triumph of virtue.[45]

– and melodrama as revolutionary –

We may now advance the hypothesis that melodramatic rhetoric, and the whole expressive enterprise of the genre, represents a victory over repres-sion. We could conceive this repression as simultaneously social, psychological, historical, and conventional: what could not be said on an earlier stage, nor still on a 'nobler' stage, nor within the codes of society. The melodramatic utterance breaks through everything that constitutes the 'reality principle', all its censorships, accommodations, tonings-down. Desire cries aloud its language in identification with full states of being.[46]

The logic of this, which Xie Jin and others would come to deal with, is that in the theatre of politics, the melodramatic nature of revolution must eventually turn melodrama *against* the revolution, once the revolutionaries are seated on the old throne. In other words, the goals and the methods of melodrama must eventually collide.

The principles of Maoist melodrama received their own 'classic' formulation as the 'Principle of the Three Stresses' by Jiang Qing, failed Shanghai actress turned Chinese culture czar in the Cultural Revolution –

Of all the characters, stress the positive ones. Of the positive characters, stress the heroic ones. Of the main [heroic] characters, stress the central one.[47]

By Jiang's definition, socialist melodrama became reductionist in form, heroic in orientation, thin in psychological characterization, happy in resolution, and in most regards closer to 'classic' French melodrama than to the standard of 'melodrama' in either China's earlier (May Fourth) or later (post-Mao) film eras. No middle characters here to blur the lines, no irresolute endings to confuse and depress the audience.[48]

176 *Hibiscus Town*. Beautiful Yuyin, the flower of Hibiscus Town, cleans house in preparation for Li Guoxiang's visit.

Maoist drama, by intent, was also close to popular Chinese opera, its conventionalized acting styles, its emphasis on acting technique rather than subtle individuation, its bold sound and colour, its emotional passion and larger-than-life heroes and villains, its epic battles-to-the-finish, and its sure (if not always bright) outcome.

But still more recently, with the decline of Maoism and the advent of a cynical 'postsocialism', the heroic fixtures and bright resolution provided by many Maoist melodramatic narratives have been challenged by an increasingly diverse audience, seen by some as artificial and holding little sway unless formally divorced from reality and couched as pure entertainment. Today, indeed, almost *any* kind of clear-cut resolution may seem to lack credibility. Indeed, looking back on twentieth-century Chinese history, is there anything more visible than the perplexing zigzag line of unending political reversals? History has been anything but clear. And so, for Xie Jin the melodramatist, history may prove to be unkind. What critics – Chinese and Western alike – seem most to expect of him (perhaps by the prompting of his own synthetic realist-melodramatic/political-entertainment mode) is a consistency between style and content, and clarity in the end. If he doesn't provide these, then what kind of melodrama is that? And yet, if he does provide them, how can he be believed?

At this juncture, some greater specificity would be helpful and the film *Hibiscus Town* is selected here to provide the viewing material. Filmed in 1986, it is the one Xie Jin film that seems best to hold a place *within* the ranks of the 'New Chinese Cinema' (alongside Zhang Yimou to be most specific, for reasons that will become clear) in the view of some Western critics. What I believe in the end one can see in *Hibiscus Town*'s dramatic strategy is a fine cut, an attempt to negotiate a successful solution to Xie's no-win situation of melodrama in an age of cynicism – namely a cinematic effort to remain true to melodramatic form by providing something of a bright ending, and yet one shaded toward reality by surrounding clouds. For the sake of what politically might be labelled a more 'humane' resolution – victory *not* bought at the price of vengeance, something learned from his own harsh Cultural Revolution experience – he does not provide a pure or cathartic conclusion through either the triumph or the vanquishing of evil. Unvanquished, unresolved, the lingering threat to the 'happy' situation established at the end of the film remains like a spectre hovering over it: the audience's catharsis is put on hold. In the fight of good citizens against nearly supernatural powers, *Hibiscus Town*'s evil forces seem to withdraw for reasons of their own, leaving the stage set for a sequel, rather like America's 1950s B-grade science-fiction movies that warned the audience at the end to 'look to the skies' and sent them skittering away nervously. It might be said that this irresolution derives not from formula but from reality, that this director has produced a more 'realistic' melodrama, a more compelling work of art for a less gullible era; perhaps this is how he has earned his enormous audience, irrespective of critical, theoretical and academic reservations about his art. Alternatively, it might be argued that he has compromised – compromised artistic form in order to safeguard political content – and melodrama is not an art of compromise. Even if Xie's model is viewed as 'realistic melodrama', how can Xie's new 'realism' avoid eroding the credibility of his melodrama? By exposing political theatricality as fraudulent, Xie Jin has (perhaps inadvertently, yet inescapably) problematized the validity of his own melodramatic means.

At the same time as one sees Xie Jin's *Hibiscus Town* awarded the Hundred Flowers Award as the most popular film of 1986 and winning the Golden Rooster for best film, best actress, and best supporting actor by the leaders of China's film industry, one can sense the old master Xie behind the scenes somewhat defensively responding to the emergent 'Fifth Generation' style, adjusting his work to accommodate a rapidly changing film era, turning to new sources to retain or reclaim leadership within it. The film is based on the novel by Gu Hua, so much of what follows in the discussion under the name of Xie Jin refers as well to Gu Hua.

Gu Hua, the son of a Hunan landlord executed soon after the Communist revolution, was a wholly unknown writer in 1981 when this first major work by him caused a 'furor' but wound up sharing the first Mao Dun writing award with five other novels.[49] The novel is focused on people and events known to Gu Hua personally and written with needle-sharp characterizations, but as the author confesses, these figures still retain the stereotypical qualities required of melodramatic form.[50] For scripting of the film, Xie Jin collaborated with the new and noteworthy Ah Cheng, a younger-generation writer whose short story trilogy, *Three Kings*, generated a bout of 'Ah Cheng fever' in Chinese literary circles during much of 1985 and one story of which, *King of the Children*, was filmed in 1986–7 by Ah Cheng's close friend Chen Kaige (discussed in the next essay).[51]

The story of *Hibiscus Town* is centred on Hu Yuyin, a pretty, popular, and industrious young woman, performed by film star Liu Xiaoqing (illus. 176). Yuyin merely runs a beancurd stall, but on the strength of her winsome personality, she and her husband have earned and saved enough money to build with their own physical labour the nicest home

177 *Hibiscus Town*. Li Guoxiang, distinctively unattractive.

in town. Politically naïve, she quickly runs afoul of the town's newly arrived manager of state-run stores, Li Guoxiang, transferred from the county's Bureau of Commerce and intent on rooting out bourgeois speculation and profiteering in the free market stalls. A creature of ideological ferocity, Li Guoxiang is unambiguously modelled on Mao Zedong's activist wife, Jiang Qing (illus. 177). Ratcheting up class hatred as the Four Clean-ups Campaign readies China for the bigger campaign ahead, Li Guoxiang is determined to make Hibiscus Town a 'fortress of socialism' and a model for the whole county. Before long, Yuyin is a cog in Li's model. Her husband is hounded to death; she is dispossessed of her business, her house, and her civic status; and she is labelled a 'new rich peasant', a counter-revolutionary, and made to serve the people as the town street-sweep.

Serving as Hu Yuyin's fellow street-cleaner is Qin Shutian – 'Crazy' Qin, he's called – a song-and-dance troupe composer, branded a Rightist in the previous decade for compositions which lamented the role of women but failed to distinguish adequately between their dark feudal past and the bright new socialist period (illus. 178).[52] As time passes, the two outcasts 'discover' each other (illus. 179). Through Qin, the despondent Yuyin learns something about coping with social ostracism and she rediscovers her own humanity. The two become illicit lovers, self-ordained newlyweds, and parents – crimes for which 'Crazy' Qin is sentenced to ten years at hard labour. Finally, in Hibiscus Town as in China, the Cultural Revolution dies of its own excesses – 'the ice was broken, the river of life raced on', as Gu Hua puts it in text.[53] Yet it takes more years still before Yuyin's status and property are restored and 'Crazy Qin' returns to his woman and their then-eight-year-old son. Of course, not everything is restored to its original order: like many Party members, Li Guoxiang, having risen repeatedly in office (manager of state-run shops, work team leader of the Four Clean-ups Movement, chairman of the people's commune), does not sink back out of sight but ascends to still higher rank (deputy secretary of the county revolutionary committee). Nor is there any assurance that the cycle of history won't turn again. Li Guoxiang has a lackey whom she has made into the town mayor and taken as her own illicit lover, Wang Qiushe (whose name the townspeople rhyme as 'Autumn Snake'). In the last scene of the film, Wang is shown having gone quite mad, marching through the town with a gong and announcing the next political movement (illus. 180). He is dismissed as 'crazy' by none other than 'Crazy' Qin, but then the fact that mass movements are shown to be crazy does not assure their elimination.

Among the central features of *Hibiscus Town* is its critique of socialist rhetoric – political melodrama – and of the controlling force of labels. From the start, Li Guoxiang is the label master. As in the 'classic'

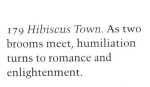

178 *Hibiscus Town.* 'Crazy' Qin, less crazy than the world around him.

179 *Hibiscus Town.* As two brooms meet, humiliation turns to romance and enlightenment.

180 *Hibiscus Town*. While Qin Shutian and Hu Yuyin stand protectively by their child, 'Autumn Snake' Wang crazily proclaims 'another movement'.

Western melodramatic formula, her skills are wickedly plied to misrepresent, discredit, silence, and bury her opponents alive.[54] Qin Shutian is the chief representative here of the Five Categories of Bad Elements (landlords, rich peasants, counter-revolutionaries, bad characters, and rightists). At the first mass meeting after her arrival, Li marches 'Bourgeois Rightist' Qin up on to the stage, baiting the townspeople and particularly their installed authorities, 'He's a class enemy, but do you hate him?' (illus. 181) As a former composer and one of the most literate folks in town, Qin has been assigned to decorate the local walls with revolutionary slogans – producing the visual labelling of Hibiscus Town as a good village, which one might well take as a suitable means for the reeducation of this 'bad element'. But at the meeting, Li turns this on its head as a means of ousting the local Party officials: 'This class enemy has gained control of the propaganda apparatus,' she proclaims. 'All the revolutionary slogans are in the hand of this Reactionary Rightist.' She asks, 'Qin, who gave you this glorious task?' to which his necessary reply is 'The authorities' (see illus. 178). With no basis in substance but simply a mastery of labels and impeccable revolutionary methodology, Li transforms the authorities into 'class enemies'. There is no resisting: when Qin himself is at first confounded by her ideologic and hesitatingly responds, 'Glorious task?', Li Guoxiang replies, 'Stammering is a sign of falsehood.' Indeed, a correct political stand allows no room for improper language or uncertain positions. 'Which side are you on?' she asks the authorities, eliminating all subtlety and leaving no middle ground.

By this point in the narrative, we've already seen that Qin Shutian also wrote couplets for the doorway of Hu Yuyin's newly built home ('A hardworking couple getting rich through socialism'), which is bound to spell future trouble. In the book when Li Guoxiang treats this home as an 'attack on the people's commune's collective economy', she counsels the mostly illiterate villagers, 'Don't underestimate written words, comrades. It's often used by class enemies as a weapon.'[55] And so, though earlier movements have passed through Hibiscus Town, the villagers who had taken no caution from it are finally brought by Li Guoxiang under the spell of labels. This demonic Hell of Labels into which all of Hibiscus Town slides is frighteningly visualized in red and black by Xie Jin's filmed melodrama. From the novel –

The townsfolk had liked to be neighbourly and treat each other to snacks, but now that bourgeois humanism was under fire, they pricked up their ears and strained their eyes to keep close watch on each other. Whereas their motto had been 'each for all and all for each,' they were now on their guard against everybody else. Besides, class alignments had been clarified. After countless meetings large and small and various political line-ups, it was clear to all that hired hands were superior to poor peasants, who were superior to lower-middle peasants, who were superior to middle peasants, who were superior to well-to-do peasants . . . and so everyone was carefully classified. Before squabbling with a neighbor you had to figure out whether his class status was higher or lower than yours. Only reckless teenagers neglected to do this. But after a few beatings-up they learned not to take on people whose parents had a higher social status . . . Grandchildren [paid] for their grandparents' crimes.[56]

The narrative structure of *Hibiscus Town* can be charted through the assigning and struggling over labels – the authority to rectify names. Having used Hu Yuyin as a wedge for her broad assault, the first of the village leaders to be dropped by Li Guoxiang is the widely respected war veteran Gu Yanshan, manager of the state-run granary whom she links to Hu Yuyin's perfidy in becoming 'wealthy'. The moment Li's interrogation of him leads to the charge 'You're a clique' (implicating Gu with Hu Yuyin and Hu's former boyfriend, Mangeng), Gu can only mumble back at the label laid on him, 'A clique!' and drop his head into his hands. To an argument, one can argue back, but the label is a noose. As in China's criminal justice system, where trials are anticlimactic, once the government presents its charge, it doesn't lose its case. There's a moment in the film, as the 'Four Clean-ups' campaign first gives way to the Cultural Revolution, when Li herself is temporarily outflanked by still greater extremists. Like many female victims, she is attacked for her sexual behaviour, made to stand in the rain next to Yuyin and Qin and to wear a necklace of worn slippers (*poxie*), 'shoes for the slut'. For

181 *Hibiscus Town*. Ideological purist Li Guoxiang toys with her subjects like a cat with a mouse. 'He's a class enemy,' she says of Qin Shutian, 'but do you hate him?'

the first time, she's reduced to a state of emotional expression, shedding tears and pleading, 'I can't stand with the Five Bad Elements. I've never been a Rightist . . . I'm a Leftist! I'm a Leftist.' But it does no good. Labels are offensive weapons with little defensive effect, best applied to others. They work best in the hands of ruthless people.

Needless to say, control of the authority to assign labels is jealously guarded and transgressions meet with severe retribution. As a disgraced former official, Gu Yanshan spends one snowy night wandering drunk and despondent through the streets of Hibiscus Town shouting that Li Guoxiang's 'a bitch'. When the comment is overheard and reported, it is instinctively understood as a usurpation of the proletarian dictator-ship's right to assign labels. 'Autumn Snake' Wang describes this to Li Guoxiang as Gu Yanshan 'attacking the movement through you', thus provoking Li's near-automatic reflex, 'We must stop people like him from grabbing power again.' In this melodrama, 'people like him' means all the innocents represented by Hu Yuyin and Qin Shutian. At the same time, the knowledge of Gu's insult is used by Wang Qiushe as a means of repairing his damaged political relationship with Li. In fact, it leads to Li and Wang initiating their own illicit sexual liaison, which turns out to further exacerbate the heroes' predicament. When 'Crazy' Qin accidentally discovers this affair, sweeping the streets one early morning as Wang slips furtively out of Li's window, he indulges in a little unauthorized labelling of his own. The next time Wang drops from Li's window, he lands in a pile of cow manure, swept there by Bad Element Qin to 'shitcoat' the revolutionary cadres for their own indiscretions. In the book, it is in retribution for this specific usurpation of their authority

that Wang and Li respond so viciously when discovering shortly afterwards that Qin and Hu Yuyin, too, have become illicit lovers and are
requesting official sanction for marriage, sending Qin off for ten years'
hard labour and ordering that Yuyin be sexually mutilated.[57]

This playful indiscretion is a costly departure from Qin Shutian's
deeper understanding of the labelling process. 'Crazy' Qin is the only
one in Hibiscus Town with the means to contend with Li's mastery of
terms. His distinctive response is to accept these terms *as terms*, to
embrace them, to manipulate them in a different way than the others
do – that is to say, to recognize their arbitrariness, their inadequacy and
their unreality. He is the first to inform Hu Yuyin that *she* has been
labelled. She's grieving by her husband's grave (illus. 182) when he first
approaches her – since no 'uncrazy' person would be found in a cemetery at night, she withdraws in fear, exclaiming, 'Are you a man or a
ghost?' 'What can I say?' he responds. 'Sometimes a man, sometimes
a ghost' (illus. 183). It's the right answer for one who's still alive but

182, 183 *Hibiscus Town.*
Brought low by radical
politics, and by the camera,
Yuyin lies on the fresh
grave of her young husband
. . . while 'Crazy' Qin looms
high over her like a dark,
disembodied ghost.

treated as less than human, adjusting the label to reality rather than the other way around. More importantly, it registers his awareness of ambiguity, of the difference between labels and reality. Yuyin, condemned in part because she had Qin sing at her wedding and write couplets for the doorway of her home, now puts the blame on him and calls out for vengeance: 'Rightist! Bad element!' Qin, accepting the term, simply responds, '*You're* a New Rich Peasant now.' It's not a label whose logic she can grasp at the moment ('Rich Peasant? A beancurd seller?' she stammers), but the stage is set for Qin to teach her the inner meaning of names. Already we can sense what he's pointing towards: labels work because people *actually* believe them. They are – like the analogical reasoning of which they are a part – a fundamental element in the Chinese ordering of things. But there is, as Qin will demonstrate, an alternative order lodged equally deep within Chinese tradition itself.

It is 'Autumn Snake' Wang who, in denying Yuyin and Qin the right to a legal marriage, provides Qin the opportunity to teach us the central lesson of the film. Qin, making his request, offers Wang the opportunity to apply a humane label to their relationship –

I'm a bachelor. She's a widow . . . We're evil but we're human beings. If we were chickens, pigs, or dogs you couldn't stop us from eating.

But that humanist approach is bound not to work. Wang's classic reply – 'Class enemies screwing on the sly!' – is accompanied by the so-called 'white couplets' he obliges 'Crazy' Qin to hang on both sides of their doorway: one of the five-character couplets reads, *Yige hei fuqi*, 'A black couple'; the other, *Liangge gou nan nü*, a 'Dog and bitch pair'. In one of the telling moments of the film, Qin hangs the couplet with pride, for all to see (illus. 184). Telling the tearful Yuyin not to grieve at this, he explains,

Don't cry. It's a good thing. Sometimes you need a deeper understanding of their meaning. It says a black couple? Who cares if its black or red? It's still a couple. It's announcing to everybody that we're a couple!

There's a patent reference here to Deng Xiaoping's distinctively un-Marxist economic formula: 'It doesn't matter whether the cat is black or white. It only matters if it catches mice.' This pragmatic step down from ideological fundamentalism also enhances the film's practical economic affirmation of individual entrepreneurship, soon to be discussed. But 'Crazy' Qin's deconstruction of labels goes even deeper than that, even farther than the pragmatic Dengists would like, and perhaps this helps to account for why the film was banned for a period

184 *Hibiscus Town*. Turning the tables on the authorities, 'Crazy' Qin happily posts self-denouncing couplets beside his doorway.

before being distributed. As Nick Browne recognizes, the film 'indicates an aspect of the person beyond that of the citizen . . . Economic modernization, to the extent that it includes a cultural redefinition of the sphere of the personal or the private, indicates a future, yet to be realized, of both rights and desires.'[58]

Put in traditional terms, however, 'Crazy' Qin's method is fundamentally an ancient Daoist one that flies in the face of political authority, seizing control of the situation through acceptance, through non-resistance, *wu wei*. In the film, Qin tells Hu Yuyin: 'Cleaning the streets isn't shameful. It's depends on how you do it.' At first, as they sweep alone, it is for her a badge of disgrace. But before too long, their brooms entwine on the pavement and afterwards dance in the streets to a distinctly anti-authoritarian rhythm. In the book, where things are made more explicit, a number of passages like the following define the subjectivity which Qin manages to establish in the midst of his ideological captivity:

One of the Five Categories, the lowest of the low, he was still so cheerful and active, as if he found nothing shameful in being labelled a monster. When publicly paraded, he always led the way boldly. At criticism meetings he flopped down on his knees, hanging his head, before being sworn at, kicked or beaten. When his left ear was boxed, he waited for another box on his right . . . At first Yuyin had thought him contemptible. Later she came to see that he was right, because this way he got off more lightly.[59]

In this way, Qin worked to undermine what dictatorships need most: a credible, fearful enemy – that by which labelling provides its clarification of 'we' and 'they'. Gu Hua's *Hibiscus Town* is explicit in its account of this need for clearly labelled enemies:

The unprecedented 'cultural revolution' saw a huge swing to the Left, and nets had to be spread everywhere to capture the Rightist devils. Documents, reports, endless meetings large and small and frenzied political movements were all to wipe out what was bourgeois and foster what was proletarian . . . If everyone had money and lived better than landlords before Liberation, with plenty to eat every day, who would make revolution? What would happen to the class ranks? Who would the cadres going down to the grassroots rely on? The poor and lower-middle peasants should always remain the majority. If they became rich that would cause complete confusion. China had endless problems, being an ocean of bourgeoisie and petty-bourgeoisie. The key for these problems was to have fierce struggles every few years. This was magnificent and became habit-forming. Yes, struggle was the key, their national treasure.[60]

Labelling in the film *Hibiscus Town* is not only verbal but also intensely visual. Li Guoxiang's given name, which implies 'excessive fervour',[61] is matched in the negative by her image: as in the novel, she's small-breasted, sallow-complected, flaccid-cheeked, grey-dressed, masculinized and painfully unattractive (illus. 177).[62] The chief agent of struggle, and wickedly cunning in her use of dialectics, she's cast in the

185 Anonymous, *Clearing Out the Mountains*, 14th century, section from a handscroll, ink and colour on paper. Palace Museum, Beijing.
The demonization of female beauty, like the feminization of demons, has a long history in China. Beauty is situated as threatening. In this Mongol-period image of clearing evil spirits from the forests, the malevolent forces may at first glance seem to have the upper hand; but many of the demonic-looking creatures have already been harnessed by the forces of good, while the court-type beauties' bestial monkey-feet show them to be demons in disguise.

214

186 *Hibiscus Town*. 'Autumn Snake' Wang is drawn mawkishly to Li Guoxiang, in stark contrast with the heroic propaganda posters in the background.

mould of the revolutionary witch Jiang Qing, combative and shrill. Contrasted with her is the high-breasted, rosy-cheeked, moon-faced, pink-clothed 'Hibiscus Fairy', as the local flower Hu Yuyin is described in both film and book, by nature generous and content to serve. Yuyin's given name, 'Sound of Jade', conveys her purity. And yet even virtue like this can be doubted, victimized, demonized in ways deeply rooted in the historic suspicion of female beauty (illus. 185). The purely melo-dramatic visual contrast between these female arch-rivals parallels the male rivalry between the wise Qin Shutian (Shutian meaning 'A Field of Books') – boyish, sheepish, self-mocking mop-head (performed by Jiang Wen, who soon after would turn into the tough skinhead, the overtly sexual Granddad of *Red Sorghum*) – and Qin Shutian's nemesis, the infantile but cunning, cowardly but bullying 'Autumn Snake' Wang Qiushe.

The moral essence of these two couples – although both are engaged in an illicit sexual union – is nowhere more melodramatically con-trasted than in the way that each of the relationships is first sexualized. 'Autumn Snake' Wang's dalliance with Li Guoxiang began after he had already betrayed her to the Red Guards and after her surprising sudden restoration to power, when he could only creep back into her good graces on her terms. This rapprochement he initiates by snitching on Gu Yanshan, who was reported to have called Li 'a bitch'. Ever the sycophant, Wang has gotten himself a new hairdo for the occasion and slicked him-self up so that he can offer Li Guoxiang a slobbery, tearful confession of his unworthiness, pushing his greased-up hair into Li's flat chest, while the two indulge in the mutual pleasure of her slapping him around repeatedly – all under the watchful gaze of heroic Cultural Revolution posters (illus. 186). At the scene's end, as he kneels at her feet, she informs him that he's forgotten to wash the back of his neck! The banality of the scene is surpassed only by its pathetic sado-masochism, which sexualizes the fundamentally sadistic relationship Li Guoxiang has with all of her political subjects.[63] From black to white: 'Crazy' Qin enters Hu Yuyin's bedchamber not for passion but, chaste, to save her from sickness and starvation. His first romantic gesture, putting hands on her shoulders, comes later, as they watch Wang Qiushe sliding away from *his* romantic tryst with Li Guoxiang. Yuyin modestly rejects Qin's gesture before acceding to it, and this is valorized by comic contrast with the slippery Wang Qiushe as he descends into the heap of manure laid by Qin at the foot of Li Guoxiang's window. There can be little doubt about Gu Hua and Xie Jin jointly exercising a 'masculinist' approach here in contrasting 'Crazy' Qin's spiritual guidance and hesitant romancing of Hu Yuyin with Li Guoxiang's political manipulation and sexually transgressive domination of the 'Autumn Snake'. Li Guoxiang's repulsive sexuality, copulating with Wang at *her own* instigation, calls to mind the ancient Chinese emblem of the northern direction and the winter season, inauspiciously known as the 'Dark Warrior' – old-*yin* symbolized as a snake and a turtle sexually entwined. The film's presentation of her as representative of lower officialdom during the Cultural Revolution has been criticized as melodramatic excess: why couldn't she have been left as a symbol of impeccable, if excessive, ideological fervour? Yet this portrayal has been defended, too. To Gu Hua's English-language translator, Gladys Yang, Li's peculiarities come as a humanizing element, breaking down stereotypes and providing a 'refreshing' look at 'real flesh-and-blood human beings with weaknesses as well as fine qualities'.[64] But in his novel, Gu Hua denies the merits of Li Guoxiang's professional success, attaching it instead to Jiang Qing's deep-seated hatred of men,[65] and establishes the melodramatic contrast between leading ladies, visually defined, that is closely followed by the film. Together, text and film, word and image, work to deny legitimacy to Li Guoxiang so as to negate the social alternative she represents: that is to say, the negation of the Cultural Revolution's goals takes place not through ideological negotiation but through dramatic form. Guoxiang's motivation, which feeds on ideology but originates elsewhere, is a jealous temperament born out of personal lack, for which vengeance is sought of the sexually better-endowed Hu Yuyin.[66] No wonder that in the book Li Guoxiang finally stoops to physical mutilation of her rival: 'Strip the rich peasant woman naked,' she commands as 'Crazy' Qin is marched off to labour camp, 'and wire her breasts!'[67]

Rather than weighing competing ideological claims, *Hibiscus Town* mechanically overdetermines the plotted narrative against Li Guoxiang, creating her clever schemes and her unabashedly mechanical manipulations only to put them on display. And by so focusing the situation in the form of this 'phallic woman' (quoting Nick Browne here), externalizing China's social wrongs, isolating it *outside* the villagers as represented by their fragrant, feminine Hu Yuyin, it may be said that *Hibiscus Town* has managed to criticize the Cultural Revolution as the work of a mere faction, misguided by personal motives, while protecting the Party and the people from excessive blame, much like Deng Xiaoping's strategy upon becoming Mao's successor.[68]

All this is pure melodrama. Had Xie Jin wished to produce instead tragic historical drama of 'Shakespearean' proportions,[69] he would have had to engage in Li Guoxiang a more complex personality, drawing perhaps on a less easily caricatured persona than Jiang Qing, and considering instead the positive qualities of Mao himself and Mao's compounding in one person such capacity for leadership and depth of venality as resist any easy understanding. Then too, the dramatic form would demand that Xie Jin lodge in Li Guoxiang some well-considered self-awareness of her own flaws, so that facing such a dramatic mirror, Xie Jin's audience would have to confront in themselves the comingling of lofty aspirations with their culpability in propagating Mao's violently failed vision in China's 'ten chaotic years'. Nonetheless, like Li Guoxiang's own dramatics, *Hibiscus Town*'s succeeds extremely well as theatre.

To achieve the dramatic visual intensity of *Hibiscus Town*, spatial realization, camera techniques (by cinematographer Lu Junfu) and lighting are all intensely manipulated. For the most part, spaces are darkened, sometimes crowded and cramped, sometimes ominously empty, using claustrophobia and isolation to heighten the feeling of paranoia (illus. 187). A feeling is created of being trapped in a predator's lair with no avenue of escape. The camerawork creates and recreates this feeling in one situation after another. The villagers at the first public meeting are viewed through Li Guoxiang's legs, dwarfed beneath her, while she seems almost literally to be 'walking over them' and they in turn look up at her like mice caught between the legs of a cat (see illus. 181). In a film focused upon opposition, as in Yuyin's first encounter with Li Guoxiang, rather than using shot-countershot camerawork, many scenes are presented with long, steady camera shots that freeze the rivals in framed, inescapable confrontation (see illus. 175). These display the predator's masochistic pleasure in toying with the victim, as the cat toys endlessly with the mouse to savour the full measure of its authority. In such cases, the still frame closely resembles many traditional tableaux of such personal encounters (see illus. 31). Before long, when Hu Yuyin first discovers how low Li Guoxiang has cast her, the camera targets her from low down through the grass of a cemetery (illus. 182) where her young husband – Li's first blood victim – has just been buried while 'Crazy' Qin looms dimly over her like the ghost he proclaims himself to be. After the onset of the Cultural Revolution, the narrow streets of this once bustling market-town become darkened and dreadful, dank and devoid of people, hauntingly quiet as the towns-people remain entombed in their homes, fearful and suspicious. It is in this abandoned social space, which proclaims to a highly social audience that something is terribly wrong, that the lonely lessons of *Hibiscus Town* are learned. In the final scene, political calm has returned to Hibiscus Town and the closeness of space is filled once again with the intense comraderie of small-town society, but it remains a tight stage, ready-made for any future revival of hostility between close-living neighbours.

In Xie Jin's melodramatic visualization of Hibiscus Town, the struggle between good and evil is projected even onto dramatic weather patterns and deeply coloured seasons. Once the political storm breaks on Hu Yuyin, Hibiscus Town's original gleam disappears, the heavens pour down rain and snow, adding to the oppressive closeness of space, and dark shadows gobble up the scenery. The distinctive exceptions to this

187 *Hibiscus Town*. Narrow passages suggest the dark and narrow corridors of human interaction.

are momentary bright spots of 'normal' human companionship, often cast in the romantic glow of distant memory: the opening scene before the political terrorization of Hibiscus Town began; the scene in the spacious, sunny hibiscus fields by the town where Mangeng recalls in flashback his courtship of Yuyin; the time when Yuyin recalls the rosy glow of her first husband's courtship and marriage; the spot of light in which Yuyin is first helped in her sickness by 'Crazy' Qin, in which they first recognize that they've become a couple, and later when she's 'married' to Qin; and finally, when Qin returns under bright blue springtime skies from his dark years at hard labour. If nature's personification here is purely melodramatic, it is entirely traditional as well, in a culture where the conjoining of Heaven and earth has long been viewed as more than mere metaphor.

In China, nature's resonance to political goings-on was displayed as a kind of dynastic performance chart, sometimes measured with auspicious manifestations, sometimes with Heavenly warnings through extremes of weather – drought and flood – celestial apparitions and earthquakes. In Chinese paintings and literature, harsh political times were signified similarly by harsh weather, snow and wind. In a lament on the political hardships of the early years under Mongol rule, Luo Zhichuan's flock of hungry crows scavenge for food in the snow like the throng of scholar-bureaucrats left without work as the Mongols replaced them with Central Asians (illus. 188).[70] Gong Xian's self-portrayal as a grove of barren willows – like them, having prematurely lost his scholarly elegance and opportunity for political advancement – takes place in the 'wintry' years of the Manchu invasion (see illus. 24).[71] Such challenging conditions nonetheless enabled the virtuous to manifest their inner qualities and distinguished the exceptional from the ordinary. As Confucius put it, 'When the year grows cold, *then* we realize that the pine and cypress will be the last to shed their foliage.'[72] Conversely, benign views of nature served as corollary themes, such as the arrival of timely spring rains (*shi yu, kuai yu,* or *gan yu*) after a period of drought, signifying the return of good government after a period of bad (illus. 189).[73] Such climatic conditions as *Hibiscus Town* has to offer, which a Western audience might readily take as exaggerated and artificial, melodramatic device, pathetic *fallacy*, might just as readily be regarded by a Chinese audience as 'natural' and wholly credible.

Among *Hibiscus Town*'s set of stock characters, the least predictable and most puzzling character for a Western audience (and thereby the least 'melodramatic', inasmuch as melodrama's typology rests on the recognizable) is one quite familiar (and conventionally melodramatic) to the Chinese. This is 'Crazy' Qin, whose role is to resist the conflict

188 Luo Zhichuan, *Crows in Old Trees*, early 14th century, hanging scroll, ink and colour on silk. The Metropolitan Museum of Art, New York.

This painting is a virtual encyclopaedia of political symbols. The withered trees are lofty scholars whose virtues, in desperate (wintry) times are concealed inside. The hungry crows circling about also represent scholars in search of support. The separation of trees (scholars) from the distant mountains (the court) by an expanse of water (symbol of isolation or exile) became a standard composition during the period of Mongol rule. Below, the pair of pheasants are birds that mate for life, remaining loyal as many Yuan scholars did to the conquered Song dynasty.

189 Guo Xi, *Early Spring*, 1072, hanging scroll, ink and colour on paper. National Palace Museum, Taipei.

Landscape as political allegory: perhaps idealizing the attainment of universal harmony with the rise of a reform faction at the royal court, Guo Xi's painting presents an orderly array of human and natural events. Peasants and fisherman occupy the lower reaches of the landscape, left and right, while scholarly travellers in the middle register head upwards toward a Daoist or Buddhist temple on the right. According to the writings of Guo Xi's own son, towering peaks above represent the emperor surrounded by his highest officials, while lofty pines supported on the flanks of that mountain represent princes of the realm ringed by lesser courtiers. Spring rains and beneficent clouds signify the arrival of good government.

190 *Hibiscus Town*. Attuned to his work, the mop-haired Qin with broom in hand.

that flares all around him by refusing to struggle back, reducing rather than elevating emotional tensions in order to make himself a less interesting target. Qin is a peacemaker in a world at war. Qin's 'craziness' is another word for Daoist or Buddhist 'wisdom', an ancient cloak of self-protection donned by many a victim in troubled times. The early Qing dynasty painter Bada Shanren, scion of the deposed Ming royal family who was sheltered in Buddhist cloisters and suffered and/or feigned both madness and muteness to assure his survival, is but one example of this complex type of behaviour well known in Chinese culture (illus. 191; see illus. 23).[74]

The broom, that most visible badge of Qin's peripheralization, is also of antique vintage and most clearly signals his unorthodox role. In Buddhism, it equates with purification, much as the monks might ritually sweep the altar with willow branches and holy water. Historically, this broom appeared in the hands of the eighth-century Buddhist recluse Shide, whose name means to 'sweep up' (for Shide was really but a young kitchen sweep and not a regular member of the community at all, a *sravaka* or naturally enlightened being); the name also means one who is 'swept up' as an 'orphan' (which Shide was; illus. 192, 193). Qin Shutian (illus. 190; see illus. 178) shares with the eccentric Shide a dishevelled, mop-like hairdo, a slightly goofy smile, and an anti-authoritarian attitude that such an appearance is meant to communicate – the renegade Shide refused to give audience to the envoy of an admiring official and took flight to the hills instead, eventually becoming a Zen Buddhist icon.[75] Through their boyish appearance, Qin and Shide are presented as pre-sexual, innocent and spiritual, although this purity is later compromised and eroded by the gradual sexualization of Qin's relationship with Hu Yuyin, transmuted from the alien-sacred into a social affirmation of family life. The dissident broom later landed in the hands of the landscape painter Gong Xian, whose political hopes were swept aside by invading Manchus like a bunch of fallen leaves; refusing

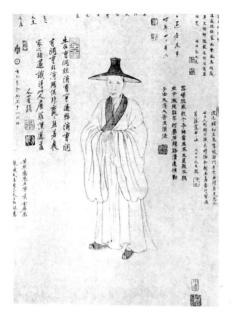

191 Huang Anping, *Portrait of Geshan* [Bada Shanren], 1674, hanging scroll, ink on paper. Bada Shanren Memorial Museum, Nanchang.

A member of the fallen Ming royal family, displaced by the Manchu invasion and shown here thirty years after that personal disaster, Bada Shanren epitomized the scholar obliged to lodge his feelings and even his identity deep inside. Contemporaneous accounts report that he was given to alternative periods of repressive muteness followed by wild ravings and gesticulations, but scholars today are unsure whether Bada was truly mad, or making the pretense of insanity for his own self-preservation, or whether perhaps he carried the pretense to the point of actual madness. Although still a Chan Buddhist at the time of this portrait, he appears in scholar's robes and a traveller's hat.

192 Attrib. Yan Hui, *Shide*, early 14th century, hanging scroll, ink and colour on silk. Tokyo National Museum.

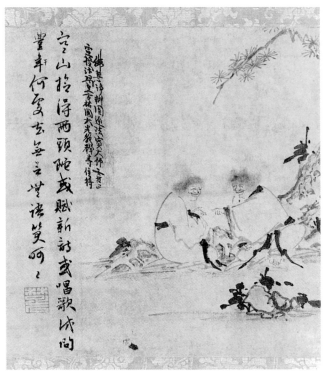

193 Yintuoluo, *Hanshan and Shide*, early 14th century, section from a handscroll, ink on paper. Tokyo National Museum.

194 Faxi (unidentified), *Portrait of Gong Xian*, mid-20th century, hanging scroll, ink and colour on paper. Sao Ye Lou, Nanjing.

This painting hangs in Gong Xian's former home in Nanjing, 'The Hall of Swept-Up Leaves,' preserved today as a memorial to this political loyalist. It depicts the master with his characteristic broom in hand.

to recognize Manchu legitimacy, he took this as an image for his painting studio, which he named the *Sao Ye Lou* (The Hall of Swept-Up Leaves) and through which he conflated the notion of monkish sweeping-as-ritual purification with his own being swept away into the otherworldly realm (illus. 194; see illus. 24).

The broom thus serves as the primary visual label of the protagonists in *Hibiscus Town* (much more is made of it in the film than in the book). Yuyin learns gradually to accept this label and to perform her *pas de deux* with it. The most romantic touch of the film occurs at the moment when the outcast couple's brooms first touch on the barren stones of the street (see illus. 179). Later on, the dismissed official Gu Yanshan reveals his deep awareness of this signifier. He appears, un-invited, as the only guest at Qin's and Hu Yuyin's wedding, announcing that 'It won't count without a go-between.' But then he acknowledges, 'I'm not the real go-between. That's the broom and the stones on the street.' In her moment of disgrace by rampaging Red Guards, Li Guoxiang is offered a broom by 'Crazy' Qin, his broom, for her to 'prac-tise' with – with which to change her moral behaviour – but she rejects it (illus. 195). 'You Reactionary! Rightist!' she spits at him, still pre-ferring antagonistic labels to the harmonizing exercise of sweeping up. He responds to this spleen with the only label he believes in, an almost pathetically simple 'You're a human being, too.'

And yet, this conflict is not simply personal, for Li Guoxiang has her own understanding of sweeping, based on Maoist rhetoric. Whereas Shide's broom was used to sweep away worldly dust, to purify and disci-pline one's own mind, in socialist rhetoric purification and cleansing meant sweeping aside class enemies: 'Sweep away all cow demons and snake spirits.' 'Sweep away all pests' (see illus. 111). And from Chairman Mao himself:

As for the reactionaries in China, it is up to us to organize the people to overthrow them. Everything reactionary is the same; if you don't strike it, it won't come down. This is just like sweeping the floor; as a rule, where the broom does not reach, the dust will not vanish of itself.[76]

Of course, for the Maoist, the phrase *dadao*, to 'strike down' or 'over-throw', packed a greater punch and thus outranked 'sweeping away' in revolutionary vigour. But street-sweeping was a common punishment in the Cultural Revolution years, humiliation for lesser victims, and hardly the worst.[77] It was Li Guoxiang who gave Hu Yuyin the broom in the first place, sweeping her out of socialist society and into the ranks of the Five Bad Elements. Thus, the broom was first of all a visual image controlled by the Party. Only secondarily did Qin and Hu,

195 *Hibiscus Town*. As Li Guoxiang is politically reduced to his level, Qin Shutian offers her his own broom, symbol of his enlightenment, urging her to 'practice'.

labelled as subversives by it, subvert it, returning it to a more traditional function.

The Chinese Communists' public application of labels to maintain control of people and events inherits and perpetuates the 'feudalistic' notion of name regulation or rectification, *zheng ming*, referred to at the outset of this essay.[78] In *The Analects*, Confucius seems forever engaged in classifying and enumerating people and behaviours in ways intended to cleave and control through the authoritative use of language. He provides ample precedent for the socialist public pedagogy of the 'three thises and five thats' with, for example (one of a great many), his 'Three Reverences':

Master Kong [Confucius] said, There are three things that a gentleman reverences: he reveres the will of Heaven, he reveres his masters, he reveres the words of the sages. The lesser man does not recognize the will of Heaven and therefore does not revere it. He disrespects his superiors and ridicules the words of the sages.[79]

Sages here are transmuted into masters and from there into bearers of Heavenly will; any reader who prefers to avoid being labelled as a 'lesser man' will, of necessity, conform to this orthodox view.

Buddhism, too, product of a caste society, is rich in categorizing, and the broadly-educated Qin Shutian, who knows his Buddhism as well as the socialist cant he's been obliged to brush all over the town's walls, doesn't hesitate to blur one system of labels with another in bringing some measure of non-sectarian enlightenment to his fellow-damned. In the book, he proclaims with more than touch of irony,

We're all on the blacklist, but some of us are blacker than others. For instance you're an ex-landlord, who grew fat off the peasants before Liberation; you're the worst. You're a rich peasant, who did some work yourself but exploited others through usury, trying to climb up to be a landlord; you're second worst. As for a counter-revolutionary like you, who treated the people as your enemy, your category is the most dangerous. Mind you watch your step . . . Me? I'm a bad element. That's more complicated, as there are different kinds: thieves, rapists, swindlers, hooligans, kidnappers, men who run gambling dens. Generally speaking, their family background's not bad. Of all the Five Categories, this is the best. We shall go to different hells after we die.[80]

Qin understands that labels are labels, regardless of creed, whether socialist, Confucian, or Buddhist. Of China's major traditional philosophies, only Daoism and its step-child, Chan Buddhism, built on this understanding of the gap between the name and the thing named.[81] Whereas Confucius names his preferred weapon as control of language, the naming of names, the *Dao de jing's* 'Laozi' seems to have no weapon. But naming no names *is* his weapon. His tactic is to disarm, to use language to neutralize language, to unname. It is a powerful tactic, and surprisingly widely practised in time and place (see illus. 171, 172).

As in Buddhism and Confucianism, class standing in socialist China came to be acquired at birth, known by the name of 'revolutionary inheritance'. As a perpetuation of religio-political superstition, like karmic reincarnation, this is subjected to mockery early in the story when a young tad stands in for his sick grandfather at the roll call of the Five Bad Categories. In the film, a woman nearby, with kids of her own, looks up and grumbles, 'Hell! Even grandkids have to join the class struggle.' In the book, this passage is more analytic: it 'struck [everyone] as strange. How could this child born after Liberation be a pre-Liberation counter-revolutionary?'[82] For political lackey 'Autumn Snake' Wang, however, the practical significance of all this is clear, as he reasons, 'So the blasted Five Categories are raising successors! The class struggle will have to go on for generations.'[83] For those like Wang who feed off class struggle, that's not such a bad thing. But for the rest of China, it's a matter of perpetuating rifts among the people rather than healing them, passing down victimization from generation to generation. In both book and film, it is noted that long before Li Guoxiang brought her ideological guns to Hibiscus Town, Hu Yuyin was prevented from marrying the town brigade's Party secretary Li Mangeng by the Party's intervention because of her bad social background, her father reputed to be a gangster and her mother a prostitute. To the Communist regime, the mockery of names and images, stripping labels of their potency by changing the rules of the game was more grave than any ideological errors conceived within the rules. And so, non-confrontational Daoism became even more abhorrent to China's Marxist philosophers than Confucianism was, as Kam Louie observes in *Inheriting Tradition*:

. . . the idealism of [the Daoist philosopher] Zhuangzi was more despicable than that of the subjective idealism of Western capitalist idealism or the idealism of Mengzi. The subjective idealism of the bourgeois philosophers in the West and of [the Confucian] Mengzi was outward-looking, and both sought the material world. Zhuangzi's, however, sought absolute freedom within one's own mind. It saw everything as being empty, life as a dream. To [Marxist philosopher] Guan Feng, such a philosophy bred nihilism, the Ah Q spirit, sophistry, and pessimism. It was an idealism which therefore had no redeeming features at all . . . Guan Feng's savage attack on Daoism would seem logically to force thinkers to turn to Communism because all other channels, including the one for taking flight, were 'banned'. It is not surprising, then, that Guan Feng's position was adopted as correct.[84]

The son born to Yuyin and 'Crazy' Qin is the physical embodiment of Xie Jin's alternative message, a positive assertion of family values, but this is formulated through a reversion to naming, Confucian style. He is the product of an illicit union, born of class struggle, but named for social reconciliation. Though illegitimate in the eyes of the state, the child was born in a military hospital after Yuyin, unable to deliver and on the verge of death, was rushed there by Gu Yanshan. When most needed, the military was prepared to help. With gratitude and presented the opportunity to write her own label, Yuyin names her son Jun, 'Army', thereby reclaiming something of the PLA – of the nation – for herself and for other victims like her.[85] At the same time, with the real father, Qin Shutian, being illegitimate and incarcerated, the war veteran Gu Yanshan lends the child his own last name, thus indicating both the craziness of the times and the bond that unites its innocent victims.[86] Punished for their transgressive parenthood, Qin and Yuyin were reduced to the lowest level of living and Qin's counsel to his 'bride' became simply, 'Survive, like an animal.' But Yuyin's pregnancy and Jun's arrival radically alter the social equation. Jun may be a melodramatic cipher, a living label – children, as innocents, are frequently used in melodrama to denote the innocence of their parents – but his presence humanizes the situation and (in the film) wins Yuyin both a probationary sentence and a modicum of sympathy from the community, which no doubt has had its own fill of ideological radicalism. Public exoneration, at any rate, comes naturally, while official rehabilitation, by contrast, comes belatedly and with reluctance.

In the book, when her name has been cleared, and Qin Shutian's too,

Yuyin laughed hysterically. 'So it was all wrong! Brother Shutian's case too! What a joke! Heavens, we're back in the new society! The Communist Party's come back – its policies too . . .'[87]

Thus, the Cultural Revolution is labelled an aberration, carried out by an anti-Party clique, rather than a legitimate Communist experience. Still, when 'Crazy' Qin returns to Hibiscus Town from more than eight years of hard labour, the normality he returns to is one of serving up customers in Yuyin's once-again thriving family doufu shop. The 'policies' affirmed by this seemingly have less to do with Marx and Mao than with the kind of small-scale, family-centred, village-based entre-preneurship traditionally supported by Confucian and Daoist values. In the book, Qin also becomes deputy head of the county's cultural center,[88] which represents a formal endorsement of 'new society' values but seems no less a Confucianistic turn; it even suggests that like many an oppressed scholar in Chinese history, Qin was but a 'Daoist' of circumstance, in response to hard times, and ready to become a social servant once again when better times permit. Gu Yanshan, too, becomes a leading office holder, secretary of the town committee. His reply in the final scene of the film to political lackey Wang Qiushe's call for a new mass movement (illus. 180) is to exclaim, 'The crazy one's sane and the sane one's crazy. Another movement and he's sane.' It's an apt description of a whole era gone awry, a twisted 'rectification of names'. Qin seemed 'crazy' because he accepted, and hence deflected, the arbi-trariness of labels, whereas Wang Qiushe was driven crazy, literally, by his inability to cope with the arbitrariness of China's political twists and turns. No longer 'crazy', the newly liberated Qin Shutian does not seem quite so interesting; indeed, he lost much of his original coher-ence when he went from boyishly innocent mop-head spiritualist to Yuyin's flesh-and-blood lover. As the melodramatic code of fascination with extremes would have it, it is 'Autumn Snake' Wang – no longer bound by sanity to his role of calculated, slavish sycophancy, his most wicked urges now emotionally unleashed – who is really interesting at the end of the film, sending the audience off with an unexpected and unforgettable chill. Gu Yanshan's comment is followed by Qin's own daunting pronouncement, 'Unless we're careful, there may be sense in his words yet'. So Qin conciliates, symbolically, by offering crazy Wang a free bowl of doufu even as he clings to his son, Jun, who signifies here the next generation and the implicit object of Wang's future threat. And there is another turn: the fact that Wang's comrade, Li Guoxiang, remains in high office is the other half of this final fright scene.

All the final twists and turns of *Hibiscus Town* are troubling matters if we are to take the film as somehow being a direct inscription of Xie Jin's own values. Melodrama may be intended to clarify, but *Hibiscus Town* leaves us with more questions than answers. Like a horror film, it presents a convulsive spectacle that an audience can be fascinated by for so long and no longer and is relieved when it is over. The audience should then return to a normality that defines the experience as 'just a movie'. But the horror in *Hibiscus Town* was part of a real-life melodrama which left China a different place, and beyond a point of no return. The streets to which one returns after viewing *Hibiscus Town* were changed forever by the events which took place in this typological 'Our Town'. What remains to be 'clarified', then, is that *Hibiscus Town* (The Movie) itself is the return, and one leaves the film instructed that one cannot really go back to Hibiscus Town (The Village) again, that never again will things seems as simple as they were then and there, that life is more complicated than its labels. The horror of *Hibiscus Town*/Hibiscus Town also left melodrama forever changed, more convoluted, more of a challenge to its critics.

Since inflexible ideological labels were the tool of Confucianists and Communists alike, it may seem ironic that Xie Jin's agenda calls not for the rejection of either of these ideologies, or of both, but for a reconciliation of the two of them. Ironic but not illogical, since Xie's primary goal is an end to conflict. Zhu Dake's previously mentioned denunciation of 'Xie Jin's [Confucian] principle' of representing women as 'entirely dependent upon men . . . used to discover and approve male values and to make men happy'[89] bears at most a passing resemblance to Hu Yuyin, whose ideological problem was her economic individualism, and far less even to Li Guoxiang, whose moral problem was her strident political disregard for individuals. But still, Zhu was not wholly wrong in attaching a Confucian label to Xie's political agenda, for social harmony, not class conflict, is Xie's model. Nick Browne understands this, putting it in terms of 'borrowing':

[Xie's] new socialism borrows a moral perspective from Confucianism in order to criticize the old ways and to justify a new concept of the self appropriate to the new economic order . . . [His] film argues that this mode of subjectivity is *not* new, but is found in the villages of the past.[90]

Nonetheless, Xie's political logic sits uneasily with his critics. Why, they seem to ask, is Xie content with mere 'borrowing'? Why is there no call to sweep away the discredited Communist system? Why – in contradiction to Zhu Dake's bogus assertion that 'Xie Jin provides his audience with a magnificent moral fairy tale in which *all social contradictions are resolved*'[91] – does Xie (and here, of course, this means Gu Hua as well) leave Li Guoxiang in high office while her former lackey terrorizes the villagers with the possibility that the last act has not yet been written. Indeed, it is the persistence of these figures, Li Guoxiang and Wang Qiushe, that is most troubling, an apparent inconsistency between political message and the stylistic mode. If downfall of evil is virtue's prime reward, why are the political villains *not*, in the 'purest' melodramatic tradition, fully vanquished? Xie instead provides a temporary resolve punctuated by an unpleasant question mark.

This issue forms the underpinning for much of the critical dialogue about this film. Nick Browne notes that by putting the blame for Hibiscus Town's debacle on Li Guoxiang and not the entire Party, Xie Jin 'neither excuses the Party nor supports a call for dismantling it'.[92] Pickowicz similarly observes Xie's irresolution:

Xie Jin's melodramas pushed far beyond the officially sanctioned condemnation of the Cultural Revolution . . . [His] films do a great deal to undermine the moral legitimacy of the Communist Party . . . [Yet he] never says that the Communist Party is hopeless and must be overthrown.[93]

Pickowicz even wonders whether the events of June 1989 might later have forced Xie to reconsider his position.[94] Naturally, Xie could hardly call *on film* for such an overthrow, either before or after Tian'an Men. But at any rate, the political logic embodied in *Hibiscus Town* is internally consistent and calls instead for reconciliation however imperfect, for a blend of old and new, a 'liberated' economy, an end to mass movements and violent revolutionism. The lesson learned is that those who prevail in revolutionary movements are those who attack the innocent and divide the people, those who 'delight in crushing others',[95] those most willing to abuse language in order to seize control for themselves and their own views. Any critic who imagines that Tian'an Men might have altered Xie's logic is perhaps more melodramatic than the establishmentarian pragamatist Xie Jin himself. Xie Jin's (and Gu Hua's) dramatic insistence on an ending that reflects current political reality is more realistic than that.

Hibiscus Town, as historical fiction, has projected itself into an external context, placed itself at the nexus of melodrama, realism, and reality, where art intersects with document. Until that outer reality has itself been resolved there can be no critical resolution over the film. By leaving Li Guoxiang on the scene, Xie has refused to bow to the unrealistic dictates of 'classic' melodrama, instead modifying the form to accord with political reality and moral choice. One might imagine here a turn of Elsaesser's historical wheel of melodrama, though hardly by a full rotation: as with all things postmodern/post-socialist, this turn is more complicated than that. With its dark, disrupted conclusion, *Hibiscus Town* no longer functions as Hegelian melodrama, that Maoist form of theatre whose narrative conventions, like the French Restoration stage, 'functioned in their most barren form as the mechanics of pure suspense', with plots and conclusions reducible to the predictable formula of 'innocence persecuted and virtue rewarded' so that they 'trivialized the [melodramatic] form'.[96] And yet, despite its embrace of a petit-capitalist ethic, it is also no return to the pessimistic, sublimated May Fourth formulations of the cinematic art, which took industrial capitalism as its demon but which, as already noted, so often ended on a hopelessly tragic note. Neither is it a full turn to that strain of post-Maoist drama in which heroes and villains are all replaced by middle characters, where the targets and meanings of morality plays are left ambiguous by the masking of labels, where virtue and evil are replaced by uncertain goals and values and the validity of melodrama itself is *openly* called into question, as in the first years of 'Fifth Generation' film-making, 1984–7. The Xie Jin model of melodrama is distinct, though critical expectations, ironically, too often seem to expect or even to desire greater simplicity than he has to offer.

As an alternative to *Hibiscus Town's* complex formulation, something closer to a 'classic' narrative was still on hand, available to its authors: Deng Xiaoping did away with Jiang Qing in melodramatic fashion, renouncing the Cultural Revolution by dissolving the Party's bonds to her and claiming thereby to have resolved all major contradictions within the Party. Presumably Xie Jin could have done the same with Li Guoxiang. But then, as 1989 amply reaffirmed, the Party still has plenty of Li Guoxiangs in high places (whatever their gender), and the violence that erupted in Tian'an Men Square was probably much more the product of contending Party factions than of their contention against unarmed youths. Sadly, speaking through the crazy 'Autumn Snake' Wang at the end of *Hibiscus Town* (see illus. 180), Gu Hua and Xie Jin were all too prescient. In an era of political and moral ambivalence, which has stripped any too-simple conclusions of their appeal, Xie Jin's ambiguous ending allowed him to adjust to a new, more realistic era, to remain credible with his changing audience, while critics went off to ponder the inconsistencies of his dramatic structure and emotional style and other questionable linkages.

As the question of how China will resolve its dilemma of a discredited but still powerful government is read back into the movie

Hibiscus Town, Western critical dissatisfaction and impatience with Chinese political reality has fed critical dissatisfaction with the film. Xie's eclectic combination of melodramatic characterization and emotionality with a more-or-less realistic conclusion, his art of rupture bearing a message of conciliation, leaves him open to criticism. Some of his critics lay blame at the foot of the melodramatic mode itself: 'a genre that severely limits the imagination', in Pickowicz's words,[97] or as Shao Mujun puts it, 'When people watch Xie Jin's films, they don't have to rack their brains to think.'[98] These are interesting charges. One wonders how Shakespeare might have responded to similar criticism. As melodramatic a history as *The Tragedy of Richard the Third* never critically judged a system that not only produced Richard as a worst-case scenario but had educated him well through apprenticeship in the practice of murderous treachery. Not even with the political system revealed by Richard's excesses for all to see do we hear the author urging that the feudal monarchy be abridged or done away with. The bard simply – melodramatically – puts it all down to Richard's physical deformity. From Richard's opening soliloquy:

> . . . cheated of feature by dissembling nature,
> Deformed, unfinished, sent before my time
> Into this breathing world, scarce half made up,
> And that so lamely and unfashionable
> That dogs bark at me as I halt by them –
> . . . therefore, since I cannot prove a lover,
> To entertain these fair well-spoken days,
> I am determined to prove a villain
> And hate the idle pleasures of these days.[99]

How like Li Guoxiang's is this *derivation* (and not mere signification) of moral deformation from physical lack: that is, morality deformed in its ontogeny, warped by its derivation from the mundane. Historically determined, the death of Richard as a dramatic fact stands in the way of the kind of questioning which Xie Jin (and Gu Hua), by leaving Li Guoxiang in office, send their audience home with. In conclusion, the victorious Richmond, mouthing words rather like Deng Xiaoping's – 'Abate the edge of traitors, gracious Lord / That would reduce these bloody days again / And make poor England weep in streams of blood!' – proclaims the past to be past and mounts the throne as Henry VII, changing nothing.[100] *Hibiscus Town*, at least in its recognition that the past may not be past, may be the more realistic of the two melodramas.

So for all this critical panning of melodrama, critics will rack their brains anyway, and for all its emotive melodrama, *Hibiscus Town* gives audience and critics alike much to ponder. Ironically, in demanding of it a clearer resolution of crises – since, in some critical formulations, Li Guoxiang (the Party) is so evil that she (it) should be swept away – many of Xie Jin's critics in effect are appealing for *more* of the melodrama, simplistically defined, which they purport to reject. That Xie Jin's melodrama is deeper in thought and richer in expression than this is recognized by Nick Browne, who writes that in China,

melodrama is the mode of representation of a historical experience that inscribes 'subjectivity' in a position between the expectations of an ethical system (Confucianism) and the demands of a political system (socialism), a condition that typifies the Chinese dilemma of modernization . . . In this sense, Xie Jin's films work explicitly to monitor and readjust these new ideological premises to old ethical standards and – through a cultural critique of ongoing antirightist violence – to explore the limits of the political administration of socialist justice. *Hibiscus Town* lays out the political process of justice – crime and punishment – but it also subjects that process to a critique that puts politicization itself on trial from an ethical standpoint.[101]

Putting political rhetoric on trial, Xie Jin also puts melodrama through a trial. But in the end, how harshly can one criticize melodrama when Chinese reality itself is so melodramatic?

6 The Children of Melodrama: No-drama, Pseudo-drama, Melodramatic Masquerade and Deconstruction Drama

The most important thing was how to make films ourselves – how we could make things different. We had seen too many propaganda films. We had the personal experience. We thought we could do something different and better.
– Chen Kaige[1]

In making an axe handle by cutting wood with an axe, the model is indeed near at hand. But the adaptability of the hand to the ever-changing circumstances and impulses in the process of creation is such that words can hardly explain.
– Lu Ji, *Essay on Literature*[2]

Xie Jin's *Hibiscus Town* demonstrates the legitimate applicability of the concept of 'melodrama' to contemporary Chinese film; at the same time, it exemplifies the way in which recent Chinese cinema is developing away from 'classic' melodrama (either as defined by post-Revolutionary French practice or during the reign of Mao Zedong) and towards what can more safely be referred to as 'the melodramatic'. Brushing away concerns that distinguish drama from melodrama, or melodrama from the merely melodramatic, is a wholly subjective matter, and unswayed by the proposal that *all* drama is melodramatic in its condensed and exaggerated staging of real life's rather diffuse morality plays, authors like Peter Brooks caution against a relativist understanding of 'melodrama':

. . . to conceive melodrama as an eternal type of the theatre, stretching from Euripides to Edward Albee, is a logical step, and one that Rosenberg, Heilman, and Smith explicitly make and document. Yet here I think the term may become so extended in its meaning that it loses much of its usefulness, at least for our purposes. When Euripides, Shakespeare, and Molière all become melodramatists at least some of the time, and when tragedy becomes only a special subset of melodrama, we lose a sense of the cultural specificity of the genre . . . The adjective *melodramatic* will take on greater critical force, greater definitional use, if we can refer back from it to a relatively well-characterized set of examples under the head of melodrama.[3]

On the other hand, Dissanayake, Elsaesser, Heilman and others suggest the virtue of an expanded definition of melodrama as providing the ability to chart cross-cultural diversity and diachronic cultural change.[4]

Simple logic suggests that without a cross-cultured application of melodrama, with no non-classic forms, then 'classic' melodrama would no longer be classic; there would only, simply, be melodrama, perhaps with nineteenth-century France as its only legitimate theatre, and who knows what would become of the merely melodramatic.⁵ The rest of theatre history (and historiography) would be impoverished by the segregation. And we would scarcely be able to recognize one of the most important motivating factors in contemporary Chinese cinema.

The 'New Chinese Cinema' producers of the post-socialist era have loudly foresworn the conventions of the previous generation of Chinese film: the stereotyping of characters, the stylistic and emotional exaggeration, and the rigidity of propagandist content. Chinese film-makers and critics alike have expressed this as a reaction against 'melodrama'. *Yellow Earth* director Chen Kaige, for example, exclaims,

I don't feel comfortable with melodrama because I don't like emotional excess. I could never make a film like Xie Jin's *Hibiscus Town*, which says that there are good people and bad people and that everything will be fine if we can just get rid of the bad people! It seems to me that all of us have positive and negative sides, and the same capacities to love and hate.⁶

Similarly rejecting – overthrowing – the conventions of his parents' era, Zhang Yimou wrote that when filming *One and Eight* (1984),

I was filled with anger whenever I set up the camera. All of us were basically fed up with the unchanging, inflexible way of Chinese film-making, so we were ready to fight it at all costs in our first film. I would set down the camera and take a look, and [say to myself], Oh, god, the composition is still the same as the old stuff! No! Turn the lens around – just turn it around, raise it, just for the sake of raising it. Actually if you ask me whether there was any concept in this kind of incomplete composition, the answer is no; but the point was simply and deliberately to be different.⁷

But theory (or rhetoric) and practice diverge. Alert to that fact, and setting rhetoric aside, critic Jianying (Jane) Zha writes of Zhang's films, with an alertness to their reversion to melodramatic form by the time of *Red Sorghum* (1987),

Zhang has clearly studied the formula of mainstream Hollywood melodrama. In China's film circles, he has been criticized for taking too much of a dramatist's approach in film-making, for paying too much attention to the plot and characterization and being too concerned with the reaction of the audience. But this concern, in part, is what saved Zhang from producing the kind of excruciatingly ponderous, sometimes, downright pretentious and dull art movies that have become a trendy plague among Zhang's fellow 'Fifth Generation' Chinese film-makers. If *Raise the Red Lantern* proved Zhang's ability to portray gripping psychological drama, it should also prove the positive side of learning from Hollywood movies – it might loosen up some of China's proud and serious artists from the stiff pedestals of 'high art,' so that they might see the virtue of telling stories, not just bestowing messages.[8]

Zha centres Zhang's melodrama on Hollywood modes. But Zhang himself implies something closer to home when he confirms that (unlike in *One and Eight* and *Yellow Earth*), 'In *Red Sorghum* I did not deliberately try to combat or contradict the *traditional* way of making film.'[9]

As these comments suggest, recent film-makers have not simply forgotten about melodrama or discarded it without a trace. Rather, just as they are locked in an examination of their cultural heritage, so too are they engaged in an intense, continuing exploration of melodrama and of diverse forms *melodramatic*. In part, the result is testimony to the persistent cultural force of melodramatic form in China. Moreover, the historic ties between generations, the personal ties, run deep, and many of the leading Maoist melodramatists, Xie Jin included, helped train the 'Fifth Generation' class. Chen Kaige's own father, Chen Huaikai (Huai'ai), was a director in the Beijing Film Studio with several major films to his credit in the 1950s, '60s and '70s;[10] his mother, Liu Yanchi, was a scriptwriter there. And in 1978, as the 'Fifth Generation' class was being selected, Chen was coached by Xie Jin for several days before his film academy entrance examination in acting.[11] Fixated as they were on the Cultural Revolutionary experiences of their youth and on the culture roots of that disaster, 'Fifth Generation' film-makers were equally fixated on the melodramatic form which they identified with the art and the thought of that era, with the socialist realism of their parents' generation. But rebel or flee as they might from their parents, they could not flee their cultural parentage, which they carried with them as a kind of cultural genetics, mutable and not always phenotypic but ever-present in the artistic cell. One of the features that distinguishes their film is how they mutated this trait, artistically speaking, into what I have called 'the children of melodrama', a series of theatrical incarnations which mark the failure – perhaps the inability – to outgrow melodramatic form and an examination of which helps one to chart the historical evolution of 'Fifth Generation' cinema.

In defining 'melodrama', a purist academician from a purer age, Peter Brooks has written that melodrama 'points, as no other word quite does, to a mode of high emotionalism and stark ethical conflict that is neither comic nor tragic in persons, structure, intent, effect'.[12] Preceding him in a similar vein, Eric Bentley attempted to set melodrama apart from four other dramatic forms: farce, tragedy, comedy, and tragicomedy.[13] To this incompatibility of forms, it could be added, or argued, that 'classic' melodrama is incompatible with allegory: the latter deals through indirection, with things suggested rather than explicit, with signs that point while actual names are masked; whereas in melodrama, to quote Brooks,

The desire to express all seems a fundamental characteristic of the melo-dramatic mode. Nothing is spared because nothing is left unsaid; the characters stand on stage and utter the unspeakable, give voice to their deepest feelings, dramatize through their heightened and polarized words and gestures the whole lesson of their relationship.[14]

But melodrama itself works by analogy; the real question is, how esoteric or evident the material, how readable are the signs, how clearly stereotyped the characters and situations? Whatever one may think of such definitions and exclusionary strictures as applied to an earlier era, in postmodern practice – in this era of 'exhaustion' and redefinition, rejection and revival, parody and synthesis, and above all, the apotheosis of the hyphen – it is scarcely surprising that a variety of hybrid forms should have appeared in Chinese film to replace an earlier stock once thought to be generically 'pure', to be named below variously as: the *no-drama*, which is drama-phobic in emotional tenor though often retaining the structural features of family melodrama; the black-comic *pseudo-drama*, parody of the real thing; the censor-conscious, identity-encrypted *melodramatic masquerade*; and the *deconstruction drama*.

With many a Chinese film in the era of Deng's so-called 'Second Liberation', even when the applicability of a 'classic' definition of melo-drama has easily been ruled out as inappropriate, the question has devolved to whether the form and effect are even truly melodramatic or not, and even then only a compromised answer is possible. *Army Nurse*, for example, while operating under great emotional restraint and a thick layer of naturalism, at the same time retains many of the hallmarks of melodramatic soap opera. Like family melodrama, it works through crisis at the personal and family (or in this case, displaced family) level; at its core are moral questions that are exempli-fied (writ small) but signified (meant large). And yet even when they represent the virtues and vices of society, the characters are portrayed as 'middle figures' rather than heroes (which Qiao Xiaoyu and Ding Zhu are not) or as demons (as Commissar Lu is not); despite melo-dramatic moments, the mood is generally understated rather than exaggerated, the pacing slow, the filming 'uncinematic'; the intellect is as much engaged as the emotions, and the conclusions to be drawn are ambiguous, left open to interpretation. Similar characteristics prevail in *My Memories of Old Beijing*, Zhang Junzhao's *One and Eight*, *Sacrificed Youth*, Tian Zhuangzhuang's *On the Hunting Ground* and *Horse Thief*, Wu Ziniu's *Evening Bell*, *The Big Parade*, *Woman from the Lake of Scented Souls*, and others. Thus, a quasi-melodrama. Many such films, to judge from their directors' statements, intend to reject socialist melodrama although in practice they still retain certain important vestiges of melodramatic form. Out of respect for their intent, this genre can be called 'no-drama', without the 'h'. It represents a return to the subtle, naturalistic, intellectual and ultimately élitist mode of visual rhetoric associated with the old scholar traditions of China (see illus. 23, 152). Wu Zhen, *Old Fisherman*; Bada Shanren, *Moon and Melon*). Films like *Yellow Earth* and *King of the Children* represent the firmest 'no', the least melodramatic of the lot; yet even in *Yellow Earth*, despite its strikingly muted emotionality and 'middling' of characters, one sees many of the structural features of the melo-dramatic genre: a family/marital crisis urged on by an intransigent father, a solution at hand but held at arm's length by the heroine's reluctance to articulate her plight to her would-be saviour (perhaps because of her repressed erotic longing for him), and an exaggerated 'resolution' in the form of her death by drowning.

The genre I have labelled the 'pseudo-drama', a genre that satirizes such labels, is perhaps best exemplified by *Black Cannon Incident* (also a pseudo-mystery), *Qiu Ju* (also a pseudo-documentary), *Back to Back, Face to Face*, and *Ermo*. The genre of 'melodramatic masquerade', beginning with *Red Sorghum* in 1987, restores popular melodrama in a variety of modified styles and structures. It infuses films of moral drama with cloaked identities, so that we know all too well who in the film is good and who is evil but are left uncertain about who or what in modern Chinese society is being referenced allegorically by their moral struggle. Examples include *The Girl From Hunan*, *Woman Demon Human*, *Transmigration* (postmodern film noir), *Judou*, *Raise the Red Lantern*, and *Farewell My Concubine*. In yet another category, *Temptress Moon*, it will be argued, is not just the bad or all-too-predictable melodrama it initially seems to be, but is self-reflexively deconstructive. In an age of hybridization, definitions here are soft and categories blurred.

Not all of the 'New Chinese Cinema' is referenced in terms of melodrama. *The Trouble-Shooters*, for example, provides satire without the drama. *In the Heat of the Sun* is a coming-of-age film – although it may also be viewed as significant satire, a spoof of the current nostalgia for the Mao Zedong era, an exercise in pseudo-sentimentality. *The Spirit of Painting* is an earnest biography of the woman artist Pan Yuliang

(1899–1977). Other films are simply romances indulgent in melo-dramatic banality and visual gloss, derivative works like *The Wooden Man's Bride*, or *Red Firecracker, Green Firecracker*, or *The Story of Xinghua*. But all of the hyphenates above emphatically make the point that in one way or another, serious and meaningful melodrama has not disappeared, not even in the no-dramas, in which it seems to be gone but is hardly forgotten. And through this new – or more accurately, revived – diversification of forms and genres is expressed much of the creative vitality of the new era of Chinese film-making.

In the first moments of *The Black Cannon Incident* (1985), on a conventionally 'dark and stormy night', a streak of lightning splits the sky (badly drawn; illus. 196) and we know that cinematically we're somewhere between Jiang Qing's Cultural Revolutionary stage and *The Rocky Horror Picture Show*. It is possible to watch the following satire in dead earnest, in which case it provides a rare education about how things really work – or fail to work – in the workaday world of post-socialist corporate China. In particular, it reveals the duality of China's institutional structure, with the parallel positioning of Party commis-sars at every level of factory organization and the infusion of Party politics into every aspect of corporate reality (illus. 197). But as with *Qiu Ju*, the commentary, and the sense of what to make of all this, is lodged in irony and satire that reminds us not to take things for what they seem to be and instead to laugh at them, however bitterly, for their pretensions and their failure to live up to their claims. The tacky-looking streak of lightning and artificial roll of thunder at the very outset of *Black Cannon* tell us immediately that this is a mystery but also provide the first cue that it really is a pseudo-mystery, a black comedy about a crime that never took place – though paranoia persis-tently suggests otherwise – and the dire consequences of thinking that it did. Described in *Black Cannon* is the clash between China's economic efforts to modernize, to enter the world of corporate capitalism and market efficiencies, and its political efforts to remain a Leninist–Maoist state, historically rooted in class struggle and a paranoic fear of class enemies forever lurking in one's midst. *Black Cannon* is dressed up like a melodrama, but its intent is to spook a system mired in a self-defeating mode of moral hyperbole about what is right and who is wrong with a semi-comic 'boo!' in the dark.

The Black Cannon Incident was the first film directed, immediately upon his graduation from the Beijing Film Academy in 1985, by Huang Jianxin, who with Chen Kaige and Zhang Yimou has remained the most steadily productive and consistently successful of film-makers of the

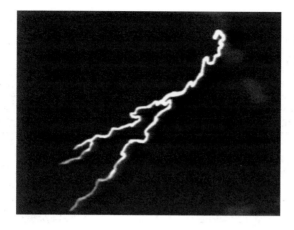

196 *Black Cannon Incident*. The story begins with a flash of lightning, a somber theme treated as farce.

so-called 'Fifth Generation'.[15] Despite its biting social critique, *Black Cannon* was named along with *In the Wild Mountains* as the best film of 1985 by China's Golden Rooster Awards selections committee, but then politics intervened, the awards were held up, and *Black Cannon* was ultimately denied its distinction.[16] Actor Liu Zifeng, however, as the film's put-upon intellectual, Zhao Shuxin, did win the award in his category and proved so popular an anti-hero that a sequel, perhaps unique in PRC film history, was made about the fictional Zhao's popularity (*Dislocation*, 1986). Zhao Shuxin is a mild-mannered German-language technical translator for a joint-venture mining concern, a nebbish whose penchant for inadvertent blundering into troubles begins with his comic entrance on to the stage: wiping the rain from his face (stormy night) as he enters a telegraph office, he immediately walks headlong into two figures who tower over him (masculine counterfoils) (illus. 198, 199) then stumbles over the nearest umbrella set out to dry. He writes out a telegram but can't do that without spoiling

197 *Black Cannon Incident*. Pragmatics runs into ideology, while the clock keeps time. At the far end of the table, the company manager (right) squares off against the Party vice-secretary (left).

240

198, 199 *Black Cannon Incident*. Anti-hero Zhao Shuxin makes his awkward entry.

his first attempt, wads up the paper and tries again. And then the real trouble begins.

Throughout the film, figuratively, Zhao can scarcely see beyond his glasses and continues to bump into things much larger than himself and unexpected obstacles are everywhere strewn across his path. His telegram message, 'Lost Black Cannon, please return', immediately arouses the suspicion of the operator. Flashing red lights come out of the darkness, a screech of brakes, and the security bureau begins surveillance of this potential threat to the state. For those to whom suspicion is a necessary watchword, Zhao's bumbling exterior, good-natured manner, and on-the-job dedication is exactly the disguise to expect of a true villain, and with this piece of counterintuitive reasoning, no piece of evidence or line of logic is sufficient to derail the presumption of guilt (illus. 200). Besides, the friendship struck up between Zhao and the German project engineer, Hans (illus. 201), is baffling and disturbing: one should be polite with foreigners, but to *really* become friends? Until the issue can be cleared up, Zhao is transferred to a make-work post and the only person who can resolve the mystery, Zhao himself, is kept out of the inquiry – in Kafkaesque fashion, uninformed of the charges against him, for his own 'protection'. Meanwhile, on the job, there is no one technically competent to take Zhao's place and his substitute cannot tell the difference in German between 'ball bearings' and 'bullets'. When the inevitable happens and the brand new, expensive German equipment that Zhao had been helping to assemble (the 'WD' – we're never quite told what that stands for or what it does) breaks down before it can even be used (illus. 202), we're left to ponder the cause, the chain of events leading

200 *Black Cannon Incident*. The comic anti-hero, Zhao Shuxin: a dangerous suspect, though what his crime might be, no one is quite sure.

201 *Black Cannon Incident*. Zhao Shuxin and Hans: an international – and suspect – friendship.

back to Zhao's dismissal from the project. Quickly then, the 'mystery' unravels: Zhao's 'black cannon' appears (illus. 203) and, true to its name, turns out to be a Chinese-chess piece, returned by a friend; the 'WD' breaks down because of a translation error about how to lubricate it before use; the Party commissars, who have been holding out against Zhao despite protests by the pragmatic project manager, are saddled with responsibility for the disaster; and the responsibility is shifted by them to Zhao – why didn't he simply replace his black cannon, when a whole new chess set would have cost less than a telegram and would not have aroused their well-intended suspicion? – who accepts the blame by renouncing the playing of chess for ever (illus. 204). In the end, the great mystery is, why did everyone think there was a 'mystery'? The paranoia that triggered this pursuit leads inexorably towards the ruin of a single, massive piece of industrial machinery, symbolizing the notion that China is building for itself an industrial disaster: it is the Party's paranoid style that proves to be the real villain of the piece.

In no other film of this era does art direction play a more vital role, here designed by Liu Yichuan, who captures the postmodern industrial image with as sardonic a vision as Charlie Chaplin brought to the factory in *Modern Times*. His translation of concept into vision is seamless, impeccable. The opening credits are typed out on a police typewriter. A palpably fake streak of lightning tells us that this is a 'melodrama' and a 'mystery' that isn't. Flashing telegram numbers tell of the absence of privacy in an age of electronic monitoring. The mysterious 'black cannon' embodies China's lingering fear of intellectuals and the confusion of public with private matters, in a land where little remains private and almost everyone is looking on. The parody of a boardroom, designed in white on white, lacks all warmth and fronts only clinical sterility, spiritual death, in place of the passionate red of an earlier, overheated era (illus. 197). The room is stuffed with a long meeting table that looks like it will never end and leaves little room for

202 *Black Cannon Incident*. Hans and Zhao's incompetent replacement sit at the foot of the WD, as far apart as space permits.

203 *Black Cannon Incident.* Zhao Shuxin, the intellectual, the loner, holds the mysterious 'Black Cannon' chess piece after its return.

204 *Black Cannon Incident.* In his final appearance, Zhao Shuxin promises his superiors, 'Anyway, I will never play chess again'.

anything else, except one thing: a gigantic, preposterously stylized clock that dwarfs everyone in its presence. Clocks everywhere remind us that it is the dawning of a new era but that it is also a time of testing and time is running out for China. How much will an outdated ideology hold China back in its efforts to catch up? The last clock we see, as Zhao forswears chess, strikes 12:00, high noon, and while the chimes still ring, we see the original clock – the sun (yellow) against a (red) sky (China's national colours but with shades of Antonioni) – in successive second-long shots counting backwards a quarter turn at a time (illus. 205–8). At the same time as the clockery urges China on, the sterility of corporate scenes, the image of monstrous machines dwarfing the working man (seen through telephoto lenses, threatening to swallow

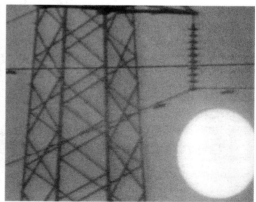

205–8 *Black Cannon Incident.* Sun-time and the time-bomb of Chinese industrial ecology.

244

people up), and the chokingly polluted red sky criss-crossed by power-lines all question the new direction. This red sky is *Black Cannon*'s one concession to revolutionary romance, but it is cast as a botched affair.

On a hot summer day, the nouveaux venture-capitalists, seated now in a circle as equals in defeat, try come to grips with the disaster of their 'WD' investment which they can't blame on Hans and can't understand except with Zhao Shuxin's help. The camera watches an electric fan go round and round in mindless repetition, while they take the heat. Utterly speechless, they've run out of words as the camera itself then goes round and round like the fan, watching them one by one, face by face, to see whether any one of them betrays a hint of understanding, of 'getting it', of breaking out of their own mindless attachment to past habits, of passing all blame on to others (illus. 209–21). The visual evidence suggests that they don't. As the camera slowly, painfully pans the entire, mute crew, it slows or stops for no one, as ultimately no one is more to blame than any other: it is the entire system that is indicted. The 'WD' itself is a blunt instrument, already obsolete before the Chinese bought it (Hans tells us so, and Zhao had warned his superiors but they wouldn't listen). What other blunt instruments out of Germany has it been chosen to represent? Perhaps Hegel, Marx and Engels? What reference is there here to an economic engine without appropriate political steerage?

Of all these striking images, the boardroom provides the most power-ful visual commentary (illus. 197). It is here, where all corporate judge-ments are made, that the judgement of Zhao Shuxin is set, and in the purest melodramatic fashion the victim himself is banished from the scene, silenced from testifying in his own behalf. The design follows a

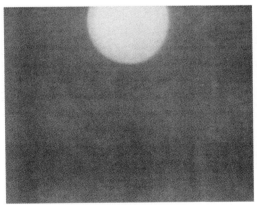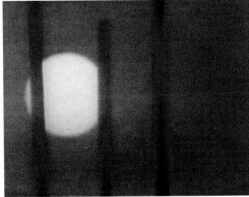

209–21 *Black Cannon Incident*. After the
failure of the WD, the camera surveys
the damage in personal terms. (The
frames should be read from right to left,
starting at top right.)

stern visual logic, like that of the modernist Chinese paintings and installations coming on to the art scene at just that time with a reality of their own that mocked and challenged the authority of everyday government-controlled reality (illus. 222). Though the walls are free of decoration, they close in oppressively, too-tightly framing the space for individual movement or emotional comfort. Crammed into this space are table and chairs that put everyone in their place, each one like each other but with a clear and rigid location hierarchy, placing the leaders farthest away at the head of the table. The camera for the most part remains steady and distant, rigidly enforcing this scheme. To the left, at the head, sits the commissar, Party vice-secretary Madame Zhou, political, dogmatic, inflexibly logical; to the right, facing her, sits the production manager, pragmatic, pleading and outgunned. Like a visual diagram, the structure mirrors the organization of all institutional life in China: every unit with a doubled, parallel structure, one part defined by the practical function of that unit, one part representing the infusion of a Party presence through political commissars who front the latest dictates and see that they are carried out, who oversee regular political study sessions and frequent self-criticisms and assure that the Party's interests and moral values are always put first. It is an image of modernity feared, much like *Street Angel*'s Shanghai skyscraper which housed the bourgeois powers-that-be in its highest reaches (see illus. 229, 230). 'Heaven is high and the emperor far away,' says the Chinese aphorism. The rigidity of the scene prevents any relaxation, intimacy, individuality, spontaneity, unpredictability, visual narrative, or ideological evolution. The clock that dominates the back wall continues to dominate our attention, and yet no one shows any awareness of it. Although, as in any melodrama, time is of the essence, no one seems to realize that while they dawdle over Zhao's case, it is only a matter of time before something goes dreadfully wrong. Once it does and the group regroups to figure out what went wrong, the hierarchy is broken. Seated in a circle, they are now all equals in error. Now, like Zhao, who has rejoined their company too late, they are all rendered speechless and left only to contemplate in stunned silence what fate has left them impotent.

The last scene of the film is a postlude in which Zhao Shuxin, the man of mystery unmasked to reveal the heart of a child, is shown watching a pair of children in a park. The kids are engaged in setting up a long row of bricks so they can knock them all down like dominoes. Once down, they enthusiastically set them up again, interrupted in their concentration only by Zhao Shuxin, who offers pieces of candy, a knowing wink and a grin, and a farewell wave (illus. 223–6). The image

222 Gu Wenda, *Untitled*, 1987, calligraphic installation as seen in artist's studio, Hangzhou.

Trained as a classic calligrapher and painter, Gu Wenda helped pioneer the avant-garde styles that made their way from the off-beat studios to the classrooms of China's elite art academies, emerging in mid-decade as the '85 movement'. Gu's bold, wall-sized, block-like forms tend to strip traditional Chinese characters of their calligraphic nuance and reduce them to their modern function as directional or instructional signs. But then he destroys that function as well, painting over his characters, crossing them out, reversing them, making up fake characters, and rendering text as unreadable. Chinese society has placed unparalleled historical trust in the written word, identified control of society with control of words; by destroying the word itself, Gu Wenda strikes at the heart of Chinese authoritarianism.

is a playful reminder of the relatedness of things. One small thing goes down, like a brick or a misunderstood telegram or a mistranslated word, and it takes the next thing with it. It also raises the question, without answer: is this intended as a critique of the mindless repetition to which China is subjected by its culture, both traditional and modern? Or is it a celebration of the ever-readiness of a hard-working people to start anew and try again? Or is it both, inseparable?

Zhao Shuxin is a parody of the melodramatic victim/hero (see illus. 198, 203). Hidden behind coke-bottle glasses, behind his homely features and his wincing smile that tells us, in effect, 'I'm hurt, but I can take it', is the stereotype of the modern Chinese intellectual, inbred by centuries of Confucian artifice, laughed at since the time of Lu Xun, beaten down by political modernity, and unwilling to take action or confront his tormentors.[17] Dramatically, he is a relative of *Hibiscus*

223–6 *Black Cannon Incident*. Bricks and children symbolize China's efforts.

Town's 'Crazy' Qin (see illus. 178). Both are buffoons, but Qin's buffoonery is intentional, self-managed, while Zhao's is uncontrolled. Their innocence is projected into an evident asexuality, but Qin eventually sheds this as he rises to the role of salvational hero fighting for the right (through his own brand of studied inaction) while Zhao retains his in remaining the anti-hero unable to resist the wrong. A study in alienation, Zhao's closest thing to a knowing friend is another male, 'another' foreigner: Hans, the only one in the film who speaks the same intellectual 'language' as he (see illus. 201). Zhao's only other natural affinity, aside from chess and machinery, is for children, his fellow-innocents. Actually – perhaps surprisingly – Zhao has a girlfriend but their relationship is chaste and it seems they may never have children of their own. Zhao once takes her to a disco performance featuring a chorus line of young, hip-shaking girls in short skirts (illus. 227), but as youths in the audience begin to respond with a touch of rowdiness, he leads her out, saying it's too noisy and gives him a headache. 'I'm too old for the new trend.' Rather than taking her home, he brings her to work with him. Easily moulded by the socialist state, the factory is Zhao's real home and fellow workers are his closest thing to family. Even so, he is a true loner, isolated even when surrounded by colleagues, alone of his kind. He plays chess by himself and can comfortably spend a whole night nosing around a piece of machinery with a wrench in hand. That this utterly emasculated and seemingly unimaginative intellectual becomes the subject of a mystery, a man without a will of his own suspected of industrial espionage, can only turn the spotlight on the mysterious paranoia of his colleagues.

At the same time, the Party commissar who demands that the investigation be fully played out, Party vice-secretary Madame Zhou, is but a

parody of the villainous female-type epitomized by *Hibiscus Town*'s Li Guoxiang (illus. 228; see illus. 177). An old granny who laments that times have changed – and who knows *what* she was capable of a few years earlier, in the heyday of the Cultural Revolution? – she tells the project manager,

Don't beat around the bush. I know what you guys say of me, calling me the 'Old Marxist Lady', 'Leftist Secretary'. Even my sons in college try to educate me with modern philosophy, try to brain-wash me. It seems Marxism and Leninism no longer count. [But] you can't change me. I've got my principles.

Then *she* calls *him* 'obstinate'. Throughout the investigation, she indulges in Party double-talk: excluding Zhao from a knowledge of the charges against him or any role in his own investigation, she tells his colleagues that in lifting him from his work assignment, 'We do it out of consideration . . . for his own safety.' Like Li Guoxiang, her old-fashioned political rhetoric is equated with inflexibility rather than presented for audience consideration as a viable alternative to post-Maoist pragmatism (devotion to socialist principle swimming against the currents of opportunism). This pseudo-drama comes down to a conflict between the obsolete (Zhou) and the emasculated (Zhao), with 'modernization' left in the lurch.

With the return of the black cannon chess piece, Zhao's innocence is proved, only to have him blamed for causing so much trouble. Zhao himself is a mute pawn to the Party hacks who play out this absurd chess game, in a process that mocks the famous slogan of Mao and Deng, 'Seek truth from facts.' His example is a warning that China's efforts to enter the modern world may be stalemated by its antiquated ideology. As an economic muse, like *Yellow Earth*, *Black Cannon* today

227 *Black Cannon Incident*. Reverse exoticism: Chinese Go-go dancers dressed as hip-shaking Pocahontases.

may appear premature in its conclusion, with authoritarian China rapidly developing its economic sphere at an overall rate not predicted even by its most optimistic planners. Yet as the millennium approaches, other 'Asian model' economies offer belated signals that a healthy economy really cannot be erected on a corrupt political base. Moreover, as Huang Jianxin's subsequent films suggest (especially his *Trans- migration*), *Black Cannon* is concerned as much with what by 1979 had already become known as the 'Fifth Modernization', humanitarian values pursued for their own sake as much as for their linkage to economic progress.

Unlike most early 'Fifth Generation' films, which relied on rural landscape settings and the past tense in their 'search for the roots' by which to explain China's modern woes and wrong turns, *Black Cannon Incident* revives a Republican period film tradition of the modern urban critique. It follows familiar Shanghai precedents in responding to the fundamental issues of modernization with a combination of pathos and satire. *Street Angel* exemplified such films a half-century earlier, blending melodrama and comedy, mime and music, high-jinks, slap-stick, and tragedy, in a period before cinema had narrowed its creative options. While that blend may appear as genre-busting by modern Western standards, *Street Angel* played more like traditional Chinese opera, unaware of rules to break. *Street Angel* begins with a downward pan of a towering Shanghai skyscraper, symbol of the new era of wealth – and of new poverty: as the camera reaches ground level, it halts for the audience to read a caption, 'Lower Depths', where the tale will be played out (illus. 229, 230). Many scenes later, the film's hand-to-mouth protagonist, Little Chen, leaves the depths for a moment, seeking out a lawyer in an upper storey of one such skyscraper in his quest to save his girlfriend from an arranged marriage with a small-time gangster. Comically, Little Chen discovers 'modern times' here, in the form of central heating, a water fountain, a bird's-eye view of the world below, and (less comically) in the form of lawyer's fees that he can scarcely imagine let alone afford. Chen's failed mission here leads to tragedy. Many other films of that era added similar moments of satire to fearful tales of misery and the inequities of urban modernization. In *Lights of Ten-Thousand Homes* (1948), the country relatives arrive like a bunch of bumpkins straight out of Dorothy's Kansas to upset things within a precariously balanced Shanghai family, much as Dorothy's arrival does to the wizard in Oz: comedy leads to crisis and on to a sublimated resolution in the reaffirmation of home and family (see illus. 137). *Black Cannon*, however, is not simply, or not really, melodrama; it is play with melodrama – melodrama decentred, diverted, the melodrama of distraction, melo-comedy, pseudo-melodrama, melodrama re-evaluated and redefined. Melodrama itself is identified in *Black Cannon* with the old political rhetoric, critiqued and rejected.

In this recast form, *Black Cannon*'s tension comes not from exaggerated emotions and high drama but rather from the evident lack of it. Though a dramatic mystery *is* unfolding, Zhao Shuxin offers not the

228 *Black Cannon Incident*. Paranoia gives way to perplexity as Party commissar Madame Zhou discovers Zhao Shuxin's innocence: how could her well-developed sense of distrust have missed the target?

229, 230 *Street Angel*. Defining the poverty zone of its activity, the film begins by panning down one of Shanghai's gleaming skyscrapers . . . ending with the words, '1935, autumn, Shanghai lower depths'.

response that melodrama expects of him, not even the kind of sheathed weapon that 'Crazy' Qin wields in *Hibiscus Town*. He remains passive, compliant, ever-loyal, and fails to come to the rescue. He represents the alienation of Chinese intellectuals, only seen through the lens of parody. Only towards the end does he seem to lose his self-comforting innocence, throwing his chess piece away momentarily – but he quickly recovers it, and then, as he pursues comfort in a Catholic church, it is not the sacrament but his encounter with an ice-cream chewing small-fry that restores him to his normal, innocent, all-too-docile self. Throughout, the unfolding industrial drama has not so much to do with Zhao as with Zhao's absence. It takes place out of sight, out of mind, with time running out as it always does in melodramatic narrative. The main characters (including Zhao) remain unaware of this ticking clock, patiently discussing unrealities and being unresponsive to the actual tensions of their situation. Only the well-cued audience is ready for lighting to strike twice, as it finally does with the destruction of the 'WD'. Reality then catches up with and demolishes rhetoric. And then we are left with the mystery of, what is the 'WD'?

In Huang Jianxin's *Black Cannon Incident*, if the on-going befuddlement over whether and how to re-label Zhao Shuxin becomes the basis of comedy, then the historical Chinese *imperative* to label is the stuff of satire. The power of the label, as seen in *Hibiscus Town*, here becomes the ridiculousness of the traditional belief that one can fix something just by labelling it correctly. If we think of melodrama as a system of signs pointing this way and that to produce a comprehensible set

254

of meanings, then what Huang Jianxin has done is to come along and change the signs, the labels, turning some in new or opposite directions, defacing parts or all of others, with the effect not only of confusing specific meanings but of scrambling the entire system. Any new meanings result from the interface of two systems, the former (melodrama) declarative and self-contained, the latter (Huang's pseudo-drama) an ironic commentary imposed on the original, turning it against itself, converting it into something contrary to its own original nature and purpose. Almost automatically, the latter renders the former old-fashioned and declares itself modern; and it proclaims modernity itself to be a form of irony, rather like Marcel Duchamp's painting a moustache on a cheap reproduction of the *Mona Lisa*. As the function of socialist drama was first to propel, later to capture the essence of Maoism and the Cultural Revolution, the function of this brand of pseudo-drama is to mock the disappearance of meaning in post-socialist China. Similarly labelling melodrama as old-fashioned, obsolete, Chen Kaige's first three films – *Yellow Earth* (1984), *The Big Parade* (1985), and *King of the Children* (1987)[18] employ a different strategy, namely to uproot the signs altogether (like the thieves who took the *Mona Lisa* right out of the Louvre earlier in this century). Huang changes the labels; Chen eliminates them. No signs, no melodrama. Huang uses a 'modern' sign to critique modernity; Chen uses labels (via their self-evident absence) to critique the rhetorical abuse of labels.

Yellow Earth questions whether the Chinese socialist experience has proved to be anything more than a rhetorical exercise. Attempting to avoid substituting one rhetorical excess for another, it refuses to clearly label PLA propagandist Gu Qing as good or bad or to clarify the nature of the film's female protagonist-victim, Cuiqiao. Cuiqiao's drowning is implied rather than explicit; Gu Qing's return is ambiguous. Images in *Yellow Earth* like that of the jar of holy water, as seen in chapter one (see illus. 1), or the moon which similarly appears three times in that film (see illus. 29), lack any clear label and embody both the esoteric meaning and the evident ambiguity of the film; they identify its message as ambiguity. Chen's *Big Parade* and *King of the Children* further extend this strategy.

So successful an exercise in ambiguity is *The Big Parade*, Chen's study of an army unit preparing – endlessly, brutally – for a National Day parade at Tian'an Men that critics have drawn entirely opposite inferences about its intentions, its perceptions of individuals and the military, and its valuation of discipline. Jianying Zha, for example, noting that it is 'the only film Chen himself openly admits to be a failure', writes,

The film tells of how the ruthless training for an honor-bound National Day military parade threatens to turn a platoon of people's Liberation Army soldiers into brutal automatons . . . [The] film is inescapably bound up with Chen's own experience as an infantryman.[19]

This 'experience' included Chen's participation in military action towards the end of the Cultural Revolution, a harrowing, bloody 'clamp down' against a minority uprising in south China, which is the basis for Zha's understanding of this as an anti-war film. When the first editing of the film was completed, it was criticized by military officials who 'said it was not a true film – that the characters in the film were not Chinese, they were like Japanese soldiers', and further production was held up by the Film Bureau.[20] Chris Berry, on the other hand, holds quite a different view. Rather than its generating 'automatons', he sees *Parade* as constructing individuals:

It features a series of voice-overs from different characters, revealing their different attitudes and constructing them as individuals rather than just clone soldiers.[21]

The training of 400 soldiers for a military parade on the 35th anniversary of the PRC (1984) requires that they march 10,000 kilometres in preparation for a sixty-second display on the parade ground, being gradually weeded out and whittled down to a core of survivors. As their training progresses, the squadron leader observes, 'Their legs are [so] swollen after a day's practice they can't even squat to shit. They [even]

231, 232 *The Big Parade*. Indoors, in the barracks . . . and out, on parade, rigid organization prevails.

256

weep in their dreams.' The outgrowth of a documentary produced by
Chen and Zhang for the airforce,[22] this version of the war-buddy film
genre configures the squadron as the nation, treating China as a military camp and asking, of what good is all the revolutionary discipline,
the indoctrination, the replication? Why so much work for so little
results? But these questions do not yield clear answers. Aware of the
disparity between months of training and moments of performance, in
the early years of post-Cultural-Revolution cynicism, the drill instructor
defends the process in terms of discipline that transcends the political:
'Do you need political principles to understand? How could we take
this if we weren't good men? Good men *do* become good soldiers. Only
good men are fit to be soldiers. Some people say we're fools. To them I
say "Fuck Off."' Tony Rayns has written, '. . . the overt concern is with
what each man has to repress, or sublimate in order to win his place in
the parade. Chen Kaige has said that he considers it a film not about the
army but about life in China today.'[23]

Zhang Yimou's cinematography and He Qun's art direction are a
study in military discipline. As brilliant in *Big Parade* as their imagery
in *Yellow Earth* was subdued, in scene after scene with formal clarity,
frontal views, and rigid symmetry, from rows of marching troops to
rows of dormitory bunk beds (illus. 231, 232), they capture the rigour of
military discipline in repetitive pattern, in the regularity and precision,
the automation, and the community space of military life. A debt to
Western films is evident, to military films from *Triumph of the Will*

through *The Long Grey Line,* and through its unusually effective use of music homage is also paid to such films as *Bridge on the River Kwai,* whose ironic study of military discipline foreshadows the many ironies found here.[24]

It is the diversity of distinctive personalities participating in this parade that generates the tension of the film, bringing forth faces from facelessness, individuality from the replicands: Instructor Sun Fang, who never smiles but keeps pace with the kids and inspires them through his own discipline; squadron leader Li Weicheng, already aged thirty-five, who's in it for a promotion before retirement, after fifteen years without one, but who voluntarily removes himself from competition at the last moment so one of his boys can march; Jiang Junbiao, so adapted to military life that he can't sleep at night unless others are snoring, not fit for the assignment because he's so bowlegged but so dedicated that he painfully binds his legs at night in the futile hope he can straighten them out in time for the big event; Hao Xiaoyuan, a peasant kid who forgoes his mother's funeral because she would have wanted to see him march on television; Lü Chun, who believes in the new individualism, not in this robotic drilling, who wants to go to military school but not to march; Liu Guoqiang, who joined the army so his wealthy would-be father-in-law would let him marry his daughter. Increasingly developed as persona, the characters also increasingly become identified collectively with their mission by the end of the film – this paradox leaves each viewer to decide where the balance lies. Have they been rolled over by the juggernaut of the system, or have they found meaning for their lives through the achievement of personal discipline?

Chen's own voice on the system of replication and suppression:

I didn't know what to do when I faced the Cultural Revolution. I was confused. You are not a human being, you are part of a machine. If you leave the machine, you can do nothing. It had become a custom – just copy everything. I think that's the base of Communist Party rule in China.[25]

Chen says that the end of the Cultural Revolution provided the first opportunity for people to become individuals again, but for many that exacted a higher price for discipline: 'At that moment China opened the door. Everybody wanted to learn from the West. They wanted to develop their own personalities. They wanted to become different people. But if somebody wanted to take part in the parade, they had to obey official orders. They had to give up being human beings and become a part in a social machine.'[26] And speaking of the Film Bureau administrators who held his film up for a year because he didn't want it to end with the parade his soldiers had prepared for, Chen again:

I said, okay, what part do you want changed? He said the ending, because it didn't show anything of the big parade, even though that was the film's title. I didn't want to do that. I explained that I was interested in how people could spend months in a very close area, stay together, and walk, walk, walk every day – what they thought about that, why they wanted to do it. He said that he agreed, and understood: it was because they were growing up under the red flag. He didn't think I was trying to do anything against the government. I really wanted to say, fuck you.[27]

Does Chen's vulgarity here confirm the anti-military implications of the film? Or is it a rejection of the censor's thinking that he can put *any* definitive interpretation on the dilemma that the film raises. And how do we read this in light of attitudes in *Yellow Earth*, whose ambiguous presentation seems to cover a deep ambivalence towards the issues raised? How does this film stretch *our* understanding of Chen Kaige or clarify *his* understanding of 'individualism' and discipline?

In addition to the interpretive directions already referred to, another alternative can be mapped out. Why do these soldiers (why do the Chinese) *voluntarily* stay together under this demanding regime rather than rebelling or simply walking away? For Chen, 'the parade' is the voluntary lining up behind authority. It is provides legitimization for the authorities. '[Mao] did a lot of terrible things, he brought tragedy to the Chinese people. But who gave him the right to do that? Who made him believe he could do everything he wanted to do? The Chinese people. I would like to break the circle.'[28] Originally, for his last scene, Chen's intention was to show an empty parade ground with the sounds of those *who didn't* participate ('. . . you hear voices laughing and talking. I prefer that ending, because people can think they didn't join the big parade.')[29] In other words, to the discipline already attained through the process of training, what Chen would like to add is *the choice* in whether and how to use it, to separate discipline, strength, and national feeling from the abuses to which they have historically been subjected. But ultimately, combined pressure from the military, the film Bureau, and the Guangxi Film Studio prevailed to reshape the ending of the film: 'If you make a decision to be a film-maker, you have to suffer.'[30] 'Don't forget, it's China,' Chen said of this. 'I have to do what I can under censorship.'[31]

The parallel of Chen's intended conclusion here to *Yellow Earth*'s last moments, where PLA propagandist Gu Qing at first seems to appear but then isn't there, is obvious. But *the form*, in both cases, is not straightforward. How, if authoritarianism is to be subverted, can this be done without asking people simply to line up *against* authority? How can it be done while still acknowledging, as *The Big Parade* clearly does, that self-discipline is a profound virtue, as positive in its spiritual potential as it is negative when abused by totalitarian authority, and that the desire to participate in the discipline of the state is a strong and benign intention on the part of the people? And how can authoritarian rhetoric be dismantled without resort to an alternative propaganda? Although Chen does not answer this in his interviews (he is not asked), he does so in his films, which reject melodrama not with more melodrama but with no-drama. The answer lies in giving no definitive answer, allowing every viewer their own interpretation.[32]

Chen's films remain indeterminate in form and avoid ultimate answers to the social questions they raise, just as he acknowledges the ambiguities of his own experience and the imponderability of his own fate: 'I went to the countryside,' he says of his Cultural Revolution experience, 'and it was a good thing, even though I was forced to go. I grew up through doing labour. I became quite strong, not only physically, also spiritually.'[33] In *The Big Parade*, like his Instructor Sun, Chen refuses to measure discipline by the ends to which it is put and instead seems to value means and ends each for their own sake. He recognizes the distinct personality of every character at the same time as he admires selflessness. Through this refusal to sort and separate, through his maintenance of an open-ended analogue, Chen demolishes the typology and the central means of signification essential to any meaningful definition of melodrama.

Ironically, *The Big Parade*, which we see not as an easy movie with pat answers but as an ambitious deconstruction of the public usurpation of individual discipline, was criticized in the film world for 'playing it safe' after Chen Kaige's risky success with *Yellow Earth*.[34] Chen's next film, *King of the Children* (1987), transfers the issues of instruction and replication from the military training ground to the classroom, looking at the conundrum of how to teach independence to an all-too-docile population so that the teacher will not remain the subject of blind obedience. The term 'king of the children', a traditional Chinese expression for 'teacher', embodies the combination of authoritarianism and passivity that Chen seeks to undermine. Based on a short story by Chen's close friend Ah Cheng,[35] who had recently helped script Xie Jin's *Hibiscus Town*, it was photographed by Gu Changwei, who would go on to serve as cinematographer for Zhang Yimou's *Red Sorghum* and *Judou* and Chen's *Farewell My Concubine*.

Xie Jin spoke to the 8th Golden Rooster Awards committee, saying, 'I feel that *King of the Children* has the most profound ideas. Such a film has already reached world level . . . it astonished us through language and words . . .'[36] But it won no awards. Worse, at the Cannes Film Festival where Chen Kaige came heralded as the leader of a new era in Chinese cinema and armed with what he considered his finest movie yet, 'He had his eyes on the Golden Palm, but he got the "Golden Alarm Clock" instead – for "the most boring picture of the year".'[37] Jianying Zha writes of Chen's first film without cinematographer Zhang Yimou that '*King of Children* sank like a stone',[38] and with it Chen's reputation plummeted, not to rise again until 1993 with his production of *Farewell My Concubine.*

The story in *King of the Children* is that of a youth, Lao Gar (the tall and gangly 'Old Pole'), sent down to the countryside in the Cultural Revolution and drafted to teach a class of teen-aged students in the rural southern backwater of Yunnan province (illus. 233). Expected only to lead his students in memorizing texts generated by the central government, he discovers he has no idea how to *really* teach and in trying to figure out how, he rebels without quite realizing it, obliging the students instead to write their own compositions. For this, he is fired. End of story, by and large: utterly undramatic. In its (un)dramatic form, it is a studio-mate to *Yellow Earth*, but even more than Chen's earlier works, this film is a meditation, a philosophical speculation not

233 *King of the Children.* Lao Gar's tightly-packed but under-equipped classroom, opening on to other classrooms beyond. The student Wang Fu rises to challenge Lao Gar's approach to teaching.

only on the state of the Chinese state – about which he appears increasingly pessimistic – but on the historical role of the all-too-childlike Chinese people in relationship to 'adult' authority. Even more directly than *The Big Parade*, it draws from the experiences of Chen Kaige and his classmate Ah Cheng as young urban intellectuals, *zhiqing*, sent down to learn from and help the rural peasantry (Chen and Ah Cheng were both sent to work on rubber plantations in the Xishuangbanna region of Yunnan).[39] The actor Xie Yuan, long and spindly as a stick of wood and looking every bit as unheroic as his name, plays Old Pole in a reflexive mode. Chen recounts this in terms of his own dual education, in the classroom and in the field:

I had a rather privileged schooling at a select boys school in Beijing [the famous 4th Middle School]. A lot of my classmates were the sons of Party leaders; one was the son of Liu Shaoqi [Mao Zedong's successor as chief-of-state in the early 1960s and Mao's archrival at the outset of the Cultural Revolution]. Others were from relatively poor families; they had got there on the strength of good results in primary school. But all of us were brought up in a big dream, believing in the Party, in Chairman Mao and in China's wonderful, perfect future. We learned nothing about the country's political and economic realities. It was only when I was sent to the countryside that I found out how the peasants did mindless, back-breaking work and still didn't have enough to eat. I used to get very angry and say that our teacher had taught us nothing but bullshit. But I don't think he deliberately set out to lie to us. The teacher was just as much a victim of the situation as we were.[40]

For Chen, it seemed a time when people were utterly subjected to the common culture, a culture of patterned repetition, 'reflected in the behaviour of every individual – from their blind worship of the leader/emperor figure to the total desecration and condemnation of individual rights'.[41] Refusing to recognize the Cultural Revolution as an historical aberration, Chen concludes,

Repetition is a characteristic of Chinese traditional culture. The children in the film copied the textbook, then the dictionary, without any comprehension. Man, in his preservation of himself, has developed culture, but in the end, the culture has become the master of man . . . Thus, what is embedded in the film *King of the Children* is my judgment on traditional culture.[42]

Explaining his film in metaphorical terms, Chen states, 'I built the school-house set at the top of that hill so that it would be like a *temple* of culture, and the symbolic meaning of the time-lapse shot at the start, with the light exchanging and clouds racing by, is that everything is changing *except* the school' (illus. 234).[43] When his fellow *zhiqing* first come to visit him, Lao Gar mocks the authoritarian pedagogy of the school-as-unchanging-temple, ordering them facetiously to stand up for him with hands behind their backs – 'If you make trouble you'll get trouble . . . today's text is important, so pay attention!' then teaching them this chant:

> Once there was a mountain
> On the mountain was a temple
> In the temple was an old monk telling a story.
> What was he telling?
> 'Once there was a mountain
> In the mountain was a temple . . .'

. . . which goes on, and on, irredeemably repetitious – but catchy and therefore dangerous, and which Lao Gar's students, overhearing his friends, immediately and instinctively begin repeating themselves.

As Chen Kaige's *Farewell My Concubine* would be narratively illustrated at beginning and end by its two leading figures,[44] *King of the Children* is tellingly framed by landscape which puts the entire theme in perspective. The last scene of the film repeats the first, only the passing clouds at the beginning are replaced by rising smoke, lush green hillsides giving way to a charred landscape (illus. 234, 235). It is an image marking the persistence of tradition succeeded by one that suggests the inexorable depletion of cultural value within that tradition, a repeated image used to suggest the destructive force of repetition. The devastation may seem terrible, but exploitation of the land is not Chen's theme here. 'The burning of the wasted mountains at the end of the film,' Chen has said, 'is a metaphor of my attitude towards traditional values. "Don't copy anything, not even the dictionary."'[45] A living tradition relies on a balance between vitality and repetition; for Chen, the latter has so much gained the upper hand in China that nothing short of a

234 *King of the Children*. The film's opening scene: the school building seen as a hill-top temple.

235 *King of the Children*. The film ends with the sounds of falling timber and the sight of smoke consuming the mountainous countryside.

'burning off' can clear the way for new cultural growth. 'In the same way, the burning of the forest at the end represents my wish to burn everything down!'[46] – this from a *zhiqing*, a young urban intellectual, son of a prominent film director, brought up in an elegant compound once owned by Manchu nobility, a youth who 'spoke with an elegant Beijing accent sprinkled with well-chosen classical phrases'[47] and spent the early years of the Cultural Revolution reading Sima Qian and Cao Xuejin, who had watched Red Guards trash the family home and burn their books,[48] who was sent down to the country- side and says 'it was a good thing, even though I was forced to go . . . I became quite strong, not only physically, also spiritually.'[49] With an ambiguity so much like Chen's own deep cultural ambivalence, these silent scenes seem to visualize a combination of nihilism and radical idealism disturbingly like that which shaped the Cultural Revolution, whose blind adherence to authority is the arch-villain of the film. Yet bracketed within these scenes is something far more subtle.

Tony Rayns has written that 'Where all earlier *zhiqing* films . . . had used the experience of being sent to a remote countryside as a means of constructing a political and moral point-of-view, *King of the Children* narrows its focus to the specific implications of the *zhiqing* experience itself – and finds them almost infinite.'[50] Politics, culture, and spirituality weave a tangled web. With its theme of liberating the individual from the grip of cultural forces and opening up space for the emergence of an individual psychology, *King of the Children* verges on authorial biography. As Chen states, '[In *King of the Children*] I tried to look for myself. If people really pay attention to *King of the Children*, they can find me.'[51] *King of the Children*, perhaps, is China's equivalent to Truffaut's *The Four Hundred Blows*. As much as it is a political parable, cast as a confrontation between a teacher and his administrators, it is also a cultural exploration engaging a teacher and his pupils, and an internal dialogue through which a teacher becomes his own pupil in quest of spiritual self-understanding.

This internal 'dialogue' is facilitated by a minor narrative episode in Ah Cheng's story that in Chen Kaige's film[52] is developed and enhanced by the creation of a new character not present in the book – possibly a mental figment, one can't be sure. To call this thematic encounter a 'subplot' to Lao Gar's classroom engagement with students would give a misleading name to the plotless, drama-free, silent, and unanticipated visual encounters by which the film records a young oxherd who repeatedly wanders through the cinematic, academic, and mental life of Lao Gar. Like the jar of holy water in *Yellow Earth*, the recurrent appearance/apparition of the herd boy seems visually to encapsulate

236 *King of the Children.* The oxherd disappearing from view.

and signify an esoteric body of possible meanings that provide for patient contemplation and thematic integration (illus. 236). In his non-physicality, the oxherd competes with Lao Gar's fellow *zhiqing* Laidi (illus. 237), the one adult woman and the most physical person in the film. Perhaps the most 'natural' woman in any of the films discussed here – spontaneous and plain-talking, sexually playful, as overweight as Lao Gar is overly tall and thin, and no closer to the uncommonly good looks of a Gong Li than Gar is to Jiang Wen – Laidi continually attempts to draw Lao Gar into a gendered relationship with her. This he constantly rejects in favor of plain friendship, egalitarian and immaterial, preserving himself instead for the inner quest associated with the oxherd.

When Lao Gar becomes a teacher, he doesn't hesitate to tell his superiors that he doesn't know how to teach. The school's headmaster replies, 'What do you mean you can't teach? Just teach, that's all, it's not hard.'[53] But to his students, he confesses that he doesn't know *what* to teach (illus. 238). When Lao Gar first faces his class, he discovers that in this impoverished part of China, not only are students too poor to buy books, the government itself cannot afford to issue books to them. Only the teacher has *the* book – 'Don't lose it,' he's warned in Ah Cheng's telling, 'If it gets lost we'll have a time finding another.'[54] His role, then, is to copy the text in its entirety on the blackboard, so that

237 *King of the Children.* Playful Laidi musses Lao Gar's hair before his departure to begin teaching. Lao Gar, as usual, rejects her advances.

238 *King of the Children.* Lao Gar's puzzle: does the teacher liberate or enslave his pupils?

students can copy it for themselves into their exercise books, learning the characters and parsing the grammar exactly as their teacher tells them to do, nothing more, exactly as the state tells him to do. In essence, of course, this is not simply a function of rural poverty and it repeats the pattern of rote learning found even in the most élite, traditional education. The copying begins in earnest, non-stop, leading right into the night. We learn that night through wordless imagery how frustrated Lao Gar is with this state of affairs when he stares and then spits at his own image in a mirror; we're showed how torn he feels and cued that he knows there is a hard choice about to be made by the way the broken mirror splits his image in two. The next day, in the midst of copying the eighth lesson on the board, a momentary distraction that draws him out into the schoolyard – the appearance, or spectre?, of a young oxherd, who then disappears almost magically from view (illus. 236). Immediately afterwards (though we only discover it later on), Lao Gar slips a phantom character into the text. Composed of the character for 'ox' written over that for 'water', the fusion means (to him) 'cow piss' (illus. 239).

In retrospect, if the herdboy's brief, almost spectral manifestation in the neighbouring classroom is hard to see (illus. 240), it is even harder for the audience to catch at once the relationship of this encounter to Lao Gar's own transformation: but the moment of his first appearance constitutes the precise beginning of a sequence in which Lao Gar begins to consider his task, to remodel his teaching, and destroy the authoritative 'king' in 'king of the children'. Within moments, Lao Gar challenges the students to interpret for themselves what they have read. He, in turn, is immediately challenged by them, resisted ('You're not much of a teacher. Why don't you teach like you're supposed to?') (see illus. 233), and while 'stunned' for an instant,[55] rather than reassert his authority in the usual fashion, he suddenly bursts out with his trademark laugh and begins for the first time to establish a personal, emotional bond with his students that will remain unbroken afterwards.

The atmosphere which develops is unusual enough that later on, the teacher next door comes over to inquire about the presence of laughter in his classroom. 'It's good to laugh,' he replies twice to her, a simple statement that issues from no Maoist or even Confucian source, and perhaps could derive only from a Zhuangzi-esque personality. Lao Gar later acknowledges it is he, the teacher, who has learned, a credit to the boy who challenged him. This teaching episode is followed the next day by Lao Gar entering the classroom, bowing twice to his students (to their astonishment), telling them that they no longer need to stand when he enters or when they speak to him ('What's the point if you don't even have books?'), nor must they hold their hands behind their backs any longer when they're not writing. He is not their king. Soon after he will dispense with the text in favour of essays written on the basis of each student's individual experience.

The made-up character, 'cow piss', should strike us as an intentional 'abuse of language', one of the modes that Chinese avant-garde art has pursued in recent years. This is based on the notion that Communist

239 *King of the Children*. Lao Gar with the underlined character for 'cow piss'.

240 *King of the Children*. The oxherd first appears as a shadowy figure, scarcely visible, in the neighbouring classroom.

241 *King of the Children*. Ignoring Lao Gar's offer to teach him to read, the oxherd turns in silence and disappears.

authorities have so abused the language with false propaganda, turning words and meanings into anything they want to, that the most effective critique is for dissident artists to openly mirror, parody, and wave this in the face of authority (see illus. 222). The best-known example of this is perhaps an installation by calligrapher Xu Bing, *A Mirror to Analyze the World/A Book from the Sky*, consisting of endless pages of calligraphy, mounted on walls, hung from ceilings, folded into albums, containing in all some 3,000 printed characters covering 300 square metres. Hand-carved by the artist, the project required three years of intensive labour, each of the characters different, made up by the artist, and all entirely unreadable (illus. 242).[56] But with Xu Bing as with *King of the Children*, there is also a deeper meaning, rooted in the ancient Daoist belief that words (not just their users or their use) are *inherently* unbelievable, that they are misleading, that they subject society to all sorts of literary lies and lead to mental slavery. This, of course, is the antithesis of Confucius's notion of the 'rectification of names'. As the first step in his awakening, this fictive character comes to Lao Gar more as an impulse than as a thought, more an undoing than a doing, something he writes for himself rather than for his students and something he himself must struggle to figure out before attempting to explain it to his class. In fact, he will only come to understand it in light of events that have yet to occur.

The *Daode jing*, quoted at the outset of the previous essay, begins with the famous phrase, 'The Way [*dao*] that can be spoken of is not the eternal way; the name [*ming*] that can be named is not the eternal name.' In different words, in his own searching way, Lao Gar will begin to elaborate this deeper lesson to himself and to his children. He will go from teaching them to write about their own experiences (which proves remarkably difficult for them to do) and awarding his best student,

Wang Fu, a dictionary for his diligence (which the pupil begins to copy daily, word for word and page for page), to denying the value of writing itself and telling Wang Fu to abandon his project. Lao Gar's final message to Wang Fu is not to copy anything, which he writes in chalk on a tree stump. The significance of this wooden stump is uncertain, though its hard to imagine there is none. Perhaps he is referencing the *Daode jing*'s 'uncarved block', an image of primordial simplicity,[57] but one can't help being reminded also of the destruction taking place in the forests all around the schoolhouse, signifying China's advanced stage of cultural decay. These alternative images, one of perfection, one of corruption, are combined in the many thematic uses of old trees in the *Zhuangzi* to signify original nature, its destruction, and the secret of its preservation.[58]

With his final instruction to Wang Fu not to copy anything, Lao Gar at last seeks to obliterate the words, the labels by which ordinary reality is constructed as ordinary and by which political abuse is constructed as part of that reality. But while Lao Gar's message engages that philosophical principle, it cannot readily escape its enigma: how can he use words to turn Wang Fu against words? How can he *instruct* his pupils to free themselves of his instructions? This parallels the historical puzzle of how Laozi could *write* the *Daode jing*, with its

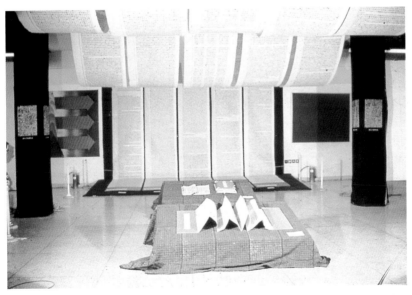

242 Xu Bing, *A Mirror to Analyse the World/A Book from the Sky*, 1988, calligraphic installation (seen here at the 1989 *China/Avant-Garde Exhibition*, National Gallery, Beijing).

imprecations against naming names (a conundrum that was not lost on those philosophical purists who criticized the Old Man for his resort to text).[59] Or to put it in modern terms, how can one destroy the destructive mentality of the Cultural Revolution without giving in to its ways? This entire semantical inversion is embodied in the character 'cow piss' which, although *freely* made up by Lao Gar, refers to a trick by which the herdsman enslaves the ox (see illus. 239).

In Ah Cheng's text, the meaning of this character is divulged immediately at the time of its creation – narratively, as Lao Gar drifts off into a private reverie at the blackboard, into a kind of philosophical meditation on his own personal experiences of ox-herding, triggered by the sounds of ox-herding drifting down from the distant mountains. Only a portion of this (italicized below) is presented in the film, in a later scene:

Cows are extremely stubborn beasts but they're also very tolerant, they just blink slowly and go on eating what they want to no matter how hard you hit them or swear at them. I always used to think that philosophers were probably like this too, or else how could they succeed in their studies? But even 'philosophers' sometimes got flustered, a*nd that was certainly when I'd go for a pee. Cows have a craving for salty things and urine is salty, so they used to jostle each other to get at my urine.* Then they'd be very happy . . . When you feed cattle with your own urine you'll find they will always obey you loyally, they'll treat you like a parent. Even I often felt like the leader of a party, happily using my urine as the source of my power.[60]

In Ah Cheng's original rendering, self, service and authority, are subtly compared to each other, intellectuals and the state are contemplated in silence by Lao Gar. In the film, instead of appearing as private musings, limited portions of this passage – minus philosophers and the Party – become Lao Gar's parting message to his pupils, withheld until the end of the story after he realizes he's just lost his job but remains unsure about whether he has failed in his mission.

The children are not expected to understand this fully, and indeed even Ah Cheng's patient reader is obliged to ponder this oddly-twisted power structure: the 'philosopher' (the intellectual, the teacher) in the service of the state may be beaten *like an ox*, even while in that service he is *like an oxherd*, exercising control over the people *through his investiture* with state authority, like the 'king' with his children. Lao Gar's analogy is rather simple, despite its trivalent structure: the weak are bound to the powerful by a material reality; those without power are nothing more than a dependent herd to those in power, able to resist only by turning to an internal reality; those with borrowed power are as much like the herd as they are like the herder – if they choose to herd others, how will they not remain part of a herd themselves? Not so simple are questions of where the *moral* authority lies, with the oxherd or with the ox (with the state, its agents, or the masses), and based on that, when and whether the herdboy should pee for the herd (serve the state, indoctrinate the children). Does the ox really need an oxherd or the oxherd his ox?

The theme of ox-herding is an ancient one in Chinese philosophy, literature, and art.[61] In its various appearances in diverse schools of thought, it is a theme of transition, figuratively negotiating the transition between city and countryside, between official service and humble retirement, demotion and exile, Confucianism and Daoism. Typically, the ox is recognized as strong but docile, as crude but virtuous, lowly yet naturally enlightened. The oxherd is the boss but seeks the wisdom of his own charge – just as the ruler seeks the service of his scholars, as the good teacher learns from his own pupils, or the mystic searches for enlightenment through nature. In the *Shuo gua* commentary on the ancient classic of divination, the *Yijing* (in the second chapter, *kun*, dealing with things earthen, receptive, pure *yin*), the ox figures as mother, as a cow with calf, as those who are hardworking but not recognized, as the masses.[62] Well before the end of the Zhou dynasty, the ox was presented as a symbol of harmony, peace, good harvest (reflected later on in paintings of 'One Hundred Oxen'): to herd (*mu*) is to govern (*zhi*).

In his commentary on the pre-Confucian classic, the *Guanzi* (chapter one, '*Mu min*' or 'Herding the People'), Qiu Jun wrote,

The one who knows well the principles of tending the ox is the one who can carefully select good land and grass to nourish the herd. Those who cannot tend oxen according to their nature, letting them thirst during the day and suffer from hunger during the night, cannot expect the herd to multiply into large numbers. The most important thing is to love them and not hurt them in any way; to make use of them and at the same time not to let them miss the conceiving and breeding period. All those herding practices merely comply with the animal's nature . . . Those who are not gentlemen will not pay attention to the meanings of pasturing and loving the herd.[63]

This is a kindly view of leadership, of leadership responsive to the needs of the people, of leaders following that which is natural as people naturally need good leaders. This sets a high standard for the herdsman, and as this rhetorical tradition developed, the emperor's herd was analogue not only for his people but for the class of scholar-statesmen who helped carry out his work: they, too, required expert herding, lest they go their own way, as scholars sometimes did. The famous Daoist alchemist Tao Hongjing, in the sixth century, wordlessly declined government service with a painting of two oxen he sent to Liang emperor Wendi, one ox wearing a golden halter (that is, serving in high office), one ox grazing freely (refusing the harness of public duty); the emperor needed nothing more to recognize that this 'ox' was one that got away (illus. 243).[64] Liu Zongyuan, in the early ninth century, wrote a 'Prose-poem on the Ox' ('Niu fu'), probably after his demotion in office; this 'ox' was one pushed to a far corner of the pen.[65] Clearly, the rhetorical tradition was long ago so well developed that no literary ox was simply an ox.

In Daoist legend, when the putative author of the *Daode jing*, Laozi, abandons urban life and courtly ways for rustic virtue, he departs westward from the capital borne by a black ox – a popular theme in Chinese painting, appropriate as a retirement gift – and leaves the Confucian gatekeeper Yin Xi his famous text (illus. 244). The next great Daoist text to follow, the *Zhuangzi*, writes of the ox,

Call in your knowledge, unify your bearing, and the spirits will come to dwell with you. Virtue will be your beauty, the Way will be your home, and, *stupid* as a newborn calf, you will not try to find out the reason why.[66]

Looking back from this at Qiu Jun's advice to the ruler, we can see that it makes sense not only for leading the people, but also for living one's life. Or for pursuing enlightenment: in Chan Buddhism, which may be thought of as the 'Daoification' of Buddhism, 'the masses' are internalized, herding is a matter of disciplining one's inner voices, and when in Chan, as in Daoism, one rides the ox of enlightenment, it comes as a mystic ten-part journey in which one looks for the ox, sees traces, sees the ox, catches it, tames or herds it, rides it 'home', forgets the ox, forgets oneself, returns to the fundamental source, and 'enters the city with hands hanging down'. In some early Chinese illustrations, the ox itself progresses from jet black to an invisible white. In the end, with the ox forgotten, one returns to a natural state of being, like the wonderfully stupid 'newborn calf' of early Daoist lore (illus. 245).[67]

In all this, the docile ox serves as a linguistic analogue for natural virtue, for the spontaneous, counter-intuitive, and anarchic, but at the same time for passivity, for banding together in herds, and for blindly serving their masters. All the while, this peculiar blend of analogues is itself analogized to the scholar's often-peculiar and perplexing state of affairs. Its logic is, literally, loopy: one has to be stupid to serve, but there is a virtue in being stupid, just as there is in serving. There is not much resolution here. As an analogical figure, the ox was used by Confucian scholars, Daoist adepts, and Chan Buddhists alike with no

243 Attrib. Han Huang, *Five Oxen*, mid-8th century, sections from a handscroll, ink and colour on paper. Palace Museum, Beijing.

These two oxen, one with a halter and one without, perhaps reflect something of Tao Hongjing's (452–536) legendary painting by which he declined court service – that is, he refused to put on the halter of public office.

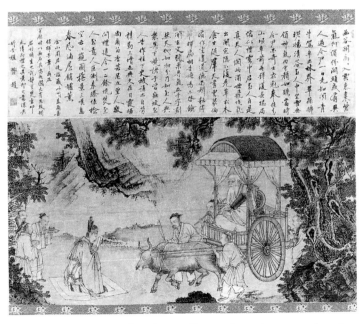

244 Shang Xi, *Laozi at the Western Pass*, early 15th century, hanging scroll, ink and colour on paper. MOA Museum of Art, Atami.

In Confucian China, the state paid respect to those who withdrew from public activity for spiritual and intellectual reasons. Here the Daoist Master Laozi, departing from China, leaves his textual legacy, the Daode jing, with the local gate official. According to some legends, Laozi headed to India where he became the Buddha, and some paintings on this theme substitute a depiction of the Buddha for Laozi. Serving as visual mediator in the space between the religious sage and the Confucian official, Yin Xi, the ox is an icon to Daoists, Buddhists, and Confucianists alike and serves as a symbol of harmony among them.

245 Zhiyong, *Herdboy Taming an Ox*, late 12th century, hanging scroll, ink on paper. Formerly in the Kozo Yabumoto Collection.

The use of ox-herding as an allegory for seeking Buddhahood can be traced back at least to the late 8th–early 9th century in China, in writings of the priest Bozhuang Huaihai, and by the 11th century had become standardized in ten-part ox-herding songs. Despite its title, this painting most likely represents the fourth of ten stages, namely catching the ox. Taming the ox comes next.

real acknowledged contradiction because it stood on common ground, in philosophical territory shared by all three. None of these philosophies imagined a world with no authority at all. Rather, they shared a view of good governance carried out according to rustic, agrarian ideals, as a minimal activity: he governs best who governs least – *wei wu wei*, do by not doing.[68] It is hardly ironic, then, that this thematic territory would be infringed by philosophers and politicians who recommended doing by doing, like the twelfth-century philosophical activist, the Neo-Confucian Zhu Xi, once known for his own paintings of oxen. Even Mao Zedong borrowed the metaphor of the ox for Communist propaganda. But as a traditionally educated revolutionary, he not only borrowed it as a metaphor for good, hard work,[69] he also found the occasion to shade its spiritual connotations with the negative import of feudal superstition and turned its traditional use against his conservative enemies with the celebrated Cultural Revolution slogan: 'Sweep away all cow demons and snake spirits!' (see illus. 111).[70]

In Ah Cheng's text, this traditional referent occurs without any explicit appearance of the oxherd. Only the made-up character, triggered by the sounds of oxen, appears, suggesting to the audience the entire range of thematic alternatives – to serve or not to serve, to nourish the people, to break from authority, to nourish the inner self. It is only in the film that Lao Gar's psychic development is enhanced by the actual appearance of the oxherd – on three occasions in all, like the three-fold appearance of the jar of holy-water in *Yellow Earth*.[71] The first time he appears is just before Lao Gar creates the character for 'cow piss' on the blackboard, indicating some spiritual bond between the two: as he is writing, Lao Gar suddenly looks up and over his shoulder, in the next classroom, he spies someone writing something on the board in that room (see illus. 240); going over to look, he sees some crude drawing of concentric circles with cow dung stuck to it; coming out into the courtyard he spies the cowherd disappearing over a fence (see illus. 236). This marks the beginning of Lao Gar's liberation as a teacher.[72] The next time they meet, in a pasture, Lao Gar's students have already begun to write their own texts based exclusively on personal experience (rather like Mao and Deng's aphorism, 'Seek truth from facts', whose sincerity the film challenges) and he, like them, has gained new insights and confidence. With this, he offers to teach the oxherd to read. But he is met with stony silence and the herdboy, who is beyond reading, disappears like a phantom (see illus. 241).[73] Their last encounter comes at the end of the film, after the authorities[74] have had Lao Gar fired for departing from the prescribed text (Mao and Deng's 'seek truth' notwithstanding), after he has explained his 'cow piss' character to the class, after he has told his star pupil (Wang Fu, who has patiently been copying the entire dictionary) not to copy anything more, not even the dictionary,[75] and on his departure from the village. This time, in an eerie hillside setting of burnt-out tree stumps meant perhaps to look like iconic dragons or the ghosts of ancient court figures, we encounter the oxherd pissing. Again he disappears, with a parting glance at Lao Gar, and this time Lao Gar responds with a smile and he, too, disappears.

Tony Rayns, who has written with interest on the relationship of sound and image in both *Big Parade* and *King of the Children*, describes this sequence of encounters:

Each subsequent appearance of the cowherd and his cattle – either in picture or, more often, on the soundtrack – is more hallucinatory. The boy speaks to his cattle but ignores Lao Gar's questions; it is as if he represents a state of existence that is somehow outside language. Inevitably, Lao Gar comes to associate the cowherd with his invented composite character. He ends his final class by explaining his shorthand invention to the pupils – and recommending them to 'renew' language for themselves.[76]

King of the Children 'renews' the language of cinema as well. In its visuality, *King of the Children* combines some of the close-knit structure and tight patternization of *Big Parade* with the openness of *Yellow Earth*.

As in the language of Chinese avant-garde painting, tropes of pattern and packing suggest a conscious critique of the repetitiveness of Chinese public behaviour (illus. 246) and the mechanically interchangeable roles of a billion-plus people seen as politically-silenced non-individuals (illus. 247). In *King of the Children*, the classroom is packed with patterned rows of shared desks, like bunks in the barracks of *Big Parade*, and it opens directly on to the next classroom in a visually unobstructed, semiotically interlocking replication system, denying whatever private space might be required for individuation (see illus. 231, 233, 240). As an object, the shed-like classroom design is rather like an ox-pen. And yet at the same time the school as a whole is set 'like a temple' on an exposed hilltop, opening outward to nature and upward to the spacious heavens, to realms spiritual rather than social (see illus. 234). As a space, it is transient between the terrestriality of the hard-working ox and the astral sacredness of this perfectly 'stupid' beast, between Marxian materialism and Daoist idealism. Here on this hilltop, the ruins of the world below filter upward only in a disembodied state, as strange sounds and smoke, or as mindless pedagogy which like so much noise and smoke tends to obscure the very existence of alternative realities but doesn't actually displace them or prevent their eventual, perhaps accidental, discovery and subsequent pursuit. The students, in their last year of studies, are expected soon to return to the fields below. Lao Gar, the oxherd, would rather guide them upward, outward, beyond the borders. But he, too, is an ox, herded about by the state and ultimately unable to do as he wishes except in his mind. Lao Gar wanders off at the end, alone, toward some unspecified liberation, as the earth below is burning (see illus. 235). We see smoke; we hear the sound of trees being chopped down and falling over, and we hear the sound of repetitive chanting: 'Once there was a mountain, on the mountain was a temple. . .'

The visually constructed meaning of these images, in large part, lies in their vagueness. Likewise, the film as a whole results in a diffuse effect, making it as meaningless for the audience as for Lao Gar's students to concentrate solely on particulars. Avoiding spatial cohesion and structural tension, embracing both learned rhetoric and the authors'

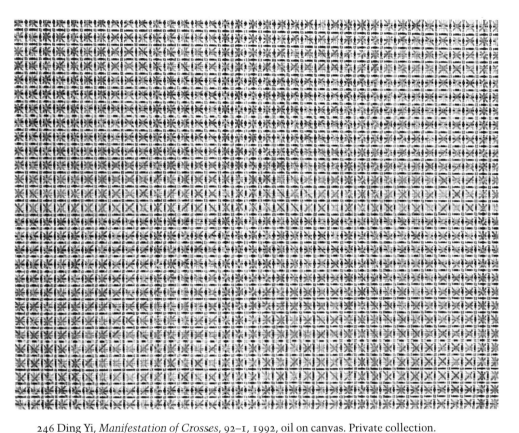

246 Ding Yi, *Manifestation of Crosses*, 92–1, 1992, oil on canvas. Private collection.

Purely abstract, purely geometrical, Ding Yi's works display no content, betray no symbolism. They can be labeled as 'op art' but that is the lesser part of their conveyance. Each and every dot or line is painted and painted over several times, single elements put together according to a carefully calculated arithmetic formula, but to what end? Reminiscent of a million marchers packed into a Tian'an Men political rally, the image appears to be about organization and control, but chaos and intentional disorder are foremost in the artist's mind. Ding's art parodies the Maoist didactics of uniformity: he first carries to extreme the notion of minds regulated by formula, and then he subtly subverts it. 'I do not want harmony . . . but an arbitrary uncontrollability of colour. . . . I want a pre-calculated chaos, caused by a complicated structure. I want the observer to feel ill when faced with the work.' The illness Ding speaks of here is not merely a visually-induced queasiness but a profound moral revulsion.

247 Wang Jinsong, *The Big Bright Day*, 1991, oil on canvas, Ludwig Museum, Cologne.

Wang Jinsong is a fan of the Chinese theatre who understands that the actor's skill is to transform himself into someone else, to change from role to role. 'On stage,' he writes, 'people do what they are told.' In China, his paintings suggest, everyone is forced on stage, one year with Mao suits, one year with Western clothing; one year as proletarian ideologues, informing on the wayward, one year as nouveau capitalists in hot pursuit of financial reward. In Wang's paintings, the figures are like stage props, one-dimensional figures with no personalities of their own. Like Ken and Barbie dolls, they can change persona as quickly as they can change their clothes: dressed up, dressed down, stripped bare, they follow the conductor. Realistic heads combine with sketchy bodies, or vice versa; plastic bodies come apart at the seams, with detachable arms and broken torsos, with feet or faces often missing. Who are they, really, beneath their disguise?

own idiosyncratic ambivalences, *King of the Children* demands a sophisticated audience at the same time as it challenges its audience to shed some of their sophistication. Of its failure at Cannes, Chen spoke to the fact that 'the people I was talking to had never been to China and knew very little about Chinese culture', and he admitted to taking 'too much for granted'.[77] But that was the lesser obstacle. If the viewers are to 'get it', they must embrace the open-ended possibilities, make believe as a young child does, join Lao Gar in his infatuated laughter, indulge his infantile play with the crude millstone in the schoolyard (an interplay, perhaps, between civilization and its discontents), identify with his 'mindless' imitations of nature (hunching over like a rock, spinning like a tree in the wind; illus. 248), accept his vision of the oxherd as a breakdown between 'phantom' (the forbidden) and (socially dictated) 'reality', and take part in his childlike search for the unnameable, for the stupid, uncorrupted 'newborn calf' within.

At Cannes, we remember, *King of the Children* was a yawn. And so it should be: with the help of Lao Gar, Chen Kaige invites us into the realm of imagination, where self merges dreamily with selflessness. By any stretch of the imagination, *King of the Children* is not a melodrama. But neither is it solipsistic and disengaged. In part, what *King of the Children* is examining is the nature of disaffection and dissent in modern and ancient China, not active opposition but the right of the disaffected to opt out. ('Everyone's fed up,' says Lao Gar in the opening scene.) Traditionally, retreat and reclusion were *the* honourable mode of dissent in China – if one didn't want to put up, one could and should have shut up. As such, it was often hard to distinguish a disaffected Confucianist in his shut-up mode from a reclusive Daoist who had no put-up mode at all and was comfortable only in isolation. But with the take-no-prisoners theorems of the Leninist–Maoist class struggle, political involvement went from an exclusive right to a universal obligation and anything short of correct and energetic support of current Party policy was a 'contradiction' in one degree or another; whether 'antagonistic' (irreconcilable contradictions between the people and the enemies of the people) as overt opposition would be, or 'non-antagonistic' (reconcilable contradictions among loyal people) as passive disaffection might be, all contradictions required 'resolution'. In early Party analyses of the 1920s, the Daoist thought of Laozi and Zhuangzi was paralleled to the anarchism of Bakunin and Kropotkin, philosophically revolutionary but of the wrong political stripe.[78] But as Kam Louie notes, in the post-Revolutionary debates on what was heritable from past philosophy, Laozi and Zhuangzi were differentiated as 'objective' and 'subjective' idealists, respectively, and it was claimed that:

248 *King of the Children.* Trying to become one with nature: Lao Gar twisting himself into a variety of tree- and stump-like forms.

Zhuangzi's ideas were self-deceptive, and that, as far as the people were concerned, the consequences of Zhuangzi's ideas were even worse [than Laozi's, or than Huang-Lao Daoism], because they encourage people to become more passive in the face of class struggle. Hence, the thinking of both Zhuangzi and Kongzi [Confucius] was adopted by the ruling classes in both the slave and feudal periods . . . [to encourage] people to be passive and so meekly submit to tyranny . . .[79]

In short, covert disaffection, once acceptable, was lumped together with overt dissent as a contradiction. And there was, therefore, no room for Lao Gar's brand of disaffection, for his befriending the students as he did and thereby abrogating his authority and undermining that of his superiors, nor for his efforts to lead his students astray from the rest of the herd. There is even less room for Chen's burning down the mountains at the end, a wordless image that sneaks past the censor an attitude more extreme than Lao Gar's disaffection. So it is a remarkable fact that Chen Kaige was able to make and distribute this critical examination of spirituality and political (in)tolerance in Deng Xiaoping's China[80] and that Ah Cheng's original editor for this short story, Wang Meng, soon after became China's liberal Minister of Culture (until sacked following the Tian'an Men tragedy). In an era when so much effort is paid to understanding Chinese political dissent and spiritual aspirations, people may yet wake up to *King of the Children*.

By the time Chen Kaige was making *King of the Children*, in 1987, his colleague of earlier times, cinematographer Zhang Yimou, was already coming into his own as an actor in *Old Well* (for which he would be named best actor at the Tokyo Film Festival) and directing his own first film, *Red Sorghum*. 'A fucking cameraman, *my* cameraman,' Chen later said of the photographer who had brought him on board to help produce *Yellow Earth*, once his own star had fallen and Zhang's was high up in the sky. 'It was like first love,' he said later of the first days of 'Fifth Generation' film-making. 'We were all so passionate.'[81] 'The most important thing,' he said of this film-making, 'was how to make films ourselves – how we could make things different. We had seen too many propaganda films. We had the personal experience. We thought we could do something different and better.'[82] Chen's early films wrapped his urbane contemplation of China's fate in a rural reverie, like an ancient landscape couched in classic restraint and balance. 'I don't feel comfortable with melodrama,' he would say, 'because I don't like emotional excess. I could never make a film like Xie Jin's *Hibiscus Town*, which says that there are good people and bad people and that everything will be fine if we can just get rid of the bad people! It seems to me that all of us have positive and negative sides, and the same capacities to love and hate.'[83] Yet Chen's characters neither loved too much nor hated much at all. And by 1987, at least seen in hindsight, the time for such understatement seemed to have quickly passed. *Red Sorghum* had already sounded the 'death knell' of the 'Fifth Generation's' *original* goals.[84] Though audiences were once stunned by *Yellow Earth*, the following few years of intellectual film-making that followed in its wake were soon dismissed as a 'trendy plague' of 'excruciatingly ponderous, sometimes downright pretentious and dull art movies'.[85]

King of the Children failed to arouse its viewers at Cannes, and many later critics, writing with their own agendas, refused to participate in its antique mysticism and quiescent sublimation or even to recognize its purely visual rage. Rey Chow, for example, deploring the lack of a strong female presence in *King of the Children*, regards this all as mere narcissistic indulgence:

The idealization of the child contains in itself a violence that is self-directed. This violence disguises itself as the love of the self, as 'narcissism.' As Freud says, 'At the weakest point of all in the narcissistic position, the immortality of the ego . . . security is achieved by *fleeing to the*

child . . .' The 'sublimated' message of the film is that the world is generated in this interplay between pedagogy and fantasy, between 'culture' and
'nature' – that is, without woman and without the physical body! . . . My
insistence, on the biological, therefore, is not an attempt to reify it as such
but a means of interrupting the tendency toward what I would call, for lack
of a better term, *mentalism* in Chinese culture.[86]

But reify, it does. It would seem that what most critics want, despite all
protestations to the contrary, is not philosophical musing, not visual
naturalism, not real-time pacing, but larger-than-life drama, more-
intense-than-our-own romance, uncommon beauty, action-packed
stories, and the return of good guys and bad – in short, melodrama.[87]
'This suspense is terrible. I hope it will last,' says one of the lead
characters at the critical moment of revelation in Oscar Wilde's comedy
of manners, coincidences, and mock-melodrama, *The Importance of
Being Earnest* – and with such a reflexive prompt tossed to the audience,
it certainly *did* continue.[88] In 1987, most 'Fifth Generation' film abandoned the abandonment of suspense and returned to entertainment –
message mixed with entertainment, in the melodramatic manner
perfected by Xie Jin but mixed with a larger dose of postmodern
ambiguity. Melodrama – like allegory and the allegorical use of gender,
all of them deeply embedded in Chinese tradition – was not to be dis-
inherited. The next time Chen Kaige made a successful film, it was the
highly dramatic, the thoroughly melodramatic *Farewell My Concubine*,
catching up with Zhang Yimou, who had already caught with and
surpassed Xie Jin. With this neo-melodrama replacing the 'Fifth
Generation's' original interest in no-drama, in the next round of under-
cutting 'Fifth Generation' film-making the critics' target would be
Zhang Yimou's films for being so un-naturalistic, so melodramatic, so
'Hollywood'.

The theme of Chen Kaige's *King of the Children* is replication, and at
the end of the film nearly everything goes up in smoke (see illus. 235).
The theme of Zhang Yimou's *Judou* (1990, China's first nominee for
a foreign film Academy Award)[89] similarly has to do with replication
and it, too, ends in flames (illus. 249). As the protagonist-victim, Judou
(actress Gong Li), burns down her own house, putting an end to her
misery there, she replicates the earlier narrowly thwarted attempt of
her wicked husband, Yang Jinshan, to send the whole family up in
flames. More than she realizes, Judou has gradually come to absorb her
husband's malevolence and to replicate his own vengeful impulses. An
even greater measure of the destructive force of replication in Chinese
culture is Judou's son Tianbai. Though a bastard by an illicit relationship, he bears none of the spirit of his nurturing mother and preserves

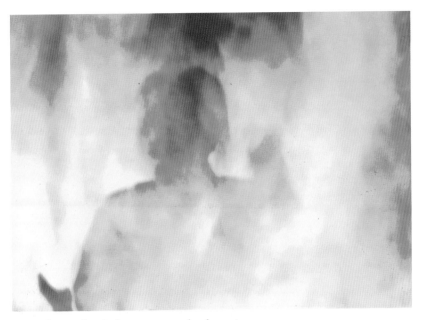

249 *Judou*. In fire, Judou puts an end to her misery.

instead the bad seed of his presumed 'father'. He is acknowledged as his 'father's' heir and the public is kept in ignorance of his true parentage because the recriminations for adultery are so horrific – 'If they knew, they'd kill us,' says Tianbai's real father.) 'Through his son, Yang Jinshan was reaching . . . from beyond the grave,' says Liu Heng's original text.[90] A major difference between these two films is that while the theme of replication is made transparent in the teacher-student relationship of *King of the Children*, which employs no dramatic means to convey its message, the dramatic affect of *Judou* smoulders and burns and somewhat obscures with smoke and flames the pervasive subtlety of the theme. Zhang Yimou's *Judou*, together with his *Red Sorghum* earlier and *Raise the Red Lantern* afterwards, are all focused on the replication of power and corruption, on intricate webs of deception and betrayal and endless cycles of exposure and revenge. At an advanced stage of the film *Judou*, the adulterous heroine accuses her illicit lover of beginning to repeat her husband's evil ways but she fails to recognize that she has already begun to do the same.

Judou details the abuses of patriarchal authority, personified by the evil wife-beater Yang Jinshan (illus. 250), and the escapist, elaborate, extended, and ultimately self-destructive affair by his wife, Wang Judou, with Jinsha's nephew, Yang Tianqing (illus. 251). Jinshan's incapacitation by accident and his subsequent dependence on the transgressive couple

250 *Judou.* Unable to sire a child by her, the abusive Yang Jinshan sits atop his bound wife Judou, whip in hand. On the window, a papercut reads 'Double Happiness' for the newlyweds.

provides Judou the opportunity, as a psychological weapon of reprisal, to flaunt before him the nephew's identity as true father of 'Jinshan's son'. But her rebellion is confirmed and the illicit couple is betrayed repeatedly in its efforts to maintain the semblance of a happy relationship outside the sanction of society: betrayed first by Jinshan's success at convincing the son, Tianbai, to regard him as his actual father, a deceit which the true parents cannot counter without exposing their transgression to the entire clan; then at the time of Jinshan's death (which might otherwise have become their moment of liberation), betrayed by clan elders, who separate them into different households for the sake of the family reputation; and finally betrayed by their own son; the son, having killed his recognized 'father', Jinshan – accidentally, but wickedly enjoying the death-throes (illus. 252, 253), grows up to kill his true father, quite intentionally avenging the mother's infidelity to his presumed 'father' (illus. 254). Overwhelmed and helplessly ensnared in this knot of evil and vengeance, Judou burns down the house as her own final act of revenge upon an entire system built on corruption and deceit.

Adapting Liu Heng's original text to cinema, Zhang Yimou has transformed it in a range of details, both broad and deep. Consistently, these changes bring out and exaggerate its melodramatic potential.

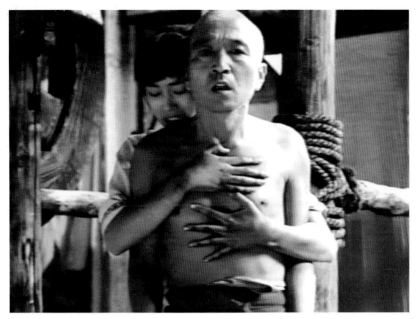

251 *Judou*. Judou seduces the cowardly voyeur, Yang Tianqing.

1. In Liu Heng's novella, Yang's brutality is the social by-product of his obsession with preserving the family line; in the film, it is an inherent moral quality lodged in a wicked and patently melodramatic character. At the very outset of the film, in order to define Yang in more extreme terms, we learn that two previous wives have been slowly tortured to death by Yang himself and Judou, just arrived, can expect to be next. In the book, Yang's first wife (of 30 years)– thought by some to be a Communist guerrilla – was killed by Japanese snipers.[91]

2. Liu Heng portrays village China as much more docile than Liu does. In the book, the villagers openly challenge Yang's brutality and only their sympathy for his tragic childlessness holds them in abeyance.[92] In the film, no villagers challenge Yang's brutality or threaten to cost him 'face', forming instead a silent, solid barrier against Judou.

3. Zhang strips Yang Jinshan of whatever redeeming values Liu Heng's text had provided. In Liu's text, Yang had wanted to adopt his orphaned nephew, Tianqing, but 'the young ingrate' (the narrator's words), resentful of his uncle's dealings with Tianqing's father, refused.[93]

4. Jinshan's death in the text results from an accident and his subsequent natural decline. In the film, he is inadvertently and yet most unsympathetically killed by the young boy Tianbai, who appears by that time as a kind of 'bad seed' – not the actual offspring of this evil man but a creature of evil circumstance.[94]

252, 253 *Judou*. As his 'father' Yang Jinshan drowns, Tianbai looks on . . . then laughs.

254 *Judou*. Tianbai delivers the coup de grace to his drowning father, Yang Tianqing.

5. Patriarchy itself is made central target of the film's critique. In Liu's text, after Jinshan's death, Wang Judou decides for herself to dwell apart from her lover; in the film, the separation of Judou and Yang Tianqing is imposed on them by the clan patriarchs.[95]

6. In the book, the young Tianbai's hatred of his uncle/father Tianqing, whom for long he doesn't even know to be his incestuous parent, is based on moral standards – his opposition to his uncle's flirtations with his mother – not an evil disposition: 'Damn it!' he says to Tianqing, 'Haven't you any decency!'[96]

7. In the book, Tianqing's death is by suicide. The film converts this suicide into a parricide by Tianbai. In the book, far from burning down her own home, Judou bears a second son by Tianqing after his death.[97]

All these changes elevate the melodramatic quality of the tale, converting characters of mixed virtue into more limited types, simpler and more clear-cut in their motives (especially, the wicked Jinshan and evil son Tianbai), streamlining the moral parameters of the original plot, redirecting its thrust from internalized guilt to a critique of social patriarchy, and facilitating an allegorical reading of the film as concerned with the current regime's obsession with self-perpetuation at all costs, with no hope of moral recovery.

The ways in which *Judou*'s cinematic visuality, photographed by Gu Changwei, enhances the narrative are just as striking as its emendations of the text. These include the bold use of colours, bright reds and yellows associated with the textile dyeing workshop run by Yang Jinshan – colours as bold as Judou, most conspicuously the blood red associated with heightened emotional timbre, with Judou's own sexuality, and with the dyeing vat where both Jinshan and his nephew Tianqing are drowned by 'their' son Tianbai (illus. 253, 254). This innovative color scheme has already been the subject of much discussion.[98] Equally potent, as in *Woman From the Lake of Scented Souls*, is the extensive use of shadowy night-time interiors, deep blue spaces vaguely defined, punctuated by the sounds of Judou's suffering at the hands of Jinshan while Tianqing roams around helplessly, aroused and angered but lacking the courage to intervene (illus. 255), and where Tianbai later stalks about like an evil phantom without the restraint to contain the darkness inside himself. The architecture of the dye-shop further dramatizes the events: the placement of the more lurid scenes upstairs, out of reach and out of view of the horrified but fascinated Tianqing; the drowning pool which yawns in wait of victims; the animal stable, with its camera-like peep-hole through which the voyeuristic Tianqing views the dehumanized Judou bathing her battered body but then is

255 *Judou*. Attracted by the nighttime sounds of Judou's torture, Tianqing peers up the darkened stairs to the master's bedroom but fears to intervene.

lured by his own obsession into becoming her means (ultimately futile, since contradictory) of flight from sexual oppression (illus. 256, 257); the textile-pounding equipment which (of course) goes to it wildly when Judou first seduces the faint-hearted nephew; and the courtyard structure, repeatedly seen from above as no neighbour or passer-by would see it, beckoning the cinematic voyeur into its frame to witness all the dreadful intimacies inside (illus. 258).

In Zhang Yimou's *Raise the Red Lantern* (1991) – which like *Judou* was nominated for an Academy Award, and like *Judou* was banned from internal distribution[99] – all these props are changed, but it's the same theme that is revisited. *Red Lantern* illuminates the corrupting power of a husband over his wife and concubines, from whom he picks a nightly favourite. With great pomp, the husband marks his nightly choice with a red lantern – certain to burn jealousy into the hearts of the non-chosen, though the master seems oblivious to the psychological dimensions of his own environment. The women remain frail and dispensable parts of the master's domain, while he remains remote and even unnamed, as fixed and firm in his authority as the solid architecture that locks each member in place (illus. 259). Disenfranchised and unable train their resentment on the master, the mistresses instead wreak vengeance on each other. The second mistress wins the trust of the fourth (Lotus, performed by Gong Li) by convincing her of the deceit of the third (Coral, actress He Saifei) then betrays both third and fourth mistresses, using a stray comment by the fourth to expose the marital infidelity of the third. The extra-legal vengeance extracted by the husband on discovering this infidelity – in Su Tong's text, having the third mistress drowned in a well and declared a suicide; in the film, she is hanged instead – drives the fourth mistress insane.[100] The fourth mistress, Lotus, in her fleeting sanity, knew this as a repetition of past events and understood the interchangeability of all these victims.[101] Moreover, she understood the seeping down of the corruption from husband to mistresses. This took form in her persecution of her maid-servant, Yan'er, who had attempted to conjure Lotus's death (with clandestine assistance from the second mistress) but instead is driven to her own death when this conjuration is discovered and Yan'er is mercilessly exposed. One point of all these intricately woven acts of deceit and exposure, betrayal and counter-vengeance, is that the master, whose abusive authority provides the agency for them all, remains largely untouched by them all. Old victims are simply replaced by new ones, the arrival of young mistresses bracketing the film at beginning and end.

Corruption and its exposure are thematic features of these three films, but the defining feature of their form is that while we know who,

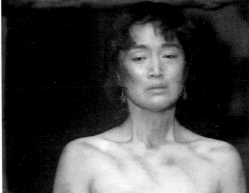

256, 257 *Judou*. Judou peers through the peep-hole where Yang Tianqing has previously peered at her . . . and afterwards displays her wounded beauty to him.

258 *Judou*. Self-reflexive voyeurism: peering into Judou's home of torment.

within the film, is 'good' and who is not – to the point of recognizing the inevitable compromising stains on 'the good' and of comprehending almost sympathetically the motives of 'the bad' – we are denied any formal reference to who and what, outside the film, in the real world, these moral designations and melodramatic struggles pertain. In *The Black Cannon Incident*, as noted earlier, the usual labels attendant to melodrama are defaced and repositioned; in Chen Kaige's *Yellow Earth*, *The Big Parade*, and *King of the Children*, melodramatic structures and their potential affect are simply uprooted. But in Zhang Yimou's three films, the markers remain unshifted and intact except that Zhang has covered them over so they are opaque and can no longer be read, as in a masquerade. We – like Chinese censors – may only guess at who stands behind the mask, which of course masks the intended clarity of 'classic melodrama'. The audience, like a 'classic postmodern' audience, is now empowered to claim who and what the film is about and to disagree mightily among itself. While each of these three films is 'safely' set in the pre-Communist era (*Red Sorghum* in the 1930s, *Judou* and *Raise the Red Lantern* in the 1920s),[102] each has been taken by audiences, critics, and censors alike as commentary on contemporary Chinese politics and culture, but just what that commentary consists of and pertains to defies singular definition.

Aside from its emotional impact and entertainment potential, a major reason why melodrama remains at the vital center of postmodern Chinese cinema may be found in the continuing capacity of *family* drama to enhance narrative with allegory, to say what it says in terms familiar and engaging while also signifying something other, something more, than that which is actually stated. This is a culture where family has long served as the primary unit of social activity and the prime analogue of the state, where family and clan integrity was the measure of public well-being. Confucius – hardly a doyen on issues of family etiquette but a stern lecturer on political practice – wrote prescriptions for behaviour at court in terms of the family model:

In serving his father and mother one may gently criticize, but even if they have seen his intent and choose not to follow it, he only increases his reverence and is not oppositional, and even if discouraged he is not resentful.[103]

In reading *Judou* and *Raise the Red Lantern* as studies of the dysfunctional family, one can hardly not read them further as critiques of a social polity deeply troubled, as was clearly intended in so many other Chinese cinematic melodramas, from *Street Angel* and *Lights of Ten-Thousand Homes* to *Family* to *Girl from Hunan, Transmigration, Woman From the Lake of Scented Souls* and *Farewell My Concubine*.

In *Lights of Ten-Thousand Homes*, a hard-pressed, downwardly mobile working family became the locus for all the conflict of traditional and modern values at war with each other in urban Shanghai. In the end, only by abandoning their flirtation with the modern nuclear

259 *Raise the Red Lantern*. Small and replaceable fixtures in the master's massive architectural domain, the wife and concubines and their maids await his nightly choice.

family unit and returning to their traditional, extended family configuration do they prove capable of withstanding the cold and impersonal forces of Western-style corporate capitalism.[104] Quite in contrast to this, in *Family* (1956), it is the extended family system of an élite scholar clan, the Gaos ('the Lofties'), which itself is corrupt and provides the locus for a condemnation of China's corrupt feudal patriarchy. Each of the Gaos' younger-generation sons, faced with harsh demands to submit to the family's collective interests and hold firm against the changes taking place in society, provides an alternate response: the elder son, though increasingly alert to his elders' corruption, conforms in the name of loyalty and with the hope of reforming from within; the middle son, less resolute than either of his brothers, opts for a modern education; and the younger, most courageous son flees the family to become a social reformer (illus. 260). 'I hate this *family*,' exclaims the youngest brother, Juehui, at one point. 'Yes, this is a vicious *world*,' replies Juemin, the middle son, confirming the analogy of private 'family' to public 'world'. Written by the anarchist Ba Jin in 1931, this allegorical *Family* could mean one thing as a Republican era novel and another as a Communist period film. If re-produced today, it could even be an attack on the rigidly structured Communist Party patriarchy itself (illus. 261).

More recently, *Yellow Earth*, for all of its implied criticism of the Party, validates the Party's critique of the traditional family and of arranged marriage. The newly-married Cuiqiao's death so closely follows the Chinese pattern of self-destructive vengeance by abused wives – traditionally by drowning themselves, so that their spirit will

260 *Family*. Young radical Gao Juehui confides in his servant, to whom he is soon proposing marriage.

261 *Family*. Throughout the film, social hierarchy is measured by a strictly prescribed spatial organization.

haunt the marital family, pollute its home and damage its public reputation – that some have taken it as an intended suicide.[105] And still more recently, in the family melodrama of *Hibiscus Town*, it is once again the integral family that is idealized and subjected to attack by wicked enemies, this time by a rampaging Party faction which prevents heroine Hu Yuyin's intended marriage to Manmeng, destroys her first marriage to Li Guigui, then tries but fails to destroy her second 'marriage' to 'Crazy' Qin. In the end, it is the Party that fails and the family which triumphs (see illus. 180). In each of these examples and many others like them, despite their different results, the family is made the operant basis for dealing with larger issues of society and government.

Judou and *Raise the Red Lantern* can stand on their own, simply, as family dramas. But we are encouraged both by cinematic tradition and by the cinematic author himself to read them broadly, systematically, and politically. Speaking of *Red Lantern*, Zhang has said,

The Revolution has not really changed things. It's still an autocratic system, a feudal patriarchal system. A few people still want to control everything and instill a rigid order. That's why I was so excited when I discovered the walled gentry mansion, which is hundreds of years old in Shanxi Province [in Baoji, where *Red Lantern* was filmed]. Its high walls formed a rigid square pattern that perfectly expresses the age-old obsession with strict order. The Chinese people have for a long time confined themselves within a restricted walled space.[106]

Since traditionally the Chinese family and state analogize each other, it is only the shortest stretch to imagine *Red Lantern*'s walled space as Beijing's Forbidden City and the unquestioned authority within this walled space as that of China's Supreme Ruler. Hegemony at court and hegemony at home maintain each other. The stretch is further reduced by the fact that both masters, at home and at court, sustain themselves by playing off subordinates against each other, a succession of whom parade to their doom proclaiming loyalty to the one who has ultimately been disloyal to them all. It is not at all hard to understand the authorities having placed a ban on this film. But exactly what they thought they were banning remains as much a melodramatic masquerade as the film itself; neither they nor Zhang dares to remove the mask. Just who does Zhang mean, above, when he speaks of 'a few people', as he uses one mask to unmask another?

In Zhang Yimou's films, whatever their Oedipal rebellion, many of the features of Xie Jin's melodramatic model are retained. Repression and anger, love and hatred – the emotionality of melodrama – are there. Like Xie Jin, Zhang 'respects' his audience and responds to their 'needs' and 'expectations' by providing them a healthy blend of entertainment and 'education'. The family base of activity is retained and a clear distinction between the positive figures and the bad is maintained, though now the good and evil figures are situated together *within* the family. And the exploration remains one of social personality and situation rather than of psychodynamics and the inner world.

In *Judou* we meet two 'classic' embodiments of melodramatic evil in Yang Jinshan and 'his son', Yang Tianbai. It is the fact that they are so much alike while *not* actually being father and son which best defines the situation (illus. 250, 254). As mentioned previously, Liu Heng's textual rendition of Jinshan had him motivated by the common desire for male offspring and gradually corrupted by his failure to attain this, while in Zhang Yimou's film this distinction dissolves into a simpler, more melodramatic image of unbridled, unmotivated patriarchal corruption. As for Tianbai, in Liu Heng's text he operates out of moral outrage rather than evil disposition, while in Zhang's film even his mother wonders darkly about his character. Judou asks, 'Tianqing, why doesn't Tianbai ever laugh?' Zhang Yimou answers the question for her, pointing not so much to the individual nor the genetics but to an entire system of unquestioning loyalty and fixed obligation:

Tianbai the boy is weird because he is the product of an abnormal relationship, which is very twisted and distorted. As he grows up, all around him is secrecy, so he does not speak. Tianbai calls the old man 'father' because he has to. In those days, his real parents would be put to death if it were found out. Even down to the 1920s, it was that strict. So you see how horrible this system is.[107]

As Zhang's listeners well know, his dates are always masked; the distorted social relationships and secrecy of the 1920s are not a thing of the past. Cinematic melodrama might once have seemed old-fashioned and outmoded, but he has updated it.

The beautiful Judou originally embodies some 'essential' goodness, but it is gradually degraded by this 'twisted' environment. Her nephew/ lover, Tianqing, also possesses goodness but, sycophant and coward that he is, he primarily directs it towards preserving his evil uncle and the misbegotten love-child who will provide his own destruction. Evil conditions prey heavily on him, too, and no sooner have they buried the old man when Tianqing slaps Judou for the first time and she accuses him of picking up where her husband left off. So fouled is everyone and everything by the end of the film that it is hard not to sympathize with Judou as she consigns it all to flames, a Pyrrhic finale that parallels the burning forests at the conclusion of *King of the Children*).

Again, wondering what and who lies behind this masquerade, with the assumption that while costumed in the period-garb of the 1920s it signifies something out of our own time, it might be guessed that somewhere in this weird family is represented the dynamics of the Communist hierarchy itself. But *Judou*'s condemnation is so broad that even within that frame of reference, one might just as easily regard the Party as having been corrupted by China as the other way around. The transition from the corrupt father to the tentative and momentary liberation of the wife followed by the reversion to corruption as a general condition under the sway of the son parallels the sequence from warlord-ruled China to the historical moment from 1949 to 1957 when hopes for the Communist regime as an alternative to internecine hostility were at their highest, to the gradual withering away of that hope with the anti-Rightist movement, the Great Leap Forward, and the Cultural Revolution. But these are just parallels. The virtue of the masquerade is that it permits multiple identification; remove the masks and the party is over.

So, melodrama has survived and thrived in post-socialist China, not in its original state but in varied forms designed by a number of film-makers, each in their own way. Unwilling (and perhaps unable) to dispose of the form they grew up with, each has been willing instead to translate it into their own terms. The exploration of melodramatic form – their artistic patrimony and their aesthetic fixation – has been as much the subject of their cinematic enterprise as the evident subjects of their filmed critiques, melodramatic form and socialist politics being inseparably linked.

Not everyone has been happy about this cultural turn, and particularly not China's own intellectuals. Beijing scholar-critic Dai Qing has written of *Raise the Red Lantern* that it

has succeeded only in raising my eyebrows and my hackles, not in touching me emotionally or aesthetically. My instinct, formed in a place like Beijing, did not betray me: this kind of film is really shot for the casual pleasures of foreigners. Although they can go on and muddleheadedly satisfy their oriental fetishisms, I do not have that luxury. The sensibilities of my generation of Chinese have already been ravaged by the Mao-style proletarian culture. How can we now stand to be cheated again by half-baked new fashions and trends?[108]

Although couched in particulars (disapproval of the Third Mistress being hanged in a rooftop building, an example that has already been noted), Dai's objections are really more fundamental than that and are very much centred around the emergence of this film genre in the international market. In a society where audience identity has always played foremost in the mind of artists (reception theory may be new in the West, but from China's scholar-painters of the eleventh century to the Maoists of our day, the question of audience has always come first), the arrival of a melodramatic style informed by Western ('Hollywood') models and successful by international standards has – ironically – seemed to constitute a sell-out of the home-based audience. Part of the irony is that international attention for Chinese film, so long sought and so hard won, has been judged by some as a failure because film styles changed in order to make this possible. And part of the irony lies in the fact that intellectual film in China had to change because it had virtually no public (with qualified exceptions like *Yellow Earth* and *Red Sorghum*), as film after film was banned from internal distribution and audience maturation was effectively thwarted, and as viewers by the late 1980s turned from serious film to entertainment cinema and from cinema to television. Asked once whether he catered only to a Western audience, Zhang Yimou replied, 'That's what the government here says too. It's really not fair, when they won't even let my films be shown in China. So they won't even let the Chinese people see if they like them or not.'[109]

Jianying Zha, not persuaded by Dai Qing's raised eyebrows, has tried to explain her attitude. 'All my American friends love Zhang's movies, all my Chinese friends hate them,' she writes.

Why? What offended the Chinese in these movies? Well . . . it could all be summed up in one thing: selling oriental exoticism to a Western audience . . . To be sure, some of the details in [*Red Lantern*] would seem exaggerated, even false, to any historically informed and realistic-minded audience, but I don't think the movie should be taken as a work of realism in a strict sense. Instead, as in almost all of Zhang's other work, it is more akin to the realm of allegorical melodrama . . . And as soon as one ceases viewing it in a realistic mode, one begins to appreciate the irony, comedy and humor in the movie's seemingly high-handed form . . . [The] fate of the new Chinese cinema had long been determined by its complicated relation with Western media and techniques, with the tastes of an increasingly international film market and its mainstream audience. To the extent that it never had a chance of escaping these circumstances, 'pure Chinese art' in the contemporary world is merely a fantasy. In this sense, not only Zhang's personal intention becomes irrelevant, the whole quarrel over 'Orientalism' seems rather simplistic and pedantic. In fact, aside from academic intellectuals from the third world countries, I have never heard of anybody else expressing anger or anxiety this way. The problem is: what is our focus in evaluating a work of art?[110]

Even before Chen Kaige joined in the melodramatic masquerade with his *Farewell My Concubine,* he too had become the object of a reaction among Chinese intellectuals which began perhaps with Zhang Yimou as its target but rapidly spread to the entire 'Fifth Generation' of film-makers. 'It was a drastic turnabout,' writes Jianying Zha, and 'soon the entire cinematic avant-garde was under attack.'

All these years the Fifth Generation had been sent out to conquer the world, to plant Chinese flags all over the cinematic map – and now, suddenly, they were getting hit from behind. To make matters worse, it came mostly from their old cheerleaders, the very critics who had once defended them from their enemies at home . . . The Fifth Generation, once heralded as brilliant enfants terribles, were now to be unmasked as a group of overrated, callow, and pretentious self-promoters.[111]

For a generation of intellectual film-makers saturated by irony and betrayal, steeped in the perception that things are not what they seem to be and not to be trusted, this greatest betrayal has been the most ironic. Mao could not be trusted, and now neither could the anti-Maoists. Chen Kaige's most recently released film, *Temptress Moon,* joins Zhang Yimou's earlier films and his own *Farewell My Concubine* in taking betrayal as one of its central themes, to which he adds distrust, the debilitating fear of betrayal. But unlike his earlier films, it is set deep within individual psychology.

Temptress Moon (*Feng yue,* literally *Wind and Moon*) is an examination (one might say a deconstruction) of the stuff of melodrama – power and intrigue, romance and deception, emotional blockage and eruption, corruption and its exposure – cast in a postmodern idiom, intellectually distilled rather than naturalistic, disjointed rather than coherent, distanced rather than participatory, alienating rather than narcissistic. It is hardly surprising then, perhaps even appropriate, that the Western reception for it generally has been as awkward and cool as the film itself (like *King of the Children,* it disappointed at Cannes). *Temptress Moon* epitomizes 'Fifth Generation' films' possibly fatal obsession with the politics of melodramatic form. With an opium-smoking heroine, a gigolo scam artist for a hero, a web of incestuous relationships, and insinuated allusions to contemporary politicians, all of which resulted in its becoming the fourth of Chen's films banned in China, *Temptress Moon* displaced the other-worldly aura of *King of the Children* with a world-weary cynicism. Set in the early years after the fall of the last dynasty, its central figure is a man whom everyone loves but whom the experience of childhood abuse and betrayal has deprived of the ability to love, and who in turn, as gigolo con artist, replicates and disseminates his own debilitating experience.

262 *Temptress Moon*. Opium-addicted Zhengda, in the background, urges his wife and brother-in-law Zhongliang into an incestuous encounter.

As convoluted in plot and artificial in style as his *Yellow Earth* is plain and natural and plotless, Chen's *Temptress Moon* turns on the improbable intersections, parallels, and collisions of lives and families – ingredients for bad realism and good melodrama, or at least for good commentary on melodrama. The rural Yu family, of no particular account, marries into the powerful Pang clan: Yu Xiuyi marries Pang Zhengda; they remain secondary but this brings into play Xiuyi's younger brother, Zhongliang, and Pang's younger sister, Ruyi (Leslie Cheung and Gong Li acting together as they did in *Farewell My Concubine*). Power corrupts, and Zhengda, perpetually sated by opium, takes pleasure in having his wife (performed by He Saifei) seduce her younger brother, Zhongliang (illus. 262). Soon afterwards, Zhengda overdoses on opium, but, like a vegetable, he lives on (illus. 263). Zhongliang flees the family and Ruyi becomes the female head of the clan.

A decade or more passes and we meet Zhongliang again in Shanghai, where he has found a new family, a clan of gangsters for whom he is the star performer and the boss's favourite. Known now as Xiao Xie, Zhongliang's evident profession is gigolo but he plays a meaner game than that, seducing wives, winning their love, and then blackmailing them. Though he would like to love, he is unable to return love and so is perfect for the role. Exterior cool, he storms inside, torn by inner conflicts (illus. 264, 265). The abused child becomes the adult abuser, facilitated by his psychological reversion to an infantile presexuality and total submission to his gangster boss as son to a substitute father. He engages in staging melodramatic situations and drawing forth from

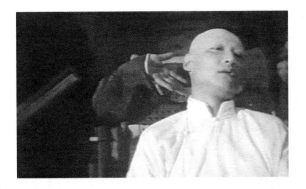

263 *Temptress Moon.*
Clan head Pang
Zhengda, brain-dead
from poisoned opium.

others the powerful emotions that he cannot let himself feel. Appropriating women as the dramatist does, attracting them to the secrecy of his game, he engages them in his deceit – all are deceiving their own spouses – and he himself coldly, analytically, gauges their response to the spectacle of his emerging drama, awaiting the best moment to betray and take final advantage, deceiving them in the midst of their own deceit of others, threatening to betray their pseudo-affairs to those they have betrayed. As his victims squirm, he searches within for the missing emotions that might have let him squirm as well and thus proved the existence of an inner life. When his hardest-fallen victim commits suicide – not for fear of exposure but because of true love betrayed – Zhongliang returns to pledge his love to the one individual he most wants to be able to love: Pang Ruyi. Then he finds himself betrayed.

Pang Ruyi was raised on an opium pipe. When brother Zhengda slips into oblivion and she's elevated as his successor, she slides onto the scene wearing all white and framed by the aura of a snow princess, not as a mark of purity but rather because she's iced with drugs (illus. 266). Zhongliang's and Ruyi's childhood acquaintance was limited to a brief encounter, on the night of his arrival at the Pang household, when she invaded the ancestral hall the night the Manchu dynasty fell from power, was caught and carried out ('What outrage! A girl in the ancestral hall!'). Who among the elders imagined that some day she would rule that ancestral roost in a later era when the whole world had turned on its cultural axis? The inheritor of power along with her opium addiction, and isolated by both from emotional reality, she lacks and longs for love. Her adult relationship with Zhongliang begins when Zhongliang's boss sends him back to his old home to seduce her and dip into her great wealth. Reluctantly, Zhongliang agrees, but his motives differ: by destroying Ruyi and the Pangs, he'll avenge himself on Pang Zhengda for his damaged psyche. In the course of this sham seduction,

264, 265 *Temptress Moon*. Product of child abuse, Yu Zhongliang combines a cool, seductive personality . . . with moments of internal fury.

Ruyi falls in love; Zhongliang of course does not, though an inner struggle rages. Ruyi falls so hard, in fact, that she is blind to Zhongliang's emotional paralysis, and she prepares for future sex with him by practising with her own cousin, Pang Duanwu – Duanwu who unbeknownst to all is gradually working his own way from a minor figure on the scene to becoming its central player. Duanwu has served Ruyi as a kind of 'regent', since as a woman she was not thought fully capable of ruling the clan. Duanwu, in fact, is in love with Ruyi but bitterly aware that he's little more to her than a teaching aid. His sexual abuse by Ruyi parallels the incestuous relationship between Zhongliang and his sister. At the same time, the growth of Duanwu's desire – first for Ruyi, whom he tries unsuccessfully to rape, then for her power, which he attains – contrasts with Zhongliang's impotence.

It *is* a little hard to believe that *Temptress Moon* was scripted by the director of *Yellow Earth* and *Big Parade* and *King of the Children*,[112] films in which story lines were cast away together with the melodrama. *Temptress Moon*, by contrast, has story lines within its story lines. The dazzling, dizzying use throughout the film of hand-held camerawork (by cinematographer Christopher Doyle) reflects Zhongliang's own brilliant inner chaos and sumptuous confusion. But the performers' frozen looks, so alienated and alienating, continually turn us away from them and back to the narrative sequence. Zhongliang's gangster boss, aware of Zhongliang's vulnerability to Ruyi, intends to assure that she is not vulnerable to him. To her, Zhongliang's corruption will be exposed. Little does the boss suspect that he will expose her to the suicide of one of Zhongliang's false loves and with that, his plot to retain Zhongliang's devotion for himself fails. Zhongliang returns to Ruyi, but now she denies her love to him, turning the tables and obliging him to deal with the rejection of his love or, perhaps more deeply, with his desire to love. At this point of betrayal, he is returned to the moment of his own deepest suffering and betrayal when in his youth (as we now learn in flashback) *he* poisoned his betrayer, his sister's husband, Pang Zhengda (illus. 267); and returning to the same room visited in his youth for that event, he prepares another draught for the husband's sister. In a tightly wrought denouement, he leaves as Ruyi smokes herself to death; moments later, as he finds the emotion somewhere in him to return and save her, it is too late: he returns from his deconstruction of melodrama to the stage proper, only to gaze in amazement at her destruction – like brother Zhengda, she is dead in mind but remains alive in body – and there to face his own melodramatic demise. As the curtain falls, Duanwu is elevated to power in the Pang clan, his way paved by Zhongliang's poisonings, while Zhongliang is assassinated by his Shanghai gang.

Out of the arbitrariness of the dramatic fate comes the least expected twist, the rise of distant cousin Duanwu as the successor to Zhengda and Ruyi, head of the Pang clan. Chen Kaige has said to his English subtitle writer that here is where the plot actually began in his mind, as he wondered once how, within the tight-knit clan of Communist Party circles in Beijing, did the Shanghai outsider Jiang Zemin rise suddenly to the pinnacle of authority. By what preposterous twist of melodramatic fate?[113] The many possible analogies between opium-smoking clans in a post-revolutionary society, blackmailing gangs in an unfettered 1930s Shanghai, and the inner workings of a no-holds-barred totalitarian Party in a post-socialist society provide interpreters of this final masquerade a field day. As for Zhongliang himself, we find that when he finally takes his mask off before Ruyi, what lies beneath it is yet another mask.

Like it or not, whether we take *Temptress Moon* as the last word on 'Fifth Generation' melodrama or simply as the latest, it occupies a

266 *Temptress Moon*. Ruyi: addicted to opium, ensconced in power, searching for love.

我把姐夫给毒了
I poisoned him.

267 *Temptress Moon*. Seen in flashback, Zhongliang reveals to his sister he has just poisoned her abusive husband.

distinctive position. Other post-socialist era post-melodramas have provided various revisions of the genre, reworking past idioms as post-modern arts are wont to do. But Chen Kaige deals with melodrama in a curious way, stepping partly outside of it in the persona of Yu Zhongliang to view it, examine it, develop it, and in many ways to condemn and reject it. In *Farewell My Concubine*, Chen directed a drama within a drama. In *Temptress Moon*, this director of 'no-dramas' like *Yellow Earth* and *King of the Children* has directed a melodrama within a no-drama. No longer content or able to sustain the sublima-tion of his earlier alter egos like Lao Gar, disappointed by the inability of his audience (Chinese or Western) to appreciate the subtlety of his transcendent no-dramas, Chen earlier reverted to the melodrama of his forebears in *Farewell My Concubine*; but now, embittered by the rejection of this by his intellectual Chinese peers, Chen seems here (less like the naive Lao Gar and more like the cynical Zhongliang) to be examining through his own work-within-a-work why he and why Chinese intellectuals distrust melodrama so deeply. Made cynical by the repeated betrayals of public and personal trust in China's 'new society', by the trampling on the public's offerings of faith and sincere emotionality, identifying melodrama with self-serving and false political rhetoric, still wishing that one *could* trust and love one's fellows but no longer daring to, Chen now *uses* melodrama (he appropriates it) to examine it, to deconstruct it, to expose it, to tread on it. But despite himself, he does not abandon it. Like Zhengda, like Ruyi, his melodrama lives on.

Melodrama, like Lu Ji's famous axe handle (referred to at the outset of this essay), retains the form of the instrument that made *it*. One may choose, as with Lu Ji, to emphasize its creative adaptation to the circumstances of a new era, or one may emphasize the persistence of tradition. What Lu Ji's metaphor provides best is the inseparability of these two alternatives. Chen Kaige might not be pleased but in the 'New Chinese Cinema', melodrama survives. And it has not merely endured, marginalized like Zhengda and Ruyi, but transfigured, it has recovered its role, been placed stage centre and shot full frame.

Film Credits

Albabetical listing. The following abbreviations are used:
d = director, c = cinematography, e = film editing, ad = art direction, mu = music,
a = actor (character), s = screenplay, t = author of original text, st = studio, m = minutes.

Army Nurse (*Nü'er lou*), d. Hu Mei, Li Xiaoqun, c. He Qing, Wu Fei, ad. Xu Maiduo,
   mu. Sun Baolin, a. Xu Ye (Qiao Xiaoyu), Hasi Bagen (Ding Zhu), Li Qingqing (Su
   Menghong), Zong Su (Ji Yamei), Zhao Gang (Tu Jianli), s. Kang Liwen, Ding
   Xiaoqi, t. Ding Xiaoqi, st. August First, 88m, 1985

The Big Parade (*Da yuebing*), d. Chen Kaige, c. Zhang Yimou, e. Zhao Qihua, ad. He
   Qun, mu. Qu Xiaosun, Zhao Jiping, a. Sun Chun (commander Sun Fang), Lu Lei
   (Jiang Junbao), Wu Ruofu (Lü Chun), Kang Hua (Hao Xiaoyuan), Wang Xueqi (Li
   Weicheng), Guan Qiang (Liu Guoqiang), s. Gao Lili, st. Guangxi, 103m, 1985

Black Cannon Incident (*Heipao shijian*), d. Huang Jianxin, c. Wang Xinsheng, Feng
   Wei, ad. Liu Yichuan, a. Liu Zifeng (Zhao Shuxin), Gerhard Olschewski (Hans
   Schmidt), Wang Yi (Party vice-secretary Madame Zhou), Ge Hui (Party secretary
   Wu), Yang Yazhou (manager Feng Liangcai), s. Li Wei, t. Zhang Xianliang (*Lang
   man di heipao*), st. Xi'an, 96m, 1985

Ermo, d. Zhou Xiaowen, c. Lu Gengxin, e. Zhong Furong, ad. Zhang Daqian, mu.
   Zhou Xiaowen, a. Alia (Ermo), Liu Peiqi (Blindman) Ge Zhijun (Chief), Zhang
   Haiyan (Fat Woman), s. Lang Yun, t. Xu Baoqi, st. Ocean Film, 94m, 1994

Family (*Jia*), d. Chen Xihe, Ye Ming, c. Xu Ji, a. Wei Heling (Old Master Gao), Fu
   Huizhen (Chen, Gao's concubine), Jiang Rui (Gao's eldest son), Han Tao (Gao
   Keming, 3rd son), Cheng Zhi (Gao Ke'an, 4th son), Yang Hua (Gao Keding, 5th
   son), Sun Daoling (Gao Juexin, eldest grandson), Zhang Fei (Gao Juemin, 2nd
   grandson), Zhang Hui (Gao Juehui, 3rd grandson), Zhang Ruifang (Li Ruiyu,
   Juexin's wife), Hu Xiaohan (Shuhua, Juehui's wife), Wang Yi (Cousin Chin), Huang
   Zhongyin (Cousin Mei), Wang Danfeng (Mingfeng), Wang Wei (Wan'er), Zheng
   Min (Feng Leshan), Zhang Ziliang (Huang Cunren), s. Chen Xihe, t. Ba Jin,
   st. Shanghai, 124m, 1956

Farewell My Concubine (*Bawang bieji*), d. Chen Kaige, c. Gu Changwei, e. Pei
   Xiaonian, ad. Yang Yuhe, Yang Zhanjia, mu. Zhao Jiping, a. Zhang Fengyi (Duan
   Xiaolou), Leslie Cheung (Zheng Dieyi), Gong Li (Juxian), Ge You (Yuan Shiqing),
   Ma Mingcheng (Xiao Douzi, youth), Yin Zhi (Xiao Douzi, child), Fei Yang (Xiao
   Shitou, youth), Zhao Hailong (Xiao Shitou, child), Jiang Wenli (Douzi's mother),
   Lü Ji (Master Guan), s. Li Pik-wah (Lilian Lee, Li Bihua) and Lu Wei, t. Li Pik-wah,
   st. Tomson (HK) Films, 157m, 1993

Garlands at the Foot of the Mountain (*Shan xia de huahuan*), d. Xie Jin, c. Lu Junfu,
   Shen Jie, Zhu Yongde, e. Zhou Dingwen, ad. Zhong Yongqing, mu. Ge Yan, p.
   Tang lixuan, Chen Junyang, a. Lü Xiaoho (Liang Sanxi), Tang Guoqiang (Zhao
   Mengsheng), He Wei (Jin Kailai), Tong Chao (Lei Zhen), Gai Ke (Han Yuxiu), Wang
   Yumei (Mother Liang), Liu Yansheng (Wu Shuang), Siqin Gaowa (Yang Gaihua),
   Ni Dahong (Duan Yuguo), He Yi (Jin Xiaozhu), Shi Lei (Lei Kaihua), Li Danjun (mess
   sargeant), Gu Yulan, Liu Song, s. Li Zhun, Li Cunbao, st. Shanghai, 150m, 1983

Girl From Hunan (*Xiangnü Xiaoxiao*), d. Xie Fei, Ulan, c. Fu Jingsheng, ad. Xing
Zheng, mu. Ye Xiaogang, a. Na Renhua (Xiaoxiao), Liu Qing (Xiaoxiao, child),
Deng Xiaoguang (Huagou), Zhang Yu (Chunquan), Zeng Peng (young Chunguan),
Ni Meiling (Chunguan's mother), s. Zhang Xian, t. Shen Congwen (*Xiaoxiao*),
st. Beijing Film Youth Studio, 1985

Hibiscus Town (*Furongzhen*), d. Xie Jin, c. Lu Junfu, e. Zhou Dingwen, ad. Jin Qifen,
mu. Ge Yan, a. Liu Xiaoqing (Hu Yuyin), Xu Songzi (Li Guoxiang), Jiang Wen (Qin
Shutian, 'Crazy' Qin), Zhu Shibin (Wang Qiushe), Zheng Zaishan (Gu Yanshan)
s. Zhong Ahcheng, Xie Jin, t. Gu Hua, st. Shanghai, 141m, 1986

Horse Thief (*Dao ma zei*), d. Tian Zhuangzhuang, c. Hou Yong, Zhao Fei, e. Li
Jingzhong, ad. Huo Jianqi, mu. Tian Zhuangzhuang, a. Tseshang Rigzin (Norbu),
Dan Jiji (wife), s. Zhang Rui, st. Xi'an, 99m, 1985

Judou, d. Zhang Yimou, Yang Fengliang, c. Gu Changwei, Yang Lun, e. Du Yuan, ad.
Cao Jiuping, Xia Rujin, mu. Zhao Jiping, a. Gong Li (Wang Judou), Li Baotian
(Yang Tianqing), Li Wei (Master Yang), Zheng Jian (Yang Tianbai, youth), Zhang Yi
(Yang Tianbai, child), t. Liu Heng, *Fuxi, Fuxi*, st. Xi'an, 98m, 1990

King of the Children (*Haizi wang*), d. Chen Kaige, c. Gu Changwei, mu. Qu
Xiaosong, Tian Zhuangzhuang, a. Xie Yuan (Lao Gar), Yang Xuewen (Wang Fu),
Chen Shaohua (Headmaster Chen), Zhang Caimei (Laidi), Xu Guoqing (Lao Hei),
Le Gang (Cowherd), Tan Tuo (production team leader), Gu Changwei (Comrade
Wu), Wu Xia (class monitor), Liu Haichen (Wang Qitong, Wang Fu's father),
s. Chen Kaige, Wan Zhi [Chen Maiping], t. Ah Cheng, st. Xi'an, 107m, 1987

The Legend of Tianyun Mountain (*Tianyunshan quanqi*), d. Xie Jin, c. Xu Qi,
e. Zhou Dingwen, ad. Ding Shi, Chen Shaomian, mu. Ge Yan, a. Shi Weijian,
Wang Fuli, s. Lu Yanzhou, t. Lu Yanzhou, st. Shanghai, 127m, 1980

Lights of Ten-Thousand Homes (*Wan jia denghuo*), d. Shen Fu, c. Zhu Jinmin, a. Lan
Ma (Hu Zhiqing), Wu Yin (Hu's mother), Shangguan Yunzhu (Lan Youlan), Qi Heng
(Qian Jianru), s. Yang Hansheng, Shen Fu, st. Kunlun, 124m, 1948

Love on Mt. Lu (or *Romance on Lushan Mountain*) (*Lushan lian*), d. Huang Zumo,
c. Shan Liangguo, Zheng Xuan, ad. Zhu Jianchang, mu. Lu Qiming, a. Zhang Yu
(Zhou Yun), Guo Kaimin (Geng Hua), Gao Cui (Zhou Yun's mother), Wu Hao
(Zhou Zhenwu), Wen Xiying (Geng Feng), Zhi Shiming (Geng Hua's mother),
s. Bi Bicheng, st. Shanghai, 83m, 1980

My Memories of Old Beijing (*Chengnan jiushi*), d. Wu Yigong, c. Cao Weiye, ad. Li
Qiming, a. Shen Jie (Lin Yingzi), Zhang Min, Yuan Jiayi, Zhang Fengyi, Zheng
Zhengyao, s. Yi Ming, t. Lin Haiyin, st. Shanghai, 103m, 1982

Old Well (*Laojing*), d. Wu Tianming, c. Zhang Yimou, Chen Wancai, e. Chen Dali,
ad. Yang Gang, mu. Xu Youfu, a. Zhang Yimou (Sun Wangquan), Liang Yujin
(Zhao Qiaoying), Lü Liping (Duan Xifeng), Niu Xingli (Wan Shuiye), Xie Zhong
(Sun Wangcai), s. Zhang Yi, t. Zheng Yi, st. Xi'an, 122m, 1986

One and Eight (*Yige he bage*), d. Zhang Junzhao, c. Zhang Yimou, Xiao Feng,
s. Zhang Ziliang, Wang Jicheng, a. Tao Zeru (Wang Jin), Chen Daoming (Platoon
Commander Xu Zhi), Lu Xiaoyan (Nurse), t. Guo Xiaochuan (Yige he bage, poem),
st. Guangxi, 86m, 1984

Plunder of Peach and Plum (Tao Li jie), d. Ying Yunwei, c. Wu Weiyun, a. Yuan Muzhi (Tao Jianping, Peach), Chen Bo'er (Li Lilin, Peach), Tang Huaiqiu (principal), s. Yuan Muzhi, t. Nie Er, st. Diantong, 110m, 1934

Raise the Red Lantern (*Dahong denglung gao gao gua*), d. Zhang Yimou, c. Zhao Fei, Yang Lun, e. Du Yuan, ad. Cao Jiuping, mu. Zhao Jiping, Naoki Tachikawa, a. Gong Li (Lotus, 4th mistress), Cao Cuifen (Cloud, 2nd mistress), He Saifei (Shanhu, Coral, 3rd mistress), Jin Shuyuan (Joy, first wife), Ma Jingwu (Chen Zuoqian, the master), Kong Lin (Yan'er, Swallow), t. Su Tong (*Qiqie chengqun, The Herd of Wives and Concubines*), st. ERA International/China Film, 125m, 1991

Red Sorghum (*Hong gaoliang*), d. Zhang Yimou, c. Gu Changwei, ad. Yang Gang, a. Gong Li (Dai Fenglian, Jiu'er, Grandma), Jiang Wen (Yu Zhan'ao, Grandpa), Sheng Jujun (Luohan), Liu Xu (father, as a little boy), Ji Chunhua (Spotted Neck), s. Chen Jianyu, Zhu Wei, Mo Yan, t. Mo Yan (*Hong gaoliang jiazu*), st. Xi'an, 91m, 1987

Rock 'n' Roll Kids (*Yaogun qingnian*), d. Tian Zhuangzhuang, c. Xiao Feng, e. Zhang Li, ad. Li Yan, mu. Xu Peidong, a. Tao Jin (Long Xiang), Ma Ling (Yuanyuan), Shi Ke (Mengdan), Zhu Xun (Xiaoxiao), Li Hu (Dalu), s. Liu Yiran, st. Youth, 80m, 1988

Sacrificed Youth (or *The Rite of Youth*) (*Qingchun ji*), d. Zhang Nuanxin, c. Mu Deyuan, Deng Wei, ad. Li Yongxin, Wang Yanjin, a. Li Fengxu (Li Chun), Song Tao, Feng Yuanzheng, Guo Jianguo, s. Zhang Nuanxin, t. Zhang Manling (*You yige meilide difang, Such a Beautiful Place*), st. Youth Studio, 95m, 1985

The Story of Qiu Ju (*Qiu Ju daguansi*), d. Zhang Yimou, c. Qi Xiaoming, Yu Xiaoqun, Lu Hongyi, e. Du Yuan, ad. Cao Jiuping, mu. Zhao Jiping, a. Gong Li (Qiu Ju), Liu Peiqi (Wan Qinglai, Qiu Ju's husband), Lei Laosheng (Wang Shantang, village chief), Ge Zhijun (Officer Li), Yang Liuchun (Wan Meizi), Ye Jun, Cui Luoren, Yang Huijun, Lin Zi, Zhu Wanqing, Wang Jianfa, s. Liu Heng, t. Chen Yuanbin (*Wan Jia Susong, The Wan Family's Lawsuit*), st. Si-Metropole/Beijing Film Academy Youth Studio, 100m, 1992

Street Angel (*Ma lu tian shi*), d. Yuan Muzhi, c. Wu Yinxian, e. Qian Xiaozhang, mu. He Lüding, Tian Han, a. Zhao Dan (Chen), Zhou Xuan (Hong), Zhao Huiran (Yun), Wei Heling (Wang), s. Yuan Muzhi, t. Monckton Hoffe (*Cristilinda*), st. Ming Xing, 93m, 1937

The Street Players (*Gu shu yiren*), d. Tian Zhuangzhuang, c. Liang Ziyong, a. Li Xuejian (Fang Baoqing), Tan Mingdi (Fang Xiulian), Zhu Xu (Fang Baosen), Chen Qing (Da Feng), s. Tian Zhuangzhuang, t. Lao She, st. Beijing, 118m, 1991

Temptress Moon (*Fengyue*), d. Chen Kaige, c. Chris Doyle, e. Pei Xiaonan, ad. Huang Xia, mu. Zhao Jiping, a. Leslie Cheung (Yu Zhongliang), Gong Li (Pang Ruyi), He Saifei (Yu Xiuyi), Lin Jianhua (Pang Duanwu), Zhou Yemang (Pang Zhengda), Xie Tian (Boss), Ge Xiangting (Elder Qi), s. Chen Kaige, Wang Anyi, st. Thomson/Miramax, 127m, 1996

Third Sister Liu (*Liu Sanjie*), d. Su Li, c. Guo Zhenting, Yin Zhi, mu. Lei Zhenbang, a. Huang Wannqiu (Liu Sanjie), Liu Shilong (A Niu), Zhang Juguang (Old Fisherman), Xia Zongxue (Mo Huairen), Liang Yin (Liu Er) s. Qiao Yu, st. Changchun and Guangxi, 117m, 1961

Transmigration (or *Samsara*) (*Lunhui*), d. Huang Jianxin, c. Zhao Fei, e. Zhang Xiaodong, ad. Yang Gang, mu. Qu Xiaosong, a. Lei Han (Shi Ba), Tan Xiaoyan (Yujing), Liu Lijun (Liu Hualing), Liu Di (Xiao Yang), Gan Lijun (Su Di), s. Wang shuo, t. Wang Shuo (*Fuqu haimian, Emerging from the Sea*), st. Xian, 153m, 1988

The Trouble-Shooters (*Wan zhu*), d. Mi Jiashan, a. Zhang Guoli, Pan Hong, Ge You, Ma Xiaoqing, Liang Tian, Sun Fengying, Li Geng, Dong Yugang, s. Wang Shuo, Mi Jiashan, st. Emei, 104m, 1988.

Woman, Demon, Human (*Ren, gui, qing*), d. Huang Shuqin, c. Xia Lixing, ad. Zheng Changfu, mu. Yang Mo, a. Pei Yanling (Pei Yanmai/Zhong Kui), Xu Shouli (Qiu Yun), Gong Lin (Qiu Yun, youth), Wang Feifei (Qiu Yun, child), Li Baotian (Father), s. Huang Shuqin, st. Shanghai, 104m, 1988

Woman From the Lake of Scented Souls (or *Woman Sesame Oil Producer*) (*Xiang hunnü*), d. Xie Fei, c. Bao Xiaoran, ad. Ma Huiwu, Wang Jie, mu. Wang Liping, a. Siqingaowa (Xiang Ersau), Wu Yujuan (Huanhuan), Hu Wanguang (Dunzi), Zhang Hui (Jinhai), Chen Baoguo (Ren Zhongshi), Lei Kesheng (Lü Ershu, the husband), Ye Linliang (Auntie Wu), Jing Cao (Zhi'er), s. Xie Fei, t. Zhou Daxin (*Xiang hun tangban de xiangyou fang, Sesame Oil Workshop by the Side of Scented Souls' Lake*), st. Tianjin and Changchun, 106m, 1992

Yellow Earth (*Huang tudi*), d. Chen Kaige, c. Zhang Yimou, ad. He Qun, mu. Zhao Jiping, a. Xue Bai (Cuiqiao), Wang Xueqi (Gu Qing), Tan Tuo (father), Liu Qiang (Hanhan), s. Zhang Ziliang, t. Ke Lan (*Shen ku hui sheng, Echo in the Deep Valley*), st. Guangxi, 86 m, 1984

References

Preface

1 Filmmakers in the People's Republic are all graduates of the Beijing Film Academy, China's only film school. In part because of the Institute's practice of accepting only one new class of students every four years, it is common to think of filmmakers in terms of 'generations', but how many generations there have actually been is not agreed upon: director Xie Fei, for example, speaks of four, while director Xie Jin describes five. None the less, with no class having graduated since the Cultural Revolution began in 1966, the graduating class of 1982 (its training initiated in 1978) marked a conspicuous new era in Chinese filmmaking and has commonly become referred to as the 'Fifth Generation'.

2 Mao Zedong, 'Talks at the Yan'an Conference on Literature and Art', in Bonnie McDougall, *Mao Zedong's 'Talks at the Yan'an Conference on Literature and Art': 1943 Text with Commentary* (Ann Arbor, 1980), p. 78.

3 Rey, Chow, *Primitive Passions: Visuality, Sexuality, Ethnography, and Contemporary Chinese Cinema* (New York, 1995), p. 94.

4 Walter Benjamin's 'The Work of Art in the Age of Mechanical Reproduction', to which Rey Chow attaches her argument (pp. 93–4), was written in 1935, one year after the filming of *Triumph of the Will* by Leni Riefenstahl, and was explicitly dependent on conditions of his own moment and place: 'We do not deny that in some cases today's films *can also* promote revolutionary criticism of social conditions, even of the distribution of property. However, our present study is no more specifically concerned with this than is the film production of Western Europe.' Benjamin, in Gerald Mast, Marshall Cohen and Leo Braudy, eds, *Film Theory and Criticism*, 4th edn (New York, 1992), p. 674 (my emphasis).

5 Whereas 'mechanicity' might seem to be 'hard' and lacking in subtlety and artistic finesse, it need not; throughout this process, what the Chinese mould seeks to replicate, to transmit – to manifest and possess – is not mere appearance but some inner (inevitably mobile and unfixed) quality of the model. See, for example, John Hay, 'Values and History in Chinese Painting', *Res*, 6 (Autumn 1983), pp. 73–111; 7/8 (Spring/Autumn 1984), pp. 102–36; Lothar Ledderose, 'The Earthly Paradise: Religious Elements in Chinese Landscape Art', in Susan Bush and Christian Murck, eds, *Theories of the Arts in China* (Princeton, 1983), pp. 165–83; Kiyohiko Munakata, 'Concepts of Lei and Kan-lei in Early Chinese Art Theory', in Bush and Murck, pp. 105–31; Jerome Silbergeld, 'Chinese Concepts of Old Age and Their Role in Chinese Painting, Painting Theory, and Criticism', *Art Journal*, 46 (Summer 1987), pp. 103–14, especially pp. 103–5; Rolf Stein, *The World in Miniature: Container Gardens and Dwellings in Far Eastern Religious Thought* (Stanford, 1990); Lothar Ledderose, *Mi Fu and the Classical Tradition of Chinese Calligraphy* (Princeton, 1979); Robert Bagley, ed., *Art of the Houma Foundry* (Princeton, 1996); *The Quest for Eternity: Chinese Ceramic Sculptures From the People's Republic of China* (Los Angeles, 1987); Klaas Ruitenbeek, *Carpentry & Building in Late Imperial China: A Study of the Fifteenth-Century Carpenter's Manual Lu Ban Jing* (Leiden, 1993).

6 T. S. Eliot, *The Sacred Wood, Essays on Poetry and Criticism* (London, 1920), p. 49.

7 Vladimir Nabokov, *Pale Fire* (New York, 1962), p. 41.

1 Drowning on Dry Land: *Yellow Earth* and the Traditionalism of the 'Avant-garde'

1 174 frames.

2 Bonnie McDougall's extensive and illuminating study, *The Yellow Earth: A Film by Chen Kaige* (Hong Kong, 1991), does not mention this detail. [All subsequent citations of McDougall without specific titles refer to this book.] In *Hua shuo Huang tudi* (Collated critical comments and interviews about *Yellow Earth*) (Beijing, 1986), it is mentioned only once, by Chen Kaige without explanation, in reference to camerawork for the rain ceremony in which this image is embedded (p. 270).

3 In his reference to this vessel (McDougall, pp. 259–60), director Chen Kaige uses the term *shengshui ping*. I would translate this *ping* as 'bottle' or 'vase' except that in the film it looks far more like a perfectly ordinary small pickle jar.

4 The use of the word 'shamanic' for the Chinese term '*wu*' is understood here as problematic, as is the unresolvable matter of when to conflate and when to separate 'shamanic' from 'Daoistic'. The avoidant solution of simply using the term 'folk' fails to distinguish traditional folk practice from the Communist opposition to such practice in the name of 'the people'.

5 The limiting of filmed critiques, prior to this time, to re-evaluations of the Cultural Revolution phase of Communist history, in accordance with the government's own agenda, can be seen in Wu Yigong's *Evening Rain* (1980), and Wu Tianming's *River Without Buoys* (1983). By 1984, only Bai Hua's harshly suppressed *Bitter Love* (1980), Xie Jin's *Legend of Tianyun Mountain* (1980) (illus. 173), and Zhang Junzhao's *One and Eight* (1984) had threatened to advance a broader critique. The latter, filmed by Zhang Yimou, also defined the possibilities of a revolution in visual style. Cf. Bai Hua, ed. T.C. Chang *et al.*, *Unrequited Love, with Related Introductory Materials* (Taibei, 1981), and Jonathan Spence's chapter on 'Film and Politics: Bai Hua's *Bitter Love*', in his *Chinese Roundabout: Essays in History and Culture* (New York, 1992), pp. 277–92; for Xie Jin, see chapter five below.

6 Popularity awards given by *Popular Cinema* magazine on the basis of a reader poll, established in 1961.

7 Presented by the Chinese Filmmakers' Association, as determined by a panel of senior directors, critics, and educators; established in 1981.

8 McDougall, p. 82. Internationally, *Yellow Earth* also won a cinematography award at the Nantes Film Festival Award, as well as prizes at the London Film Festival and the Hawaii International Film Festival; *ibid.*, p. 113.

9 Geremie Barmé and John Minford, eds, *Seeds of Fire: Chinese Voices of Conscience* (New York, 1988), introduction, unpaginated.

10 McDougall, p. 87.

11 *Ibid.*, p. 165.

12 See Bonnie McDougall, *Mao Zedong's 'Talks at the Yan'an Conference on Literature and Art': 1943 Text with Commentary* (Ann Arbor, 1980).

13 At the Fourth Congress of Chinese Writers and Artists, October 1979, Deng Xiaoping complemented the principles of his Four Modernizations campaign with this pronouncement on culture:

> The basic standard for judging all our work is whether it helps or hinders our effort to modernize . . . The bureaucratic style of work must be dropped. There must be no more issuing of administrative orders regarding the creation and criticism of literature and art . . . We must get rid of all stereotypes and conventions and study new situations and solve new problems in conformity with the

characteristics of the new historical period China is in . . . It is essential that writers and artists follow their own creative spirit. What subjects they should choose for their creative work and how they should deal with those subjects are questions that writers and artists themselves must examine and gradually resolve through practice. There should be no arbitrary meddling in this process.

Deng Xiaoping, *Selected Works of Deng Xiaoping (1975–1982)* (Beijing), p. 206.

In July 1980, what had been proclaimed at Yan'an, 1942 – 'Literature and art in subordination to politics' – was toned down to read 'Literature in service of the people and in service of socialism'. Cf. Perry Link, *Stubborn Weeds: Popular and Controversial Chinese Literature After the Cultural Revolution* (Bloomington, 1983), pp. 19–24.

14 Yu Huiyong, 'Let Our Theater Propagate Mao Tse-tung's Thought For Ever', *Chinese Literature* (July–August 1968), p. 111.

15 Judy Stone, *Eye on the World: Conversations with International Filmmakers* (Los Angeles, 1997), p. 99.

16 Barmé and Minford, p. 261.

17 McDougall, pp. 164, 151, 155.

18 *Ibid.*, p. 6.

19 On censorship, see p. 317, n. 11.

20 McDougall, p. 211.

21 Literally, he asks this about Cuiqiao's older sister, who was married, beaten, ran away, and was sent back to her husband by her father, who analogizes her as 'a beaten wife, kneaded dough' (McDougall, p. 212).

22 McDougall, p. 212.

23 *Ibid.*, p. 238.

24 Haun Saussy, *The Problem of a Chinese Aesthetic* (Stanford, 1993), p. 107.

25 See Wai-fong Loh, 'From Romantic Love to Class Struggle: Reflections on the Film *Liu Sanjie*', in McDougall, ed., *Popular Chinese Literature and Performing Arts*, pp. 165–76. Also comparable is the film *Du Shiniang*. Apparently, the original story of *Yellow Earth* by author Ke Lan had this type of musical propaganda in mind, set in a flowery valley with no reference to the Yellow River or the yellow earth. But in the film-makers' radical overhaul of Ke Lan's work, the songs became fewer and progressively more sober, like the film itself and like its title, which progressed from Ke Lan's up-beat *Echo in the Deep Valley (Shen gu hui sheng)*, to *Silent is the Ancient Plain (Gu yuan wu sheng)* and finally to *Yellow Earth (Huang tudi)*. Participating in the transition were Zhang Ziliang who made the initial conversion to filmscript without much change in its character, cinematographer Zhang Yimou who first brought the script to director Chen Kaige's attention, art director He Qun, composer Zhao Jiping, and most importantly Chen Kaige himself. McDougall, pp. 27, 32, 34.

26 Kam Louie, *Inheriting Tradition: Interpretations of the Classical Philosophers in Communist China, 1949–1966* (Hong Kong, 1986), p. 89.

27 *Ibid.*, 28.

28 Roxane Witke, *Comrade Chiang Ch'ing* (Boston, 1977), p. 154, suggests the marriage was arranged when Mao was fifteen and never consummated. But Anne Thurston, in Li Zhisui, *The Private Life of Chairman Mao* (New York, 1994), p. 639, n. 7, indicates Mao's first marriage as dating from 1908 when the young bride moved into the family home, to 1910 when the young wife died, and that 'reports on whether the marriage was consummated differ'. In Edgar Snow, *Red Star Over China* (New York, 1938), p. 130, Mao himself reports that

he and his friends 'had no time for love or "romance" and considered the times too critical and the need for knowledge too urgent to discuss women or personal matters. I was not interested in women. My parents had married me when I was fourteen to a girl of twenty, but I had never lived with her – and never subsequently did. I did not consider her my wife and at this time gave little thought to her. Quite aside from the discussions of feminine charm, which usually play an important role in the lives of young men of this age, my companions even rejected talk of ordinary matters of daily life.'

29 Some eleven years after his own childhood marriage, Mao wrote nine such articles in a mere thirteen days' time, precipitated by the death of a Changsha girl by suicide after her forced marriage. For extracts, see Roxane Witke, 'Mao Tse-tung, Women and Suicide', in Marilyn Young, ed., *Women in China: Studies in Social Change and Feminism* (Ann Arbor, 1973), and Stuart Schram, *The Political Thought of Mao Tse-tung* (New York, 1963), pp. 334–7. In the theatre of propaganda, Tian Han's 1922 play *A Night in a Coffee Shop* was an early example directed against arranged marriage.

30 McDougall, pp. 187, 190–91.

31 *Ibid.*, pp. 232–3.

32 *Ibid.*, p. 43.

33 *Ibid.*, 250–51.

34 *Ibid.*, p. 255. 'Cuiqiao's song is suddenly broken off', reads the director's script.

35 Paradoxically, if one reads this allegory even more cynically, Gu Qing's instrumentality in Cuiqiao's demise suggests that the red revolution has had great impact, shattered the age-old relationship between the people and their land, leaving nothing of spiritual value to take its place.

36 McDougall, p. 156.

37 Esther C.M. Yau, '*Yellow Earth*: Western Analysis and a Non-Western Text', in Chris Berry, ed., *Perspectives on Chinese Cinema* (2nd edn, London, 1991), p. 146; originally in *Film Quarterly*, 41.2 (1987–8), pp. 22–33.

38 McDougall, p. 6.

39 The 'Three Obediences' are defined in the *Li Ji*: 'The woman follows (and obeys) the man: – in her youth, she follows her father and elder brother; when married, she follows her husband; when her husband is dead, she follows her son.' *Li Chi: Book of Rites*, trans. by James Legge (New Hyde Park, 1967), I, p. 441 (book 9, section 3). As for the 'four Virtues', women were to be virtuous in their actions, in their conversation, in their appearance, and in their work about the home; cf. Dorothy Ko, 'Pursuing Talent and Virtue: Education and Women's Culture in Seventeenth- and Eighteenth-Century China', *Late Imperial China*, 13.1 (1992), pp. 28–30.

40 McDougall, p. 36.

41 *Ibid.*, pp. 209–10.

42 This relationship corresponds more closely to theory than to traditional practice, which saw many rural women work hard both out of doors and in.

43 McDougall, pp. 192–3.

44 Roxane Witke, 'Mao Tse-tung, Women and Suicide'. Margery Wolf, who discusses the possible marital-suicidal scenarios, also reports, 'The most striking single fact about Chinese suicide that makes it so different from Western suicide is its relationship to gender. In contrast to every other country for which we have statistical data, Chinese women are as likely as men to kill themselves and in some time periods more likely'. 'Woman and Suicide in China', in Margery Wolf and Roxane Witke, *Women in Chinese Society* (Stanford, 1975), p. 117.

At a symposium entitled 'Non-Economic Aspects of China's Economic Reforms' (Harvard University, September 1996), Arthur Kleinman presented current data to the effect that 42 per cent of all the world's suicides occur in China (four times the per capita rate of the United States); that unlike most nations, China's suicides are predominantly rural (five to seven times greater than the urban suicide rate); and that only in China do more women than men commit suicide.

45 McDougall, p. 225.

46 Esther Yau regards the marital theme as a key signifier in *Yellow Earth*, treating the relationship between Gu Qing and Cuiqiao as structural rather than individual and personal:

Inasmuch as the sense of social identity defines the person within Chinese society, individuals in Chinese films are often cast as non-autonomous entities within determining familial, social, and national frameworks. Ever since the 1920s, the portrayals of individuals in films have been inextricably linked to institutions and so do not reach resolution outside the latter. Hence, unlike the classical Hollywood style, homogeneity is not restored through the reconciliation of female desires with male ones, and the ways of looking are not structured according to manipulations of visual pleasure (coding the erotic, specifically) in the language of the Western patriarchal order.

Yau, pp. 69–70. She goes on to write that 'With an integration of socialism with Confucian values, film texts after 1949 have often coded the political into both narrative development and visual structures, hence appropriating scopophilia for an asexual idealization. In the post-Cultural Revolution context, then, the critique of such a repressive practice naturally falls on the desexualising (hence dehumanising) discourses in the earlier years and their impact on the cultural and human psyche'. Yau, p. 70. *Yellow Earth*, however, must be understood as engaging at least somewhat in that 'repressive practice' rather than in its critique. It remained for films like *Army Nurse* and *Sacrificed Youth* (both 1985) to advance that critique of desexualization.

47 Rubie Watson, 'Chinese Bridal Laments: The Claims of a Dutiful Daughter', in Bell Yung, Evelyn Rawski and Rubie Watson, *Harmony and Counterpoint: Ritual Music in Chinese Context* (Stanford, 1996), p. 108.

48 *Ibid.*, p. 114.

49 *Ibid.*, p. 126.

50 *Xintianyou* is translated by McDougall (pp. 31, 173) as roughly meaning 'following the flow of nature'.

51 Chen Kaige speaks laconically of this in an interview, saying only, 'I think my first three films were very sexual, especially *Yellow Earth* and *The Big Parade*. Maybe that's something very personal!' Tony Rayns, 'The Narrow Path: Chen Kaige in Conversation with Tony Rayns', in John Boorman and Walter Donohue, eds, *Projections 3: Filmmakers on Film-making* (London, 1994), p. 55.

52 Laurence Schneider, *A Madman of Ch'u: The Chinese Myth of Loyalty and Dissent* (Berkeley, 1980), p. 200; see especially chapter five, 'A Touch of Class: Ch'u Yüan in the People's Republic'.

53 *Ibid.*, pp. 179, 180, 182.

54 David Hawkes, trans., *Ch'u Tz'u: The Songs of the South* (Boston, 1959), p. 90 (slightly modified).

55 In the *Nine Songs*, three of the nine deities are usually thought of as female: the Mountain Goddess, the Xiang Princess and Lady of the Xiang (the latter two possibly alternate identities of the same figure); in these cases, presumably,

the role is played by a male shaman. The male gender of the Yellow River lord suggests a female supplicant or sacrificial victim. Cf. Arthur Waley, *The Nine Songs: A Study of Shamanism in Ancient China* (London, 1955); Hawkes, *Ch'u Tz'u*; Edward Schafer, *The Divine Woman: Dragon Ladies and Rain Maidens in T'ang Literature* (Berkeley, 1967); and Laurence Schneider.

The authorship of the *Nine Songs* has been held in doubt throughout much of this century, though the politically driven treatment of this question during Mao's era strongly reasserted the traditional view of Qu Yuan as author (Schneider, pp. 169–70).

56　Qu Yuan, 'The Nine Songs: The Greater Master of Fate', Hawkes, pp. 39–40.

57　Cf. Hans Frankel, *The Flowering Plum and the Palace Lady: Interpretations of Chinese Poetry* (New Haven, 1976), including an example by Han poet Zhang Heng (pp. 183–5) and with regard to Tang practice, by which time the temporal disguise was so commonly practiced and well understood as to afford little or no protection anyhow (pp. 141 ff.).

58　For an account of the resurgence of Qu Yuan imagery in recent years, see Ralph Croizier, 'Qu Yuan and the Artists: Ancient Symbols and Modern Politics in the Post-Mao Era', *The Australian Journal of Chinese Affairs*, 24 (July 1990), pp. 25–50.

59　Cuiqiao's songs were performed by a professional musician to a romanticized, Western orchestral accompaniment, much to the consternation of critics and ultimately to the dissatisfaction of the director himself; McDougall, 46.

60　McDougall, p. 221.

61　*Ibid.*, pp. 240–42.

62　*Ibid.*, p. 252.

63　Hawkes, p. 40.

64　McDougall, pp. 10–11.

65　*Ibid.*, p. 13.

66　*Ibid.*, p. 10.

67　*Ibid.*

68　This predicament is strikingly reminiscent of Juehui's silence which leads to Mingfeng's death in Ba Jin's 1931 novel, *Family*, filmed in 1956; for that text, see Ba Jin, trans. by Sidney Shapiro and Lu Guanghuan, *Family* (Garden City, 1972), pp. 211 ff.

69　See Wang Fangyu and Richard Barnhart, *Master of the Lotus Garden: The Life and Art of Bada Shanren (1626–1705)*, ed. Judith Smith, (New Haven, 1990), pp. 104–6.

70　Jerome Silbergeld, 'Kung Hsien's Self-Portrait in Willows, with Notes on the Willow in Chinese Painting and Literature', *Artibus Asiae*, XLII/1 (1980), pp. 5–38. For a more recent study along these lines, see Alfreda Murck, 'Paintings of Stem lettuce, Cabbage, and Weeds: Allusions to Tu Fu's Garden', *Archives of Asian Art*, XLVIII (1995), pp.32–47.

71　See Fu Shen, 'An Aspect of Mid-seventeenth Century Chinese Painting: The "Dry Linear" Style and the Early Work of Tao-chi', in *Journal of the Institute of Chinese Studies, Chinese University of Hong Kong* (December 1976), pp. 579–616.

72　A lengthy defense of the notion of vessel as female might be called for. But a shortcut could be offered, to the effect that while men have similarly been likened to vessels – archetypically, Confucius' student Zigong, whom the master likened to a sacrificial vessel (a *hulian*; *Analects*, 5.3) – the male ideal structured by Confucius and admired by his followers through the ages is

steeped in traditionally 'feminine' virtues, a receptacle of virtue, lovely and
sedate rather than assertive and confrontational.

73 In traditional terms, this drought might be thought of as Heaven's response,
    bao ying, to Cuiqiao's death.

74 Sima Qian, *Shi ji* (Hong Kong, 1958), vol. X, pp. 3211–2 (ch. 126); for a
    complete translation and discussion of the phenomenon, see J. J. M. de Groot,
    The Religious System of China (Leyden, 1910), 6:1197-8. A painting by Zhang
    Hong (1577–c. 1652) illustrating this narrative episode, from Zhang's *Album of
    Figures from Tales of Sima Qian*, is illustrated (poorly) in Wang Bomin,
    Zhongguo huihua shi (Shanghai, 1982), p. 521.

75 Cf. Richard Barnhart, *Marriage of the Lord of the River: A Lost Landscape by
    Tung Yüan* (Ascona, 1970), pp. 11–12.

76 From Wang Chong of the first century, we get: 'When the sun is eclipsed, it is
    because the Yin vanquishes it; on this account attacks are then made by man
    upon things which are yin. So also, at the time of a drought, when the Yang
    predominates, the allies of the Yang are made to smart; and therefore, whereas
    the wu are allies of the Yang, Xi of Lu in a time of draught resolved to burn the
    wu [because] the wu contain the breath of the Yang in themselves'. de Groot,
    6:1194. See also Edward Schafer's study of rain-making in Shang and Zhou
    China, 'Ritual Exposure in Ancient China', *Harvard Journal of Asiatic Studies*,
    XIV (1951), pp. 130–84.

77 Chow, p. 45.

78 McDougall, pp. 9, 17. Chen Kaige has defended against this, saying 'Praying for
    rain is one of the most ancient rituals of our people, and one which survives
    even today. In the *Book of Songs* [the *Odes*] there are descriptions of peasants
    praying for rain during celebrations for good harvests. . . Our aim in filming
    this scene was not at all voyeuristic or calculated to show up the ignorance of
    the peasants, but rather to express the formidable energy and force of the
    peasants.' Barmé and Minford, p. 268. Needless to say, the prayer scenes
    express more than just that; the *Odes* are by no means the source for this
    scene, but see for example *The She King* [*Shi jing*], trans. by James Legge (*The
    Chinese Classics*, IV; Hong Kong, 1960), pp. 377–9.

79 McDougall, pp. 29–31.

80 Pang Jin, *Long de xisu* (Popular customs regarding dragons) (Xi'an, 1988).

81 McDougall, pp. 258–9.

82 Pang Jin, pp. 106–7, text and translation supplied by Judy Boltz, with my
    modifications. Ellipses and placement of the term *shengshui ping* (jar of holy
    water) in quotation marks follow Pang's original text.

83 In Zheng Yi's novel *Old Well*, a similar kind of ceremony takes place in northern
    Shanxi province, in the Taihang Mountains region. In 1983, although such
    prayer ceremony is prohibited and the local villagers' Dragon King idol has
    been destroyed, the peasants are so frustrated in their well-digging efforts that
    they surreptitiously offer a three-night theatrical performance for the Dragon
    King's pleasure. Unfortunately, he gives but lightning and a splattering of
    water. The villagers believe they've been outbid by a visiting bridge construc-
    tion brigade, which has given prayers and blood offerings on behalf of drought
    so that they can complete their work. Zheng Yi, *Old Well,* trans. David Kwan
    (San Francisco, 1989), pp. 117–18. The film of *Old Well* (1987, directed by Wu
    Tianming from Zheng Yi's filmscript) does not include this scene. Zheng Yi
    (p. 28) also notes the frequency with which successful Dragon King idols were
    abducted by other villages near and far and returned with honours, especially
    celebratory if he answered their prayers.

84 McDougall, p. 6.

85 A classic commentary on this philosophical condition is Su Shi's 'Red Cliff' prose-poem (fu) of 1082, which pivots on this lament made during a trip down the Yangzi River: 'Fishermen and wood gatherers by the banks of streams, companions to fish and crayfish, friends of deer and elk, riding this leaf of a boat, dipping gourds into the wine jar and pouring for each other – we are no more than summer flies between heaven and earth, a grain of millet on the waste of the sea? It grieves me that life is so short, and I envy the long river that never stops. . .' Trans. by Burton Watson; cf. Jerome Silbergeld, 'Back to the Red Cliff: Reflections on the Narrative Mode in Early Literati Landscape Painting', *Ars Orientalis*, xxv (1995), pp. 19–38.

86 The relationship of cinematographer Zhang Yimou to the local 'Xi'an School' of painting, heir to the Song landscape tradition, has been noted; a native of Xi'an, Zhang studied photography in the Shaanxi Provincial Museum in the late 1970s before his acceptance into the Beijing Film Academy in 1978.

87 It is worth noting that were this a stage entry and Gu Qing the conquering hero, he would enter from stage left, the *yang* direction (the villain would be vanquished to stage right, the *yin* direction). Entering along the central axis seems to pose Gu as neither hero nor villain but rather, just as he is in the ideological text, as ambiguous middle figure.

88 For the ideological battles that took place over traditional Chinese painting during the first four decades of Communist rule, see Jerome Silbergeld with Gong Jisui, *Contradictions: Artistic Life, the Socialist State, and the Chinese Painter Li Huasheng* (Seattle, 1993), and Julia Andrews, *Painters and Politics in the People's Republic of China, 1949–1979* (Berkeley, 1994).

89 Yau (p. 75) writes that 'Almost uninscribed by culture and, to some extent, by the text itself, Hanhan has the greatest degree of differentiation (i.e., Hanhan = X) and exists to be taken up by the three other narrative strands [Cuiqiao, the father, and Gu Qing] for signification'.

90 Chen Kaige's comments in note 78 above would further this interpretation; but then he has taken various positions in various interviews.

91 McDougall, pp. 18–19.

92 Schneider, p. 197. '[The] post-Cultural Revolution historiography is really aiming at a reappraisal of the historiographic premises of the lore rather than of the lore itself. . . To speak on behalf of the common masses in Ch'ü Yüan's time is not to speak for the most progressive forces, since (according to this historicist approach) the masses only began to develop and represent an advanced revolutionary consciousness in modern times and under socialism. . . Now, History wields the whip and drives before it the Revolution. The First Emperor and Ch'ü Yüan, both of them, are just along for the ride.' (pp. 198–9)

93 McDougall, *Mao Zedong's 'Talks'*, p. 61; 'Our professional musicians should give their attention to songs sung by the masses. Our professional artists should give their attention to mass art'. *Ibid.*, p. 73.

94 E.g., Chow, chapter 2; An Jingfu, 'The Pain of a Half Taoist: Taoist Principles, Chinese Landscape Painting, and *King of the Children*', in Linda Ehrlich and David Desser, eds, *Cinematic Landscapes: Observations on the Visual Arts and Cinema of China and Japan* (Austin, 1994), pp. 117–27.

95 Other allusive elements in *Yellow Earth* deserve a similar exploration: the wild pear tree that appears in the opening scene (like the jar) and three times altogether, first in full foliage and finally (according to the directorial notes) barren of leaves (illus. 27); the moon, which similarly appears in three sequences and seems to codify Cuiqiao's haunted relationship with Gu Qing

(illus. 29); and the use of the colour red, which conflates Cuiqiao's status as bride/victim (illus. 14, 15) with her Communist aspirations and also helps establish her linkage to the jar of holy-water with its attached red fabric (illus. 1–3).

2 Ruins of a Sorghum Field, Eclipse of a Nation: *Red Sorghum* on Page and Screen

1 Chen Kaige, *Playboy* (Chinese version), XXII (May 1988), p. 48; quoted in Chow, p. 94.
2 For discussions of *yingxi*, see George Semsel, Xia Hong, and Hou Jianping, eds, *Chinese Film Theory: A Guide to the New Era* (New York, 1990); George Semsel, Chen Xihe, and Xia Hong, eds, *Film in Contemporary China: Critical Debates, 1979–1989* (Westport, 1993), Part III, pp. 63 ff.
3 Stories by Ba Jin (1931), Mao Dun (1932) and Lu Xun (1924), respectively. By this time, the Party had (speciously) claimed the May 4th Movement as catalysed by the Soviet revolution.
4 McDougall, pp. 175, 32.
5 Chapter one, note 25.
6 The film credits do not formally list a scriptwriter.
7 Pp. 285–7.
8 Focusing on their lack of cinematic mobility, critics have typically ignored the transformation of content in adaptation from the page or the stage to screen. An example of such radical adaptation occurred with *Street Angel* (1937), scripted and directed by Yuan Muzhi. This was inspired by the 1928 American film of the same name and by Monckton Hoffe's 1922 stage play *Cristilinda*, from which both films claimed derivation. The play (set in England) concerns a crippled but pure-at-heart circus performer who refuses to partake in the black-mail of her former boyfriend, a rags-to-riches painter, after his angelic portrait of her has been passed off by scoundrels as a Renaissance-period religious masterpiece. The American film (set in Naples) elaborates on the romance between this idealistic painter and the circus beauty, set against the relentless pursuit of her by the authorities (Jean Valjean-like) for an attempted theft by her in order to buy medicine for her poor dying mother. Although their differ-ences are considerable, the linkage between the Western play and Western film remains recognizable. On the other hand, one can scarcely detect the basis in either of these two sources for Yuan Muzhi's film. Cf. Monckton Hoffe, *Cristilinda* (New York, 1925); see chapter four, pp. 151–3 and n. 53, for further discussion of *Street Angel*.
9 Jerome Silbergeld, 'Art Censorship in China: A Do-It-Yourself System', in Elizabeth Childs, ed., *Suspended License: Censorship and the Visual Arts* (Seattle, 1997), pp. 299–300. See also Jerome Silbergeld, *Contradictions*.
10 A few unauthorized exceptions to this have emerged in recent years, such as Zhang Yuan's *Beijing Bastards* (1993), which met with harsh government opposition.
11 After the establishment of the People's Republic in 1949, the Film Bureau, with membership including political commissars from the Communist Party's Propaganda Department, was housed in the Ministry of Culture, as were the various national artist associations. In the early years of the Cultural Revolution, the Ministry was dismantled, coopted by Wu De's Central Cultural Activity Group under the auspices of Jiang Qing's Central Cultural Revolutionary Leadership Group, but it was re-established in 1971 under Wu

De's direction. In 1986, however, film and electronic media were elevated in stature compared to other cultural media, and the Film Bureau was made part of a new Ministry of Radio, Film, and Television. Much work is still needed on the sensitive subject of Chinese film censorship. The most useful writings come from Paul Clark, who gives emphasis to a complex and ever-changing three-way relationship between film-maker, audience and government/Party: 'The Film Industry in the 1970s', in Bonnie McDougall, ed., *Popular Chinese Literature and Performing Arts in the People's Republic of China, 1949–1979* (Berkeley, 1984), pp. 177–96; *Chinese Cinema: Culture and Politics Since 1949*, (New York, 1987); 'Two Hundred Flowers on China's Screens', in Chris Berry, ed., *Perspectives on Chinese Cinema* (2nd edn, London, 1991), pp. 40–61. See also Paul Pickowicz, 'Velvet Prisons and the Political Economy of Chinese Cinema', in Deborah Davis, Richard Kraus, Barry Naughton and Elizabeth Perry, eds, *Urban Spaces in Contemporary China* (Cambridge, 1995).

12 Mayfair Mei-hui Yang, 'Of Gender, State Censorship and Overseas Capital: An Interview With Chinese Director Zhang Yimou', *Public Culture*, V/2 (1993), pp. 306–7.

13 'Some people are for this film. Some are against it', Zhao proclaimed. 'We'd best not interfere'. Stone, p. 117.

14 Mo Yan, translated by Howard Goldblatt, *Red Sorghum* (New Publishing House, 1987). The novel has generated a considerable body of scholarly literature both in China and the West.

15 The numbers three and nine are universally associated with *yang* in China, two and four with *yin*. Jiu'er was born on the ninth day of the ninth month. She comes to reside at 18-Mile Slope, where her family brews a wine known as '18-Mile Red' from the 900 tons of sorghum they raise annually. The film is set in a nine-year period.

16 For various perspectives, see Yuejin Wang, '*Red Sorghum*: Mixing Memory and Desire', in Berry, ed., *Perspectives*, pp. 80–103; Zhang Yangjin, 'Ideology of the Body in *Red Sorghum*: National Allegory, National Roots, and Third Cinema', *East-West Film Journal*, IV/2 (June 1990), pp. 38–53, and also in Wimal Dissanayake, ed., *Colonialism and Nationalism in Asian Cinema* (Bloomington, 1994), pp.30–41; Tonglin Lu, '*Red Sorghum*: Limits of Transgression', in Liu Kang and Xiaobing Tang, eds, *Politics, Ideology, and Literary Discourse in Modern China: Theoretical Interventions and Cultural Critique* (Durham, 1993), pp. 188–208; Zhu Ling, 'A Brave New World? On the Construction of "Masculinity" and "Femininity"', in *The Red Sorghum Family*, in Tonglin Lu, ed., *Gender and Sexuality in Twentieth-Century Chinese Literature and Society* (Albany, 1993), pp. 121–34.

17 Mo Yan, p. 4.

18 One thinks immediately of historical figures like Xiang Yu, hero of the play *Bawang bieji* or *The Prince's Farewell to his Concubine*, who failed to gain the mandate of Heaven due perhaps to his moments of ruthlessness, and Cao Cao, who brought the Han dynasty to an end but couldn't take its place largely due to his own violent temperament, in plays like *Zhuo fang Cao, The Capture and Escape of Cao Cao*.

19 E. Ann Kaplan, 'Problematising Cross-cultural Analysis: The Case of Women in the Recent Chinese Cinema', in Berry, ed., *Perspectives*, p. 141; Kaplan's film subject here is not *Red Sorghum* but Xie Fei's *Girl from Hunan*.

20 Mo Yan, pp. 69–71.

21 Mo Yan also worked directly on the film script.

22 This issue will be taken up in the next chapter, pp. 142 ff.

23 For bringing forth this topic, I am grateful to Wu Hung and Eugene Wang, at whose conference on 'Ruins in Chinese Visual Culture' (University of Chicago, May 1997) I first presented the outlines of this chapter.

24 Rose Macaulay, *Pleasure of Ruins* (New York, 1953).

25 See especially, Stephen Owen, *Remembrances: The Experience of the Past in Classical Chinese Literature* (Cambridge, MA, 1986).

26 A survey of this topic by Wu Hung yielded only five such paintings, and in contrast to poetry he finds 'no traditional Chinese painting [of] a ruined city or a man looking at a ruined city'. Wu Hung, 'Ruins in Chinese Art: Site, Trace, Fragment' (unpublished paper presented at the symposium on 'Ruins in Chinese Visual Culture', University of Chicago, May 1997), 1, p. 15. As if to prove the point by way of contrast, a number of artists resident in Nanjing in the first years of Qing rule (Gong Xian, Shitao, Gao Cen, Gao Yu, Hu Yukun) covertly painted the only major building not destroyed by Manchus at the tomb of the Ming dynasty founder, the stele tower, in order to express their continuing loyalty to the earlier dynasty; demonstrated by Jonathan Hay, 'Dangerous Reminders: Ruins and the Openness of History' (unpublished paper, presented at this same symposium), material forthcoming in Hay's *Shitao's Late Life and Art: Topographies of Modernity in Chinese Painting Around 1700* (Cambridge). Changes in this attitude from traditional to modern times are noted by Wu Hung in his paper and exemplified in Eugene Wang's paper for this conference, 'Site, Sight, and Sore Eyes: The Leifeng Pagoda and Its Spectators'.

27 Terms related to 'ruins' include *xu*, which refers to a former site now wholly bereft of physical remains, and *ji*, referring literally to 'tracks' or to traces, the actual detritus. These and other terms (*yi wu, sheng ji*, and so forth) are discussed in Wu Hung's paper.

28 Winner of the 'Golden Eagle' for best picture at the 2nd Manila International Film Festival; Wu Yigong also won China's Golden Rooster Award as best director of the year.

29 Lin Haiyin, *Cheng nan jiu shi* (Taibei, 1960); mainland Chinese publication came about in 1981.

30 Two years earlier, Wu Yigong's *Evening Rain (Ba shan ye yu)* provided an early critique of the wrongs of the Cultural Revolution in a narrative about a falsely-arrested poet whose fellow travellers on a boat down the Yangzi decide to help escape.

31 Wu Hung's 'Ruins in Chinese Art' discusses how in Chinese painting, ancient trees often served to depict or imply what ruined architecture did not, bearing witness to the ravages of time (illus. 24 provides such an example); what follows here, however, refers to man-made ruination of landscape rather than its gradual degradation by nature.

32 *Ibid.*, p. 71.

33 *Ibid.*, p. 358.

34 *Ibid.*, pp. 63–74.

35 *Ibid.*, p. 359.

36 *Ibid.*, p. 71.

37 *Ibid.*, p. 4.

38 *Ibid.*, p. 358.

39 *Ibid.*, p. 4.

40 Irving Howe, *William Faulkner: A Critical Study* (2nd edn, New York, 1962), p. 26.

41 For example, in one of the most controversial scenes of the film, as Grandma is borne to her wedding, the sedan bearers give her bridal sedan a customary

violent shaking. Typically, Mo Yan's magic-realism spares us no detail: 'The two eggs she'd eaten for breakfast churned in her stomach; the flies buzzed around her ears; her throat tightened, as the taste of eggs surged up into her mouth. She bit her lip. . . But to no avail. She opened her mouth and spewed a stream of filth, soiling the curtain, toward which the five flies dashed as though shot from a gun' (pp. 44–5). In cinematic terms, however, while Gong Li bites her lip throughout this symbolic shaking, she remains gorgeous throughout and hardly breaks into a sweat.

42 Mo Yan, p. 273. Mo explores the psychological dimensions of this degeneracy, enumerating the 'three ingredients' of the family's love affairs, from Granddad's generation down to the narrator himself, as: fanaticism ('heart-piercing suffering'), cruelty ('merciless criticism: each partner in the love affair wants to skin the other alive, physically and psychologically'), and frigidity ('icy emotions . . . their teeth chatter so violently they can't talk, no matter how much they want to') (Mo Yan, pp. 272–3). Lu Xun would have understood this, perhaps, but it is wholly alien to the heroic tone of film.

43 Mo Yan, pp. 22 ff.

44 Trinh Minh-ha, *When the Moon Waxes Red: Representation, Gender, and Cultural Politics* (New York, 1991), pp. 1–2. She does not write about *Red Sorghum*.

45 Five minutes earlier in the film, Jiu'er's grandson pairs cinematic anticipation with textual reminiscence in a voiced-over narration: 'Dad told me, after he saw the sun that day his eyes got worse and worse. Everything was red'.

46 *She King [Shi jing]*, Legge, IV, pp. 320–21.

47 This eclipse itself is datable by the first lines to 29 August 775 BC, once thought to be the earliest undisputed concordance between Chinese and Western dating; *She King*, Legge, IV, p. 321. For an explanation of the historical persistence of this traditional attitude towards eclipses – despite a clear understanding of their astronomical mechanism by the first century AD and a predictive use of this by the early third century – see Joseph Needham, *Science and Civilization in China* (Cambridge, 1959), III, pp. 409 ff.

48 The book allows us to date Grandma's death to 1939 (Mo Yan, p. 253).

49 Jiu'er's grandson, as film narrator, comments at the outset of the battle sequence, 'I've been back there. The bridge is still there but there's no sorghum now'.

50 'Mother – Mother – head southwest – a broad highway – a long treasure boat – a fleet-footed steed – lots of traveling money – Mother – rest in sweetness – buy off your pain.' This is sung three times over in the film. In the book, it is sung only once before father's voice chokes with tears as Grandma's spirit refuses to go where its ordered, returning instead to serve fistcakes to the spirits of Grandfather's ill-fated troops (Mo Yan, p. 261).

51 McDougall, p. 6.

52 Ah Cheng, *Three Kings: Three Stories from Today's China*, trans. Bonnie McDougall (London, 1990); for the film script, see Chen Kaige and Wan Zhi, introduction by Tony Rayns, trans. Bonnie McDougall, *King of the Children and the New Chinese Cinema* (London, 1989).

53 *Ibid.*, pp. 61–2.

54 *Ibid.*, p. 62.

55 Chen was sent down to the Xishuangbanna region of Yunnan province, then spent five years building roads in Laos; Zhang Yimou spent seven years doing common labour in a cotton mill in Xianyang, near Xi'an.

56 Editor Stevan Harrell's introduction to *Cultural Encounters on China's Ethnic Frontiers* (Seattle, 1995), pp. 3–36, outlines Confucian, Christian, and Marxist

'civilizing projects' in Chinese history, particularly the calculated 'primitive-ness' of China's ethnic minorities in the Marxian project. Providing an intro-duction to the Chinese adaptation of Lewis Henry Morgan, Marx, Engels, and Stalin into their socialist definition of minority status, Harrell (9) demonstrates how of these three civilizing projects, 'The Communist project has been the most explicit and systematic in its process of definition'.

57 Based on Zhang Manling's novel, *You yige meilide difang* [*Such a beautiful place*] (Beijing, 1984).

58 During the Maoist era, films like *Third Sister Liu* (*Liu Sanjie*, 1961) and *Ashima* (1964) portrayed the 'soft' southern minorities, while *Serfs* (*Nongnu*, 1963) covered the harsher lives of China's northern ethnicities.

59 See Dru Gladney's critique of the modern fabrication of 'Han' identity and his discussion of how definitions of the minority cultures have served to establish a self-conscious dominant majority, in 'Representing Nationality in China: Refiguring Majority/Minority Identities', *Journal of Asian Studies*, 53.1 (February 1994), pp. 92–123.

60 Harrell, 4.

61 Just which village this landslide destroys, and when, remains most unclear in the film and is explicit only in the book (Zhang Manling, p. 52). Moreover, the book is set among Han villages, which Zhang Nuanxin's film script transforms into minority territory.

62 Xia Hong, 'The Debate over *Horse Thief*', in Semsel, *Film in Contemporary China*, pp. 44–6.

63 Six, according to Wu Tianming, in Stone, p. 115; seven according to Chris Berry, 'Market Forces: China's "Fifth Generation" Faces the Bottom Line', in Berry, ed., *Perspectives on Chinese Cinema*, pp. 118, 124 note 17.

64 Yang Ping, 'A Director Who is Trying to Change the Audience: A Chat With Young Director Tian Zhuangzhuang', originally published in *Popular Cinema* (Beijing), 1986.9, p. 4; trans. in Berry, *Perspectives on Chinese Cinema*, p. 127.

65 Trans. Tseng Hsien-ch'i and Richard Edwards, 'Shen Chou at the Boston Museum', *Archives of the Chinese Art Society of America*, 8 (1954), p. 31; cf. Jerome Silbergeld, 'Chinese Concepts of Old Age', pp. 109–10.

66 Eugene Wang's examination of *Samsara* as a study of self and self-denial extends this alienation to include a reflexive cinematic reference: 'Thus, while the shadow play and shadow watch [of Shi Ba, in the next-to-last scene] act out the tropological structure of the self, they at the same time become an explicit gesticulation of cinematic self-referentiality . . . The only way cinema here claims its power is by reverting to the silent mode of shadow play, the origin of the cinematic medium. Thus the film retrospectively questions itself by disavowing and negating the modalities of representation. As if in keeping with the screen character's painful soul-searching and self-questioning, the film itself needs its parallel interrogation of its own mode of existence/ expression.' Eugene Wang, 'Samsara: Self and the Crisis of Visual Narrative', in Wimal Dissanayake, ed., *Narratives of Agency: Self-Making in China, India, and Japan* (Minneapolis, 1997), p. 44.

67 A phrase unfortunately omitted from the English subtitles.

68 The 1934 film *Plunder of Peach and Plum* similarly begins and ends its unmitigated plunge into pessimism with the Chinese school anthem, inspiring at the outset but leaving the audience to wonder at the conclusion whether the song is played as lingering hope or in dire cynicism.

69 Quoted in Andrew Solomon, 'Their irony, humor (and art) can save China', *New York Times Sunday Magazine*, 19 December 1993, p. 66.

70 *Ibid.*, p. 66. For thoughts on the changing but continuing attachment to Chairman Mao (his 'fall and rise'), see Geremie Barmé, *Shades of Mao: The Posthumous Cult of the Great Leader* (Armonk, NY, 1996).

71 Stone, p. 122. For her role as Ermo, Ailiya won the Golden Rooster award as best actress of the year; *Ermo* won the Swissair/Crossair special award at the Locarno International Film Festival.

72 From the artist Wu Zhen: 'Men of today and those of the past cannot see each other; / But through surviving works, it is as if they had never died.' Inscription on his copy of a painting of bamboo by Su Shi, trans. James Cahill, 'Wu Chen, A Chinese Landscapist and Bamboo Painter of the Fourteenth Century' (Ph.D. dissertation, University of Michigan, 1958), p. 23.

73 Jianying Zha writes, 'Only much later did critics come to see that *Red Sorghum* was the film that, in a way, sounded the death knell of the Fifth Generation. It was still an art film, but it left the back door open a crack, and a star crept in: Gong Li . . . as she tumbled into the fire island of a sorghum and made it with a man she hardly knew. Sex had finally come to "serious" Chinese cinema'. Zha, *China Pop: How Soap Opera, Tabloids, and Bestsellers Are Transforming a Culture* (New York, 1995), pp. 88–9.

74 Quoted in Chow, p. 236, n. 58.

75 Wang Yuejin, 'The Old Well: A Womb or a Tomb?', *Framework*, 35 (1988), pp. 73–82. But the film *Old Well* omits the earlier episode in Zheng Yi's novella in which a frustrated effort was made to raise water by means of a stolen dragon-king idol; see chapter one, n. 83.

76 The logic of this is not new. Du Yu, governor of Jingzhou in the third century, once had duplicate stelae commissioned: 'one of these he set up on the mountain, and the other he threw into the deepest part of the river [because] he understood quite well that valleys and hills would someday change places'. 'What he did not understand', the eleventh-century author of this passage goes on to say derisively, 'was that the stone would someday wear away'. Ouyang Xiu, trans. Owen, *Remembrances*, 28. Wu Hung, 'Ruins in Chinese Art', discusses the importance of stelae, which initially serve to record and perpetuate but with age can become part of their own preservationist context. See also Eugene Wang's comments on the stele in this film, 'The Old Well', pp. 78 ff.

3 A Farewell to Arts: Allegory Goes to the Movies

1 *Analects*, 16.8; cf. Legge, I, p. 315.

2 Zha, p. 98.

3 *Ibid.*, p. 79, noting the *San Francisco Chronicle*, which may have been first to do this. In earlier decades, this title was usually bestowed on *A Spring River Flows East*, dir. Cai Chusheng and Zheng Junli (1947).

4 Cinematographer Gu Changwei was also nominated by the Academy. *Farewell My Concubine* shared the Cannes award for best film with *The Piano* and was selected as best foreign film by the National Board of Review, the New York Film Critics, and the Los Angeles Film Critics Association. Gong Li was named best supporting actress of the year by the New York Film Critics.

5 Lilian Lee, *Farewell to My Concubine*, trans. Andrea Lingenfelter (New York, 1993), p. 118; Lee's original was published in 1992.

6 *Ibid.*, p. 123.

7 *Ibid.*, p. 2.

8 This ending does not occur in the book but occurs with the radical conversion

of the book to filmscript by director Chen Kaige, with the participation of Lilian Lee and Lu Wei.

9 Ann Kaplan, who does equate body parts, sensitively emphasizes the 'double shock of castration (the finger) and of abandonment – both by his mother' and she discusses psychoanalytically the way in which Douzi's childhood abandonment points the way toward his sexual conversion. E. Ann Kaplan, 'Reading Formations and Chen Kaige's *Farewell My Concubine*', in Sheldon Hsiao-peng Lu, ed., *Transnational Chinese Cinemas: Identity, Nationhood, Gender* (Honolulu, 1997), p. 270.

10 For a detailed explication of this sequence, see Bruce Kawin, *How Movies Work* (Berkeley, 1992), pp. 275–85.

11 In Lilian Lee's text (p. 33), it is Master Guan, at an earlier moment, who carries out this act.

12 Lee, pp. 56–7. In the film, not the book, Douzi literally substitutes for a female, who is sent packing by the eunuch on the young actor's arrival.

13 Also called Yuan Siye.

14 Saussy, p. 28. *Allos*, other, plus *agoreuei*, to speak in assembly – 'other than the words', requiring explication 'in other words'.

15 Zha, p. 98.

16 *Ibid.*, p. 98.

17 In Klaus Eder and Deac Rossell, eds, *New Chinese Cinema* (London, 1993), p. 98.

18 Zha, pp. 97–9.

19 *Ibid.*, p. 99.

20 Saussy, p. 30 (describing, not arguing, this view).

21 Pauline Yu, *The Reading of Imagery in the Chinese Poetic Tradition* (Princeton, 1987), pp. 32–3; Saussy, p. 25.

22 Yu, *The Reading of Imagery*, p. 31.

23 *Analects*, 16.8; cf. Legge, I, p. 315.

24 *Ibid.*, p. 23.

25 See chapter one, n. 70–71, and chapter five, n. 70. For a bibliographic guide to some of these coded works, see Jerome Silbergeld, 'Chinese Painting Studies in the West: A State-of-the-Field Article', *Journal of Asian Studies*, XLVI/4 (November 1987), pp. 849–97, especially pp. 870 ff.; for a recent, contextualized discussion of this issue, see Martin Powers, 'Discourses of Representation in Tenth and Eleventh Century China', in Susan Scott, ed., *The Art of Interpreting* (University Park, 1996), pp. 89–125.

26 Lee, pp. 181–2.

27 In the words of Craig Owens, 'The Allegorical Impulse: Toward a Theory of Postmodernism', in Brian Wallis, ed., *Art After Modernism: Rethinking Representation* (New York, 1984), p. 209.

28 *Ibid.*, pp. 206, 209, 212.

29 Paul de Man, *Allegories of Reading* (New Haven, 1979), p. 242; Owens, p. 228.

30 Miklós Haraszti, *The Velvet Prison: Artists Under State Socialism* (New York, 1987), p. 121.

31 Ding Yinnan's *Dianying ren (The Filmmakers)*, constitutes a minor exception. From Hong Kong, on the other hand, comes Stanley Kwan's sophisticated *Ruan Lingyu (Centre Stage,* 1991), and acting in France, Maggie Cheung plays herself being filmed in *Irma Vep* (dir. Olivier Assayas, 1997).

32 In a different reading of this, rather than constituting a healthy, alternative vision that is tragically entwined and politically destroyed along with Dieyi's uncompromising commitment to art, Juxian's normative commitment to

family is made central to a negative critique of the director by Wendy Larson: 'This female road is, of course, deficient in imagination and creative reproductive power, and herein lies Chen's misogynist vision'. ('The Concubine and the Figure of History: Chen Kaige's *Farewell My Concubine*', in Sheldon Hsiao-peng Lu, ed., *Transnational Chinese Cinemas*, p. 343.) Female author Lilian Lee's original role in constructing this vision is not accounted for. Dieyi's own artistic ideals are cast by Larson as a 'fantasy and illusion of pure cultural form' (p. 343). His determination to perform regardless of audience (Japanese, Communist, whatever) is described in terms of a 'concubine [who] prostitutes her art – the essentially Chinese art – before the art-loving audience, whose imperializing position corresponds to that of the international (Western) film spectator and critic' (p. 340), an equation that leads to Larson's concluding pronouncement on the international success of *Farewell My Concubine*: 'When Chinese film is positioned within the transnational and transcultural market, any innocent notion of cultural representation immediately becomes simplistic and reductionist and reinforces the consumerist commodification of culture.'

33 In Lilian Lee's text, young Douzi's encounter with an abandoned child – a female – reminds him of his own abandonment but does not lead to her adoption (pp. 58–9). The film conflates that uneventful scene with the tale of Xiaosi, who first appears in Lee's text (pp. 73, 86) as a thirteen-year-old attendant to the adult Dieyi and Xiaolou.

34 See above, 107–8.

35 The third 'female', the 'new Concubine' Xiaosi, also meets his downfall in a short scene just before the final one, edited out of American-released versions but available in Japanese distribution.

36 The visual desecration of Juxian's beauty, indeed of her sexual identity, which appears in the book – she is given in public a hideous 'yin-yang' haircut (half a haircut) which when displayed in her suffering and death leaves her pathetically with a 'somewhat comical appearance' – is avoided in the film (Lee, p. 222).

37 *Farewell's* bracketing mechanism reveals that what could be taken as fiction is in fact a reality, opposite to the 'normal' practice as seen in films like *The Cabinet of Dr Caligari* (1919). There the bracketing narrative, added by the film-makers, casts the tale as an hallucination, transforming the original revolutionary tale, derived from a true story and directed towards the 'real horrors' of German authoritarianism, into a glorification of authority, which according to Kracauer 'perverted, if not reversed' the meaning and intention of the text authors; Siegfried Kracauer, 'The Cabinet of Doctor Caligari,' in Mast, Cohen and Braudy, p. 25 (originally published in Kracauer, *From Hitler to Caligari*, 1947). A comparable phenomenon resulted with the ending tacked on to *The Invasion of the Body Snatchers* (1956).

38 They are not, however, as in *Farewell*, lead figures who 'tell' the tale in flashback and then, the tale told, reappear just as they were at the outset.

39 Wang Jinling, *Zhongguo wenxue lilun shi* (Taibei, 1985), p. 168; trans. in Saussy, p. 61.

40 *Ibid.*

41 *Ibid.*, p. 32: '. . . metonymy passes for the most nearly "literal", the least tropical of the tropes, the trope anchored in some relation of fact.'

42 *Qiu Ju* won Golden Rooster awards for best film and best actress (Gong Li) and shared with Zhang's earlier *Raise the Red Lantern* the Hundred Flowers award for most popular film of the year. *Qiu Ju* and Gong Li were also awarded Golden Lion prizes for best film and best actress at the 49th Venice International Film Festival.

43 Zha, p. 95: '. . . in a curious way, Chen and Zhang traded places.'
44 Chen Yuanbin, *The Story of Qiuju* [original title: *Wanjia susong, The Wan Family's Litigation*] , trans. Anna Walling (Beijing, 1995), p. 8.
45 In Zhang Yimou's words, 'What Qiu Ju wants is a *shuafa* – a word used in the film that does not mean an "apology" but an answer, an explanation, a clarification'. Quoted in Ann Anagnost, 'Chili Pepper Politics', in Ann Anagnost, *National Past-times: Narrative, Representation, and Power in Modern China* (Durham, 1997), p. 138; this article regards the film as an ironic commentary on the insincerity of the village compacts drafted in the early post-Mao era.
46 See Paul Pickowicz's account, below, p. 129.
47 John Cawelti, '*Chinatown* and Generic Transformation in Recent American Films', in Mast, Cohen and Braudy, p. 510 (originally published 1978).
48 Yang, pp. 308–9.
49 Moreover, following the international success of the film, the Ministry of Post and Telecommunications issued a commemorative envelope with photographs of Chen Yuanbin, Zhang Yimou and Gong Li.
50 Paul Pickowicz, 'Velvet Prisons', pp. 212–3.
51 From *The Story of Qiu Ju* laser disc jacket, Sony Pictures Classics, 1992.
52 Mayfair Yang, pp. 306-7.
53 What is displayed [in his films] is not so much woman or even feudal China *per se* as the act of displaying, of making visible. What Zhang 'fetishizes' is primarily cinematography itself. If we speak of a narcissism here, it is a repeated playing with "the self" that is the visuality intrinsic to film'. Chow, p. 149.

4 The Veil of Tradition: Victims, Warriors and the Female Analogy

1 Yang, p. 300.
2 Fredric Jameson, 'Third World Literature in the Era of Multinational Capitalism', *Social Text*, 15 (Autumn 1986), pp. 69, 85–6 (Jameson's italics).
3 Jameson remarks also address not an objective reality as much as cultured perceptions of 'reality'. Immediately preceding the first part of this statement is the following passage:

Let me try to state this distinction in a grossly oversimplified way: one of the determinants of capitalist culture, that is, the culture of the western realist and modernist novel, is a radical split between the private and the public, between the poetic and the political, between what we have come to think of as the domain of sexuality and the unconscious and that of the public world of classes, of the economic, and of secular political power: in other words, Freud versus Marx. Our numerous theoretical attempts to overcome this great split only reconfirm its existence and its shaping power over our individual and collective lives. We have been trained in a deep cultural conviction that the lived experience of our private existences is somehow incommensurable with the abstractions of economic science and political dynamics. . . I will argue that, although we may retain for convenience and for analysis such categories as the subjective and the public or political, the relations between them are wholly different in third-world culture. (Jameson, p. 69)

Putting the second part of this statement in a similarly subjective context is the following:

'The truth of the Master', Hegel observes grimly, 'is the Slave; while the truth of the Slave, on the other hand, is the Master.' . . . the slave is called upon to labor for the master and to furnish him with all the material benefits befitting his supremacy. But this means that, in the end, only the slave knows what reality and the resistance of matter really are; only the slave can attain some true materialistic consciousness of his situation, since it is precisely to that that he is condemned. The Master, however, is condemned, to idealism. . . It strikes me that we Americans, we masters of the world, are in something of that very same position. The view from the top is epistemologically crippling, and reduces its subjects to the illusions of a host of fragmented subjectivities, to the poverty of the individual experience of isolated monads, to dying individual bodies without collective pasts or futures bereft of any possibility of grasping the social totality. . . All of this is denied to third-world culture, which must be situational and materialist despite itself. And it is this, finally, which must account for the allegorical nature of third-world culture, where the telling of the individual story and the individual experience. . . (Jameson, p. 85)

The contextualized reading, thus, is entirely different from phrases read in isolation.

4 Walter Benjamin, *The Origin of German Tragic Drama*, quoted in Chow, p. 55.
5 Chow, p. 150.
6 *Ibid.*, pp. 146–7; Chow's emphases.
7 *Ibid.*, 149.
8 Lydia Liu, 'Invention and Intervention: The Making of a Female Tradition in Modern Chinese Literature', in Ellen Widmer and David Der-wei Wang, eds, *From May Fourth to June Fourth: Fiction and Film in Twentieth-Century China* (Cambridge, MA, 1993), p. 196.
9 Chow, p. 51.
10 Saussy, pp. 48–9.
11 Stuart Schram, ed., *Chairman Mao Talks to the People; Talks and Letters: 1956–1971* (New York, 1974), p. 215; cf. Julia Kristeva, *About Chinese Women* (New York, 1986), p. 77.
12 Robert Rorex, *Eighteen Songs of a Nomad Flute: The Story of Lady Ts'ai Wen-chi* (New York, 1974).
13 Bo Juyi, 'Pipa xing', in *Tang shi sanbai shou xiangshi* (Taibei, 1970), pp. 96–8; for a complete translation see Witter Bynner and Kiang Kang-hu, trans., *The Jade Mountain* (New York, 1964), pp. 100–03.
14 Li He, 'A Girl Combs Her Hair', trans. A.C. Graham, *Poetry of the Late T'ang* (Baltimore, 1965), p. 115. Li He died in 816 at the age of 26.
15 *Red Cherry*, centred on a Nazi atrocity committed symbolically against a young Chinese woman living in the Soviet Union – literally, on her body – won the Golden Rooster and Hundred Flowers awards as best film while Guo Keyu won the Hundred Flowers award as best actress.
16 Yang, p. 300.
17 Cf. chapter three, note 25.
18 See chapter one, pp. 38–9.
19 Esther Yau, '*Yellow Earth*: Western Analysis and a Non-Western Text', in Berry, ed., *Perspectives on Chinese Cinema*, p. 69.
20 See chapter two, pp. 62–3.
21 Lydia Liu, 'The Female Body and Nationalist Discourse: Manchuria in Xiao Hong's *Field of Life and Death*', in Angela Zito and Tani E. Barlow, eds, *Body, Subject and Power in China* (Chicago, 1994), p. 161.
22 Wang Yuejin, '*Red Sorghum*', p. 97.
23 *Ibid.*, p. 81; my italics.

24 *Ibid.*

25 *Ibid.*, p. 83.

26 *Ibid.*, pp. 91, 92.

27 *Ibid.*, p. 100.

28 'In a world ordered by sexual imbalance, pleasure in looking has been split between active/male and passive/female. The determining male gaze projects its phantasy on to the female figure which is styled accordingly . . . Desire, born with language, allows the possibility of transcending the instinctual and the imaginary, but its point of reference continually returns to the traumatic moment of its birth: the castration complex.' Laura Mulvey, 'Visual Pleasure and Narrative Cinema', *Screen*, 16/3 (Autumn 1975), p. 11; also in Mulvey, *Visual and Other Pleasures* (Bloomington, 1989).

29 Linda Williams, 'When the Woman Looks', in Mast, Cohen and Braudy, p. 561 (originally published 1984).

30 First seen for sale by Douzi and Shitou as impoverished youths (Lee, p. 65), this sword (a real sword, not a blunt stage fake) appears throughout the text at moments that invest it with its own narrative. This is Xiang Yu's sword, symbol on stage of his heroism and also the implement of Concubine Yu Ji's destruction. More problematically, it came to Dieyi as a kind of 'wedding present' from the opera patron Yuan Shiqing, once Yuan had possessed Dieyi sexually (playing Xiang Yu to Dieyi's Yu Ji in the seduction). Dieyi immediately presented it to Xiaolou for his wedding to Juxian, a transmission laden with psychological implications. The sword then appears in the actors' various entanglements with the Nationalists and the Communists.

   Too late, Juxian had fretted, 'Why did we keep that sword, Xiaolou?' Juxian was frantic. 'We haven't had a moment's peace since it came into this house.' (Lee, p. 206) During the Cultural Revolution, it became associated with the bourgeois culture of the theatre and as dangerous to its owner as before it had been powerful. Xiaolou disowns it in public and throws it to the flames, but Juxian stares straight ahead and snatches the sword back. From that moment, she is targeted, and just before her suicide she carries it back to Dieyi. One day Dieyi himself will commit suicide with it.

   Ironically, in Lilian Lee's text (pp. 214–15), it is Dieyi who recovers the sword from the flames. And it is the male director, not the female author, who empowers Juxian to achieve this feat.

31 Chow, pp. 47 (her italics), 45.

32 Williams, p. 570.

33 Cultural confusion and social repression has been framed in an increasing number of recent Taiwan and Hong Kong films in gay male situations, reassigning the exemplification of 'other' away from the category of heterosexual female; among these, Tsai Ming-liang's *Vive L'Amour* (*Aiqing wansui*, 1994) and *The River* (*He liu*, 1997), and Wong Kar Wai's *Happy Together* (*Chung zha xie*, 1997). Mainland social and cultural policies make it much harder for film-makers there to develop this genre. Neither the homosexuality of *Farewell My Concubine* nor the incest of *Temptress Moon* initially met the standards for internal distribution.

34 Chow, p. 152.

35 Wang, p. 83–4.

36 Wang, p. 92.

37 See chapter six, pp. 282 ff.

38 Chow, p. 167 (her italics).

39 Owens, p. 228.

40 Anagnost, p. 154.

41 In Ding Xiaoqi, *Maidenhome* [and other stories], trans. Chris Berry and Cathy Silber (San Francisco, 1994), p. xiii.

42 Chris Berry, 'Chinese "Women's Cinema"', *Camera Obscura*, 18 (1988), p. 6.

43 Dai Jinhua and Mayfair Yang, 'Conversation with Huang Shuqing [sic]', *Positions*, III/3 (Winter 1995), p. 795.

44 *Ibid.*, pp. 792, 797.

45 *Ibid.*, p. 798.

46 *Ibid.*, p. 803.

47 *Ibid.*, p. 805.

48 *Ibid.*, p. 802.

49 *Ibid.*, pp. 802–3.

50 *Ibid.*, p. 794.

51 *Ibid.*, pp. 804–5.

52 Chris Berry, 'Interview with Hu Mei', *Camera Obscura*, 18 (1988), p. 40.

53 For all its apparent Chineseness, *Street Angel* was derived from the 1928 American silent film *Street Angel*, directed by Frank Borzage and based on Monckton Hoffe's 1922 play, *Cristilinda*. To these sources, which end not in tragedy but reconciliation, Yuan Muzhi's film owes far more for setting and social circumstance than it does for the derivation of its plot (see chapter two, note 8). Janet Gaynor won the first Academy Award for best actress for her role in *Street Angel* and two earlier films, *Sunrise* (1927) and *Seventh Heaven* (1927), while in the following year, 1930, *Street Angel* was belatedly nominated for best cinematography (Ernest Palmer) and interior (set) direction (Harry Oliver).

54 From endnotes by Chris Berry in Ding Xiaoqi, unpaginated. Hu Mei's father was a symphony conductor, her mother a voice teacher, and their home a cultural gathering place. For another account of her experiences during this period, see Stone, pp. 104–5.

55 Chris Berry, 'Interview with Ding Xiaoqi', *Modern Chinese Literature*, 7 (1993), pp. 109–11.

56 Berry, 'Interview with Hu Mei', pp. 38–9.

57 *Ibid.*, p. 112.

58 Berry, 'Interview with Ding Xiaoqi, p. 17.

59 *Ibid.*, p. 34.

60 *Ibid.*, p. 113.

61 *Ibid.*, pp. 110–12.

62 Berry, 'Interview with Hu Mei', p. 36.

63 Berry, 'Chinese "Women's Cinema"', p. 17. Ann Kaplan writes, similarly, '. . . finally she returns to her old remote army hospital position, where at least she has memories of her short happiness'. Kaplan, 'Problematising', p. 146.

64 Berry, 'Interview with Ding Xiaoqi', p. 113.

65 Berry, 'Interview with Hu Mei', p. 34.

66 Kaplan, p. 149.

67 Virtually every illustration published in Chinese film studies could be analyzed for the misinformation provided. This situation is no better than illustrating a text on art with some combination of forgeries and pastiches, and it speaks of a lack of detailed attention to Chinese film imagery. One can scarcely conceive of an analogous situation in literary studies (writing about Shakespeare, perhaps, while quoting only Holinshed or Marlowe) or imagine its being tolerated academically.

68 Berry, 'Interview with Ding Xiaoqi', p. 110.

69 *Ibid.*, p. 111. (Actually, the commissar is not the one who introduces Xiaoyu to her fiancé.)

70 Kaplan, p. 152.

71 *Ibid.*, p. 153.

72 Stone, p. 106.

73 Berry, p. 111.

74 Shared with Ang Lee's *Wedding Banquet*.

75 Zhou Daxin, 'Xiang hun tangpan de xiangyou fang', in Zhou Daxin, *Xiang hun nü* (*Hongfan wenxue congshu*, vol. 249; Taipei, 1993), pp. 1–44.

76 This is a Chinese perception as well. Female director Huang Shuqin, for example, has also described Xie's work as 'sort of feminine'. Dai Jinhua and Mayfair Yang, p. 804.

77 See chapter one pp. 40ff.

78 Notably, in *Girl From Hunan*, one male transgressor 'merely' had his legs broken, while his female partner was drowned. The female victim left an orphaned daughter – most likely, if she had a son to care for she would have been spared, as was the case with 'the Hunan girl', the adulterous protagonist Xiaoxiao herself, in bearing a male heir.

79 Dai Qing, 'Raised Eyebrows for *Raise the Red Lantern*', *Public Culture*, 5.2 (1993), pp. 334–5. In Su Tong's original novella, a number of polygamist Chen Zuoqian's previous wives were originally drowned in a garden well for their marital transgressions ('jumped in and committed suicide', is the way Master Chen masks the truth of their murders); at the end, third mistress Coral is drowned in that well for her own infidelities; and the chief protagonist, fourth wife Lotus, who long was haunted by that well and tormented by the prospect of drowning in it herself, goes mad at Coral's death, her final words in the book being, 'I won't jump, I won't jump'. Su Tong, *Raise the Red Lantern: Three Novellas* [original story title: *Qiqie chengqun, The Herding of Wives and Concubines*], trans. Michael Duke (New York, 1993), pp. 36, 53–4, 97–9. Although Dai Qing has called the film's hanging unrealistic, it is no more so than the master polluting his own well. For further discussion, see chapter six, pp. 288–91.

80 The two divinities, Xiang River Princess (Xiang Jun) and the Xiang River Lady (Xiang Furen), were traditionally treated as elder and younger sisters, daughters of mythic ruler Yao, bestowed as wives to his hand-picked successor, Shun; this belief dates back at least to Sima Qian's *Shi ji*, in its account of the First Emperor's travels. But Arthur Waley expresses a common modern view when writing that 'I cannot, however, help thinking that the Lady of the Hsiang (Hsiang Fu-jen) is merely another name for the Princess of the Hsiang (Hsiang Chün), and that the two hymns [used by Qu Yuan] represent local variants of a hymn addressed to the same deity'. Waley, *The Nine Songs*, p. 35.

With few exceptions, early paradigms of the noble (male) political suicide were rarely done by water; women drowned and their spirits then ruled the waters (cf. Edward Schafer, *The Divine Woman: Dragon Ladies and Rain Maidens in T'ang Literature*). Qu Yuan's non-exemplary suicide-by-drowning is sometimes said, on weak grounds, to have imitated an earlier drowning by the all-but-unknown Peng Xian (a shaman/occult leader? a statesman?) mentioned in the final line of Qu's *Li sao* poem ('I will go and join P'eng Hsien in the place where he abides'; Hawkes, p. 34). See Schneider (p. 218 n. 28, pp. 131 ff.) for Peng Xian and the drownings of Shentu Di, the shaman Cao Xu, and possibly Zhong Kui. Qu Yuan's strongest historical defender, Wang Yi, suggested that (as paraphrased by Laurence Schneider, with my italics) Qu 'would have done better not to be so compliant to his lord, to whom he related *in the passive role of a wife*. Instead, he should have been more aggressive, assuming a father's or teacher's role' (Schneider, p. 29.) For more on the appropriation of Xiang River scenery into allegories of political lament, see Alfreda Murck, 'The *Eight Views of Xiao-Xiang* and the Northern Song Culture of Exile', *Journal of Song-Yuan Studies*, 26 (1996), pp. 113–44.

81 Cf. Patricia Ebrey, *The Inner Quarters: Marriage and the Lives of Chinese Women in the Sung Period* (Berkeley, 1993), chapter seven, 'Women's Work Making Cloth'; Susan Mann, *Precious Records: Women in China's Long Eighteenth Century* (Stanford, 1997), chapter six, 'Work'.

82 Cf. Ellen Johnston Laing, 'Erotic Themes and Romantic Heroines Depicted by Ch'iu Ying', *Archives of Asian Art*, 49 (1996), pp. 68–91.

5 The Force of Labels: Melodrama in the Postmodern Era

1 *Analects*, 13.3; cf. Legge, I, p. 263.

2 *Daode jing*, p. 1; cf. Ch'u Ta-kao, p. 11.

3 Filmscript by Lu Yanzhou from his own original text, cinematography by Xu Qi, art design by Ding Chen and Chen Shaomian.

4 Xinhua News Service (Beijing), 11 May 1997. A thoroughly conventional historical epic, *Opium War* has yet, at the time of this writing, to receive general American distribution, having played at Cannes, the Toronto Film Festival, and the Seattle Film Festival.

5 George Semsel, ed., *Chinese Film: The State of the Art in the People's Republic* (New York, 1987), p. 111.

6 Cf. Semsel, *Film in Contemporary China*, p. 83.

7 Film administrators conventionally discuss how the government's support for film is allocated among the first three of these categories and every director seems to have his or her view of the ideal proportion. Director Xie Fei once recommended that propaganda and education films constitute 30–40 per cent of the films produced, entertainment 60 per cent, and art the 'remaining' percentage (that is, anywhere from 10 per cent to zero), a somewhat accurate gauge of the past decade's output.

8 Cf. Zhang Junxiang, in Semsel, *Chinese Film Theory*, p. 29.

9 Rousseau, in reference to the stageplay *Pygmalion*, written in 1774 or 1775; cf. Peter Brooks, *The Melodramatic Imagination: Balzac, Henry James, Melodrama, and the Mode of Excess* (New Haven, 1976), pp. 14, 217 n. 14.

10 Nick Browne relates diverse characterizations of melodrama to the particular critical perspectives from which each definition emerges, for example: European studies (which tends to lodge its definition in 'the subjectivity of the European bourgeoisie in its struggle against the authority of a declining feudalist system'), psychoanalysis (deriving from the French 'postrevolutionary attempt to institute in the Republic a morality founded on an ethical imperative centered around a new and troubled figuration of the self in its relation to the unconscious ... a theatre of social misfortune in which personal virtue is contested, hidden, misrecognized, or subverted'), Marxist studies ('the characteristic form of nineteenth-century bourgeois aesthetic thought that marks out the impasses and the paralysis of Western revolutionary programs and aspirations, involving even the theatrical metaphors and schemes of Marx's *Kapital*'), contemporary film studies ('the contradiction between a potentially transgressive feminine sexuality and a social system that seeks to delimit and

contain it . . . [exemplifying] the instability of the ideology of private life under capitalism'), and feminist studies ('a dominant mode of mass culture and the site of the central contradictions of patriarchy . . . the chosen ground for the delineation of the affective stakes of social constraint and transgression'). Browne, 'Society and Objectivity: On the Political Economy of Chinese Melodrama', in Nick Browne, ed., *New Chinese Cinemas: Forms, Identities, Politics* (New York, 1994), pp. 40–41.

For a discussion of the influence of 'pure' or 'classic' (French) melodrama in *melodramatic* literature, see Brooks, *The Melodramatic Imagination*. His list of melodramatic characteristics (pp. 11–13) includes 'allowing us the pleasures of self-pity' and the 'final reward of virtue', the latter of which will come in for discussion later on. Eric Bentley contrasts melodramatic excess with naturalism yet writes that 'melodrama is the Naturalism of the dream life' and that it 'corresponds to an important aspect of reality' as a 'spontaneous, uninhibited way of seeing things' ('as one can see from the play-acting of any child'); Bentley, *The Life of the Drama* (New York, 1964), pp. 205, 216. See Thomas Elsaesser, 'Tales of Sound and Fury: Observations on the Family Melodrama', in Mast, Cohen and Braudy, pp. 512–35 (originally published 1972), for important distinctions between French, German, British, American, and other melodrama, also discussed below.

11 Paul Pickowicz, 'Melodramatic Representation and the "May Fourth" Tradition of Chinese Cinema', in Widmer and Wang, p. 301.

12 Peter Brooks refers to the hidden quality of melodrama as the 'moral occult', 'the domain of operative spiritual values which is both indicated within and masked by the surface of reality. The moral occult is not a metaphysical system; it is rather the repository of the fragmentary and desacralized remnants of sacred myth. It bears comparison to unconscious mind, for it is a sphere of being where our most basic desires and interdictions lie, a realm in quotidian existence may appear closed off from us, but which we must accede to since it is the realm of meaning and value. . . We may legitimately claim that melodrama becomes the principal mode for uncovering, demonstrating, and making operative the essential moral university in a post-sacred universe.' Brooks, pp. 5, 15.

13 *Ibid.*, p. 302.

14 Browne, p. 40.

15 Elsaesser, pp. 514–15.

16 Owens, p. 212.

17 Wimal Dissanayake, ed., *Melodrama and Asian Cinema* (New York, 1993), introduction, p. 1.

18 *Ibid.*, p. 3.

19 Elsaesser, pp. 516–17.

20 *Garlands* won the Golden Rooster award as best film of the year and the Hundred Flowers awards for most popular film, actor, and supporting actor.

21 *Ibid.*, p. 517.

22 *Ibid.*, p. 110.

23 Semsel, *Chinese Film Theory*, p. 110.

24 Semsel, *Chinese Film*, p. 115.

25 *Ibid.*

26 The layered structures of this film are appreciatively analyzed in Ma Ning, 'Spatiality and Subjectivity in Xie Jin's Melodrama of the New Period', in Nick Browne, ed., *New Chinese Cinemas: Forms, Identities, Politics*, pp. 15–39, especially 24 ff.

27 Li Jie, in Semsel, *Chinese Film Theory*, p. 147.
28 Paul Pickowicz, 'Popular Cinema and Political Thought in Post-Mao China: Reflections on Official Pronouncements, Film, and the Film Audience', in Perry Link, Richard Madsen, and Paul Pickowicz, eds., *Unofficial China: Popular Culture and Thought in the People's Republic* (Boulder, 1989), pp. 46–7.
29 Deng never recanted his central role in the anti-Rightist movement, although he acknowledged some excessive application of a basically correct policy.
30 In Semsel, *Chinese Film Theory*, p. 147.
31 In Eder and Rossell, pp. 29–30. For Shao, the 'New Cinema' movement was broadly based (even in its weaknesses) – it arose when the 'Fifth Generation' was still in film school and 'bore no traces of a conflict between generations'. 'It would be a naive mistake', says Shao, 'to use Western Terminology to contrast "art films" (the Chen Kaige phenomenon) and "commercial films" (the Xie Jin model) [to] explain the way New Chinese Cinema was created and has developed.' (Eder and Rossell, pp. 23–4.)
32 Semsel, *Chinese Film Theory*, pp. 144–6.
33 Klaus Eder, 'New Chinese Cinema: A Preliminary Introduction', in Eder and Rossell, pp. 14–15.
34 Semsel, *Chinese Film Theory*, pp. 144–5.
35 Pickowicz, 'Melodramatic Representation', p. 323.
36 *Ibid.*, pp. 321, 323, 326.
37 *Ibid.*, pp. 322, 323.
38 Rayns, 'The Narrow Path', p. 52.
39 Brooks, pp. 12, 20.
40 *Ibid.*, p. 43.
41 Elsaesser, p. 516.
42 *Ibid.*, p. 515.
43 *Ibid.*, p. 516. Why Catholic France differed from Catholic Spain and Mexico is not clarified.
44 McDougall, *Mao Zedong's 'Talks'*, p. 19.
45 Brooks, p. 15.
46 *Ibid.*, p. 41.
47 Yu Huirong, 'Let Our Theatre Propagate Mao Tse-tung's Thought For Ever', *Chinese Literature* (July–August 1968) p. 111.
48 Cf. Roxane Witke, *Comrade Chiang Ch'ing* (Boston, 1977), especially chapters sixteen, seventeen.
49 Gu Hua, trans. Gladys Yang, *A Small Town Called Hibiscus* (Beijing, 1983); introductory comment by Yang, 8. Gu Hua was born in 1942. After the Tian'an Men demonstrations, in 1989, he migrated to Vancouver, British Columbia. Pickowicz distances Xie Jin's film from Gu Hua and his book, of which he says only that it 'is not an especially distinguished work of fiction' (p. 316); Browne discusses *Hibiscus Town* without mentioning Gu Hua.
50 As Gu Hua notes in his postscript (p. 260), 'I have tried to avoid writing in a stereotyped, generalized way, but hitherto I have made very little headway in this respect, and I need to redouble my efforts'.
51 Ah Cheng was born Zhong Acheng in 1949. His father was the once-prominent Zhong Dianfei, whose career as a film critic was damaged by the anti-Rightist movement of 1957.
52 Gu Hua, p. 49; this, like many details, are evident only in the book.
53 *Ibid.*, p. 204.
54 Cf. Brooks, p. 33.

55 Gu Hua, p. 92.

56 *Ibid.*, p. 131.

57 *Ibid.*, p. 200.

58 Browne, p. 53.

59 Gu Hua, p. 185.

60 *Ibid.*, p. 203.

61 Literally, 'excessively fragrant', this fragrance refers to revolutionary senti-
    ment.

62 *Ibid.*, pp. 21, 25.

63 Early on, Guoxiang hangs the label of adultery on Gu Yanshan for a sexual rela-
    tion with Hu Yuyin, which Gu can dislodge only by a humiliating
    demonstration that he was rendered impotent years earlier in his service as
    war hero.

64 Gu Hua, p. 10.

65 'A few years earlier', reflects the narrative shortly after the end of the Cultural
    Revolution, 'a woman leader in Beijing [i.e., Jiang Qing] had tried to follow in
    the steps of Lü Zhi [Han dynasty empress, d. 180 BC], Wu Zetian [Tang dynasty
    empress, r. 694–705], and the Empress Dowager Cixi [Qing dynasty,
    1835–1908]. During the campaign to repudiate Lin Biao and Confucius she
    stressed the need to train able women successors. "What's so wonderful about
    you men?" she demanded. "You just have an extra prick." This showed her
    thoroughgoing materialism. Her favour was extended throughout the country,
    manifested in all revolutionary committees. And so Li Guoxiang, the secretary
    of the commune, was made the woman secretary of the county committee.'
    Gu Hua, p. 208.

66 A scene omitted from the film describing their first encounter makes this
    explicit at the outset: 'Like the old-style wife of a town head, [Li Guoxiang]
    thrust out her small breasts to make a tour of inspection of the market, finally
    zeroing in on the beancurd stall. She was struck by the "Beancurd Beauty's"
    [Yuyin's] attraction for customers, quite apart from her good service and
    winning ways. "Confounded men!" she swore to herself. "They're like greedy
    cats prowling around that beancurd stall." Obviously Sister Hibiscus was her
    chief rival.' *Ibid.*, p. 21.

67 *Ibid.*, p. 200.

68 Browne, p. 54.

69 See Xie's comment on p. 195.

70 See Charles Hartman, 'Literary and Visual Interactions in Lo Chih-ch'uan's
    Crows in Old Trees', *Metropolitan Museum of Art Journal*, 28 (1993),
    pp. 129–67.

71 See chapter one, n. 70.

72 *Analects*, 9.27; cf. Legge, I, p. 225.

73 James Cahill, 'Awkwardness and Imagery in the Landscapes of Fa Jo-chen',
    paper for a symposium held at the Cleveland Museum of Art, March 1981, not
    published. Alfreda Murck has read Guo Xi's famous landscape in similar terms,
    noting its possible association with the ascendancy of the 'reformist' Wang
    Anshi faction at court in the early 1070s and the dismissal of many from the
    'conservative' opposition; Murck, 'The Meaning of the "Eight Views of Hsiao-
    Hsiang": Poetry and Painting in Sung China', Ph.D. dissertation, Princeton
    University, 1995, pp. 35 ff.

74 Cf. James Cahill, 'The "Madness" in Bada Shanren's Paintings', *Ajia bunka
    kenkyu* (Tokyo), XVII (March 1989), pp. 119–43; Wang Fangyu and Barnhart,
    pp. 37–9.

75 From the prefatory notes of this envoy, Lü-ch'iu Yin, who was introduced at the Guoqing Temple to Shide and his recluse friend Hanshan by the abbot Feng'gan:

> I then proceeded to the kitchen, where I saw two men standing in front of the stove warming themselves and laughing loudly. I bowed to them, whereupon the two raised their voices in chorus and began to hoot at me. They joined hands and, shrieking with laughter, called out to me, 'Blabbermouth blabbermouth Feng'gan! You wouldn't even know the Buddha Amitabha if you saw him! What do you mean by bowing to us?' The monks all came rushing in and gather around, astonished that a high official like myself should be bowing to two such poor men. Then the two joined hands and dashed out of the temple. I sent someone after them, but they ran too fast and had soon returned to Cold Cliff.

Burton Watson, *Cold Mountain: 100 Poems by the T'ang Poet Han-shan* (New York, 1970), p. 8; Watson suggests that these notes may be part of a fabricated hagiography. See also, Wu Chi-yu, 'A Study of Han-shan,' *T'oung Pao*, 45.4–5 (1957).

76 Mao Zedong, speech on 'The Situation and Our Policy After the Victory in the War of Resistance Against Japan', August 1945, in *Quotations From Chairman Mao Tse-tung* (*The Little Red Book*) (bilingual 2nd edn, Beijing, 1967), pp. 20–21, translation slightly modified here.

77 In the mid-90s, the government's sweep against pornography has been known as *sao huang*, or 'sweeping out the yellow'.

78 Rey Chow writes that in upheavals of the late Zhou period, '*Zhengming* became a weapon that assured the immovability of an already established political hegemony and in that sense a paradigmatic case, in Derrida's terms, of *logocentric* governance. By extension, we understand why, in their mobilization of class consciousness, the Chinese communists have actually been following the Confucian model of language as it is inherited in Chinese politics in spite of their overt ideological contempt for the Master [Confucius].' Chow, 'Against the Lures of Diaspora', in Tonglin Lu, *Gender and Sexuality in Twentieth-Century Chinese Literature and Society* (Albany, 1993), pp. 30–31; also published in Chow, *Writing Diaspora: Tactics of Intervention in Contemporary Cultural Studies* (Bloomington, 1993). Kam Louie's research in *Inheriting Tradition* emphasizes that 'the Master' came to be held in such contempt by the Marxist philosophical historians only gradually, after a decade of academic debate in the 1950s about his inheritability and only after his name had gradually been forged into a weapon.

79 *Analects*, 16.8; cf. Legge, I, p. 313.

80 Gu Hua, p. 32.

81 The less successful so-called 'White Horse' school of philosophy (from the query, 'Is a white horse a horse?') was actually predicated on this linguistic issue.

82 Gu Hua, p. 54.

83 *Ibid.*, p. 55.

84 Louie, pp. 125, 128.

85 Such a benign view of the People's Liberation Army was perhaps conditioned by the role the PLA played in 1976 in helping to arrest the Gang of Four in putting an end to the decade of chaos.

86 This occurs in the film without explanation; see Gu Hua, p. 224.

87 *Ibid.*, p. 240.

88 *Ibid.*, p. 249.

89 Above, p. 198.

90 Browne, pp. 52–3.

91 Semsel, *Chinese Film Theory*, pp. 144–5 (my italics).

92 Browne, p. 54.

93 Pickowicz, 'Melodramatic Representation', pp. 321–3.

94 *Ibid.*, p. 324.

95 Gu Hua, p. 141.

96 Elsaesser, p. 515.

97 Pickowicz, 'Melodramatic Representation', p. 326.

98 Shao Mujun, 'Chinese Films, 1979–1989,' *China Screen*, III/11 (November 1989), p. 11.

99 *Shakespeare: The Complete Works*, ed. G. B. Harrison (New York, 1948), p. 226.

100 *Ibid.*, p. 269.

101 Browne, pp. 46–7.

6 The Children of Melodrama: No-drama, Pseudo-drama, Melodramatic Masquerade and Deconstruction Drama

1 Chen Kaige, with introduction by Robert Sklar, 'Breaking the Circle: The Cinema and Cultural Change in China', *Cineast*, XVII/3 (February 1990), p. 28.

2 Lu Ji [261–303], *Essay on Literature (Wen fu)*, preface, trans. Shih-hsing Chen, in *Anthology of Chinese Literature: Volume I, From Early Times to the Fourteenth Century*, ed. Cyril Birch (New York, 1965), p. 204.

3 Brooks, xi.

4 See pp. 107, 111; Robert Heilman, *Tragedy and Melodrama: Versions of Experience* (Seattle, 1968).

5 In refusing to dismiss the importance of 'the melodramatic', I am reminded of the resonant response by comedian Jerry Seinfeld to a radio interviewer's question, 'Are you a Jew?' 'I don't know if I'm a Jew,' he said soberly, pausing for timing, and then concluded, 'but I'm Jew*ish*!'

6 Rayns, 'The Narrow Path,' p. 52.

7 Translated in Chow, *Primitive*, pp. 153–4, from Zhang Yimou, *'Gaoliangdi de chuanshuo – yi zhi shengming de zange'* ('Legend from the Land of Sorghum – A Eulogy to Life'), in *Hong gaoliang*, edited by Jiao Xiongping (Taibei, 1992), p. 93.

8 Jane Ying [Jianying] Zha, 'Excerpts from "Lore Segal, Red Lantern, and Exoticism"', *Public Culture*, V/2 (1993), p. 331.

9 Chow, *Primitive*, p. 153 (my emphasis).

10 Chen Huaikai was co-assistant director of *Family* and *New Year's Sacrifice* (both 1956) and co-director of *Song of Youth* (1959), *Haixia* (1975), and *The Great River Rushes On* (1978).

11 McDougall, p. 139.

12 Brooks, p. 12.

13 *Ibid.*, with chapters on each of these forms.

14 *Ibid.*, p. 4.

15 *Black Cannon* was based on a novel by China's popular author, Zhang Xianliang, *Langman de heipao (Romance of the Black Cannon)*. Chris Berry reported that as of early 1988, *Black Cannon* had sold more copies (99) than any 'Fifth Generation' film other than *Secret Decree* (1984, 240 prints; Berry, 'Market Forces,' p. 124 n. 17). Subsequent films directed by Huang include *Dislocation* (1986), *Transmigration* (1988), *The Wooden Man's Bride* (1993),

Stand Up, Don't Bend Over (1993), *Back to Back, Face to Face* (1994), *Signal Left, Turn Right* (1996), *Surveillance* (1997).

16 Semsel, *Chinese Film*, p. 182.

17 Zhao is a reminder that even in China, victims come in two genders, male as well as female, though figuratively he could be regarded as a silenced female-in-disguise; Huang Jianxin's graduation project at the Beijing Film Academy, *Reminiscences in a Light Rain* (1985), was about 'a shy girl student's unvoiced crush on a popular boy student' (Tony Rayns, in Chen Kaige and Wan Zhi, p. 36).

18 The first two of these were made with Zhang Yimou as cinematographer and He Qun as art director.

19 Zha, *China Pop*, p. 85.

20 Semsel, *Chinese Film*, p. 182.

21 Berry, 'Chinese "Women's Cinema"' p. 19.

22 In 1984, after *Yellow Earth*, Chen and Zhang were invited to make a fifteen-minute television documentary for the air force at Tian'an Men on National Day. The result was *Forced Takeoff* (*Qianxing qifei*), which despite the failure of the air show due to 'heavy pollution which obscured the planes as they flew in formation over Tiananmen', still was shown 'several times' on television in 1985 and 1986 and won a third class National Television Drama Award (a 'Flying Apsara'). McDougall, p. 142.

23 Rayns, in Chen Kaige and Wan Zhi, p. 30.

24 Zhang's cinematography here was foreshadowed by the crisply-patterned waist-drum scene at Yan'an in *Yellow Earth* (illus. 20).

25 Chen Kaige, 'Breaking the Circle', p. 31.

26 *Ibid.*, p. 30.

27 *Ibid.* Finally, 'to make them happy', Chen cut in some footage from the parade shots for *Forced Takeoff*.

28 *Ibid.*, p. 31.

29 *Ibid.*

30 *Ibid.*

31 Stone, p. 96.

32 Tony Rayns builds an interpretation of *The Big Parade*'s ending based on the premise that the sounds heard are those of the parade. 'More subversively, the film then goes on to establish a larger dialectic between what is seen and what is heard. . . Had Chen been allowed to end the film as he first intended – with the sound of the "big parade" itself laid over images of a deserted Tiananmen Square in the centre of Beijing – then the closing moments would have provocatively reversed the terms of the dialectic: authoritative sound would have cut against a questioning image' (Rayns, in Chen Kaige and Wan Zhi, p. 31). While it contradicts Chen's explanation above, it might very well be welcomed as contributing to the pluralistic writing and re-writing of text that Chen has espoused.

33 Eder and Rossell, p. 91.

34 McDougall, p. 144.

35 Ah Cheng, trans. Bonnie McDougall, *Three Kings: Three Stories From Today's China*. The other two 'kings' of Ah Cheng's trilogy are 'King of Chess' (by Hong Kong directors Yim Ho and Tsi Hark in 1989 in a greatly modified but fascinating cross-cultural form) and 'King of the Trees'. For the shooting script of *King of the Children*, trans. Bonnie McDougall, see Chen Kaige and Wan Zhi.

36 Eder and Rossell, p. 62.

37 Zha, *China Pop*, p. 81.

38 *Ibid.*, p. 89.

39 After a period cutting bamboo to make way for rubber plants, which he later said was 'just like killing people' (Stone, p. 94), Chen was recruited by the PLA to play basketball but wound up building roads for five years in Laos.

40 Chen Kaige and Wan Zhi, p. 5 (slightly modified).

41 *Ibid.*, p. 61.

42 *Ibid.*, p. 62.

43 Rayns, 'The Narrow Path', p. 52 (italics original).

44 See pp. 117–19.

45 Chen Kaige and Wang Zhi, p. 62.

46 Rayns, 'The Narrow Path', p. 52.

47 Zha, *China Pop*, pp. 82–3, 85.

48 McDougall, p. 135.

49 Eder and Rossell, p. 91.

50 Rayns, 'The Narrow Path', p. 55.

51 Chen Kaige, 'Breaking the Circle', p. 31. We must be cautious here about the dual authorship and merged identity of Chen Kaige and Ah Cheng.

52 Chen co-wrote the script with Chen Maiping, a high school friend of Chen's who appears in the credits under his literary name 'Wan Zhi'.

53 Ah Cheng, p. 166.

54 *Ibid.*

55 Quoting the shooting script, in Chen Kaige and Wan Zhi, p. 84.

56 See Britta Erickson, 'Process and Meaning in the Art of Xu Bing', in *Three Installations by Xu Bing* (Madison, 1991); Gao Minglu, 'Meaninglessness and Confrontation in Xu Bing's Art', in Judy Andrews *et al.*, *Fragmented Memory: The Chinese Avant-Garde in Exile* (Columbus, 1993). Artists Gu Wenda (illus. 222), Qiu Zhijie and Wu Shanzhuan have also laid important groundwork for this kind of 'meaningless' writing; cf. Gao Minglu, *Inside Out: New Chinese Art* (Berkeley, 1998), pp. 158–62.

57 *Daode jing*, chapters fifteen, fifty-seven.

58 'The hundred-year-old tree is hacked up to make bowls for the sacrificial wine, blue and yellow, with patterns on them, and the chips are thrown into the ditch. Compare the sacrificial bowls with the chips in the ditch and you will find them far apart in beauty and ugliness; yet they are alike in having lost their inborn nature.' 'Zhuangzi was walking in the mountains when he saw a huge tree, its branches and leaves thick and lush. A woodcutter paused by its side but made no move to cut it down. When Zhuangzi asked the reason, he replied, "There's nothing it could be used for!" Zhuangzi said, "Because of its worthlessness, this tree is able to live out the years Heaven gave it".' *The Complete Works of Chuang Tzu*, trans. Burton Watson (New York, 1970), 140, 209 (transliteration altered); cf. also 35. The second short story in Ah Cheng's 'Kings' trilogy, *King of the Trees*, is rooted in this traditional imagery.

59 The old legend is that Laozi, on his way out of China on the back of an ox, composed his 5,000-character classic at the request of gatekeeper Yin.

60 Ah Cheng, pp. 170–71.

61 See Scarlett Ju-yu Jang, 'Ox-Herding Painting in the Sung Dynasty', *Artibus Asiae*, LII/1–2 (1992), pp. 54–93.

62 *The I Ching or Book of Changes*, trans. Richard Wilhelm and Cary Baynes, (Princeton, 1961), pp. 275–6. The ox is also associated in chapter thirty, *li*, with perseverance and patient dedication (p. 119).

63 *Jang*, pp. 69–70.

64 The work no longer survives but may be reflected in a later painting, the *Five Oxen* handscroll attributed to Tang painter Han Huang, in the Palace Museum, Beijing; cf. Chu-tsing Li, 'The Freer "Sheep and Goat" and Chao Meng-fu's Horse Paintings', *Artibus Asiae*, xxx (1968), pp. 313–14. It is said that the emperor 'sighed with respect for [Tao Hongjing's] high ideals and did not force him'.

65 Jang, pp. 55–6.

66 *The Complete Works of Chuang Tzu* (ch. twelve, 'Heaven and Earth'), p. 131.

67 Cf. Jan Fontein and Money Hickman, *Zen Painting and Calligraphy* (Boston, 1970), pp. 113–18; Helmut Brinker, *Zen in the Art of Painting* (London, 1987), pp. 103–10.

68 Daoism, from the time of its earliest philosophical pronouncements, actually helped open the door to totalitarian thought with its suspicion of intellect and readiness to rely on the anti-intellectual sage-ruler:

> Therefore the Sage rules
> By emptying their hearts,
> Filling their stomachs,
> Weakening their ambitions
> And strengthening their bones.

Thus he gives the crafty ones no chance to act. He governs by non-action; consequently there is nothing un-governed. *Daode jing*, 3, trans. Ch'u Ta-kao, p. 14.

69 At the 1942 Yan'an Forum, Mao quoted Lu Xun, 'Head bowed, I'm glad to be an ox for little children', an acceptable conceit even in the case of an ox who ordered the little herdboys around; McDougall, *Mao Zedong's 'Talks'*, trans. McDougall, p. 85.

70 The phrase 'cow demons [ox ghosts] and snake spirits' (*niu gui yu she shen*) has its own antiquity; the ninth-century poet Du Mu used it rhetorically in describing the demonic verse of his departed contemporary, Li He: '. . . fallen kingdoms and ruined palaces, thorny thickets and gravemounds cannot describe his resentment and sorrow; whales yawning, turtles spurting, ox-ghosts and serpent-spirits cannot describe his wildness and extravagance.' *The Poems of Li Ho*, 791–817, trans. J. D. Frodsham (Oxford, 1970), p. 2. During the Cultural Revolution, the 'ox pen' (*niu peng*) was the term for the closet or other tortuously small place of confinement to which thousands of intellectuals were sentenced.

71 Or other three-fold presentations in *Yellow Earth*: the wild pear tree at the beginning, the moon, the reappearance of Gu Qing.

72 Chen Kaige and Wan Zhi, p. 82.

73 *Ibid.*, p. 101.

74 Represented by Comrade Wu, performed by the film's cinematographer Gu Changwei.

75 Chen Kaige departs here from Ah Cheng, surpassing him in iconoclasm. In Ah Cheng (p. 215), Lao Gar's last act is to add his name to the dictionary which he leaves for Wang Fu, so that Wang Fu can go back to the source of writing and reshape language in his own way. In the film, perhaps because *it is a film* and not a written text, Chen can take the extra step, beyond all written words and names. But he takes another step as well, in the burning of the hills (not in Ah Cheng's text) to represent *his* (Chen's, not the Communists') destruction of traditional culture, which as remarked upon both here and in the second essay above, on ruins (p. 80), becomes as iconoclastic as the Red Guards themselves.

Rey Chow, however, has denied the moral basis of Chen's departure from Ah Cheng, ascribing it entirely to a matter of media: 'The drastic questioning of the traditional authority of the written word (and thus of the primacy of the verbal language) is, I would contend, not a questioning of a moralistic kind. As I argue in the previous chapter, the film medium allows Chen to explore the much larger issue of technological reproduction in a modern "third world" culture. . .' (Chow, p. 121).

76 *Ibid.*, p. 57.

77 Rayns, 'The Narrow Path', p. 53.

78 Cf. Robert Scalapino and George T. Yu, *The Chinese Anarchist Movement* (Berkeley, 1961).

79 Louie, p. 121.

80 *King of the Children* was the only one of five successive Chen Kaige films, from *Big Parade* through *Temptress Moon*, not to be banned from internal Chinese distribution.

81 Zha, *China Pop*, pp. 81, 87.

82 Chen Kaige, 'Breaking the Circle', p. 28.

83 Chen Kaige, 'The Narrow Path', p. 52.

84 Zha writes that *Red Sorghum* 'sounded the death knell of the Fifth Generation' (*China Pop*, p. 88); the insertion here of 'original goals' is my own and, I believe, more accurate.

85 Zha, 'Excerpts', p. 331.

86 Chow, pp. 137, 139–40.

87 Rather than applauding Laidi's naturalism and Chen Kaige's rejection of cinematic artificiality, Rey Chow finds that 'she [Laidi] has been turned [by Chen] into a comic spectacle whose palpable physical dimensions exceed the closed circuit of male pedagogy and fantasy' (pp.134–5) so that Lao Gar can turn away from her towards his own 'narcissistic' pursuits; Lao Gar's ignoring of Laidi's own 'healthy narcissism' represents for Chow 'the road not yet taken,' an alternative path obliterated by Chen's 'hope to rewrite culture without woman' (pp. 140–41).

Chen Kaige presents a rather different perspective on the matter, reminding us that it is his life experience which is so integral to *King of the Children*, and reminding us also that the factor, the blunt reality, of Chinese film censorship is largely missing from this critical equation. 'I think my first three films were very sexual [as the first essay in this series has already argued with regard to *Yellow Earth*] . . . [But the] reason I came late to sexual questions is that I grew up without contact with girls and women. I went to a boys' school, and then I was sent to the countryside and lived with a lot more boys, and then I joined the army and found no women there either. I played basketball in the army, and there was a women's basketball team too. One woman in that team came from Beijing, like me, and I tried to find a way to talk to her, but it didn't work out. I'd become self-conscious about dealing with sexual matters by the time I made *King of the Children*, and I wanted the film to contain a love scene. But it simply wasn't possible in China at the time' (Chen, 'The Narrow Path', p. 55).

88 Oscar Wilde, *The Complete Works of Oscar Wilde* (New York, 1989), p. 379.

89 This while banned from internal distribution; it received no awards in China.

90 Liu Heng, *The Obsessed*, trans. David Kwan [original title, *Fuxi, fuxi*] (Beijing, 1991), p. 107.

91 Liu Heng, p. 17.

92 *Ibid.*, pp. 40–41.

93 *Ibid.*, p. 23.

94 *Ibid.*, p. 100.
95 *Ibid.*, p. 106.
96 *Ibid.*, p. 119.
97 *Ibid.*, pp. 122–5.
98 Most notably, Jenny Kwok Wah Lau, '*Judou*: An Experiment in Color and Portraiture in Chinese Cinema', in Ehrlich and Desser, pp. 127–45.
99 Both *Judou* and *Raise the Red Lantern* were banned from internal distribution until July 1992. Nonetheless, in award ceremonies conducted the following year, *Red Lantern* shared the Hundred Flowers honours for best film and Gong Li won the award for best actress. In addition, *Red Lantern* was selected as best foreign film of the year by the New York Film Critics, the National Society of Film Critics, and the British Academy Awards, while Gu Changwei was named best cinematographer by the National Society and the Los Angeles Film Critics Association.
100 For discussion of this controversial change from text to script, see chapter four, n. 79.
101 In Su Tong's text, Lotus was haunted by the spectre of becoming the next to drown in this well (pp. 53–4, 84) and as previous noted, her final, demented words are, 'I won't jump, I won't jump' (p. 99).
102 Judou's tale, in Liu Heng's text, begins in 1944 and continues into the period of Communist land-redistribution in the north.
103 *Analects*, 4.18; cf. Legge, I, p. 170.
104 See chapter four, pp. 153–4.
105 See chapter one, p. 37 and n. 64.
106 Mayfair Yang, pp. 300–304.
107 *Ibid.*, pp. 304–5.
108 Dai Qing, p. 336.
109 Mayfair Yang, pp. 305–6.
110 Zha, 'Excerpts from "Lore Segal"', pp. 329, 331–2.
111 Zha, *China Pop*, p. 94.
112 Chen Kaige produced the script together with Wang Anyi.
113 I am grateful to Andrea Lingenfelter for this information.

Bibliography

Ah Cheng, *Three Kings: Three Stories From Today's China*, trans. Bonnie McDougall (London, 1990)

An Jingfu, 'The Pain of a Half Taoist: Taoist Principles, Chinese Landscape Painting, and *King of the Children*', in Linda Ehrlich and David Desser, eds, *Cinematic Landscapes: Observations on the Visual Arts and Cinema of China and Japan* (Austin, 1994)

Anagnost, Ann, 'Chili Pepper Politics', in Ann Anagnost, *National Past-times: Narrative, Representation, and Power in Modern China* (Durham, NC, 1997)

Andrews, Julia, *Painters and Politics in the People's Republic of China, 1949–1979* (Berkeley, CA, 1994)

Bai Hua, *Unrequited Love, with Related Introductory Materials*, ed. T. C. Chang *et al.* (Taibei, 1981)

Barlow, Tani, ed., *Formations of Colonial Modernity in East Asia* (Durham, NC, 1997)

——, ed., *Gender Politics in Modern China: Writing and Feminism* (Durham, NC, 1993)

Barmé, Geremie, *Shades of Mao: The Posthumous Cult of the Great Leader* (Armonk, NY, 1996)

——, and John Minford, eds., *Seeds of Fire: Chinese Voices of Conscience* (New York, 1988)

Bentley, Eric, *The Life of the Drama* (New York, 1964)

Berry, Chris, 'Chinese "Women's Cinema"', *Camera Obscura*, 18 (1988)

——, 'Interview with Ding Xiaoqi', *Modern Chinese Literature*, 7 (1993)

——, 'Interview with Hu Mei', *Camera Obscura*, 18 (1988)

——, 'Interview with Zhang Nuanxin', *Camera Obscura*, 18 (1989)

——, 'Market Forces: China's "Fifth Generation" Faces the Bottom Line', in Chris Berry, *Perspectives on Chinese Cinema*, 2nd edn (London, 1991)

——, 'Neither One Thing nor Another: Toward a Study of the Viewing Subject and Chinese Cinema in the Eighties', in Nick Browne, ed., *New Chinese Cinemas: Forms, Identities, Politics* (New York, 1994)

——, and Mary Ann Farquhar, 'Post-Socialist Strategies: An Analysis of *Yellow Earth* and *Black Cannon Incident*', in Linda Ehrlich and David Desser, eds, *Cinematic Landscapes: Observations on the Visual Arts and Cinema of China and Japan* (Austin, 1994)

——, ed., *Perspectives on Chinese Cinema*, 2nd edn (London, 1991)

Brooks, Peter, *The Melodramatic Imagination: Balzac, Henry James, Melodrama, and the Mode of Excess* (New Haven, 1976)

Browne, Nick, ed., *New Chinese Cinemas: Forms, Identities, Politics* (New York, 1994)

Callahan, W. A., 'Gender, Ideology, and Nation: *Ju Dou* in the Cultural Politics of China', *East–West Film Journal*, VII/1 (1993)

Chan, Anita, *Children of Mao: Personality Development and Political Activism in the Red Guard Generation* (Seattle, 1985)

Chen Kaige, 'Breaking the Circle: The Cinema and Cultural Change in China', intro. by Robert Sklar, *Cineast*, XVII/3 (February 1990)

——, and Wan Zhi, *King of the Children and the New Chinese Cinema*, trans. Bonnie McDougall, intro. by Tony Rayns (London, 1989)

Chen Kaiyan, ed., *Heipao shijian: cong xiaoshuo dao dianying* [*Black Cannon Incident: From Novel to Movie*] (Beijing, 1988)
——, ed., *Hua shuo Huang tudi* [*Collated Critical Comments and Interviews about Yellow Earth*] (Beijing, 1986)
Chen Xiaoming, 'The Mysterious Other: Postpolitics in Chinese Film', *Boundary 2: An International Journal of Literature and Culture*, XXIV/3 (Fall 1997)
Chen Yuanbin, *The Story of Qiuju* [original title: *Wanjia susong*, *The Wan Family's Litigation*], trans. Anna Walling (Beijing, 1995)
China Avant-Garde: Counter-Currents in Art and Culture (New York, 1993)
Chow, Rey, 'Against the Lures of Diaspora', in Tonglin Lu, *Gender and Sexuality in Twentieth-Century Chinese Literature and Society* (Albany, 1993); also published in Rey Chow, *Writing Diaspora: Tactics of Intervention in Contemporary Cultural Studies* (Bloomington, 1993)
——, *Primitive Passions: Visuality, Sexuality, Ethnography, and Contemporary Chinese Cinema* (New York, 1995)
——, *Woman and Chinese Modernity: The Politics of Reading Between East and West* (Minneapolis, 1991)
Clark, Paul, *Chinese Cinema: Culture and Politics Since 1949* (New York, 1987)
——, 'Ethnic Minorities in Chinese Films: Cinema and the Exotic', *East–West Film Journal*, I/2 (June 1987)
——, 'The Film Industry in the 1970s', in Bonnie McDougall, ed., *Popular Chinese Literature and Performing Arts in the People's Republic of China, 1949–1979* (Berkeley, 1984)
——, 'The Sinification of Cinema: The Foreignness of Film in China', in Wimal Dissanayake, ed., *Cinema and Cultural Identity: Reflections on Films From Japan, India, and China* (Latham, MD, 1988)
——, 'Two Hundred Flowers on China's Screens', in Chris Berry, ed., *Perspectives on Chinese Cinema*, 2nd edn (London, 1991)
Cui, Shuqin, 'Gendered Pespective: The Construction and Representation of Subjectivity and Sexuality in *Ju Dou*', in Sheldon Hsiao-peng, ed., *Transnational Chinese Cinemas: Identity, Nationhood, Gender* (Honolulu, 1997)
Dai Jinhua, 'Invisible Women: Contemporary Chinese Cinema and Women's Film', trans. Mayfair Yang, *Positions: East Asia Cultures Critique*, III/1 (Spring 1995)
——, and Mayfair Yang, 'Conversation with Huang Shuqing [*sic*]', *Positions: East Asia Cultures Critique*, III/3 (Winter 1995)
Dai Qing, 'Raised Eyebrows for *Raise the Red Lantern*', *Public Culture*, V/2 (1993)
Davis, Deborah, Richard Kraus, Barry Naughton and Elizabeth Perry, eds, *Urban Spaces in Contemporary China* (Cambridge, 1995)
De Man, Paul, *Allegories of Reading* (New Haven, 1979)
Ding Xiaoqi, *Maidenhome* [and other stories], trans. Chris Berry and Cathy Silber (San Francisco, 1994)
Dissanayake, Wimal, ed., *Cinema and Cultural Identity: Reflections on Films From Japan, India, and China* (Latham, MD, 1988)
——, ed., *Colonialism and Nationalism in Asian Cinema* (Bloomington, 1994)
——, ed., *Melodrama and Asian Cinema* (New York, 1993)
Ebrey, Patricia, *The Inner Quarters: Marriage and the Lives of Chinese Women in the Sung Period* (Berkeley, 1993)
Eder, Klaus, and Deac Rossell, eds, *New Chinese Cinema* (London, 1993)
Ehrlich, Linda, and David Desser, eds, *Cinematic Landscapes: Observations on the Visual Arts and Cinema of China and Japan* (Austin, 1994)
Elsaesser, Thomas, 'Tales of Sound and Fury: Observations on the Family

342

Melodrama', in Gerald Mast, Marshall Cohen and Leo Braudy, eds, *Film Theory and Criticism*, 4th edn (New York, 1992)

Farquhar, Mary Ann, 'The "Hidden" Gender in *Yellow Earth'*, *Screen*, XXXIII/2 (Summer 1992)

Gilmartin, Christina, Gail Hershatter, Liso Rofer and Tyrene White, eds, *Engendering China: Women, Culture, and the State* (Cambridge, 1994)

Gladney, Dru, 'Representing Nationality in China: Refiguring Majority/Minority Identities', *Journal of Asian Studies*, LIII/1 (February 1994)

——, 'Tian Zhuangzhuang, the Fifth Generation, and Minorities Film in China', *Public Culture*, 8 (1995)

Goldman, Merle, ed., *Chinese Intellectuals and the State: In Search of a New Relationship* (Cambridge, MA, 1987)

——, *Literary Dissent in Communist China* (Cambridge, MA, 1967)

Gu Hua, *A Small Town Called Hibiscus*, trans. Gladys Yang (Beijing, 1983)

Hao Dazheng, 'Chinese Visual Representation: Painting and Cinema', in Linda Ehrlich and David Desser, eds, *Cinematic Landscapes: Observations on the Visual Arts and Cinema of China and Japan* (Austin, 1994)

Haraszti, Miklós, *The Velvet Prison: Artists Under State Socialism* (New York, 1987)

Harrell, Stevan, ed., *Cultural Encounters on China's Ethnic Frontiers* (Seattle, 1995)

Heilman, Robert, *Tragedy and Melodrama: Versions of Experience* (Seattle, 1968)

Jameson, Fredric, 'Third World Literature in the Era of Multinational Capitalism', *Social Text*, 15 (Autumn 1986)

Jang, Scarlett Ju-yu, 'Ox-Herding Painting in the Sung Dynasty', *Artibus Asiae*, LII/1–2 (1992)

Kaplan, E. Ann, 'Melodrama/Subjectivity/Ideology: Western Melodrama Theories and Their Relevance to Recent Chinese Cinema', in Wimal Dissanayake, ed., *Melodrama and Asian Cinema* (New York, 1993)

——, 'Problematising Cross-cultural Analysis: The Case of Women in the Recent Chinese Cinema', in Chris Berry, *Perspectives on Chinese Cinema*, 2nd edn (London, 1991)

——, 'Reading Formations and Chen Kaige's *Farewell My Concubine'*, in Sheldon Hsiao-peng Lu, ed., *Transnational Chinese Cinemas: Identity, Nationhood, Gender* (Honolulu, 1997)

Kawin, Bruce, *How Movies Work* (Berkeley, 1992)

Larson, Wendy, 'The Concubine and the Figure of History: Chen Kaige's *Farewell My Concubine'*, in Sheldon Hsiao-peng Lu, ed., *Transnational Chinese Cinemas: Identity, Nationhood, Gender* (Honolulu, 1997)

Lau, Jenny, '*Judou*: A Hermeneutical Reading of Cross-Cultural Cinema', *Film Quarterly*, XLV/2 (Winter 1992)

Lau, Jenny Kwok Wah, '*Judou*: An Experiment in Color and Portraiture in Chinese Cinema', in Linda Ehrlich and David Desser, eds, *Cinematic Landscapes: Observations on the Visual Arts and Cinema of China and Japan* (Austin, 1994)

Lee, Leo Ou-Fan, 'The Tradition of Modern Chinese Cinema: Some Preliminary Explorations and Hypotheses', in Chris Berry, ed., *Perspectives on Chinese Cinema*, 2nd edn (London, 1991)

Lee, Lilian, *Farewell to My Concubine*, trans. Andrea Lingenfelter (New York, 1992)

Leyda, Jay, Dianying, *Electric Shadows: An Account of Films and the Film Audience in China* (Cambridge, MA, 1972)

Li, H. C., 'Chinese Electric Shadows: A Selected Bibliography of Materials in English', *Modern Chinese Literature*, VII/2 (Autumn 1993); VIII/2 (Autumn 1994)

343

——, 'Color, Character, and Culture: On *Yellow Earth*, *Black Cannon Incident*, and *Red Sorghum*', *Modern Chinese Literature*, v/1 (Spring 1989)

Lin Haiyin, *Cheng nan jiu shi* (Taibei, 1960)

Link, E. Perry, *Evening Chats in Beijing: Probing China's Predicament* (New York, 1992)

Lipman, Jonathan, and Stevan Harrell, eds, *Violence in China: Essays in Culture and Counterculture* (Albany, 1990)

Liu, Lydia, 'The Female Body and Nationalist Discourse: Manchuria in Xiao Hong's *Field of Life and Death*', in Angela Zito and Tani E. Barlow, eds, *Body, Subject and Power in China* (Chicago, 1994)

——, 'Invention and Intervention: The Making of a Female Tradition in Modern Chinese Literature', in Ellen Widmer and David Der-wei Wang, eds, *From May Fourth to June Fourth: Fiction and Film in Twentieth-Century China* (Cambridge, MA, 1993)

Liu Heng, *Judou* [includes filmscripts for *Judou* and *The Story of Qiu Ju*] (Beijing, 1993)

——, *The Obsessed* [original title: *Fuxi, fuxi*], trans. David Kwan (Beijing, 1991)

Loh, Wai-fong, 'From Romantic Love to Class Struggle: Reflections on the Film *Liu Sanjie*', in Bonnie McDougall, ed., *Popular Chinese Literature and Performing Arts in the People's Republic of China, 1949–1979* (Berkeley, 1984)

Louie, Kam, *Inheriting Tradition: Interpretations of the Classical Philosophers in Communist China, 1949–1966* (Hong Kong, 1986)

Lu, Sheldon Hsiao-peng, ed., *Transnational Chinese Cinemas: Identity, Nationhood, Gender* (Honolulu, 1997)

Lu, Tonglin, *Gender and Sexuality in Twentieth-Century Chinese Literature and Society* (Albany, 1993)

——, '*Red Sorghum*: Limits of Transgression', in Liu Kang and Xiaobing Tang, eds, *Politics, Ideology, and Literary Discourse in Modern China: Theoretical Interventions and Cultural Critique* (Durham, NC, 1993)

Ma Ning, 'Spatiality and Subjectivity in Xie Jin's Melodrama of the New Period', in Nick Browne, ed., *New Chinese Cinemas: Forms, Identities, Politics* (New York, 1994)

——, 'Symbolic Representation and Symbolic Violence: Chinese Family Melodrama of the Early 1980s', in Wimal Dissanayake, ed., *Melodrama and Asian Cinema* (New York, 1993)

Mast, Gerald, Marshall Cohen and Leo Braudy, eds, *Film Theory and Criticism*, 4th edn (New York, 1992)

McDougall, Bonnie, *Mao Zedong's 'Talks at the Yan'an Conference on Literature and Art': 1943 Text with Commentary* (Ann Arbor, 1980)

——, *The Yellow Earth: A Film by Chen Kaige* (Hong Kong, 1991)

Mo Yan, *Hong gaoliang jiazu* (Taibei, 1988)

——, *Red Sorghum*, trans. Howard Goldblatt (New York, 1993)

Mulvey, Laura, 'Visual Pleasure and Narrative Cinema', *Screen*, xvi/3 (Autumn 1975)

Ni Zhen, 'Classical Chinese Painting and Cinematographic Signification', in Linda Ehrlich and David Desser, eds, *Cinematic Landscapes: Observations on the Visual Arts and Cinema of China and Japan* (Austin, 1994)

Owen, Stephen, *Remembrances: The Experience of the Past in Classical Chinese Literature* (Cambridge, MA, 1986)

Owens, Craig, 'The Allegorical Impulse: Toward a Theory of Postmodernism', in Brian Wallis, ed., *Art After Modernism: Rethinking Representation* (New York, 1984)

Parish, William, and Martin Whyte, *Village and Family in Contemporary China* (Chicago, 1978)

Pickowicz, Paul, 'Huang Jianxin and the Notion of Postsocialism', in Nick Browne, ed., *New Chinese Cinemas: Forms, Identities, Politics* (New York, 1994)

——, 'Melodramatic Representation and the "May Fourth" Tradition of Chinese Cinema', in Ellen Widmer and David Der-wei Wang, eds, *From May Fourth to June Fourth: Fiction and Film in Twentieth-Century China* (Cambridge, 1993)

——, 'Popular Cinema and Political Thought in Post-Mao China: Reflections on Official Pronouncements, Film, and the Film Audience', in Perry Link, Richard Madsen and Paul Pickowicz, eds, *Unofficial China: Popular Culture and Thought in the People's Republic* (Boulder, 1989)

——, 'Velvet Prisons and the Political Economy of Chinese Cinema', in Deborah Davis, Richard Kraus, Barry Naughton and Elizabeth Perry, eds, *Urban Spaces in Contemporary China* (Cambridge, 1995)

Rashkin, Elissa, 'Rape as Castration as Spectacle: *The Price of Frenzy*'s Politics of Confusion', in Tonglin Lu, ed., *Gender and Sexuality in Twentieth-Century Chinese Literature and Society* (Albany, 1993)

Rayns, Tony, 'The Narrow Path: Chen Kaige in Conversation with Tony Rayns', in John Boorman and Walter Donohue, eds, *Projections 3: Filmmakers on Film-making* (London, 1994)

——, 'The Position of Women in New Chinese Cinema', in Wimal Dissanayake, ed., *Cinema and Cultural Identity: Reflections on Films From Japan, India, and China* (Latham, MD, 1988)

Riley, Jo, *Chinese Theatre and the Actor in Performance* (Cambridge, 1997)

Rothman, William, '*The Goddess*: Reflections on Melodrama East and West', in Wimal Dissanayake, ed., *Melodrama and Asian Cinema* (New York, 1993)

Saussy, Haun, *The Problem of a Chinese Aesthetic* (Stanford, 1993)

Schafer, Edward, *The Divine Woman: Dragon Ladies and Rain Maidens in T'ang Literature* (Berkeley, 1967)

Semsel, George, Chen Xihe and Xia Hong, eds, *Film in Contemporary China: Critical Debates, 1979–1989* (Westport, CT, 1993)

Semsel, George, Xiao Hong, and Hou Jianping, eds, *Chinese Film Theory: A Guide to the New Era* (New York, 1990)

Semsel, George, ed., *Chinese Film: The State of the Art in the People's Republic* (New York, 1987)

Shao Mujun, 'Chinese Films, 1979–1989', *China Screen*, III/11 (November 1989)

——, 'Notes on *Red Sorghum*', *Chinese Literature*, 1 (1989)

——, 'On the Ruins of Modern Beliefs', in Klaus Eder and Deac Rossell, eds, *New Chinese Cinema* (London, 1993)

Silbergeld, Jerome, 'Art Censorship in China: A Do-It-Yourself System', in Elizabeth Childs, ed., *Suspended License: Censorship and the Visual Arts* (Seattle, 1997)

——, with Gong Jisui, *Contradictions: Artistic Life, the Socialist State, and the Chinese Painter Li Huasheng* (Seattle, 1993)

Spence, Jonathan, 'Film and Politics: Bai Hua's *Bitter Love*', in Jonathan Spence, *Chinese Roundabout: Essays in History and Culture* (New York, 1992)

Stone, Judy, *Eye on the World: Conversations with International Filmmakers* (Los Angeles, 1997)

Su Tong, *Raise the Red Lantern: Three Novellas* [original story title: *Qiqie chengqun, The Herding of Wives and Concubines*], trans. Michael Duke (New York, 1993)

Su Xiaokang and Wang Luxiang, *Deathsong of the River: A Reader's Guide to the Chinese TV Series Heshang*, trans. Richard Bodman and Pin Wan (Ithaca, 1991)

Sullivan, Michael, *Art and Artists of Twentieth-Century China* (Berkeley, 1996)

Trinh, T. Minh-Ha, *When the Moon Waxes Red: Representation, Gender, and Cultural Politics* (New York, 1991)

Wang, Eugene Yuejin, 'Samsara: Self and the Crisis of Visual Narrative', in Wimal Dissanayake, ed., *Narratives of Agency: Self-Making in China, India, and Japan* (Minneapolis, 1997)

Wang, Jing, ed., *China's Avant-Garde Fiction* (Durham, 1998)

——, *High Culture Fever: Politics, Aesthetics, and Ideology in Deng's China* (Berkeley, 1996)

Wang, Yuejin [Eugene], 'Melodrama as Historical Understanding: The Making and the Unmaking of Communist History', in Wimal Dissanayake, ed., *Melodrama and Asian Cinema* (New York, 1993)

——, '*The Old Well*: A Womb or a Tomb?', *Framework*, 35 (1988)

——, '*Red Sorghum*: Mixing Memory and Desire', in Chris Berry, ed., *Perspectives on Chinese Cinema*, 2nd edn (London, 1991)

Widmer, Ellen, and David Der-wei Wang, eds, *From May Fourth to June Fourth: Fiction and Film in Twentieth-Century China* (Cambridge, MA, 1993)

Williams, Linda, 'When the Woman Looks', in Gerald Mast, Marshall Cohen and Leo Braudy, eds, *Film Theory and Criticism*, 4th edn (New York, 1992)

Wolf, Margery, *Revolution Postponed: Women in Contemporary China* (Stanford, 1985)

——, and Roxane Witke, *Women in Chinese Society* (Stanford, 1975)

Xia Hong, 'The Debate over Horse Thief', in George Semsel, Chen Xihe and Xia Hong, eds, *Film in Contemporary China: Critical Debates, 1979–1989* (Westport, CT, 1993)

Yang, Mayfair Mei-hui, 'Of Gender, State Censorship and Overseas Capital: An Interview With Chinese Director Zhang Yimou', *Public Culture*, V/2 (1993)

Yau, Esther C. M., 'Cultural and Economic Dislocations: Filmic Phantasies of Chinese Women in the 1980s', *Wide Angle*, XI/2 (Spring 1989)

——, 'Is China the End of Hermeneutics? Or, Political and Cultural Usage of Non-Han Women in Mainland Chinese Films', *Discourse*, XI/2 (Spring–Summer 1989)

——, '*Yellow Earth*: Western Analysis and a Non-Western Text', in Chris Berry, ed., *Perspectives on Chinese Cinema*, 2nd edn (London, 1991)

Yau, Esther Ching-Mei, 'Filmic Discourse on Women in Chinese Cinema: Art, Ideology and Social Relations (1949–1965)', PhD thesis, University of California at Los Angeles, 1990

Young, Marilyn, ed., *Women in China* (Ann Arbor, 1973)

Yu, Pauline, *The Reading of Imagery in the Chinese Poetic Tradition* (Princeton, 1987)

Yung, Bell, Evelyn Rawski and Rubie Watson, *Harmony and Counterpoint: Ritual Music in Chinese Context* (Stanford, 1996)

Zha, Jane Ying [Jianying], 'Excerpts from "Lore Segal, Red Lantern, and Exoticism"', *Public Culture*, V/2 (1993)

Zha, Jianying, *China Pop: How Soap Opera, Tabloids, and Bestsellers Are Transforming a Culture* (New York, 1995)

Zhang Manling, *You yige meilide difang* [*Such a Beautiful Place*] (Beijing, 1984)

Zhang Xudong, *Chinese Modernism in the Era of Reforms: Cultural Fever, Avant-Garde Fiction, and the New Chinese Cinema* (Durham, 1997)

Zhang, Yangjin, *The City in Modern Chinese Literature and Film: Configurations of Space, Time, and Gender* (Stanford, 1996)

——, 'From "Minority Film" to "Minority Discourse": Questions of Nationhood and Ethnicity in Chinese Cinema', in Sheldon Hsiao-peng Lu, ed., *Transnational Chinese Cinemas: Identity, Nationhood, Gender* (Honolulu, 1997)

——, 'Ideology of the Body in *Red Sorghum*: National Allegory, National Roots, and Third Cinema', *East–West Film Journal*, IV/2 (June 1990); also published in Wimal Dissanayake, ed., *Colonialism and Nationalism in Asian Cinema* (Bloomington, 1994)

Zheng, Yi, 'Narrative Images of the Historical Passion: Those Other Women – On the Alterity in the New Wave of Chinese Cinema', in Sheldon Hsiao-peng Lu, ed., *Transnational Chinese Cinemas: Identity, Nationhood, Gender* (Honolulu, 1997)

——, *Old Well*, trans. David Kwan (San Francisco, 1989)

Zhou Daxin, 'Xiang hun tangban de xiangyou fang' [*Sesame Oil Workshop by the Side of Scented Souls' Lake*]', in Zhou Daxin, *Xiang hun nü* (*Hongfan wenxue congshu*, 249) (Taipei, 1993)

Zhu Ling, 'A Brave New World? On the Construction of "Masculinity" and "Femininity" in *The Red Sorghum Family*', in Tonglin Lu, *Gender and Sexuality in Twentieth-Century Chinese Literature and Society* (Albany, 1993)

Zito, Angela, and Tani E. Barlow, eds, *Body, Subject and Power in China* (Chicago, 1994)

Photographic Acknowledgements

The author and publisher wish to express their thanks to the following artists and photographers or other sources of illustrative material and/or permission to reproduce it:

Museum of Fine Arts, Boston – Denman Waldo Ross Collection (photo: © Museum of Fine Arts, Boston, all rights reserved): 126; courtesy of Chang Tsong-zung: 76, 246; *China Avant-Garde: Counter-Currents in Art and Culture*: 45; Cleveland Museum of Art – purchase from the J. H. Wade Fund: 22, John L. Severance Fund: 166; © 1987 and 1990 FARWORKS, INC, cartoons from *The Far Side*, used by permission, all rights reserved: 171, 172; *Gong Banqian shoutu huagao*: 24; courtesy of the artist [Gu Wenda]: 222; Harvard University Art Museums, Cambridge, MA (gift of Earl Morse) (photo: Michael Nedzweski/© President and Fellows of Harvard College, Harvard University): 23; Scarlett Jang, 'Ox-herding Painting in the Sung Dynasty': 245; Mayching Kao, *Twentieth-Century Chinese Painting*: 66; The Nelson-Atkins Museum of Art, Kansas City, MO – purchase: Nelson Trust (photo: © The Nelson Gallery Foundation): 128; © 1997, Newsweek, Inc., all rights reserved, reprinted by permission: 131; Chris Perry, *Perspectives on Chinese Cinema*: 151; Michael Sullivan, *Art and Artists of Twentieth-Century China*: 141; Wang Fangyu and Richard Barnhart, *Master of the Lotus Garden*: 191; *Woodcuts of War-Time China, 1937–45*: 55; courtesy of the artist [Wang Jinsong]: 247.

Index

Page numbers in *italics* contain illustrations.